PENGUIN BOOKS

STARTING FROM SCRATCH

Pam Johnson-Bennett is a Certified Animal Behavior Consultant and one of the best-known experts on feline behavior. She is vice president of the International Association of Animal Behavior Consultants and the founder and chair of the cat division of the IAABC. She is the author of six other books on cat behavior and has been the recipient of numerous awards.

Pam speaks on behavior at veterinary conferences and humane organizations and makes numerous television appearances, including CNN, Fox News Channel, and the National Geographic Channel. She is also a frequent guest on national radio.

In addition to running a private veterinarian-referred behavior service, Pam is the cat behavior expert at Friskies.com and Yahoo.com. She serves on the advisory board of the Tree House Animal Foundation and is on the PR committee for the Winn Feline Foundation. She was also the national spokesperson for Friskies. Being dedicated to improving the lives of shelter cats, Pam also served as the spokesperson for the Friskies Shelter Program, where she helped design a prototype cageless shelter-cat habitat.

Pam was the behavior columnist for *Cats* magazine and *The Daily Cat* and the resident behavior expert at ivillage.com. She has authored articles for scholarly journals and cat magazines and is frequently quoted in national magazines and newspapers.

Pam lives in Nashville, where she runs Cat Behavior Associates, LLC.

Also by Pam Johnson-Bennett

Psycho Kitty

Twisted Whiskers

Hiss and Tell: True Stories from the Files of a Cat Shrink

Think Like a Cat: How to Raise a Well-Adjusted Cat—Not a Sour Puss

Cat vs. Cat: Keeping Peace When You Have More Than One Cat

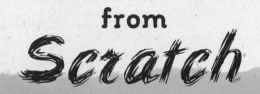

Starting
from
Scratch

How to Correct Behavior Problems
in Your Adult Cat

Pam Johnson-Bennett

Certified Animal Behavior Consultant

Penguin Books

PENGUIN BOOKS

Published by the Penguin Group

Penguin Group (USA) Inc., 375 Hudson Street, New York, New York 10014, U.S.A.
Penguin Group (Canada), 90 Eglinton Avenue East, Suite 700, Toronto, Ontario, Canada
M4P 2Y3 (a division of Pearson Penguin Canada Inc.)
Penguin Books Ltd, 80 Strand, London WC2R 0RL, England
Penguin Ireland, 25 St Stephen's Green, Dublin 2, Ireland (a division of Penguin Books Ltd)
Penguin Group (Australia), 250 Camberwell Road, Camberwell, Victoria 3124, Australia
(a division of Pearson Australia Group Pty Ltd)
Penguin Books India Pvt Ltd, 11 Community Centre, Panchsheel Park, New Delhi–110 017, India
Penguin Group (NZ), 67 Apollo Drive, Rosedale, North Shore 0632, New Zealand
(a division of Pearson New Zealand Ltd.)
Penguin Books (South Africa) (Pty) Ltd, 24 Sturdee Avenue, Rosebank,
Johannesburg 2196, South Africa

Penguin Books Ltd, Registered Offices:
80 Strand, London WC2R 0RL, England

First published in Penguin Books 2007

3 5 7 9 10 8 6 4

LIBRARY OF CONGRESS CATALOGING-IN-PUBLICATION DATA

Johnson-Bennett, Pam, 1954–
Starting from scratch : how to correct behavior problems
in your adult cat / Pam Johnson-Bennett—1st ed.
p. cm.
Includes index.
ISBN 978-0-14-311250-1
1. Cats—Behavior therapy.   I. Title.
SF446.5.J636   2007
636.8'0887—dc22   2007013935

Printed in the United States of America
Set in Filosofia
Designed by Lynn Newmark

For my wonderful family, Scott, Gracie, and Jack,
and my precious feline family, Bebe and Mary Margaret

Acknowledgments

I must first thank my husband, Scott, for his unending amount of patience and support. Being the spouse of a writer isn't easy. Being the spouse of a cat behavior consultant isn't easy. Being the spouse of a writer who is also a cat behavior consultant certainly takes a very special person. My husband is that special person.

Thank you to my agent, Linda Roghaar, who always provides the motivation, support, and guidance needed. You are a writer's dream.

Thank you to my editor, Clifford Corcoran, and my family at Penguin, for your ongoing support and belief in what I do.

Thanks to Ellen Pryor for years of incredible PR work and even more years as a cherished friend.

I have had so many wonderful clients over the years. Thank you for putting your trust in me. I have thoroughly enjoyed getting to know all of you and hope I have contributed to improving the lives of your cats.

The International Association of Animal Behavior Consultants is an organization that has a very special place in my heart. The animal kingdom is very fortunate to have Lynn Hoover, the founder and president of the IAABC, as a best friend. Lynn, you are an inspiration to so many people and it's an honor to work with you.

A special thank-you to Marilyn Krieger for your dedication to this profession and assistance in the cat division of the IAABC, and for your friendship.

Thank you to Mark Waldrop, DVM. If you ever move, I'll have to follow you, as will most of Nashville's residents.

Thank you to all the veterinarians I work with on a daily basis. I am in awe of the dedication, endless hard work, and compassion you show each of your clients. I deeply appreciate the trust you have in me to take care of the behavior problems your clients have with their cats.

Thank you to my assistant, Renee.

Contents

Acknowledgments   vii

Introduction   xvii

1. Get Reacquainted with Your Feline Einstein   1

Body and Posture   4
Ears   7
Eyes   8
Whiskers   9
Nose   11
Mouth   12
Tongue   12
Tail   13
Vocalization   14
Pay Attention to What Your Cat Is Saying   16

2. Real Estate Reality Check   17

Is Your Cat's Environment Part of the Problem?

Indoor/Outdoor   17
Vertical Thinking   25
Hideaways and Tunnels   30
Scratching and Climbing   32
The Litter Box Environment   33
The Feeding Station   33
Bedtime   33

Feline Home Makeover: Operation Enrichment   34
    Climbing and perching   35
    Stimulation   37
    Safety   41
    Familiarity   42

3. Serious Fun   45

Play Therapy

Obesity   46
How to Use Play Therapy to Your Advantage   48
Interactive Play   48
Choosing Interactive Toys   49
Interactive Play Therapy Techniques   52
Play Therapy Schedule   57
Interactive Play Sessions for Multiple Cats   58
Interactive Play Therapy for Retraining   60
Solo Play   64
Catnip   67
Clicker Training   70
Clicker Training in a Multicat Home   76
Beyond Basic Training   77

4. Retraining Old Habits and More Serious Problems You Thought You Had to Live With   79

Retrain with the Right *Starting from Scratch* Attitude   79
Rebuilding Trust   80
Correcting Those Little Annoying Problems   81
    Counter hopping   82
    Door dashing   87
    Plant nibbling   91
    Curtain climbing   93
    Computer crashing, cat-style   93
    Interior decorating with toilet paper   94
    Toilet water fascination   95
    Faucet fixation   96

Nightly noises and crack-of-dawn wake-ups   97
Oliver Twist syndrome   101
Correcting More Serious Problems   102
Boredom   102
Depression   104
The grieving cat   105
The fearful cat   108
Fear of people   110
Separation anxiety   118
Compulsive Behaviors   121
Psychogenic alopecia   123
Compulsive licking   123
Wool sucking, chewing, and pica behavior   124
Feline hyperesthesia   127
Medicating a Cat Who Doesn't Want to Be Medicated   129
Know your options   130
Pilling   130
Administering liquid medication   134
Applying ointment or cream   135
Eye medication   136
Ear medication   137

5. Tired of Those Out-of-Box Experiences?   138

Retraining to the Litter Box

Reevaluate the Current Setup   140
What we assume cats want   140
What your cat really wants you to know   141
Why problems occur   142
Spraying and indiscriminate urination   142
Back to the Box   144
Products you'll need   144
Spraying   146
Retraining a sprayer   151
Indiscriminate urination   157
Retraining an indiscriminater   163

Location strategies   169
Turf claims and overcrowding   172
Other deposits that occur outside the box   173
Toilet training cautions   176

6. Tattered and Shredded   178

Retraining Inappropriate Scratching

The Need to Scratch   179
Declawing   179
Nail Caps   181
Refresher Course on Scratching   182
Rethink the Current Scratching Post Setup   184
The Retraining Process: Operation Velvet Paws   186
　　Furniture armor: Set the stage for retraining   187
　　The right post   188
　　The right location   191
　　Retraining   191
　　Bonus retraining tips   193

7. Mealtime   195

I Want What I Want When I Want It!

Maybe the Bowl Is the Problem and Not the Food   196
The Bottomless Bowl: Pros and Cons of Free-Feeding   199
Pros and Cons of Scheduled Feeding   199
Finicky Eating Syndrome and Fixed Food Preference   200
Retraining the Finicky Eater   203
Bowl Bullies   204
Cats on Different Diets   206
Tubby Tabbies: Safe Mealtime Retraining   207
Stick to the Plan   211

8. Spits and Spats   212

Aggression, Biting, and Fighting

The Biter   213
Aggression   215

Fear aggression   215
Petting-induced aggression   219
Redirected aggression   221
Pain-induced aggression   225
Territorial aggression   226
Play aggression   228
Predatory aggression   229
Intercat aggression   230
Status-related aggression   233
Maternal aggression   234
Idiopathic aggression   235
The *Starting from Scratch* Reintroduction Technique   235
Other Uses and Variations on the Reintroduction
  Technique   241
When Professional Help Is Needed   242
Psychopharmacological Intervention   243

9. Why Can't We All Just Get Along?   245

Your Cat and Other Family Members

Is Your Cat Meant to Be the Only Cat in the Home?   246
Dislike or Fear of the New Cat in the Home   246
  Starting from scratch with a proper introduction   246
Dog Panic   257
Birds, Hamsters, and Other Small Pets   263
When the New Baby Creates Kitty Crisis   264
  If the baby isn't home yet   264
  After the bundle of joy arrives   266
Kids and Cats   271
Fixing Blended-Family Cat-astrophes   275
The Cat-Avoiding Spouse   277
The Spouse-Avoiding Cat   283

10. Travel Retraining   286

On the Road with Your Own Mr. or Miss Grumpypaws

Look at Travel from Your Cat's Point of View   286

Retrain Your Cat to the Carrier   287

  The *starting from scratch* retraining process   289

  The emergency technique for getting a
    carrier-hating cat into the carrier   293

Long-Distance Car Travel   294

Air Travel   300

Home Alone Kitty: Retraining the Cat Who Hates
  Pet Sitters   302

Boarding Woes   307

How to Reduce Anxiety for Veterinarian Visits   311

Leash Training an Adult Cat   313

Moving to a New Home   319

  Start early   319

  Moving day   322

  The new home   322

11. Cat Versus Brush   325

Groom Your Cat and Live to Talk About It

Look at Your Current Grooming Technique
  from Kitty's Point of View   325

How the Grooming Session Should Be Viewed
  by Kitty and the Cat Owner   327

The Retraining Process   327

Time for Tools   330

Brushing and Combing   330

Nail Trimming   333

Ear Cleaning   335

Teeth Cleaning   336

Bathing   338

Hairballs   341

12. Looking Ahead   346

Senior Cat Behavior

Behavior and Physical Changes   347

Make Adjustments as Needed   351

The Litter Box   352
Feline Cognitive Disorder   353
Other Companion Animals in the Home   355
Show Patience and Tolerance   356
Enjoy This Time Together   356

Appendix   357
Index   364

Introduction

I have to start by telling you what this book *is not*. It's not a kitten training book. It won't tell you how to choose a cat or what nutrients or vaccinations your cat needs. This is a book focused on adult cats with big or little behavior problems. Whether you've lived with problems for years or you just want to make sure problems don't develop in the future, this *is* the book that will cover those issues in detail. Since behavior problems cause more cats to be relinquished to shelters than medical issues do, it's important that you have the correct tools to help you and your cat get back to the relationship you've always wanted.

Inspirations for books can come from many different places. It's not unusual for a passing comment made by an acquaintance or a brief interaction with someone to spark an idea or trigger a life-changing moment. My inspiration for this book came from meeting Mr. Grumpypaws, a cat who is living proof that it's never too late to work on behavior problems and make life better for you and your kitty. You'll learn a little more about Mr. Grumpypaws in a moment.

When you first decide to share your life with a cat, whether the cat in your life has been with you since kittenhood or found his way into your heart as an adult, you don't usually go into the relationship expecting to endure behavior problems or develop an antagonistic relationship with that ball of fur.

Picture some of the touching scenes from cat food or litter commercials in which cats lovingly cuddle with their human family or happily trot to the food bowl when dinner is served. These cats always use the litter box, never scratch the furniture, and wouldn't dream of coughing up a hairball on the very expensive comforter in the beautifully decorated bedroom. How about biting the hand that feeds them? Unheard of!

If you're looking across the room at your cat and wondering what went wrong, don't be discouraged. It's not too late to turn things around. Many of the behavior consultations I do are the result of the human family members not understanding what their cats truly need and what they are communicating by their so-called misbehaviors. So many people have just given up and resigned themselves to living with cats in situations in which neither they nor their cat is really happy. They feel they've lived with it this long, they can suffer through a few more years. You and your cat don't have to live that way anymore. Many times the problem is that the cat owner has never received accurate information about how cats should be trained. Cats are not little dogs, and yet many people continue to look at them that way. When that happens, the cat and the human family both lose.

You can and should love your cats as cherished family members, but it's crucial to always recognize that they *are* cats and not furry human children. Cats have their own way of communicating; they have specific needs emotionally, physically, and medically. Imagine how much better your relationship with your cat would be if you had the tools to understand what he was communicating by his behavior and could effectively use that knowledge to solve problems. Surprisingly, interpreting his language is not hard at all.

For many people, life with their cats goes smoothly for years or even throughout the cats' lifetimes. Unfortunately, though, that isn't the case for many others. You and your cat may be hitting that bump in the road right now—or maybe in your case it's more like a roadblock or a total detour. Many of us have found ourselves sharing our lives with cats through rescue, shelter adoption, or taking in strays. In these cases, the cats are not clean slates. They come into our lives with a history that influences their current and future behavior. Those influences are powerful, but they can, in many cases, be changed or at least improved through behavior modification so the cats can blossom in their new lives.

If you bought this book, chances are your cat is exhibiting a behavior problem, or maybe you just want to make sure you learn to read warning signs before a problem begins. If you're dealing with a behavior problem, what do you think went wrong? Do you think it's your fault? It's not. Is it your cat's fault? Absolutely not. For so many people, the idea of being able to train a cat seems impossible. Cats have been the subject of endless jokes about being aloof, independent, and untrainable. So many people assume that if they're going to live with a cat, they'll just have to accept the hand they're dealt. You may not have realized your cat even had a behavior problem until suddenly, one day, everything changed. Maybe he doesn't actually have a problem at all—maybe he's scratching on furniture because he's trying to fill a normal need and there isn't a more acceptable option for him.

You may have found lots of people with opinions on how you should train your cat or, better yet, how impossible it is to even _think of_ training a cat. It's easy to find bad information and you may have been led in the wrong direction. Family, friends, and neighbors can be well meaning, but that doesn't make their cat advice sound.

Behavior problems are often made worse because cat owners misunderstand the underlying cause and assume the _misbehavior_ is deliberate. If you take nothing else away from reading this book, please remember that no cat deliberately and willfully tries to misbehave. Your cat is facing a problem and attempting to solve it according to what he knows as a cat. That's why it's crucial for you to find the underlying cause of the behavior in order to come up with the right solution. Whether it's just a pesky little annoying behavior you'd like to tweak or a major problem that has you at the end of your rope, you must shift your thinking in order to look at the possible true cause, as well as determine whether it's truly a behavior *problem* or a *normal* behavior that needs a better alternative. In either case, I'll do my best to help you come up with a solution. This book will guide you as you play detective in order to figure out what's wrong and then I'll map out your behavior modification plan.

Back to Mr. Grumpypaws. He was twenty years old and one of the oldest cats I've been asked to consult about. Veterinarians see many eighteen-, nineteen-, and twenty-year-old cats, and some even older than that, but behavior consultants don't tend to fill their schedules with such geriatric kitties.

Mr. Grumpypaws was in surprisingly good health for such an elderly feline. His cat owner called me because the cat had always been grouchy and unpredictable, kept everyone awake at night with his howling, and had a somewhat hostile relationship with his companion cat of six years.

I was called so late in this cat's life because the client had only recently heard of cat behavior consulting. She happened to see me on television and then did an Internet search to track down my office. Up until that point, she had always just assumed that Mr. Grumpypaws was unchangeable. She loved her cat, whom she had gotten from a shelter when he was six months old. Originally named Oscar, his name became unofficially but permanently changed to Mr. Grumpypaws five years later.

When I did the house-call consultation, I saw that there were a number of little things that needed changing that would make a huge difference to Mr. Grumpypaws. He was being pushed out of his favorite spots by his younger companion, something the client hadn't noticed because of the subtle body language the younger cat was using. Ever since Mr. Grumpypaws was a young adult, he had lots of energy but no healthy outlet for it. That led to destructive behavior that resulted in punishment. The cat became confused and frustrated, and developed an antagonist relationship with his human family. There were numerous changes we were able to make that improved Mr. Grumpypaws's disposition. By creating more vertical space for the two cats to climb and perch, we increased their territories and eased the tension. We made changes to their litter box setup to create more security. I also put the clients on a schedule of doing low-intensity, age-appropriate interactive play therapy with Mr. Grumpypaws to help him gain confidence and work off his anxiety. Since he was a very active cat, even at twenty years old, we were able to use environmental enrichment techniques to keep him occupied so he would be less likely to keep everyone up at night. The play sessions, combined with some other activities to win Mr. Grumpypaws's trust back, enabled the human family to get close to him again—something everyone had missed very much. Those modifications, along with other very specific techniques I mapped out for the family, allowed Mr. Grumpypaws to turn back into Oscar again.

Oscar is now twenty-three years old, and the last three years have been problem-free, other than some health issues, which are certainly to be expected at his advanced age. Although the family doesn't know how much longer he has to live, they're grateful that he has had the last three years of security, contentment, and fun, and has been able to get the most out of his life. Let Mr. Grumpypaws inspire you to take the steps necessary to correct your feline behavior problem, no matter how long you've lived with it. Even if the problem is so deeply rooted that you can't completely correct it, you should be able to improve the situation and gain a better understanding of what caused it.

So what typically goes wrong in the cat-human relationship? One thing you may not realize is that your cat, being the smart creature that he is, is learning from you, even when you're not aware of it. You may have been reinforcing the very behaviors you don't want. It's a common problem that I see daily in my consultations. In so many cases, the only time the cat gets attention is when he's being reprimanded for a misbehavior. Here's an example of reinforcing an unwanted behavior: giving your cat a treat, praise, or petting in order to quiet him or stop him from being aggressive or frightened. The attention you showed toward the behavior told the cat that he was correct in behaving that way. How many times have you picked up your cat and petted him when he was hissing or growling at a visitor? It's very natural to want to comfort him, but the message you send is that he should do that very same behavior again the next time a guest visits.

Other reasons why behavior problems occur are changes in the household—such as the addition of another cat, a new family member, or a move to a new house—or the fact that the cat has reached social maturity (around two to four years of age). Most cat owners don't even know that there is such a thing as *social* maturity, so how in the world would they know how it could affect a cat's behavior?

In trying to correct behavior problems, you need to work with the cat's nature so you can better understand where he's coming from. Cats are cautious creatures who are suspicious of change. They're territorial and most comfortable in familiar surroundings, but they need stimulation and activity within that familiar environment. Cats have a prey-drive, and everything about their bodies was built for hunting. They also have a need for cleanliness. Cats use multiple forms of communication. All of these things will be used in behavior modification as you work on solving behavior problems.

As you go through this book and learn about behavior modification, you'll see a pattern develop. The pattern is centered around *choice*. You won't be forcing your cat to do anything at any time. What you'll be doing is creating choices for him. He'll be making choices concerning things that matter very much to him, such as his litter box, feeding station, sleeping area, play technique, affection, social interaction. By giving him acceptable choices, his anxiety level decreases. He'll let you know what he prefers, and with that communication you can create an environment that inspires desirable behavior. Everybody wins.

No matter where you are in your relationship with your cat, you can improve the situation. If you've used inappropriate techniques or punished your cat in the past, then some fence-mending may need to be done. If you've lived with a problem for so long you don't know how you'll ever find the original cause, don't worry; this book will guide you through that process. *Starting from scratch* is a method that stops you from continuing down the wrong road and puts you on the right path toward a happy life with your cat.

Here's hoping we can turn your own Mr. Grumpypaws back into Oscar again.

1

Get Reacquainted with Your
Feline Einstein

How well do you really know your cat? You may have been living with him for many years, but do you truly believe you know what goes on inside his mind or what he's trying to say by his various behaviors?

You may be sitting there shaking your head, thinking you know your cat all too well. You may be able to predict how he's going to behave in a particular situation and whether he's going to react negatively to one thing or another. Maybe you can easily label your cat as finicky, ornery, mean, unsociable, or spiteful, or maybe the label could be loving and affectionate. Is your cat too needy? Timid? Shy? Skittish? Do you joke about how he rules the roost? Is he very playful, or is he a furry couch potato?

Maybe you're reading this and thinking how you don't have the first clue about what goes on inside that feline head of his. Maybe he totally perplexes and frustrates you.

What I see in so many of my consultations is that my clients really don't know what it is their cats are trying to communicate by particular behaviors. Cat owners often misinterpret feline behavior, and as a result, problems can't be effectively corrected.

Your cat is an amazing communicator. His mind and body work perfectly together. If you take some time to get a better understanding of what he might be trying to communicate, there's an excellent chance you'll look at so-called misbehaviors in a whole new light. You'll develop a new appreciation for that cute ball of fluff you've lived with all these years.

For example, you may have commented many times about how your cat always faces away from you when he sits on your lap. Maybe you've considered this rude, since your dog always wants to be eye to eye with you. In reality, this posture is very positive. When he sits with his back toward you, he's showing ultimate trust. It's very comforting for him to feel you there. It's a source of security that he might be trying to provide for you as well. Become more aware of how a cat shows trust instead of expecting him to show it in the way your dog does, or even the way a human does.

Your cat is also a hunter who is extremely in tune with his environment, so when he lounges on your lap, he wants all of his sensory receptors facing forward. If you always keep in mind that your cat is hardwired as a predator, regardless of whether he has ever caught a mouse, you'll better understand how and why he positions himself in certain ways.

Another misinterpreted behavior is when your cat stands on your lap and presents his hindquarters to you. While that may appear to be the ultimate in rudeness, he's actually trying to follow appropriate feline protocol. In the feline world, two familiar cats will approach each other for a little nose-to-nose sniffing and then anal sniffing. What may seem repulsive to you is crucial to cat etiquette because, unlike us, cats rely on scent as a very important tool in communication and social structure.

The cat's use of scent is very much misunderstood by humans, since we're such a verbal and visual species. Many of our assumptions about how and why our cats use scent are inaccurate. If a cat sprays, what's the first thing you think of? He's marking territory, right? Well, that's not always the case. Urine marking is a complex form of communication that's used not only for marking territory but also as a form of covert aggression. When a cat is unsure of how much of an opponent he may have to face in his territory, he might spray as a way of leaving a calling card. This scent-mark lets the other cat know about him. He'll also use the information gathered from the other cat's urine-mark to learn about him. What we may view as just a troublesome behavior your cat views as a necessary information exchange. It's also how a cat may combine his scent with yours as a way of comforting himself. Confident cats may spray, but cats who aren't confident can also spray. Both males and females can spray. If you're experiencing a spraying problem in your multicat home, don't assume it's the male doing the spraying. It might actually be the female.

When your cat rubs on you or an object, do you again think that he's merely marking his territory? There are actually various reasons why a cat may rub. Where and how he does it communicates what he's feeling. When he comes up to you, lowers his head, and seems to butt it gently (or sometimes not so gently) right in your face, he may be doing what is referred to as *bunting*. This is a very affectionate behavior that is displayed only toward another companion animal or a human family member. Bunting is a very respectful way that a cat shows affection.

How about when you see your cat rubbing his cheek along an object? Is he marking? Yes, he is, but do you know what he's feeling when he displays this type of marking versus urine marking? Facial rubbing releases pheromones (scent chemicals) on objects, and these facial pheromones are the "friendly" ones. When a cat facially rubs an object, he's marking it in a calm way to reaffirm that he's in familiar surroundings. The emotion associated with facial rubbing is very different from the high-intensity, anxiety-related emotion connected to urine marking.

When you walk to the kitchen, does your cat weave in and out of your legs, rubbing his flanks along your shins and almost tripping you? Is he just excited? He's certainly excited because he's anticipating dinner, but flank rubbing is a respectful form of marking that shows he acknowledges his place in the social status and knows that you're the higher-ranking member. I'll bet you weren't aware of how much respect your cat was showing you on a day-to-day basis.

There are many signals your cat gives with his body that convey what he's feeling. Becoming more familiar with some of those signals may reduce misunderstandings that result in your getting bitten, scratched, or having your cat run from you. Even if you have a wonderful relationship with your cat except for a few pesky little behavior problems you'd like to correct, familiarize yourself with his method of communicating and you'll strengthen the bond between the two of you. Communication is key in any relationship, and when it comes to your cat, it can make solving a behavior problem so much easier.

BODY AND POSTURE

Your cat's body is quite a magnificent and efficient machine. It is extremely flexible with loosely connected vertebrae. There are more bones in the cat's body than in ours. Did you ever wonder how your cat manages to squeeze into the tightest spaces? His clavicle (collarbone) "floats" by being attached to muscle, as opposed to being attached to bone, as our fixed clavicle is.

He's a swift and silent sprinter, since he walks on his toes and not the entire foot, the way we do. This is very important for a hunter who relies on silently and swiftly stalking his prey. The positioning of his shoulder blades allows for long strides, and that gives him quite an advantage when hunting.

As a hunter, he depends on being able to keep his senses fixed on his target and not lose sight of it. Watch your cat when he's stalking something and you'll notice that his shoulder blades rise and fall but his head remains still and locked on his intended target. The cat's body is very efficient.

A cat's amazing ability to jump from the ground to a high perch is not only useful for hunting but also keeps him safe when he needs to get out of reach of a potential opponent. A cat can jump five times his height.

Let's look at some basic feline body language that can be easily misinterpreted.

One of the most misunderstood postures is when the cat rolls onto his back and exposes his belly. Many people interpret this to mean the cat is asking for a tummy rub or is showing a sign of submission the way a dog would. Wrong! If you rub or pet your cat's exposed stomach, you'll most likely end up with eighteen claws sinking into your skin and maybe quite a few teeth as well. Belly up is the ultimate defensive position because it enables the cat to engage all of his weapons. For many cats, when you pet the exposed belly, you automatically trigger the response, regardless of how easygoing the cat is normally. What the cat is saying with this defensive posture is that he doesn't want to fight, but if the opponent proceeds, all weapons will come into use.

Your cat may also display an exposed belly when he's stretched out relaxing. If he's in that position under calm circumstances, he feels comfortable being so vulnerable. He may be expressing trust, affection, relaxation, or even love, but that comfort level can change in a heartbeat if you pet his stomach.

Kittens often display belly-up posture during playtime as well as when they feel defensive. Kittens tend to use all sorts of mixed signaling as they learn about their bodies' abilities and how to communicate.

Your cat's body language communicates whether he wants interaction with you or would prefer to be left alone. You can also tell whether he's uncertain, feeling threatened, or just relaxed. If your cat walks up to you with a confident gait and a spring in his step, holding his tail high over his back, he's looking for interaction. His tail may have a slight curl on the end or he may even give it a little twitch as a friendly greeting.

Since the cat's tail is easily visible when upright, he may use that position when walking in grass or brush to indicate to another cat that closer interaction is wanted or at least allowed. Compare that to the cat who is crouched with his tail tucked tightly around him.

While in this position he also avoids making direct eye contact. This posture is saying he doesn't want to interact with you and may be fearful or trying to appear invisible.

By becoming familiar with the crouched posture of a cat who wants to be left alone, you can help him feel more trusting around you because he will know he doesn't have to worry about being approached when he doesn't want to be.

Body language ultimately comes down to two messages: distance-increasing or distance-decreasing. With distance-increasing, the cat may be saying go away or that he doesn't wish any further interaction. Distance-decreasing can indicate an invitation to come closer or can signal indifference. Distance-decreasing posture can turn into distance-increasing if an approaching cat oversteps his boundaries.

In a multicat household you may have noticed one of your cats displaying a stiff-legged, forward-facing posture toward another cat. The forward-facing cat's head is lowered, his pupils are constricted, and his ears are flattened back against his head. His whiskers are erect and fanned forward. Your other cat may be sideways-facing, not looking directly at his opponent. What's going on here? The forward-facing cat is displaying offensive aggression. The cat facing sideways is being defensive and may go into the "Halloween cat" posture by displaying a piloerection of fur. He may arch his back and tail to try to appear as large and threatening as possible. His sideways stance is to make him look large, but it also says he'd rather not do battle. He'd rather the opponent just turn around and retreat. The defensive posture also says that if the opponent continues to advance, the defensive cat will certainly engage in battle. Become familiar with which cat is displaying a particular posture and you'll have more clues to help you determine who is being the offensive aggressor and who is being defensive.

Signaling can be uniform and consistent or it can contain conflicting messages. With concordant signaling, the cat's body parts are in agreement (tails, ears, whiskers, eyes), so you know the cat is certain about whatever message he's trying to relay. With conflicting signaling, the cat may have his feet facing one way, hoping for a chance to get away, but his head or body language is saying something completely different. Fear aggression is a good example of conflicting messages because the cat's vocalization, eyes, ears, whiskers, and head are in a position to do battle but his body and feet are turned sideways, hoping there'll be an opportunity to get the heck out of there.

If your cat really wants to make sure another cat understands that he poses no threat whatsoever, he may engage in repetitive messaging just to make sure there are no miscommunications. If you have a multicat household, you may notice that when two cats are engaged in a potentially hostile confrontation, there are numerous "pauses" in the action. They may stop in whatever positions they're in and stare at each other. One cat may have a paw raised at the time, and during the pause the paw remains frozen in midair. These pauses in their hostile dance give them each time to do more information gathering. Cats would prefer not to have a physical confrontation, so the pauses give both of them time to reconsider or back down.

EARS

Your cat's ears have more than thirty muscles. He can rotate them independently of each other, and that enables him to accurately pinpoint the location of a sound. Your cat may be sitting on your lap, facing away from you with his ears forward, but if someone walks into the room on one side, he may turn one ear toward the sound while keeping the other ear tuned in to the goings-on on the other side of the room. The cone shape of the cat's ears captures and funnels sound. His ears are so much more efficient than ours, which are nonflexible and cup-shaped.

A cat's hearing is extremely sensitive, and he can hear at higher frequencies than humans or even dogs. High-frequency hearing is exactly what a cat needs in order to catch those little squeaks from mice and other potential prey.

There's an organ in the cat's ear that helps him right himself in midair. You may have heard the phrase "Cats always land on their feet," but that's not always true. In order to right himself, the cat needs a certain amount of time in midair. If the distance is too short, then he will not have adequate time. If the distance is too long, regardless of whether he rights himself, he will suffer injuries—possibly severe or fatal.

We take our sense of balance for granted, but your cat truly depends on the efficiency of his inner ear to help him remain balanced during those fast changes in direction when pouncing on prey, making high leaps, or balancing on narrow tree branches.

His ears can also provide clues concerning his mood. Ears that are held erect and forward usually indicate that the cat is alert and interested. Should he change them to a T position, also known as the airplane-wing position, it probably means he has become fearful or is developing increasing irritation or aggression. This position may also be displayed if your cat has an ear infection or ear mites.

When the ears are rotated and flattened against the sides of his head, he may be in a defensive, aggressive state of mind. If the ears rotate completely back but there is some inside pinnae (the cone-shaped part of the ear) visible, then his mood may be one of extreme offensive aggression. This flattening of the ears is how the cat protects them from injury during battle.

A cat may twitch his ears to indicate possible frustration. If one ear faces forward and one is flattened sideways, he may be uncertain of whether he's in a threatening situation.

EYES

Since he's a hunter, your cat has forward-facing eyes with binocular vision. His visual field is greater than that of a human. He's a *crepuscular* hunter, meaning he's most active at dawn and dusk. His eyes are equipped with a reflective layer at the back to maximize light. This layer reflects light that didn't get absorbed on the first pass, which makes his eyes much more efficient. This reflective layer is what gives your cat's eyes that glow when there's sudden light in a darkened room.

Your cat has color vision but it is limited to blues, grays, yellows, and greens. As a crepuscular hunter, what matters most to him is movement rather than color. To trigger your cat's prey-drive, movements need to go across his visual field or away from it.

Cats have a third eyelid that extends up from the inner corner of the eye. This thin membrane protects the eyes when walking through brush as the cat hunts. It also provides extra lubrication to the eye. When your cat's eye gets injured, the third eyelid may be visible as an extra form of protection while the eye is healing. This membrane is also often visible when the cat is sick. If your cat's third eyelid remains visible, you should have your cat checked by the veterinarian because he may be ill or have had an injury to his eye.

Your cat's eyes can also provide valuable clues regarding his mood. When a cat is excited or interested in something, the pupils are generally round. Depending on the circumstances, it could also indicate fear or defensive aggression. Should the pupils become totally dilated, he may be becoming more fearful or the defensive aggression may be increasing.

Constricted pupils may mean your cat is displaying offensive aggression, or he may be in predatory mode, especially if there's a toy or potential prey in sight. Keep in mind that pupil size is affected by the amount of light in the environment, so you always have to take that into consideration when trying to interpret mood.

Pupils that are slightly oval usually indicate relaxation. If the eyelids appear droopy or even half closed, he's probably extremely relaxed, if not almost asleep.

WHISKERS

Your cat's whiskers are fascinating devices that serve many functions. There are four rows of whiskers on either side of his muzzle.

The top two rows can move independently of the bottom two. The follicle of the cat's whisker is very sensitive and surrounded by blood vessels and nerve endings. When your cat is hunting, he fans his whiskers forward to catch all vibrations or changes in air currents. When he captures his prey, his whiskers help him detect movement. He can't see his prey very well when it's that close to his face or in his mouth, so he depends on his whiskers for movement detection.

In low-light situations, the cat uses his whiskers to help detect air currents. This helps him navigate around objects in the dark. His whiskers are also important tools for helping him determine whether he can safely squeeze into a tight spot. Typically, the whiskers extend to the same size as the widest part of the cat's body. If your cat is obese, he loses this ability because his body width far exceeds the extension of his whiskers.

CATWISE CAUTION

Never cut your cat's whiskers or pull on them. They're extremely sensitive. Cutting your cat's whiskers may greatly affect his ability to navigate and can cause pain and extreme stress.

There are whiskers above your cat's eyes that act like extensions of his eyelashes. They help to trigger protective eye blinks when your cat is walking through brush or if something dangerous is near his eyes. There are also whiskers located at the temples. Having whiskers above the eyes, at the temples, and on the muzzle helps your cat maximize his ability to gauge his environment and detect the presence of prey or danger.

On the back of his forelegs are also a few whiskers that become very useful when the cat has captured prey with his paws. The carpal whiskers are able to detect movement so the cat knows whether the prey is still struggling to get away. When hunting, sight and sound may come first, but once the cat has made contact with his prey, his sense of touch takes center stage.

The whiskers also provide some clues as to what your cat may be feeling. When he's relaxed, his whiskers extend sideways. Should prey come on the scene or if you exhibit a little toy, your cat's whiskers may suddenly fan forward to capture all the information he can.

If your cat has a hostile relationship with a companion cat, his whiskers will fan forward during the initial stage of offensive aggression. The cat who flattens his whiskers against his face is displaying defensive aggression. Should an all-out battle take place, both cats' whiskers are usually flattened against their faces.

NOSE

Your cat's nose is not as sensitive as your dog's, but it's much better than ours. Cats have several million more scent-sensitive cells than we do.

If you've watched your cat smell his food before tasting it, especially if you've heated it, he's using his nose to detect even the tiniest temperature change. His sensitive nose is what gives him the ability to detect even the smallest amount of medication you may have tried to sneak into his food. This sense of smell is necessary for survival in the wild because it helps him determine if a food is safe. A cat who hunts prefers to eat fresh-killed prey because he knows it's safe. If he must eat already dead prey, or if he's forced to raid a neighbor's trash, his nose helps him determine whether food has gone bad. If you've ever left a dish of wet food out until it turned into cement, imagine what his nose told him about the palatability and safety of that meal.

Your cat comes equipped with a very special organ that serves as a bridge between scent and taste. It's called the vomeronasal organ, or Jacobson's organ, and it sits between the roof of the mouth and the nasal cavity. This organ allows the cat to smell and taste a scent. The odor is flicked from the tongue to the roof of the mouth, where it's then transferred to the vomeronasal organ. Its primary function is for further analysis of other cats' pheromones. Intact males use this vomeronasal organ to analyze the pheromones in urine to determine whether it comes from a male or a female, and if it does come from a female, whether she's in heat. Through analysis of the pheromones, the cat can also determine the social status of the one who left the urine-mark. Cats use this organ when they feel that any interesting or unfamiliar scent requires further analysis. You can tell when your cat is using his vomeronasal organ because his facial expression will almost resemble a grimace with mouth slightly open. This is called the flehmen reaction.

MOUTH

Cats are obligate carnivores, which means they must eat meat to survive. Unlike many other animals, they can't convert beta-carotene from vegetable sources into vitamin A, so they must get it from animal sources. Although you may choose to be a vegetarian for health or ethical reasons, your cat can't. Serious health complications will result.

Your adult cat has thirty teeth. Since the cat is a carnivore, his teeth are designed to tear and strip meat from the bones. He doesn't grind food the way an omnivore or herbivore would. A carnivore's teeth are designed for tearing and chopping.

The fanglike teeth in the cat's mouth are his canine teeth. They're intended to perform the "killing bite." In theory, when a cat pounces on his prey, his canine teeth, if well placed on the prey, sever the spinal cord. Unfortunately, it doesn't always happen that easily during a hunt.

TONGUE

I'm sure you're familiar with how rough your cat's tongue is. That's because it contains backward-facing barbs. These barbs help the cat rasp meat from the bones of his prey. They also help him groom his hair coat, removing dead hair and debris. Unfortunately, this comes with a downside. Because of the backward-facing barbs, the cat is unable to spit things out of his mouth. When he grooms, he has to swallow the hair. That's why there's a danger of choking when cats play with dangerous items such as yarn, rubber bands, or string. He's unable to remove them from his mouth, so he has to swallow them.

Your cat drinks by forming a spoon with his tongue. He takes several laps and then swallows the water.

The tongue is also used for cooling by evaporation. He'll groom himself to allow the saliva to evaporate from his hair coat.

Considering how much grooming a cat does, isn't it amazing how sweet-smelling his coat remains? That's because there's a deodorizing component to his saliva. His tongue isn't just used for grooming in order to remove hair and look good, it's also a survival necessity. After he has eaten his prey, he grooms to remove all traces. This is important because he doesn't want to alert any other potential prey in the area that a predator is nearby. Removing the traces of prey through grooming is also done to make sure the cat himself doesn't end up the victim of a bigger predator.

TAIL

The tail is an extension of the spine and it actually makes up about one-third of it. Your cat uses his tail for balance. It acts as a counterbalance, allowing him to shift his center of gravity as he jumps on a fence or makes high-speed directional changes.

The tail is also an important communication device that can help a cat reduce the number of potential physical confrontations he might have with an opponent. It can be seen from far away and its position can be read by an approaching cat.

It is also an excellent mood indicator. If you pay closer attention to the position of your cat's tail, you'll probably get bitten or scratched less. A vertical tail held erect and slightly curled usually indicates friendliness. A tail held in a horizontal, half-lowered position while the cat is walking may indicate that he's relaxed. If the tail is very lowered, however, it can indicate aggression.

You may have the image of the wagging tail of a happy dog. Although that's not always accurate when relating to dogs, many people also assume a cat's wagging tail means the same thing. That assumption will almost always result in getting scratched. A lashing tale indicates agitation. The more intense the lashing, the greater the agitation.

If you have a multicat household in which the cats are very close and friendly, you may have noticed them sleeping together in such a way that one cat has his tail wrapped around the other. This affectionate position also indicates total trust. The cat who wrapped his tail around the other one is saying that he doesn't feel there's any threat whatsoever. That feeling can be confirmed by the cat's actual body posture. He may be stretched out (very vulnerable) or facing away from the other cat. This is total trust.

VOCALIZATION

Humans are the ones who spend so much time talking, but your cat vocalizes as well and he has quite a vocabulary. He meows, trills, purrs, chirps, chatters, murmurs, hisses, spits, and growls, and those are just a few vocalizations in his repertoire. Some sounds are reserved strictly for cat-to-cat conversations, while others are directed at us, and some, such as chattering, seem to be just a displacement behavior for frustration or excitement.

The purr is a very misunderstood form of communication. Many people assume the cat is happy and content whenever they hear that sweet little motorboat sound. While the cat does purr when he's relaxed, happy, and content, he also uses the purr in other situations that have nothing to do with being happy. A cat may purr as a self-soothing mechanism when sick or injured. Many cats have been known to purr when terminally ill or when they are close to death. A cat may purr when cornered by an attacker in an effort to soothe the opponent. A queen will purr in order to help her young kittens locate teats for nursing. Newborn kittens are deaf but they can feel the vibrations of her purr.

Cats utter several murmur sounds, which are produced with a closed mouth. There are numerous vowel sounds that originate with an open mouth (such as the all-important "meow"). There are also strained-intensity sounds where the mouth is open.

If you listen carefully, you can start to recognize and interpret your cat's vocabulary. A closed-mouth murmur may be used as a greeting, or it may be the sound your cat makes right before he purrs when he curls up in your lap.

When your cat is looking out the window and spots a bird, you may hear a fast chattering sound coming from him. This indicates excitement and also some frustration because he can't get to his intended target.

You may have a cat who loves to trill when you walk into the room. This is a happy sound that's a little more musical than a chirp.

The standard meow may be used as a greeting or a request. A variation on that is the mew, which one cat might use when trying to locate another cat in the household.

If your cat has a tendency to vomit up hairballs, you may hear him moan right beforehand.

Then there's the hiss. This is something you've probably heard from time to time, maybe only when your cat is on the examination table at the veterinarian clinic, but if you have a cat who shows fear aggression in many situations, the hiss may be something you hear on a regular basis. This is a snakelike sound produced when the cat arches his tongue and forces a blast of air out of his mouth. It's a defensive aggression vocalization. Some cats also add a spit right before or after a hiss. The spit is a popping sound that's produced more often when the cat is startled.

The growl is a low sound produced with an open mouth that is used in either defensive or offensive aggression. This is the ultimate warning signal to back off.

Pay attention to the sounds your cat makes on a regular basis and you'll probably find he's using the same patterns. In no time you'll be able to interpret just what he's trying to tell you.

PAY ATTENTION TO WHAT YOUR CAT IS SAYING

Observe the sounds your cat makes as well as his body positioning and what he does with his ears, tail, whiskers, and eyes, and you may be able to develop a better relationship with him. He might not feel as frustrated because you'll be picking up on what he thinks are very clear signals. Your cat is an amazing communicator, and with a little more awareness on your part, you can discover more about him, even after all these years. You can also teach your children how to read signals so they can avoid approaching the cat when he doesn't want to be approached. Just remember that when trying to read your cat's body language, you must take into consideration his immediate environmental circumstances. For example, his pupil size may have changed suddenly due to sighting a bird outside the window and not because of a change in mood. Behaviors don't occur in a vacuum, so part of the interpretation process involves the environment the cat is in.

Interpreting Body Language

- Body posture and position
- Size and shape of pupils
- Ear position
- Whisker position
- Vocalization
- Degree of piloerection, if any
- Immediate environmental circumstances

2

Real Estate Reality Check
Is Your Cat's Environment Part of the Problem?

An often overlooked element in behavior modification is the environment in which the cat lives. How it is set up influences how stimulated or bored the cat becomes, her level of security, how companion cats interact with each other, and how social the cat may choose to be with humans. The environmental choices you make for your cat also affect her physical health. No behavior modification program is complete without reevaluating your cat's living conditions. Even if you think you've done a good job with the environmental setup, there's always room for improvement. As you read through this chapter, I'm sure you'll find some ways to tweak your cat's environment to make life better or assist in solving behavior problems. Remember, no *starting from scratch* retraining plan is complete without taking the environment into consideration.

INDOOR/OUTDOOR

This is a major issue, so we must start here. This is a subject that can create division among cat owners faster than the twitch of a whisker. Decisions you have made regarding if or when you let your cat outdoors may be contributing to her behavior problems.

The indoor/outdoor decision has many underlying issues and

each one can have an effect on behavior. Indoor/outdoor life ranges from cats who are kept outdoors exclusively to ones who live only indoors. In between, there are many variations. Some owners allow their cats to roam outdoors during the day but bring them in at night. Others do the reverse. Some cats are allowed outdoors only while owners are there to supervise. Others are leash-trained and go outdoors only while harnessed. Frighteningly, I have also seen cats tethered to deck railings to keep them in a confined area. Many cat owners buy or build outdoor enclosures to keep their cats confined while outside. There are also companies selling electronic containment systems (such as invisible dog fences) modified for use with cats (a very bad idea, by the way).

I have strong opinions on the indoor/outdoor issue, but I believe most cat owners make decisions about it with their cats' best interests at heart. Sadly, though, many of those decisions are made without being fully informed. It's not just a black-and-white issue of in versus out. You have to know the possible dangers of your decision if you are choosing to let your cat outside. If you're thinking of letting your cat go outdoors, you must also take into account the area in which you live, the personality, health, and age of your cat, and what your true motivation is for your decision.

If you're at all familiar with my books and behavior modification techniques, you know I'm a firm believer in keeping cats indoors. My stance isn't the emotional one you may have experienced from others in your life who might strongly disagree with your decision. If you allow your cat outdoors, you should know not only the hazards your cat faces but also how being outside may be contributing to a current behavior problem.

Let's go through the dangers first. Your motive for letting your cat outdoors may be based on wanting her to enjoy the sunshine and fresh air, and to let her indulge her natural hunting desire. In theory, that sounds great, but your cat may pay a high price for it. First, depending on where you live, she is at risk of injury or death from being struck by a vehicle. Even if you think your cat is street-savvy,

her focus can be diverted if she's stalking prey or escaping an attacker. You also have to keep in mind that a cat who was street-savvy
in the past isn't as capable as she ages and her senses decline.

An outdoor cat, though very fast and smart, is at risk of confrontation with dogs, other cats, and also cruel people. As fast as a
cat is, she's not built for long runs. She has the lung capacity of a
sprinter, so a dog giving chase might overtake her.

Cats are territorial, and every time your kitty heads outside, she
may have to face other cats in the neighborhood who are rougher
and tougher. There may be a cat in the area who wants to limit your
cat's ability to roam. You may think your cat is happy every time you
open the door to let her out, but she may actually be anxious over
what awaits her out there. She may even be the rough and tough cat
herself. Either way, it puts her at risk.

Even though you may keep your cat's vaccinations up-to-date,
there are numerous diseases that she can still acquire outdoors. If
you don't keep your cat vaccinated, then she is totally vulnerable to a
number of debilitating and deadly diseases.

When your cat comes in contact with another cat, she may get injured in a fight in ways you may not be aware of at first. Cats are very
susceptible to abscesses. An abscess is typically formed when a cat
sustains a bite wound from another cat. The canine teeth of the cat
are very sharp and they create a narrow but deep puncture wound. If
the wound seals over on top, the bacteria remain trapped beneath.
As the infection grows beneath the skin, the cat may be in much pain
in that area. Eventually, the area swells with pus and is usually warm
to the touch. The cat might cry out in pain when petted or touched in
that spot. She may also develop a fever. Immediate veterinary care is
needed so the abscess can be flushed and cleaned. A drain is usually
sewn in surgically to allow the wound to heal from the inside out, and
the cat is put on a course of antibiotics. Abscesses are painful and
the recovery is uncomfortable. Unfortunately, many people are unaware of the injury until it does actually abscess and create a possibly life-threatening situation. Your cat doesn't necessarily have to

willingly engage in a confrontation to end up with an abscess. When I was a veterinary technician, I saw plenty of cats with abscesses on their hind quarters. They just weren't fast enough when attempting a retreat.

While outdoors, your cat is at risk of acquiring parasites. Depending upon where you live, fleas, ticks, and mosquitoes could be a health concern. Many cats commonly have flea-bite allergies as well and end up with hair loss. Fleas are also hosts to tapeworms, so if your cat has fleas, chances are she has tapeworms as well. Many times a cat owner is fooled into thinking the cat doesn't have any fleas because none is seen in the hair. Keep in mind that the cat's fastidious nature and self-grooming can make it hard for you to find a flea. Heavy flea infestation can result in anemia, especially in young, old, or weak cats. Tick bites pose a risk of tick-borne illnesses. Mosquitoes can carry heartworm. While dogs are the more common target of heartworm, cats are still susceptible. If you allow your cat outdoors, even for a few minutes, she must be protected against fleas, ticks, and heartworm. Be sure you talk to your veterinarian about which products are best for your cat. Don't buy over-the-counter products at pet supply stores or supermarkets. Your veterinarian will help you choose the safest and most effective product based on your cat's health, weight, and age.

Your cat may love to hunt while outdoors, but there are dangers associated with eating prey. Prey can carry parasites and disease. Cats also ingest whatever poisons the prey may have eaten.

Fresh air and sunshine are wonderfully beneficial, but there are also weather-related dangers for your cat while outdoors. In very hot weather, your cat is susceptible to heatstroke if she can't get into a cool enough environment and doesn't have access to drinking water. Because there is less hair on the cat's ears and nose, she is additionally at risk of sunburn. Repeated sun exposure can lead to the risk of skin cancer. Hot surfaces such as asphalt or concrete can burn the cat's paw pads. At the very least, they can create pain if the cat has to walk on those hot surfaces. In very cold weather your cat is susceptible to frostbite, especially the ear tips. Paw pads are vulnerable as well to frostbite and extreme discomfort due to contact with cold, icy surfaces. Another cold weather danger is antifreeze poisoning. Cars notoriously leak antifreeze, and it's not unusual for it to be spilled when someone is pouring it into the radiator. The taste of ethylene glycol is sweet, which attracts animals to it. Many cats die from antifreeze poisoning every winter. Car engines also pose a deadly risk in winter. Cats are attracted to the warmth of the engine and often crawl up in there to escape the cold. I'm sure you can imagine how horrific it is for the cat who is sleeping there when the engine is started up. A painful death, for sure.

Because of your cat's fastidious grooming nature, she's also at risk of being poisoned if a toxic substance gets on her fur. She may rub against something or a chemical may spill on her as she investigates the neighbor's garage. She'll groom her fur to remove the substance and ingest the poison.

You may want your cat to enjoy outdoor life but your neighbors may not share your sentiments. They may strongly object to the appearance of your cat in their yards, stalking birds at the feeders. Your cat may also eliminate and/or spray in someone else's yard— something that is not welcomed, even by the most tolerant of cat lovers. There may be a neighbor with an indoor cat who gets highly reactive whenever your cat comes onto the property.

While some neighbors may only mutter to themselves about what a nuisance your cat is, others may take more drastic measures. Your cat may be chased (perhaps into the road and into oncoming traffic), squirted with a water hose, shot with a BB gun (or worse), poisoned, or trapped and brought to a shelter. Even if your neighbors wouldn't dream of harming your cat, there are cruel people out there, adolescents and adults, who take sick pleasure in abuse of animals.

If your cat wanders far enough, she may get picked up by someone who decides to keep her. If she's a sociable, friendly cat, she becomes vulnerable to being an addition to someone else's family, or worse, ending up in the home of someone with cat-hoarding syndrome.

Intact cats who are allowed outdoors add to the very sad overpopulation problem. They also end up in more fights and are more at risk of disease. The fights that males engage in for the opportunity to mate with an available female can be very bloody. The mating ritual itself is very violent and a female cat may end up mating with several males. That creates multiple opportunities for injury and the spreading of disease.

When you let your cat outdoors, you give up control over what can and cannot be included in her diet. She is free to hunt and eat whatever she can catch. She may also visit nearby houses to munch out of available outdoor food bowls. The food that your neighbor puts out for the stray cats in the area may not be the best for your own cat. Your kitty may also be sharing a food bowl with several other outdoor cats who carry diseases that are spread through saliva. If obesity is a problem with your cat, you can't effectively put her on a weight-management program if she's visiting several houses for her between-meal snacks.

Another drawback to outdoor life is that you're less able to monitor your cat's health. If your cat is eliminating outdoors, you may not be alerted to potential health problems if you can't see your cat's waste or her elimination habits. Cats are susceptible to urinary tract problems, but if your cat eliminates only outdoors, how will you know she is having a problem? How will you know if your cat's urethra is totally blocked, a life-threatening medical emergency? This is a very real concern for male cats especially, because the urethra in males is long and narrow. If a stone forms in the bladder and can't pass through the urethra, it can block it completely. This is an absolute emergency because a painful death will occur in a short amount of time. How will you know if your cat is constipated and unable to pass a stool? What if your cat has severe diarrhea? What happens in the litter box is valuable information in helping you monitor your cat's health, since she can't verbally tell you that something's wrong. Even if you maintain an indoor litter box for your indoor/outdoor cat, you won't be able to fully monitor what is or isn't happening.

In addition to all of those health and injury risks, outdoor life might be contributing to a current behavior problem. If a cat who is allowed outdoors is spraying when she returns inside, it may be due to an encounter with another cat. Your cat may be spraying as a way of solidifying familiar territorial perimeters. Your cat may also not feel comfortable having a physical interaction with the outdoor cat and so engages in a more covert method of aggression.

 **CATWISE CLUE**

Many people don't realize that males aren't the only cats who can spray. Female cats spray as well.

In a multicat environment, if there is aggression between your indoor/outdoor cats, it might be because one cat doesn't feel confident enough to stand up to another outdoor cat, so she chooses to turn her aggression on a lower-ranking companion cat. There is also a possibility of redirected aggression if one cat returns indoors after seeing another cat while outside or having an encounter with that cat.

Not every cat is emotionally equipped to handle life outdoors. Your cat's behavior problem may be connected to the fear of being placed outdoors when she's really too timid or frightened to be in that unfamiliar environment. I have had many clients with fearful cats, and the problems were due to the fact that they placed the cats outdoors during the day, totally unaware that they feared being there. The cats would find hiding places while their owners were at work. One cat stayed planted on the back porch, terrified to step into the yard because of the large dog next door.

The fact that the indoor environment is familiar is very comforting to cats. They want to get up from their naps and know that they won't encounter any strange scents or have to worry about who might be coming around the corner. The outdoor environment constantly changes. There are so many animal scents, weather changes, unfamiliar and sudden noises, and so forth. Some cats are confident in how they handle these things, but some are not.

You may also be in a situation in which your indoor/outdoor cat has actually trained *you*. She may meow demandingly when she wants to go out, regardless of whether or not it's convenient for you. Perhaps she scratches at the door or even climbs the screen to get you to pay attention to her request. Maybe she's one of those in-out-in-out-in-out cats who can't make up her mind what side of the door she wants to be on from one minute to the next. Perhaps you have a cat who long ago bypassed vocalizing and goes straight for the bite if you don't let her out when she wants. You may also be one of those lucky kitty owners who has a door darter—a cat who sees the opportunity of the open door and bolts out whenever she wants.

If you think your cat's behavior problem may be due to her indoor/outdoor life, or if I've convinced you that it's safer to keep your cat indoors, don't worry about the transition. I know you may have avoided keeping your cat inside because the transition process seemed impossible, what with the yowling of your unhappy cat or the constant escape attempts whenever the door was cracked an inch. Don't be afraid—there's a method to retraining your cat to stay indoors. The simple fact is that if you make the indoors as interesting as the outdoors, your cat will have everything she needs and wants while staying safe. If you don't create an interesting and secure indoor environment, though, there is no motivation for her to follow the plan. So the first step is to create a kitty haven indoors. Once you understand what your cat needs in her environment, you can then move on to the behavior modification technique of the actual transition.

Regardless of whether your cat stays in or goes out, a stimulating and secure indoor environment is a must. As I said in the beginning of this chapter, the environment plays a key role in creating or solving behavior problems. The following sections will walk you through the must-have components in the environment. If you're attempting to keep your outdoor cat indoors, first prepare the environment in the ways listed below. You'll then find behavior modification techniques later in this book. Chapter 3 covers how to use distraction to help change your cat's focus when she's whining at the door and chapter 4 covers how to prevent door dashing.

VERTICAL THINKING

When your cat goes outdoors, there are usually two major things on her mind. One creates a feeling of fun anticipation and the other creates anxiety. The fun anticipation comes from the possibility of successful hunting. Your cat was born to hunt and there are so many creatures out there who stimulate that prey-drive. The anxiety comes from the possibility of encountering another cat or other rival or predatory animal. Whether or not your cat is confident, there's anxiety associated with the unknown—and the outdoor environment is filled with the unknown. What we're going to do is create a fun and stimulating indoor environment that gives her all the good things, and we'll remove that big anxiety-provoking negative aspect. If you're worried that I'm going to instruct you to start bringing live mice or crickets into the house for your cat's entertainment, you can relax. Your cat's prey-drive can be stimulated and satisfied through the correct type of playtime. We'll get to that later. First we have to set the stage and construct the framework for our make-believe outdoor environment. I want to start by changing the way you think about your living space.

As humans, we tend to think of our environment in horizontal terms. If you have a dog, her world is pretty much horizontal as well. Look around the room and you'll see what I mean. Furniture is all placed on the floor. We move through the room horizontally. Your dog probably has a comfy bed on the floor, or she's content to curl up on the bed or sofa with you. Look at your walls now. There's probably some artwork hanging there or maybe a mirror or a TV. You've carefully maximized your horizontal space and used the vertical space in the typical way suited to humans. Your cat, however, doesn't limit herself to living in a horizontal world. Her world is very vertical. Cats can jump five times their height. They climb trees and perch on high spots to watch for prey or to widen their view when looking out for possible danger. Think of the more common places you might find your cat and I'll bet many of them are off the ground. Your cat may enjoy being on top of the refrigerator—a place you'll never find your dog. Perhaps she can scale the entertainment center and perch on top of the TV. A typical cat lounging area is to curl up on a bookshelf. Perhaps one of the reasons you bought this book was to find a way to stop your cat from walking on the kitchen counter or the dining room table. She isn't misbehaving by wanting to be on those elevated places; she's doing what comes naturally as a cat. Vertical space is important to her. Vertical space will also play an important role in modifying behavior problems. Your cat is very much connected to her environment, so it would make sense that an anxiety-provoking environment or one where there isn't enough stimulation could contribute to unwanted behavior.

Look again around your room and at the walls. There's some vertical space there that's going unused. If you're willing to make a few modifications, you can actually double and triple the size of your cat's territory without having to break down a wall and add on to your home. A little increase in vertical space will go a long way in making the indoor environment more appealing.

If your cat likes to hang out on the counter or on furniture where you'd prefer she not go, you can create more appealing options for her by increasing her allowable vertical territory. Look at the vertical places she currently uses to get an idea as to why she might like them. She might be on the counter because it's an open area where she can see who comes into the room. There may also be a window there and being on the counter is the best way for her to look out. Food left on the counter can be strong motivation for her being there. If you have a multicat home, the counter may be where your cat feels safest when everyone comes in to eat. The feeding station can be a hostile place in some multicat homes.

If the back of the sofa is where your cat likes to sleep, she may be there because it's very comfortable or maybe she can lounge in the sun and look out the window. If she curls up on a shelf in the bookcase, she may be looking for a safe, out-of-the-way spot to nap where no one can sneak up behind her. Perching on top of the refrigerator is also a feline favorite, and that's because it's very often the highest place in the home that the cat can reach.

In a multicat home, vertical spaces can help keep peace because the cats can more easily maintain any status they may have established. A high-ranking cat may claim the highest elevated spot as a way to oversee the area. It can also be a show of ranking, as her high elevation lets the other cats know who's boss. If a high-ranking cat has access to the highest elevation, she may be content to use that display rather than engage in any aggression. Your frightened cat may perch up high so she stays out of the line of fire and to get a better view of who might be around. With every form of elevation, you add a level to the territory. That's one of the important factors in why many people with small apartments can have multiple cats living in harmony—they creatively increase the territory just by making use of vertical space. Even at that, though, there is only so much overlapping of the home range you can ask of cats who must share one environment.

Vertical thinking doesn't apply just to high elevations. If you have a multicat home, you especially have to think of all levels—high, middle, and low. You might have a cat who is in the middle of the pecking order and feels more comfortable on middle perches. A very timid, shy cat would appreciate having several hiding places low to the ground or slightly elevated. Some frightened cats feel more secure being safely up high on an elevated perch. No matter how many cats you have, even if it's just one, she'll appreciate having this increase in her territory. It'll provide her with more options for exercise and play as well as creating more areas of security.

One of the easiest ways to increase vertical territory is with a cat tree. A cat tree that has multiple perches can allow more than one cat to share a close space. This works well if the tree sits by a window, because two or three cats can enjoy the view while maintaining social ranking. The multiple perches are beneficial even if you have only one cat, because she can easily climb to the top perch. Cat trees can be purchased from pet supply stores, through mail order, or online. They come in a wide range of prices, depending upon how elaborate you want to get. Some online companies will let you design the height you want, as well as the perch style and type of carpet covering. If you're interested in a cat tree, don't be fooled by how elaborate it looks. What matters most to your cat is stability and comfort. Choose a tree that has a rock-solid base. The last thing you and your cat want is to have the tree wobble or tip over when kitty takes a flying leap. Comfort is important, especially when you consider how much time your cat may spend napping there. Trees come with everything from flat perches to elaborate minipagodas. If possible, choose a tree with U-shaped perches. Cats tend to feel more secure when they can rest their backs against something. If the perch is flat, your cat may feel vulnerable on all sides. The enclosed, pagoda-type perches don't allow your cat to see out very clearly. They also tend to be too small. The more elaborate the perch, the more it drives up the cost of the tree. A simple, sturdy tree with U perches will work just fine. When shopping, take the size of your cat into consideration. Some trees have perches fit for only small cats. If you have a fifteen-pound cat, she'll need enough space for comfortable lounging on the perch. Take your cat's personality into account as well. If you have a very timid cat who prefers hiding places, then a tree with at least one pagoda-style perch or other semienclosed perch would be a good idea. Just make sure the size of the perch is appropriate for the size of your cat.

Cat trees may seem expensive when you first start shopping, but a good-quality one will last a very long time. We've had our cat trees for more than fifteen years and they still look great.

Another benefit of the cat tree is that it can serve double duty. In addition to providing multiple perching space, the support posts are usually tall and thick enough to serve as very effective scratching posts. Some trees have rope-wrapped support posts, which are ideal. You can also wrap the posts with rope yourself or cover them with sisal.

Cat trees can provide security for a cat if you have a dog or young children, or even if your cat is timid around visitors. The tree becomes a spot the cat knows is hers only. If it's tall enough, it becomes out of reach of a small to medium-sized dog. It also serves as an off-limits area for the children. We taught our children right from the start that when the cats are in the cat tree, it means they want to be left alone. Once your cat starts to feel a sense of security and knows that when she feels anxious she can find safety on the top perch of her tree, she may start staying in the room rather than disappearing under the bed. The cat tree provides an added sense of security in that it contains only your cat's scent, unlike the rest of the furniture in the home. When a visitor comes into the home, your cat may quietly sit in the cat tree to observe the guest, feeling comfort in the fact that she's in her safe spot.

If the cat tree is high enough, you can even put a walkway or some added shelving on the wall. Your cat will then have an easy way to climb up to the catwalk from the tree.

If a cat tree isn't in the budget or you have very limited space, consider a few window perches. Although they won't provide as much height as a cat tree, they still increase the vertical space. Perches can also widen the window ledge enough to allow your cat to be more comfortable. They come in many styles and some even contain heating elements. Choose a perch that'll attach securely to the wall. If you have more than one cat and you have enough window space, get more than one perch. This will give your cats the option of getting cozy together on one perch or choosing perches of their own. In a multicat home, the more choices you provide, the less tension is created. This applies to so many things in the environment—scratching posts, litter boxes, feeding bowls, perches. Let them choose if they want to share. If your cats are best buddies, then sharing isn't such a big issue, but if your cats have some tension in their relationship, or if one or more is experiencing a behavior problem, the more options they have, the better.

To increase vertical territory, you can be as creative as you'd like and you can work within your own budget needs. A table by the window that has a folded towel on it can serve as a window perch. You can get as elaborate or basic as you want. What's most important is that the elevated areas are sturdy, safe, comfortable, and in appealing locations, and that there are enough of them for each cat in the home. I have had clients with limited space create catwalks around the room, installing climbing perches on the wall that lead to the walkways. You don't have to get that creative; you could install a couple of perches by adding ordinary shelving on the wall—just make sure all shelves are wide enough to be comfortable and are very secure. Cover the shelving with a nonslip material, fleece, or carpeting.

Make use of mid-level vertical territory, especially in a multicat home. Do this by making sure there are some perches or cozy places off the ground but not as high as the top perches. If you have a cat tree, then the mid-level vertical territory can be a window perch or even the back of a sofa or chair, provided your cat is allowed on the furniture. If you don't allow your cat on the furniture, then you have to create mid-level vertical spaces that are permissible.

Vertical space shouldn't be limited to one room. While you don't have to modify every room in your home, make sure the rooms your cat spends time in are equipped with more vertical space. If you have a cat tree in the family room, maybe you can put a few window perches in other areas of the home. The more behavior problems you're dealing with, especially ones involving multicat issues, the more vertical space you'll need.

HIDEAWAYS AND TUNNELS

To fully maximize your environment's appeal, you also have to consider that your cat will want some places where she can become invisible or secure areas where she can navigate through a room without having to draw unwanted attention to herself. A couple of cozy little hideaways are great for taking those much-enjoyed cat-naps. If the hideaway is comfortable and secure, it can reduce your cat's need to hide under the bed. If what you're trying to accomplish is to get your timid cat out into the main part of the house more often in order to help socialize her, you have to start by creating safe options for her. If your cat is the type who prefers hideaways, then try placing an A-frame or semicovered bed behind a chair in the corner (just make sure it's easy for her to get in and out of so she doesn't feel trapped there), on a shelf, or someplace where she would feel safe and secure. You can find semicovered cat beds in pet supply stores or you can simply create your own by using an open paper bag and a towel. When you open the bag, fold a one- or two-inch cuff around the edge to help it hold its shape. Place the bag on its side and line it with a towel. You can do this with a cardboard box as well.

Tunnels are a good option for creating low-level escape routes for timid or low-ranking cats. They're also lots of fun for any kitty. If your cat tends to walk along the perimeter of the room more than through the center, she may feel intimidated, or is a lower-ranking cat in a multicat home. The higher-ranking cat tends to occupy the center space, so a lower-ranking cat may feel more comfortable walking along the baseboard or even going behind furniture to get from one room to another. If the cat who walks the perimeter has more options, it may reduce her anxiety and the chances of confrontation by the other cat.

You can purchase cat tunnels in many pet supply stores or online. They come in various styles such as soft-sided ones that allow you to buy the individual pieces to make the tunnel as long as you want or to make it wind around a corner. To make a homemade tunnel, you can use sturdy cardboard or PVC and then cover it with fabric or carpet. You can even make a basic tunnel by connecting narrow boxes (cut out the bottoms) or paper bags. To keep the paper bags from collapsing, line the inside with foam-core board and glue or Velcro it to the top and sides. If you Velcro it, you can reuse it with another bag should that one get ripped.

If you make your own tunnel, cut out an escape hole midway through. This is important in order to provide a way out for the cat if she doesn't feel safe in the tunnel or if two cats enter the tunnel from opposite directions. Again, the more options you create for your cat, the less chance of unwanted behavior.

For a perimeter-walking cat, place the tunnels behind furniture. For example, if you slide your sofa out from the wall a bit, you can put the tunnel behind it and no one but the cat will know it's there. You can also put the tunnels in front of furniture that can't be moved. This can be a temporary option for a timid cat, as you work on behavior modification with her. As she becomes more secure, you'll eventually be able to remove the tunnels that are inconvenient to the humans in the family. Reposition them somewhere else in the room, though, so your cat will always have the option of using them.

SCRATCHING AND CLIMBING

These are two vital parts of a cat's daily life. They need to scratch for claw conditioning, stretching, and emotional release, and they also love to climb, as evidenced by their extremely flexible bodies. If you've been battling with your cat over furniture scratching or if she's climbing into forbidden areas, the way to resolve this is by giving her acceptable options for those behaviors. If you try to deny your cat the natural and normal behaviors that make up being a feline, then you're setting yourself up for behavior problems. It's so much easier to direct the behavior to a place that you and your cat find acceptable. The climbing part of this can be accomplished by providing cat trees and access to other acceptable elevated areas, as explained above. If you need help in setting up appealing scratching posts and creating deterrents as you direct your cat to the more acceptable areas, specific information is in chapter 6, which deals with furniture scratching. For help in directing your cat away from forbidden areas such as counters and into acceptable areas, refer to chapter 4.

THE LITTER BOX ENVIRONMENT

If you want to know where most of the environmental problems start in a cat's home, you usually don't have to look any farther than the litter box. As you walk through your home during your evaluation of how appealing the environment is, you need to take a long, serious look at the litter box setup. This is a huge part of your cat's world, and if you don't have a secure and appealing setup, it can start a domino effect in terms of behavior problems. For many people, litter box maintenance is the least enjoyable aspect of life with a cat, but if you shortchange this in any way, your cat will suffer. In order to know whether you're on target or have missed the mark with your litter box decisions, refer to chapter 5.

THE FEEDING STATION

If your cat is exhibiting food-related behavior problems, or if you have a multicat home, there may be some environmental modifications needed. They can range from where you feed your cat to the type of bowl you use. It's amazing how sometimes the smallest adjustment can make a huge difference to your cat. You'll find ideas for setting up creative feeding stations in this chapter, but more solutions to mealtime problems are covered in chapter 7.

BEDTIME

For some people, this is a time of bonding and relaxation with their cats. For others, it's a time of territorial disputes, a.k.a. who gets to sleep on the owner's bed. It can also be a time of constant wake-ups, nightly noises, and cat fights. From an environmental standpoint, you need to work with the personality of your cat and create satisfying nighttime surroundings. If there have been disturbances at night, look at what might be triggering them so you can create an effective option for retraining. For example, if you have a multicat home and a couple of cats fight for the prime space on the bed, then you need to create a second sleeping area for one of them that'll be just as appealing. This might be where a cat tree in the bedroom would work if you have the room, or maybe a window perch. If you have enough privacy that you can leave the curtains open or raise the blinds just enough for your cat to peek out, that might help the spot become a good second choice. Since many cats enjoy warm beds, consider using a heated or thermal cat bed (don't use an ordinary heating pad). If you're dealing with this particular behavior problem during the colder months, a thermal cat bed may be the perfect choice for one or more of the kitties. In fact, you may end up having to purchase more than one, or choose a large one if both cats decide they'd prefer that instead of the bed.

If the problem you're having is that you don't want your cat in the bed at night at all, instead of just locking her out of the room, create her own interesting area in another part of the house. Again, this is where a cat tree can be very beneficial. If you've been having trouble retraining your cat to stay out of the room, it might be because you have been approaching it from the negative instead of the positive. Create an appealing option for her. You also have to be consistent in your retraining. Don't allow her in the bed on weeknights but then banish her on weekends because you want to sleep late. Consistency is crucial in retraining.

If your cat is making noise, getting playful at night, or waking you up too early, you can find retraining techniques in chapter 4.

FELINE HOME MAKEOVER: *OPERATION ENRICHMENT*

If you are trying to do a transition to indoor life for your outdoor kitty, this is the information you'll need. From what you've read so far, you already have a pretty good idea of what might be lacking in your cat's current environment that could be contributing to behavior problems. Now, as Emeril says, *let's kick it up a notch* and create a stimulating environment that'll be the envy of other cat families. The great part about your feline home makeover is that you can go as wild as you'd like or stay simple and basic. If you're handy, you can make some of the components yourself. You don't have to blow your budget to make life more interesting for your cat. Simple objects, with a little creative input from you, can be turned into toys or kitty furniture. A cardboard box lined with a thick towel works just as well as an expensive pet bed. Your cat won't know the difference, but your wallet will. The object of the feline home makeover isn't to turn your home over to your cat, making your neighbors think you've lost your mind, but rather to create a cat-friendly environment that works for both the feline and human members of the family.

Throughout this book you'll see that I mention some products by brand name. The reason I do is because those products are ones I have had personal experience with. My clients have tried many products and these have shown results. If you're going to spend money, use the recommendations as starting points. You may find other brands that work better for you. You don't need to buy everything and break the bank. One or two products combined with homemade ones may be just what your cat needs. Only you know your budget limitations, your creative skill, and how your environment is set up. I don't want you to waste your money on things that don't work.

Provide what your cat needs to correct current behavior problems and prevent future ones. If you're going to create an indoor environment that has all the good aspects of the outdoors, then you need places to perch, climb, sleep, eat, and play, plus a few bonus components.

Climbing and perching

For climbing and perching, the cat tree is ideal to simulate the natural tree a cat would use in the wild. If you have the cat tree but don't know where to place it, put it by a window that has an interesting view. A backyard where birds come and go would be great. If you really want to create stimulation, set up a bird feeder outside the window for your cat's viewing pleasure. Keep in mind, though, that the feeder may attract other outdoor cats. If that should occur in your yard, the feeder will actually create stress for your indoor cat. If your cat likes to keep up on the happenings of the neighborhood, then put the tree near a front-facing window. Consider your cat's personality when placing the tree. If your cat is very timid and fearful, the tree should be placed near a quiet window or, in some cases, not near a window at all. For an older kitty who loves napping in the sun, choose a location that'll bathe the tree in sunlight. If placed by a window for your older cat, make sure it's not drafty. Use your knowledge of your cat's temperament to help you find the ideal location. If you have more than one cat, set up a couple of bird feeders outside in different locations and have a tree at one window and a perch at another. This way, if there's tension between the cats or if one has claimed a certain spot, another cat can still enjoy bird watching.

If the idea of a cat tree really turns you off because you're worried about it looking like a sore thumb in your house, there are ways to make it more attractive. First, you can look for the fancier trees that are made to appeal to the human eye. They're carpet-covered in colors that make them look more "treelike," such as leaf green for the perches, dark brown for the trunk, and grass-colored on the bottom. The problem with these trees is that they usually aren't good for scratching. If the perches are wide enough for your cat and you think she'll be comfortable, they're fine for perching but you'll still need to get scratching posts. Instead of spending money on the aesthetically appealing tree, it would be a better idea to get one that meets the needs of your cat, as previously described in this chapter. A good, sturdy basic cat tree will also be less expensive than one created to please the human eye. If you hate the look of it, place a silk tree in front of it or some silk plants of various heights around it. Don't use live plants unless you're sure your cat doesn't chew on houseplants. It's better not to tempt fate, so the silk tree is a safer option. In addition to disguising the cat tree, the silk trees sur-rounding it may make a cat feel more hidden there. This would be beneficial for a timid cat. When I brought two feral cats into my home, in an effort to help them feel more protected and less out in the open, I put silk trees around the cat tree.

In addition to the cat tree, replace those ineffective scratching posts that are just gathering dust with sisal- or rope-covered scratching posts. Place a couple of corrugated cardboard scratchers around the house for added horizontal scratching fun. Refer to chapter 6 for specifics on what to look for in a scratching post. Don't forget about window perches for those lonely windows in need of cat company.

If you have a room without crown molding or other architec-tural detail, consider creating a catwalk that goes partially or to-tally around the room. This is over-the-top for many owners, but if you'd like to have something fun and different for your cats, this could be a great way to increase space. Create staggered perches on the wall to lead to the walkway or construct a cat-sized stairway. Make sure you have perches or a walkway on at least two sides so a cat never gets cornered up there by an opponent in a multicat home.

Perches can be placed in various areas of the home to help with behavior issues. For example, if your cat likes to lounge on the com-puter monitor or hang out on your desk while you're trying to pay bills in your home office, you can create a kitty perch for her—put a padded perch on the wall above the computer monitor. You can also create a cubby for the computer monitor that can be covered on top with fleece.

Stimulation

Stimulation is a big part of what makes the outdoor environment at-tractive, so you now have to create stimulation indoors. In the wild, a cat would have a dozen or so opportunities to hunt throughout the day. Your indoor cat can easily get bored if there are no hunting opportunities or stimulating activities. You don't have to provide live mice for your cat, but you do have to create mock hunting sessions so she can use those incredible senses of hers and exercise that flexible body. These opportunities to hunt will come in two forms: *interactive* and *solo*. Interactive play involves the use of a fishing pole–type toy, with you controlling the motions. Solo playtime involves toys and other activities that your cat controls. Specifics on both of these types of playtime are found in chapter 3. Playtime can go a long way in helping your cat enjoy her environment more. The correct type of playtime will also be a valuable tool in behavior modification whether you are trying to help an outdoor cat get used to the indoors or you're trying to help two companion cats develop more tolerance toward each other.

Add more stimulation and fun to the feeding station as well. Instead of feeding your cat in one location, hide small bowls of dry food around the areas where she plays. This way she gets to "discover" the food. You can add interest to mealtime by using puzzle feeders such as the *Play-N-Treat* balls. These are hollow balls that have a hole on one side. You fill the ball halfway with dry food, and as the cat rolls the ball around, food periodically falls out. These balls can be used only in homes without dogs, though. Another puzzle game that can be used as a puzzle feeder is the *Peek-a-Prize*. This is a well-made wooden box with multiple paw-sized, strategically placed holes. Normally, you put toys in the box for your cat to paw at, but it can also be used as a puzzle feeder by dropping several pieces of dry food in there. The *Kitty Kong* can also be used as a puzzle feeder, especially if your cat isn't getting the knack of the *Play-N-Treat* ball. The *Kitty Kong* is open-ended on one side. Place several pieces of dry food inside and you have an instant and easy puzzle feeder.

You can create homemade puzzle feeders as well. Cut several paw-sized holes on all sides of a sturdy cardboard box, tape the flaps closed, and toss numerous pieces of dry food into the box. Your cat gets to reach in with her paw to get the food. You can also make a puzzle feeder by punching holes in the round cardboard center insert from a roll of toilet paper or paper towels. Cut out two round circles of paper and then securely tape them onto each end. Put numerous pieces of dry food inside. Test your homemade toy before giving it to your cat by making sure that it rolls easily and that you've made the holes large enough so dry food easily falls out as the toy moves on the floor or carpet. If your cat chews paper, stick to the *Play-N-Treat* ball, *Peek-a-Prize*, or *Kitty Kong*, but otherwise, the homemade puzzle feeders can be a wonderful and inexpensive way to increase stimulation and activity. You may even come up with your own idea for a puzzle feeder. Just make sure it's safe and not frustrating. It should create a challenge but it should never cause anxiety. More specifics on how to correct mealtime issues can be found in chapter 7.

Another fun part of outdoor life for a cat is to be able to munch on some grass. Many indoor cats share that desire and end up chewing on houseplants, which is extremely dangerous. Grow some kitty greens for your cat so she has a supply of fresh grass. You can find kits at pet supply stores or you can grow your own using oat, rye, or wheat grass. Leave the grass out for your cat to enjoy. More specifics on this can be found in chapter 4.

Many cats love the sound and sight of running water. It becomes an opportunity for play and is often more desirable to drink because it stays oxygenated. In addition to having a regular water bowl, how about getting your cat a drinking fountain? Several companies make pet water fountains, so they're easy to find in just about any pet supply store as well as online. They're actually very beneficial to cats because they can encourage increased water consumption—something that's of greater concern for cats fed dry food, older cats, or those with diseases such as chronic renal failure, lower urinary tract disease, kidney infection, or diabetes.

Did you know your television could be a source of entertainment for your cat? To add to the stimulation in the environment, there are cat-interest DVDs and videos that showcase prey. These DVDs show mice, fish, birds, and insects and include realistic sounds to further appeal to your cat's senses. Not all cats are interested in these DVDs but many enjoy them. In the *Friskies Cat Habitat* that Frank Bielec, Lou Manfredini, and I created, we placed small TV screens in the wall right near the perches of the cat tree. The cats enjoyed sitting on a perch and watching their own TVs. You don't have to get that elaborate; just popping one of the DVDs in for your cat every once in a while may increase stimulation. The DVD many of my clients' cats seem to prefer is *Video Catnip*, but there are numerous other brands out there. The DVDs and videos can be found in pet supply stores and online. One way to use the DVD is to set the time for it to come on while you're at work and kitty is home alone.

If you don't need to use tunnels in your home because your cat isn't timid, use them for fun. Place a soft-sided tunnel on the floor so it snakes around a corner and hide a treat or toy inside. Make a tunnel out of paper bags and hide toys inside such as a glitter ball or a catnip-infused mouse. Line the inside top and sides with foam-core board, using glue or Velcro. This will keep it rigid and sturdy. Change the tunnel's location every so often to keep things interesting. You can also purchase soft-sided cat tunnels at your local pet supply store or online. Make them long so they can wind around corners and create lots of opportunities for your cat to explore and have fun.

In addition to tunnels, cat sacks are great fun and serve as comfortable hideaways. You can make one with a simple paper bag. Open the bag, and roll a cuff around the edge to increase its sturdiness. Lay it on its side and line it with a towel. For use as hideaways, place several paper bags in corners on various levels. Don't put them on the floor unless you know your cat enjoys sleeping that low. Most cats tend to feel more comfortable sleeping up off the ground. To use the bags as playtime cat sacks, forgo the towel and toss a Ping-Pong ball or other small toy in there. Place these playtime cat sacks out in the open for your kitty to discover as she goes about her day.

CATWISE **CAUTION**

Never use a plastic bag as a toy or as a hiding place for a cat. Cats can become tangled in the plastic handles and may end up choking. Also, some cats chew on plastic and that can pose a serious health risk. Only use a paper bag and make sure it doesn't have handles. If you decide to use a paper shopping bag that does have handles, cut them off first.

Boxes are great toys for cats. When you get a delivery, save the box for your cat to enjoy for a couple of days. Cut out a few holes and turn the box upside down so your cat can hide in there. Toss in a ball or toy for her to bat around.

Safety

Since cats love to climb and explore, sometimes a vase or a picture may accidentally get knocked to the floor. Once you've created more acceptable elevated areas for your cat, the hope is that she'll spend less time perusing your mantle or bedroom dresser. You can use training techniques to let her know what is and isn't an acceptable area by following the instructions in chapter 4. You also need to make sure breakable items are not in places where your cat could get to them, not just for the sake of the valuable item but for the safety of your cat. Part of creating a feline-friendly environment involves safety. Breakable items that are on display and can't be put away can be secured with museum wax. This keeps the item in place and no one will know the wax is there. Items that are top-heavy and can be knocked over should be placed on tables against the wall so your cat can't get behind them to push them off.

Secure electrical cords so they aren't dangling. With an adult cat you may have thought you were beyond the kitty-proofing stage, but while you're doing environmental improvements, make sure cords are tucked behind furniture or concealed at the baseboard with cord covers. I had one client with a twelve-year-old cat who had never bothered the electrical cords, even when she was a kitten. The owner didn't give the cords a second thought after her cat reached adulthood. One day the cat was batting a toy mouse around the room and it got tangled in the many cords behind the owner's computer desk. In an effort to get to the mouse, the cat chewed one of the wires. Fortunately, the cat survived the incident with only minor injuries. The owner made sure all wires were secure from that point on. Look around your home and make necessary adjustments to things that could pose a potential danger, such as dangling wires, open trash cans, harmful chemicals, and torn window screens.

The air in your house is another consideration in your feline home makeover. Cats can have allergies, just as people do. If you smoke, your cat is vulnerable to the secondhand smoke. Indoor air purifiers won't totally eliminate that risk but they will help keep the air a little cleaner. Limit your use of air-freshener sprays because of how they may affect your cat's respiratory system.

Familiarity

Even though you're trying to create a stimulating and fun environment, your cat still needs comfort and familiarity. She takes comfort in knowing that everything in her home will not suddenly have a strange cat's scent on it, a familiar object won't abruptly disappear, and a potentially threatening object will not appear. One way she helps identify objects in her territory as hers or as something she's familiar with is through the use of scent. A cat will often facially rub an object to deposit her facial pheromones on it. Pheromones are scent chemicals that contain information about the cat. Facial pheromones are known as the "friendly" pheromones. A cat tends to facially rub in areas where she feels comfortable. You can use this information to help create more comforting familiarity in the environment for your cat. You can do it in two ways. First, there's a product called *Feliway* that contains a synthetic version of feline facial pheromones. It was originally created for use in homes where there are urine-marking problems because cats don't tend to urine-spray where they facially mark. The side benefit of *Feliway* is that it can be used on unfamiliar objects in the home to help a cat more quickly feel comfortable with them. The product is often used when a family is moving into a new house and *everything* is unfamiliar to the cat, or when a new piece of furniture is being brought into the home. If there is an area in your home where you think your cat doesn't feel as comfortable (maybe she has a fear of being near the front door) or if you are bringing in a new object—even if it's a cat tree—use *Feliway* on it. The product comes in a spray bottle and you spray a little on the corner of the object once or twice a day. Spray it eight inches up from the floor, which is the approximate distance from a cat's nose to the ground. If you have multiple cats, *Feliway* can still be used because each cat will think the pheromones are her own. *Feliway* also comes in a plug-in diffuser called *Comfort Zone*. If your cat isn't comfortable in an entire room or if numerous things are new in the room, the diffuser may be the best option. It covers approximately 650 square feet and lasts about a month. *Feliway* is available in pet supply stores, online, and through many veterinarian offices. If you are bringing an outdoor cat inside, the diffuser is a good addition to the behavior modification process. Another option for putting facial pheromones on a new object is to place a soft clean sock on your hand and then gently rub your cat around the head and face, paying particular attention to the sides of her mouth. Don't do this if your cat doesn't enjoy being petted, though. Take the scent-filled sock and rub it on the corners of your new object. If you have more than one cat, use a different sock for each and place the scents on different parts of the object's corners. Don't rub one cat's scent over another's.

Last, but certainly not least, your feline home makeover must include an honest evaluation of the litter box setup. It may just need a little tweaking, or you may be facing a major litter box overhaul. This is the time to clean up, make necessary substrate (litter) changes or location transitions, and add extra boxes if needed. If you're dealing with a serious litter box problem, you may be facing the chore of ripping up carpeting or replacing badly soiled furniture. Remember that it isn't enough just to remove the soiled items and replace them with new ones—you must find the cause of any underlying problems so you'll be able to make the best decisions when it comes to creating the most cat-friendly home for your kitty. More specific information on litter boxes can be found in chapter 5.

3

Serious Fun
Play Therapy

As you go through the retraining process, *play* may not be high on your list. You may even have gotten to the point where your relationship with your cat is so disconnected that you can't imagine playing with him. Your cat might be so consumed with stress that he no longer finds joy in playtime. Play may seem like the last thing you would want to concern yourself with when you have a cat with a behavior problem, but it's actually going to be one of the most important tools in your behavior modification toolbox.

Cats are playful creatures and they benefit physically, emotionally, and mentally from the experience. Since a cat is a hunter, his body is made for flexibility, speed, and accuracy. If he's not able to flex those muscles and enjoy a good play session, there can be a chain reaction of negative consequences. Physically, he needs a certain amount of exercise on a regular basis to keep his body in good shape.

As a hunter, the cat's senses are extremely sharp. He's tuned in to his environment and is alert to the slightest sounds, sights, and scents. The mental aspect of playtime is important because it allows the cat to satisfy his prey-drive, and that's a normal part of being a cat.

Emotionally, playtime can be used to help build confidence, reduce stress, fight depression, and combat behavior problems.

The type of play therapy I'm referring to isn't just the fuzzy mouse you bought for your cat that sits in the corner gathering dust—it's targeted play therapy specifically designed for your cat's physical, mental, and emotional needs. Even though you'll know this play therapy is serious stuff, as far as your cat is concerned, he'll just think you've increased the fun factor in your home.

OBESITY

Based on the high number of obese cats I see in my consultations, too many are getting way too much food and little or no exercise. The result of that combination can put the cat at risk for arthritis, diabetes, or heart disease. It can also lead to other problems if the cat becomes too overweight to groom himself. He may no longer be able to reach around to groom his hindquarters. If the cat can't keep his body as clean as he'd like to, that not only leads to potential skin and hair coat problems, but also can lead to depression. Cats were not meant to look like they swallowed a football. Their legs and joints weren't meant to carry an enormous amount of weight. I have seen cats who were so fat, their legs became invisible beneath the overstuffed pillows of body fat—all that I could see was their paws.

If your cat is overweight, it may be contributing to the behavior problems he's having. For example, he may be eliminating outside the litter box because he's no longer comfortable getting inside it. Based on the location of the box, it may take too much effort for him to reach it, especially if he has to go up or down stairs.

An obese cat who cannot get around as quickly as he used to may become the victim in a multicat home. He may begin to display personality changes if he feels his place in the pecking order has shifted. If he can no longer get away from a more aggressive cat, he may start hiding more.

If your overweight cat is unable to groom himself or is experiencing weight-related pain such as arthritis, his disposition may change to one of a grumpy, irritable kitty. This may affect his relationship with you as well as the relationship he has with any companion pets in the home.

Problems around the feeding station may be contributing to the cat's weight increase. If your cat is worried that other companion cats are going to get the food, he may be overeating. If that's the case, you not only have the problem of the obese cat, but also the problem of the intercat relationships. The cat's increased weight can be the symptom of a behavior problem occurring within the home.

The overeating can be due to boredom. Cats were built to *do something*. Regardless of the type of cat you have, he was born to hunt. Some breeds are more efficient at that than others, but basically being a hunter is at the core of every feline. That doesn't mean your cat must go out and drag home every mouse, bird, or snake in the yard, but if your cat is overweight, it does mean that there's too much emphasis on food and not enough on fun.

You may think your cat doesn't have much of a prey-drive because his stomach is always full. Not true. Some cat owners used to believe they could reduce the amount of prey their cats dragged home if they let them outdoors only after a meal. The truth is, a full stomach doesn't cut down on the amount of hunting a cat (of a healthy weight) will do—it cuts down only on the amount of prey the cat may actually ingest. The problem the obese cat has is that it becomes too much effort physically to haul that big body around to hunt. The prey-drive is buried deep in there, though, and once you find just a spark, you can motivate your cat to move again.

A weight-reduction plan requires the combination of an appropriate nutritional program for your cat as well as an increase in activity. For information on how to start a weight-reduction program and behavior problems associated with mealtime, refer to chapter 7. Combine that with the play-therapy information in this chapter, and hopefully your cat will be on his way to better health and better behavior.

HOW TO USE PLAY THERAPY TO YOUR ADVANTAGE

There are so many reasons to make play therapy work for you to improve life for your cat. It starts, of course, with the physical benefits, as I mentioned previously. That alone should be reason enough to retrain your cat and yourself to the idea of regularly scheduled playtime. The extra benefit, though, is that play therapy can be used as part of a behavior modification program. It can be a powerful way to change a cat's mind about a negative experience or location. For a cat eliminating outside the litter box, play therapy can help him change his impression about the area where he's inappropriately eliminating. Used correctly, play therapy can defuse a tense situation between companion cats or help a timid cat develop more confidence. If your cat is terrified of visitors in the home, play therapy will be one of the methods you can use to ease his fears and increase his comfort level. When destruction or disturbing nocturnal activities are the issue, play therapy may be what saves the cat from being banished to another room or, worse, rehomed.

One of my favorite reasons to teach cat owners about play therapy is that it can help strengthen the cat-human bond. If you've been dealing with a long-term behavior problem or you've used inappropriate methods of behavior modification, your relationship with your cat may be distant, one of mere tolerance, or even hostile. Your cat may have learned to fear you because he knows he's going to be chased, yelled at, put in "time-out," or physically hit. These are things that can damage the relationship, and sometimes can turn the cat and owner into enemies under one roof. So whether you're dealing with a tiny behavior problem or a major one, play therapy should be a required activity. It won't just be fun for the cat; it'll be fun for you, I promise!

INTERACTIVE PLAY

If you're like most kitty owners, you probably have a basket in the corner of a room filled with cute little toys for your cat. There's a reason why they continue to just sit there gathering dust day after day, and that's because they're *dead prey*. For your cat to get any use out of them requires him to create all the movements, and that means he has to play the part of both the hunter and the prey. As a hunter, he's attracted to movement, sound, sight, and smell. Those fuzzy mice sitting in that basket hold no interest. That's where interactive playtime works so well, because the cat doesn't have to do the extra work to make the prey come to life. When you use an interactive toy with your cat, he gets to fully enjoy being the hunter.

Many people love to tell me how unique their cats are because they play fetch just like a dog. They think their cats are so amazingly smart because they picked up that trick on their own. Well, the truth is, their cats are actually extremely smart, but the behavior is not all that unusual. After the person has thrown the ball or toy a few times, the cat realizes that the only way this "prey" comes to life is when the person has it. So, smart kitty trots back with the toy in his mouth and deposits it at the human's feet. When your cat plays fetch, it's usually a sign that he's in need of a better quality of playtime, and that's where interactive play comes in.

This type of play involves the use of a toy that you hold to control the movements. There are many types of interactive toys on the market. Some are fishing-pole designs with a pole, string, and a toy dangling from the end of the string, but that's just the beginning. There are poles with feathers, streamers, or jingly toys attached directly to them (without strings), and there are some with a long, snakelike piece of material attached. Not all interactive toys are good or well made. Since a successful interactive play therapy session starts with the right kind of toy, I'm going to help you navigate your way through the toy aisle.

CHOOSING INTERACTIVE TOYS

Your cat may end up with one favorite toy, but it's good to get a variety of types so you can trigger different hunting techniques. Some toys are meant to simulate the motion of a bird while others may imitate a snake. When a cat hunts in the wild, he may have a taste preference, but if he's needing a meal, he'll hunt what's available. So although he may prefer a bird, he might have to settle for a mouse or a chipmunk. When you do your play sessions, it's good to vary the types of toys so your cat can exercise different hunting techniques. A very athletic cat may excel at air hunting and leap high to accurately capture the birdlike toy. An obese cat or a very timid one may need to start with ground hunting techniques, and so a toy that mimics snake or mouse movements would be best.

When you first start shopping, think carefully about the personality of your cat and how active he is currently. If you have more than one cat, you might find they'll end up with different favorites. Whatever toys are chosen should be well made, and you need to be able to move them in a way that'll trigger the cat's prey-drive. You don't want to choose a toy that has a very short wand because that will put your hand too close to where the cat will be biting or pawing. A long pole with a string and a toy on the end of it is ideal because it puts a very safe distance between your fingers and the cat's teeth. It also allows the toy to be the main focus because the string will essentially become invisible once the cat's prey-drive kicks in. The long pole and string also help maintain the comfort zone for the cat. This is of vital importance if you're working with a timid or poorly socialized cat. If the toy is short and you're too close to the cat, it can prevent him from focusing on the play session because he has to keep an eye on you. For the play therapy to work, the cat has to be able to turn all of his attention to the toy and not have to worry about anything else around him. Keep this in mind as you look at the toys in the store. A toy may look like a lot of fun from a human's point of view—small wand, big bright feathers—but will it work for an effective interactive session?

Don't get any toys that are designed like gloves with extended fingers. Even if the glove is heavy-duty enough to prevent injury from scratches (and I have yet to see one made that strong), you will be sending a mixed message to your cat. Your fingers should never become a part of the toy itself.

If you have a robust, active cat, you can choose a larger toy, but if your cat is timid or depressed, you may have to start with something less intimidating. You want the toy at the end of the string to be the approximate size of prey or even smaller. A cat wouldn't hunt something his own size or larger. He goes after prey that's within his conquering capabilities. A cat also has a small stomach, so he hunts something he'll generally be able to consume. The toy doesn't have to be pretty; it has to be effective. It also doesn't have to be expensive, but it does have to be well constructed.

You may find that the types of toys you initially buy for your timid or obese cat, or one who is not used to playtime, will change as he gets more skilled and confident. Ground hunting may be the preferred playtime method for a few weeks or months. You'll watch your cat's abilities, and as he gets more comfortable or active, you can incorporate more athletic forms of interactive play therapy.

All the toys you purchase for interactive play must be put away out of the cat's reach when the play sessions are over. This is to protect the cat from injury and also to keep the toys special. You'll have other safe solo toys for your cat to have around the house 24/7, but the interactive toys need to keep their strong appeal. This controlled access is one of the important ways they're able to be used for behavior modification.

For air-hunting toys, a fishing-pole type is best because the toy on the end of the string can move freely. The one that has topped my list for many years is *Da Bird*. This outstanding toy is a basic fishing-pole design with actual feathers attached at the end of the string. The wow factor comes from the fact that the feathers are attached to a swivel device. When you move the toy through the air, the feathers twirl around to move and sound like actual bird wings. This toy is available in pet supply stores, online, and through mail order. If your cat becomes too enthusiastic and destroys the toy, you can purchase a replacement piece to reattach to the string.

My second favorite toy for cats is the *Cat Dancer*. This isn't a fishing-pole design, but rather a strong springy wire with a little rolled cardboard handle on one end and a tightly rolled cardboard target toy on the other end. It sounds too simple to work, but trust me, this is one terrific toy. When you hold the handle end, rest your index finger on the wire, and with gentle movements you can make the toy dart like a cricket. There are so many benefits to this toy, and you'll learn about them a little later. The *Cat Dancer* is very inexpensive and available just about everywhere.

Another great toy along the same lines as the *Cat Dancer* is the *Dragonfly*. This toy consists of a Mylar dragonfly suspended from a strong and flexible wire. The Mylar makes the toy's movements and sounds very irresistible to many cats. The toy is available in some pet supply stores, but the easiest place to find it is online.

For a snake toy, there are several options. The *Cat Charmer* (made by the company that makes the *Cat Dancer*) is a well-made basic toy with a long, thin fleece ribbon attached to a pole. Our *Cat Charmer* has withstood countless cat pounces and attacks for many years. There are other snakelike toys available as well. Just make sure the one you choose is well made so the snake doesn't separate from the wand after a few play sessions.

There are so many terrific interactive toys available. The ones I mentioned are just a few of the foundation toys you should have as you begin the retraining process. As you familiarize yourself with your cat's play techniques, you'll continue to tweak your toy repertoire.

CATWISE REMINDER

Put all interactive toys away when the session is over to prevent the risk of your cat chewing on strings or breaking off pieces, which could cause choking.

INTERACTIVE PLAY THERAPY TECHNIQUES

Now that you have the right toys, the next step is learning how to use them correctly. Oh, I know you're probably rolling your eyes at the thought of having to be taught how to use a cat toy, but there's a right way and a wrong way. If you do it the wrong way, as many people do, you won't be engaging the cat's brain and benefiting him emotionally. The wrong technique may work the cat physically, but it also annoys or frustrates him. It's time for a retraining checkup to see whether you've been playing the wrong way.

Many cat owners use two general approaches to interactive playtime, both of which are counterproductive. The first involves dangling the toy in the cat's face. The cat responds by swatting or biting the toy. Often, the posture he takes is to sit up on his haunches and box the toy. That's not playtime—that's a defensive reaction. The second way I often see owners play with their cats is to take the toy and move it wildly about, sometimes having the cats doing nonstop flips and chasing it until their sides are heaving and their mouths are open in desperate panting.

The reason the above methods are wrong is that both of them create a *negative* reaction. Playtime is supposed to be fun, not annoying and frustrating. It's also supposed to imitate the way a cat would naturally hunt, so the movements of the toy have to simulate that of prey. I don't know of any suicidal prey who would willingly dangle themselves in a cat's face, hoping to be captured. And although a hungry cat in the wild might have to exhaust himself to catch a meal, his technique most often involves stalking and then pouncing—not chasing until his heart is about to leap out of his chest.

For a cat, the hunting technique is very efficient. He uses his brain as much as his body. If you have never seen your own cat in a hunt (even if it's to capture a tiny spider in the house), I'm sure you've seen the image on television. The cat silently stalks his prey, using whatever is around for cover. The hunter is silent and invisible as he inches closer and closer. In the wild, he may hide behind a tree and then slink low to the ground as he moves to the next tree or bush. A cat will also often hunt in tall grass, as it's an ideal place to find prey such as mice, but also because he can move through it without detection. When the cat gets within striking distance, he pounces with amazing speed. If all goes well, he is able to inflict what is known as the killing bite by severing the prey's spinal cord with his two sharp canine teeth. Otherwise, he grasps the prey with his front paws. The technique is based on the cat's incredible senses, his stealth, and his speed.

If you want to have a successful and beneficial interactive play session with your cat, you have to trigger his prey-drive, and the way to trigger it is to move the toy like prey. If you have been playing with your cat the wrong way in the past, you and your kitty are about to discover a fun new world.

Play therapy will function in two ways. One way is for maintenance and should be scheduled on a regular basis. The other way is targeted specifically for behavior problems. We'll start with the maintenance version of interactive play therapy.

Since cats don't prefer to hunt in flat open areas, you'll need to set the scene to be a more natural environment for him. If you're playing in a room with several free-standing furniture pieces, then you're already in good shape. If your room has furniture that's all set against walls, then the area in the middle is too open and vulnerable for him. When he hunts/plays, he needs opportunities for cover. The cover will simulate bushes, trees, logs, tall grass—things that would naturally be in the environment where a cat might hunt. You can add to the atmosphere by placing open paper bags or boxes in the open center of the room. Even a pillow tossed on the floor will work in a pinch. You want to create things for him to hide behind, over, and underneath.

How to use the toys comes next. If you are using a toy that mimics air hunting, such as *Da Bird*, don't wave it in the air nonstop. Since you want this to be a fun and satisfying experience, alternate between having the prey fly through the air and walk on the ground. Very often, it's when the bird is feeding on the ground that the cat sneaks up and pounces. Make the toy hide behind a piece of furniture and "peek" out at the cat. Even a subtle quivering of the toy will put the cat's eyes and ears on alert. It's the time between the prey's frantic movements that the cat inches up and plans his attack. You want your cat to use his brain as much as his body. Don't keep the toy in constant motion. Watch as your cat does his best and most stealthy maneuvering when the toy is momentarily still.

With a wire toy such as the *Cat Dancer* or *Dragonfly*, you can mimic a cricket, grasshopper, or fly. When you subtly twitch the wire with your finger, notice the erratic movements of the target toy at the end. This is similar to the erratic way a cricket might jump or a fly might buzz around. The unpredictable movements cause the cat to really lock his focus on the prey. You can make the *Cat Dancer* dart in and out of a bag or box and dash behind the leg of a chair or underneath the sofa. Alternate with a few movements through the air and you've created the next best thing to having a grasshopper in your living room, but without the panic from human family members.

Snake toys such as the *Cat Charmer* can slither around a corner or up and over a piece of furniture. It's not the waving-in-the-air motion that'll trigger the prey-drive, but the slowly-disappearing-out-of-sight movement.

If you don't have the three toys I've listed, use whatever ones you've chosen and try to create preylike movements. Think of it as the feline version of hide-and-seek. Alternate fast and slow, high and low. The toy doesn't have to actually look like the type of prey you're imitating. What matters is that it is *acting like prey*.

 CATWISE **CLUE**

When you move the toy like prey, move it *away* from your cat or *across* his field of vision. This is the movement that sparks the prey-drive.

You can start the game by triggering his prey-drive through sound. Very often it's the squeak of a mouse or the sound of something rustling through leaves that alerts the cat. Use sound often throughout the game by having the toy "walk" on a surface such as the floor or the inside of a box, which can be irresistible to your cat. The sound of the *Cat Dancer* darting around inside a box or paper bag will be hard for your cat to ignore. If you're using a silent toy such as a long feather, make those movements count to compensate for the lack of sound. The feather can slowly inch its way out from under the chair and very slightly wiggle to catch your cat's eye.

An extremely important rule of interactive play therapy has to do with success. If this is to be beneficial and fun, your cat needs to have multiple captures. Don't make it too much of a challenge for him to successfully grab the toy in his mouth or his paws. Sometimes a cat owner gets carried away with trying to keep the toy out of the cat's reach and it ends up being frustrating for the poor kitty. Periodically, let your cat successfully pounce on or grab the toy. If he starts to walk away with it or won't let go, give the toy some slack and let him enjoy his capture for a few moments. When he notices that the prey isn't resisting, he may loosen his grip or drop it from his mouth. That's when you can have it come back to life. Don't try to yank the toy out of his mouth or engage in a tug-of-war, because that will only make him hold on to it harder, which could cause injury to his teeth, or, at the very least, the toy could break. The game isn't about how long you can keep the toy away from the cat—it's about how rewarding the session is for him.

When you're ready for the game to end, don't abruptly stop, or you'll leave the cat still revved up and wondering what the heck happened to his prey. When the game is over you want your cat to be relaxed, satisfied, and feeling like the mighty hunter. Snatching the toy away won't accomplish that. The proper method is to slowly wind down the movements, almost as if the prey is getting tired or injured. If you're using an air-hunting toy, pretend the bird can no longer fly, so have all movements be low to the ground. As the toy gets slower and slower and eventually the prey "dies," your cat will start to relax, feeling as if he accomplished his final grand capture.

PLAY THERAPY SCHEDULE

When I do consultations and ask clients how often they play with their cats, many times I get blank stares. Sure, the cats have plenty of toys, but the clients don't recall exactly when they last engaged in interactive play. Some cat owners try to do the play sessions but end up haphazardly fitting them in once every week or so. That does nothing for the cat.

Play therapy for maintenance should ideally be done twice a day. In general, a maintenance play therapy session can last about fifteen minutes. I know everyone is so busy these days, but that's just thirty minutes out of your day to provide your cat with a tremendously rewarding activity. The playtime, which simulates a hunt, is in keeping with what is a natural part of a cat's daily life. Provide this on a regular basis and your cat gets the activity and stimulation essential to being feline—and you get a powerful tool to help keep your cat healthy. You also get a tool that helps in preventing behavior problems.

The key here is consistency. Do the play sessions every day, not every two or three days. Some days you may be able to get in only one session; that's understandable, but the more you stick to the schedule, the better it is for your cat. Your cat needs this stimulation and activity on a regular basis. If you don't have a full fifteen minutes to devote to a play session, do whatever you can. Your cat will enjoy any amount of time you can give him, and no matter how long your play sessions are, whether they're five minutes or thirty minutes, remember to wind down the action at the end in order to leave your cat relaxed and satisfied.

Since play therapy simulates a hunt, it can be especially rewarding for the cat to enjoy a feast after his capture. You don't have to offer a literal feast—it can be just a treat or you can divide up his daily portion of food in order to offer a small serving. Serving a portion of food works only if you feed on a schedule and don't free-feed. If you free-feed, you can offer a piece of a treat. You don't have to do this last part of offering food, but if your cat is on a weight-reduction program, this may help if he gets used to "working for food" and burning off some calories beforehand. It can also be a wonderful reward if two cats did a good job of parallel play without any negative reactions or intimidation. You don't always have to time it so that food is offered after playtime; it's something extra you can put in your behavior modification toolbox to use if it helps in the retraining process.

Once you get on a consistent schedule, you'll find that your cat starts to get right into it when he sees you with the toy. It's very rewarding when you notice your normally sedentary cat perk up when he sees you walking toward the closet where the toys are kept.

If you have a cat who isn't responding to play therapy no matter how realistic your toy movements are, try other toys. With some cats it can take a few tries before you hit on the one that creates a reaction. For a fearful cat who isn't responding, take the toy off the end of the fishing pole and just entice him with the dangling string. Add the toy later, when he starts to develop more confidence. Catnip can also be used in most cases to jump-start a sluggish cat's desire to play, since it reduces inhibition.

INTERACTIVE PLAY SESSIONS FOR MULTIPLE CATS

One way to exacerbate a current behavior problem is to ask two or more cats to compete for one toy during a play session. If you have two cats who get along famously and enjoy playing cooperatively with one interactive toy, then you can consider having them share. For the most part, though, it can be frustrating for one cat to have to sit back and watch another get the capture. If one cat is intimidated by a companion cat in general, you'll see that show up during interactive playtime. The more confident cat will take charge of the game and the less confident one will either reluctantly attempt to participate or just sit back and watch. Either way, the event triggers stress and possibly fear in that cat, and that's certainly not what you intended when you brought out the toy. If you have a couple of cats, pay attention to how they have played together in the past. Do they seem to be equal in who gets to be the aggressor, or is one cat always in charge? You don't want to continue any negativity in the relationship by giving the bossier cat another way to be intimidating.

Group interactive playtime will involve the use of more than one toy. If you have another family member in the home, then group playtime will go smoothly as you take a toy and the other family member takes a toy. You each concentrate on one cat and this becomes a game of parallel play. The cats are aware of each other in the room, but they aren't competing for one toy. The distance between your toy and your family member's toy will depend on how well the cats get along. Be careful, though, you don't want them crashing into each other as they stalk and pounce.

If you're alone and want to conduct a group session, take two interactive toys and hold one in each hand. It's easier if you use two of the same type of toy so you don't have one arm doing one type of movement while trying to have the other arm do something totally different. It may seem awkward at first to handle two toys, but with practice you'll develop more coordination. The room has to be large enough so that things don't get too chaotic.

If you're using two toys and one cat seems to lose interest in his own toy and starts focusing on the other cat's toy, just make his toy's movements more enticing than the other's temporarily, until you can get him refocused. If he pounces on the other cat's toy, quickly get the other kitty interested in the new toy. It doesn't have to be so strictly set up that one cat must play only with his assigned toy. The point of the dual toys is to prevent competition and intimidation.

If you're alone and you have three or more cats, use two toys and do the best you can to evenly distribute stalk/pounce opportunities. If one of the cats is especially aggressive and makes it hard for the other two to enjoy the game, then group play isn't a good option right now. Put the aggressive kitty in a separate room during your playtime with the others. Do a group play with the two cats who get along, and then do an individual play session with the other cat. After you work on the behavior modification for whatever that cat's problem is, you may be able to include him in the group session with one or both of your other cats.

INTERACTIVE PLAY THERAPY FOR RETRAINING

There are several ways to use play therapy to help in behavior modification. It may not seem as if playtime would be appropriate for a cat who is misbehaving, but it can actually be a powerful way to refocus him and defuse tension.

First of all, if your cat is displaying any type of behavior problem, you must incorporate the maintenance version of play therapy on a daily basis. Previously, I mentioned that sessions can be done once a day if you occasionally can't find the time to conduct them twice a day. If your cat has a behavior problem, however, you need to find that extra time in your schedule to fit in two sessions. If you're trying to retrain a serious behavior problem, then you're in crisis mode right now and you need to pull out all the stops. Your plan must be focused and intense. Very often a behavior problem creeps up, gradually getting worse and worse over time. It's not unusual for a cat owner not to notice what's occurring until something dramatic happens, such as overt aggression or urination outside the litter box. That means this problem has been incubating for a while, and your efforts have to be more concentrated, rather than casual and convenient. Another thing to remember is that you are your cat's whole world. All of his attention, affection, food, safety, and so forth come from you. We humans have so much going on in our lives that it's easy to forget how much our cats may look forward to our arrival home at the end of the day. Cats and dogs are *companion* animals, and when we take on the responsibility of having companion animals in our lives, we need to do our share in those relationships. Retraining a cat with a behavior problem may mean we don't get to watch an extra half hour of television or we have to stay up an extra fifteen minutes at night in order to get a play session in, but the rewards will outweigh

the inconvenience. Think of this as an investment in avoiding behavior problems in the future in addition to correcting the current
issue. The eight weeks or so (depending on the severity and type of
problem) you spend retraining the cat and faithfully doing the interactive play therapy will be well worth it when you start to see your
cat get along with his companion cat, successfully use the litter box,
remain calm when visitors come, or whatever it is you want to see
your cat do.

In addition to maintenance, you can use play therapy for *redirection.* This type of play is quick and immediate but timing is crucial.
When your cat shows signs that he is about to display the unwanted
behavior, redirect his attention toward a toy. As I said, timing is crucial, because you need to refocus him before the actual behavior takes
place. If your timing is off and he has already engaged in the unwanted behavior, then your play therapy will be a reinforcement of
that behavior. You have to catch him while it's still a thought in his
head or he's walking toward an area where the unwanted behavior
usually takes place. The redirection changes his mind-set from negative to positive because you're instantly triggering his prey-drive.
You don't have to do a full-scale play session; you just have to create
preylike movements to distract him and then let him have a capture.

Redirection works well in several circumstances. Here are a few
typical examples. Let's say you're trying to retrain your cat out of his
behavior of spraying. In the past, if you caught him walking toward
an object and thought he might spray, or if he backed up to the object, you may have yelled or chased him away. Although that prevented the one incident of spraying, he probably sprayed somewhere
else when you weren't looking. Your negative reaction also created
anxiety, and possibly fear, in him. Your new approach is going to be
to come at things from the positive side in order to reduce stress and
put your cat in a frame of mind where he feels more secure. So now
when your cat starts walking toward an area and you suspect he's
going to spray, redirect his attention toward a toy. Since his frame
of mind is negative or anxious when he is headed toward the spray

target, your play therapy redirection technique sparks his prey-drive, which immediately creates excited anticipation. Another important aspect of the redirection technique is that if you misread your cat's intentions and he isn't going to spray, then all that happens is he gets a little bonus playtime. With the previous technique of yelling or chasing, imagine how confused and scared the cat would be if he had no intention of spraying.

Another typical example of the power of redirection is when you're working on intercat relationships. One cat may be bullying another cat on a regular basis, and you notice he's walking toward his victim, who happens to be looking out the window, unaware of what's about to happen. If your previous technique was to yell or chase, that sent the aggressor out of the room, but it also probably startled the unsuspecting cat. It also does nothing to help the cats develop tolerance toward each other. Instead, use the redirection technique to quickly refocus the aggressor on the toy instead of his victim. Although he may be intent on stalking his victim, the opportunity to pounce on a mouse is usually too hard to pass up. The result of this is that the aggressor's mind-set shifts from negative to positive and the victim remains unharmed. As with the previous example of spraying, your timing is important, so you have to make sure you redirect the behavior before the cat attacks his victim. And again, if you misread your cat's intentions, there is no harm done in that he receives an extra opportunity for play.

Use redirection whenever you need to refocus a cat away from something or away from a behavior you suspect is about to occur. In order for it to work, though, you have to have a supply of interactive toys conveniently located. You'll miss the opportunity for redirection if you have to run downstairs to the closet to search for a toy. During the retraining period, keep a stash of interactive toys in various locations around the house. The *Cat Dancer* is great for redirection because the wire can be coiled around so it fits neatly in a drawer or behind a picture. The toy is also inexpensive enough that it won't break the budget to buy in multiples. When it comes to redirection, you don't have to use big, inconvenient toys; use whatever will get a positive reaction. If your cat likes Ping-Pong balls, Mylar balls, or fuzzy mice, keep a supply in several locations so you can toss or roll one to trigger the prey-drive. As you start doing the maintenance interactive play sessions, you'll become more familiar with what toys are hard for your cat to resist. Use that knowledge to develop a stash of toys for redirection. Once I was in my kitchen and needed to defuse some mounting tension between my two cats nearby, and I used the ring from the milk container (a cat fave). I quietly opened the refrigerator, took the ring off the plastic jug, and then tossed it so it skidded along the floor. Prey-drive kicked in instantly.

When you use redirection, don't toss the toy at your cat. Remember that the prey-drive is triggered by objects moving away from or across your cat's visual field.

Play therapy can be used in another variation to change a cat's mind-set. This involves creating a positive association with something that is currently viewed by the cat as negative. Do this by conducting one of your play sessions in a negatively viewed area. For example, if your cat is frightened of a certain room or an object within that room, start by doing a play session near but not in that area. You need to be far enough away at first so the cat remains within his comfort zone. After a few sessions, move closer, but be very conservative in how quickly you think you can progress. It's always better to go more slowly than you think you need to in order to prevent the cat from having a negative reaction. These play sessions can be your regular maintenance ones or you can add a few extra ones in these areas. If your cat has urine-sprayed in certain areas, do play sessions in each of the areas to change his association with those spots. For a cat afraid of a particular room, inch your way in gradually through play sessions. Sometimes the problem is that the cat is frightened of coming out of a particular room. The play therapy starts in the room for several sessions, and then you can inch your way to the threshold and, hopefully, beyond. Let the cat set the pace of how quickly he's ready to advance. Fear of an object such as a vacuum cleaner can often be reduced through gradual desensitization and play therapy. Specifics on this can be found in chapter 4. I can't stress enough how gradually you have to do this if the problem is fear-based.

Play therapy for positive association can be used during group play if you have two cats who have a tense relationship. Do parallel play, so that the cats are aware of each other in the room yet each can remain within his comfort zone. They'll hopefully start to realize that having the other one around isn't such a bad thing.

Play therapy also works when you need to change your cat's mind-set after a negative event. If your cat has had a bad experience, such as being ambushed in the litter box, do a casual, comforting version of play therapy to trigger some degree of prey-drive. Depending upon what happened, he may not jump right into the game, but if you can show through your body language that you're relaxed and the toy is moving like prey, you just might see a spark in his eye. I always try to leave things on a positive note with a cat so he doesn't stay curled up somewhere, turning what might have been a momentary negative occurrence into a major trauma. A note of caution, though, is that this method shouldn't be used if your cat is aggressively reactive due to something traumatic. He needs time to calm down and get his bearings again before you attempt to elicit a positive response from him.

You now have a better understanding of the importance of play therapy and how it can help facilitate the retraining process. The coolest part about all of this is that while you're using it to modify behavior, exercise, desensitize, redirect, and so on, your cat is just having fun.

SOLO PLAY

Your cat benefits from stimulation and activity in his environment, and there are ways you can provide that even while you aren't at home. A cat typically spends about nine to twelve hours a day alone in the house without you there as the source of his entertainment.

Help him make the most of that time alone by creating activities for his enjoyment during solo play.

Solo play is not a replacement for interactive play, but it can add to a cat's enjoyment of his environment tremendously. We can start with the toys you already have. Gather up all of those fuzzy mice and other little toys and put most of them away in the closet. If you have too many toys just lying around, they don't become special anymore. Rotate toys on a regular basis so that you're putting out only a few at a time. That way, when the other toys come out, they'll seem fresh again. You should also use this time to throw out toys that are ripped with stuffing exposed or have loose pieces in danger of coming off. If the toys are favorites of your cat and you can do some repair work on them, that's fine—just make sure the toys are safe.

You may also need to purchase a few new toys for solo playtime, especially if the toys you have for your cat are old and he hasn't shown any interest in them in quite a while. When you go to the store, look for toys that will create an interesting movement when the cat bats at them, and ones that seem as if they would be fun to paw at. For example, many cats love the ring from around the milk containers. You can buy safer versions of those at the pet supply store. They're light and move easily across the floor with just the lightest touch of the paw.

Mylar crinkly balls are practically indestructible, make a great sound when touched or batted, and move across the floor with ease. They are widely available at pet supply stores.

You can find toy mice in a wide variety of styles, fabrics, sizes, and shapes. Get a small assortment but choose them based on your cat's personality and size. If your cat is small, don't get a large stuffed mouse.

Feathered toys are always popular with cats; just make sure the feathers are securely attached to the toy. Peacock feathers are usually a hit with cats.

Sound should also factor into some of your toy choices. Not all toys have to make a sound, but you may find a couple that create great little squeaks and noises. Bells in toys are very popular, but they don't make the type of sound that typically triggers the prey-drive. It's those little rustling sounds, like the one the Mylar balls make or the sound of a toy skidding across the floor. The squeak of a mouse can be what triggers your particular cat to go on the hunt. *Play-N-Squeak* is a stuffed mouse that contains a sound-generating chip inside. When the mouse is batted at or moved, it squeaks. The toy is well made and many cats love it. If you have a very small cat, though, the size of the mouse may be too large, so consider that as you look it over. If you have a small cat who loves to tackle the larger toys, then the *Play-N-Squeak* may be just what he needs. This toy is widely available in stores and online.

There's such a variety of toys for solo play that I'm sure you'll be able to find several that will be perfect for your cat. No matter how wild you get when you go on your shopping spree, remember to put out only a few and rotate all toys.

When you put out these toys, don't just toss them in a basket. Instead, strategically place them in spots around your cat's play area for him to discover. Put one toy on the cat tree and have another peeking out from under a chair. I love to set the stage for my cats' daytime fun before I leave the house in the morning. The fact that all the toys are in different locations when I return tells me they enjoyed the extra activity while I was gone.

Use boxes and bags for solo playtime as well. You've probably seen how much fun it is for a cat to investigate an open paper bag. Now, instead of having him jump in with your groceries, give him a couple of bags of his very own. Fold a cuff around the edge of the bag to help it stay open and then toss a toy in there. Boxes can be wonderful toys for cats, so get creative with one when you purchase a boxed item or receive a delivery. Leave the box open and toss a toy in there for your cat to bat around, or cut some holes in the box and turn it upside down as a hideaway. A Ping-Pong ball can be placed inside an empty tissue box for your cat to paw at. Use the rectangular large-size tissue boxes instead of the small square ones so there's room for the ball to roll around. Ping-Pong balls make a great sound as they roll across the floor. Just be sure your cat doesn't tend to bite hard when playing with Ping-Pong balls so there's no risk of puncturing the ball. Don't use Ping-Pong balls in a home with a dog, to avoid the risk of the dog's puncturing the ball or swallowing it.

Play tunnels can serve as fun places and also napping hideaways. You can find soft-sided tunnels at pet supply stores and online. Puzzle-type games and puzzle feeders are terrific for providing stimulation for solo play. Use the *Peek-a-Prize* and the *Play-N-Treat* balls for added hunting opportunities and stimulation. For more puzzle-feeding ideas, refer to chapter 2.

Some motion toys can be used for solo playtime. The *Panic Mouse* is a motorized toy on a wire that flips and flops around its base. You can vary the speed, which is important for customizing it to your cat's personality. However, it can be easily tipped over when the cat grabs the target toy, so this is one motion toy you should use only when you're nearby in case it needs to be put back right side up. The *Panic Mouse* isn't a substitute for interactive play, but it can be a fun addition if your cats are in need of play and you have something else you need to do. This toy is widely available in stores and online.

When you're considering a motion toy, think about your cat's personality before you purchase it. A timid cat may not do well with one of these toys; it would be better to stick to your manual interactive play sessions and nonthreatening solo toys. One of my cats is basically fearless and could play twenty-four hours a day without sleep, so she enjoys those extra play sessions with her *Panic Mouse*.

CATNIP

When you go toy shopping, you'll come across many catnip-filled or catnip-scented toys. Some companies make top-quality catnip toys, but others use the lowest grade of catnip. If you know that the quality of the catnip is good and your cat responds to it, that's great, but if you're in doubt, it's better to buy plain toys and rub catnip on them yourself.

CATWISE CLUE

When shopping for loose catnip, choose brands that state that only leaves and blossoms are used. Lots of stems in the catnip indicates lower quality.

Catnip or catnip-filled toys should be given to your cat only once or twice a week. Don't leave anything with catnip around all the time because a cat can actually lose his ability to respond to it.

Catnip can be a wonderful addition to the retraining process. Keep a container of good-quality catnip on hand for those special once- or twice-weekly catnip-party play sessions. Catnip is a totally harmless herb, and when a cat inhales it, he experiences about fifteen to twenty minutes of fun. It allows the cat to be less inhibited, and that can be a great way to reduce stress or jump-start a play session. It's the component *nepetalactone* in the volatile oil that causes the wonderful reaction. To release the oil, rub the dried catnip between your fingers before giving it to your cat.

You can use loose catnip in several ways. Put some in the bottom of a clean sock, knot the end, and let your cat have his way with this homemade kick bag. You can rub it on toys to make them more appealing or you can keep a few fuzzy mice or crinkly balls in a container of catnip so they'll be primed and ready to go when you need them. Catnip can be rubbed on a scratching post to entice your cat to it. You can even just sprinkle loose catnip on the floor or on a paper plate and let your cat roll around and have a blast. Although the catnip effect is created through inhalation, it's not surprising to find a cat licking or eating it. Don't worry, that's totally harmless.

In addition to the regular schedule you have for catnip parties, use it for behavior modification when needed. If your cat has seemed tense or nervous, a souped-up play session with catnip might be perfect. If you've had visitors over and your cat is still reacting negatively even after they have gone, offer a little catnip.

Amazingly, cat owners tend to forget about how powerful and useful this herb can be. I find that they either don't use it to their advantage enough or have given it to their cats so much that it has lost its effect. Use it correctly and it will be a wonderful tool.

CATWISE CLUE

Not every cat responds to catnip, so don't be concerned if it has no effect on your cat. The catnip response is inherited, and about one-third of the cat population lacks this gene.

If you have a male cat in your multicat home, the first time you expose him to catnip, do it individually before throwing a group party. Some males respond too enthusiastically to catnip and cross over the line into aggression.

Some Uses for Catnip

- Rub dried catnip on toys that your cat has lost interest in.
- Use catnip as a reward after grooming or nail trimming.
- Place a little loose catnip on the examination table at the veterinary clinic to distract your cat.
- Throw a catnip party after your cat has had a stressful experience.
- Jump-start an interactive play therapy session for a sedentary or overweight cat.
- Rub catnip on a scratching post to entice your cat to scratch there.
- A catnip-spiked toy tossed on the floor can help distract a cat from a potentially unwanted behavior.
- Catnip is a good way for a very active cat to work off his energy.
- Throw a catnip party once or twice a week just for . . . well, just for fun!

CLICKER TRAINING

You may have heard this phrase as it applies to dogs, but there's a good chance you have never imagined clicker training your cat. Surprise, surprise, cats are actually excellent candidates for clicker training and the technique is very valuable when you're working on behavior problems. The basic premise is that the clicker "marks" exactly what you want and then you can build a wanted behavior from that using positive reinforcement. The clicker is basically a little plastic noisemaker that sounds like a cricket. There's nothing especially magical about the clicker; it's just an easily identifiable sound for the cat and is unique to the typical sounds in your home.

I love clicker training because it allows you to mark the behavior you want from your cat instantly. Every behavior your cat exhibits has a consequence, and it can either be good or bad. With clicker training, you show the cat that desirable behavior results in a good consequence. Your cat is smart and he'll soon make the connection between behaviors that pay off in a good consequence and ones that don't have any payoff. This method of training focuses on positives. If the cat doesn't perform the desired behavior, he doesn't get rewarded and his brain will quickly tell him that getting rewarded is far better than not getting rewarded. Also, clicker training allows the cat to "work for food," which is a natural part of being feline. It can be a stress-free and fun way to change negative behaviors and help your cat develop confidence.

Before you can use clicker training for actual problem solving, you have to teach your cat what the sound of the clicker means. It's easier than you think and it actually requires no work on the cat's part. To start, you'll need a clicker. You can find them in just about any pet supply store as well as online. Get more than one just in case it gets misplaced. When you hold the clicker in your hand, depress the indentation or the button (depending on the type of clicker) and you'll hear a *click* sound.

The reward you'll use when clicker training will be food. It's the most basic reinforcer and, since cats are food-motivated, it's a natural. If you free-feed your cat, he may not be hungry enough when you do your clicker training session. If that's the case, switch to scheduled feeding (see chapter 7) or take up the food well in advance of a session. The main reason a session may fail is because the cat simply isn't hungry. If you schedule-feed, divide up his portions so that you can reserve a little for clicker training sessions.

You can use treats for clicker training, but if you do, break them up into small pieces so you aren't interfering with the cat's normal nutrition. Whole treats also take too long to chew and can distract the cat from the session. Some commercial treats, even if broken up, require too much time to chew, so keep that in mind when deciding on the appropriate treat. A tiny morsel of wet food is usually best, but use what works best for your cat. If your cat isn't on a special diet, you can use a small amount of baby food, but don't buy baby food that contains onion powder or garlic powder because both of those ingredients can pose potential health risks to cats.

The training session starts with you showing the cat the connection between the clicker and the reward. He has to learn that the click means an immediate food reward. Start by having a small container of food or some broken-up pieces of treats handy. Offer him a tiny amount of food and click at the same time. The amount of food offered should be no larger than a pea. If you're using broken treats, you can hand-feed or toss it on the ground. If you're feeding wet food, put a tiny drop on the edge of a spoon. I like to use a baby food spoon that has a soft tip instead of an ordinary metal spoon so the cat doesn't get an unpleasant surprise if he tries to bite it. Click each time you offer the food but click only once for each offering. You're doing what's referred to as "charging the clicker." This session teaches the cat that the click means an instant food reward. Right now he doesn't know why he's getting these little rewards, but that education will come later. If the sound of the clicker bothers your cat initially, put it in your pocket or wrap it in a small towel when you click until he gets used to it.

It may be tempting to click repeatedly, but the message you're preparing him for is the single sound of the click and its association with the immediate food. During these sessions, don't talk to your cat or distract him. These initial training sessions are all about the cat, the clicker, and the food.

Once you have done some of these sessions and your cat has been exposed to the click/reward combination, you can begin your first trick. Don't be turned off by the word *trick*; it's merely a basic movement your cat will do so he can learn the connection between a specific behavior, the click, and the reward. It's basically a three-step process:

1. Get the specific behavior.
2. Mark the behavior with the clicker.
3. Reward the cat for the behavior.

You're not going to start out attempting to have your cat jump through a hoop or stand up on his hind legs. You'll start with a random behavior that your cat does naturally. Keep the clicker and the food handy and choose a behavior that you're going to mark and then reward. Sitting, for example, is something your cat will do several times a day, so you can mark the exact moment he sits with the clicker and then offer a reward. At first he won't know what he did that earned him the reward, but after a few times he'll start to put it together. Don't push his bottom down or coax him to sit—just let it be a random movement, and when he does it, reward him. To accelerate the process you can also hold the spoon of food or the treat right over his head and move it slightly toward his back. He'll probably look up, and as he does his rear will usually go into a sit position.

The first behavior doesn't have to be a sit. You can choose lying on his side, stretching, pawing a particular object, and so on. Whatever movement your cat does that you can successfully and consistently mark will be fine. This phase of the training teaches him that he must now perform a specific act in order to get the payoff. It's something he does anyway, so it's easy for both of you. So far, so good.

Since right now you're rewarding seemingly random behaviors, click and reward your cat as he does various movements that are positive. Don't go overboard and click for everything, but choose a couple that he does more than once in a day and use those for training.

CATWISE CLUE

Use a fanny pack or buy a trainer's treat bag to keep around your waist. This will make it easy to move around your house and be ready to click/reward as your cat performs the desired behavior.

Once you feel your cat has made the connection between the particular behavior and the click/reward, you can give that behavior a name or "cue." So if you've been rewarding the cat for sitting, now you will either say "Sit" or use a hand motion or both. Give the cue consistently now so your cat gets familiar with the particular word cue relating to the behavior he performs.

The next phase involves clicking and rewarding only when you have given the cue for that behavior. At first your cat may not understand why he isn't getting a payoff, but you need to establish that this is now a trick that will be on your timing, not his. Say "Sit." Wait for the behavior, and the second he does it, click and reward. Timing is important, so don't be late with your click and, for goodness sake, don't be late with the payoff. There's an important reason for giving cues, and it is so the cat doesn't just "throw" behaviors or tricks at you, expecting to be rewarded. Once your cat has learned the cue, don't fall into the trap of repeating cues if he isn't exhibiting the behavior. Once you're sure the cat fully understands the cue, it shouldn't take eight repetitions of the verbal command before he decides to respond.

Keep training sessions short so they remain positive and so you don't tire out your cat. A session shouldn't last more than a few minutes. If your cat isn't responding to the session, he may not be hungry enough, or maybe he's tired. Keep everything positive and try again later. Don't get frustrated if he doesn't perform the behavior. Every cat learns at his own pace.

Use clicker training to teach your cat to come when called. You've probably already done this by offering him food or treats, but now add the clicker to continue the training process. You can do this as a regular training session, and you can also do it when you prepare his dinner. Most cats' ears are keenly aware of when the food hits the bowl. As you're setting the bowl down, call out your cat's name, and when he comes, click and reward.

There's an additional method you can use with clicker training, and it includes incorporating a target stick. This is merely a wand used for pointing. Some target sticks have a little ball attached to the end to catch the cat's attention. Train the cat to the concept of the target stick by holding it out in front of him. When he approaches it to sniff it (as curious cats will always do), click and reward. Move the stick away and try again. Move the stick at varying distances and click and reward every time his nose touches it. The stick can then be used to help you point to what you want done. For example, if you want the cat to walk to a certain spot, or reach up, or turn around, the stick can help you train him. You can use the target stick to lure your cat to go through a hoop, over or under an object, and so forth. After all, if you're going to use clicker training to help solve behavior problems, why not also impress your friends with a few tricks!

Once your cat has gotten the hang of clicker training, you can use it to identify desirable behaviors and assist you in correcting behavior problems. If you have companion cats who aren't getting along, clicker training may help them focus on the payoff when they display a positive behavior rather than a negative one. Clicker training may help if you've been trying to train your cat to accept being picked up, or groomed, or even petted. The key is to keep the training short, rewarding, and consistent. You'll find multiple opportunities to incorporate clicker training into your behavior modification plan because it tells the cat exactly what behavior you want at the second the cat displays it. It's a powerful way to pinpoint your desires in a language the cat understands completely.

After you've established the basics of clicker training with your cat, back off on some of the food rewards. Keep up with the clicker part of the training, but every once in a while you can substitute praise or petting for food. Intermittent food rewards actually help maintain the training because the cat will perform the behavior knowing there's a *possibility* that it will bring him the reward. A common mistake in clicker training is failing to graduate to intermittent rewards. That mistake will end up backfiring on you because the cat may perform wanted behaviors only when he's certain food is present. Intermittent rewarding is what will keep the cat motivated to continue the particular behavior. It's similar to playing poker. The possibility of a reward keeps the player coming back.

I keep my clicker on a little coiled spring cord attached to my belt loop so that it's always handy if I need to mark a behavior. You don't want to be digging in your pockets to locate the clicker because you'll be too late and the behavior you wanted to mark will have passed.

Again, when you're marking a behavior, click only once. Your timing must be accurate. Don't get excited at a particular behavior and click, click, click, click. The cat will have moved by then and he won't know exactly what you're marking.

Don't talk a lot during the clicker training sessions. Say the cat's name and give the verbal cue. Praise him when he performs the behavior. Don't try to coax him by chattering away or using baby talk. It's the connection between marking the behavior with the clicker and the payoff of food that the cat will be focusing on.

If you'd like to learn more about clicker training or the science behind operant conditioning, there are a number of books available.

I've just scratched the surface here of what you can do with clicker training, but if you and your cat really enjoy it, there are many more advanced behaviors you can do.

CATWISE REMINDER

- Keep sessions brief.
- Train in a quiet place that's free of distractions.
- Train when your cat is hungry but not starving.
- Keep the sessions positive and fun.
- Be consistent in the cues you give.
- If you're clicker training more than one cat, don't expect them to learn at the same pace.
- Never punish, yell, or show frustration if your cat isn't picking up on the behavior you want.
- Choose behaviors and tricks that are appropriate for your particular cat.
- After your cat understands the behaviors and clicker training, switch to intermittent rewards.
- Timing is crucial in clicker training, so mark a behavior at the exact second it is displayed.
- Click only once to mark a behavior.

CLICKER TRAINING IN A MULTICAT HOME

It's not as tricky as you might think. Start with the cat whose behavior you want to change and do your sessions in a separate room. Once he starts responding, you can do your clicker training with the other cats around. Cats are very smart and they learn through observation. You may find that another cat has picked up on the cue without your having to train him.

If you have several cats with behavior problems, start clicker training the cat you think will be the most responsive and let him then guide the other cats.

Once your cats all know their names and come when called, you can include individual names when you give a cue.

BEYOND BASIC TRAINING

Throw caution to the wind and try to train your cat to perform a couple of fun tricks. It's not a waste of time because it continues to solidify clicker training in your cat's mind and also does a few other very valuable things. The more your cat uses his brain and has a fun job to do, the more he's satisfying that natural part of being a feline. Another great side effect of clicker training is that it improves the communication between you and your kitty. My favorite part about clicker training, especially when you get into fun tricks, is that it helps to strengthen the bond between the two of you. If your cat is having behavior problems, you need to find fun ways to spend time together, and clicker training is ideal.

If you've worked on the basic behaviors, such as "Sit," "Roll over," and so forth, there are other fun sessions you can have. How about a jump through a hoop? Get a large embroidery hoop and hold it on the ground. Use your target stick or a treat on the other side to lure your cat through, and the second he walks through the hoop, click and reward. Gradually, during the following sessions, you can raise the hoop a little at a time until he actually has to jump through it. You'll also work toward not visibly holding the treat on the other side of the hoop. He'll eventually know that if he goes through the hoop, he'll get a payoff. If you get in the habit of always showing him the treat, you risk having him perform the behavior only if he sees it.

If you're using wet food or baby food, one thing that I've done to make life simpler when teaching more complex tricks is to tape my clicker to the end of a baby spoon. If the spoon is very short, you can tape the spoon on one end of a stick and the clicker on the other end where you'll be holding it. This frees up one hand so you can do hand cues or hold the embroidery hoop more easily.

Teach your cat to go through a tunnel by using the target stick as well. Use a cat tunnel or make one of your own out of a paper bag or box. Cut out the bottom and place it on its side. Just make sure you have reinforced the bag so it doesn't collapse. Lure the cat through the tunnel with the target stick or a toy. Click the instant he goes through the tunnel and then give him the immediate payoff.

If your cat masters both the tunnel and the hoop, you may be able to combine them. Line them up but place them far enough apart so that your cat can maneuver out of one and into the other easily.

Pay attention to the types of behaviors your cat likes to do naturally or does with ease and develop that into a fun trick. The key word here is *fun*. Although it's called clicker *training*, the whole experience should be fun and rewarding for your cat.

A terrific thing is going to happen when your cat understands the clicker training process. He'll have *learned how to learn* and will pick up on your cues faster. You'll find that his attention span has increased, and that he'll be eager to display the behaviors that may garner rewards. Every behavior has a consequence, which can be positive or negative and delayed or immediate. With animals, immediate consequences are what work and delayed consequences are ineffective. When you clicker-train, your cat receives an immediate and positive consequence. When a behavior results in a positive consequence, the cat will more likely want to repeat it. By following this technique, you're able to retrain your cat in a way that strengthens the cat-human bond and focuses on helping your cat succeed. It's a simple concept that will have profound results.

4

Retraining Old Habits and More Serious Problems You Thought You Had to Live With

RETRAIN WITH THE RIGHT *STARTING FROM SCRATCH* ATTITUDE

Whether you're trying to correct a major problem that has your cat on her last chance or simply attempting to change a few annoying little habits, *how* you approach the situation is extremely important. You may be at odds with your cat by now and the two of you might have a severely damaged relationship, but you have to put aside your emotional reactions to what has occurred in the past in order to bring about a constructive and healthy solution to the problem. Instead of getting angry or disheartened because your cat has failed to do something, change your attitude to focus on helping her succeed.

As you've learned from the chapters you've read so far, my technique is based on creating an atmosphere that puts the cat in a better position to direct herself toward the desired behavior and away from the undesired one. My approach with cats is to focus on the underlying cause or need for the undesirable behavior and what they are saying through that behavior. I then create an atmosphere that meets their needs in a way that's acceptable to both cats and humans. I concentrate on the positive steps the cats take toward the behavior I want, giving them an incentive to keep going that way. Any so-called negatives that I might incorporate don't come directly from me. I know the cats aren't deliberately misbehaving, and I certainly don't want to damage the cat-human bond, so negatives are used sparingly in the form of appropriate deterrents. From a cat's point of view, these deterrents seem to appear mysteriously rather than being directly created by a human. Anytime a deterrent is used, I balance that negative with a positive by offering the cat a better option so she soon sees that what has happened is a good thing, not a negative one, after all. I'm the only one who has to know that this was all carefully planned behavior modification. I've become very good at appearing innocent and nonsuspicious whenever a cat looks at me.

If the behavior problem you're trying to resolve has been a long-term one, remain patient as you and your cat work through the behavior modification. The problem didn't occur overnight and it won't be corrected overnight either. When you do the proper behavior modification, you'll have the joy of watching your cat take baby steps in the direction you want. The more you concentrate on those positive little steps, the easier the process will be for both you and your cat. It's easy to get discouraged if, after things have been going well for a while, you experience a sudden setback, but that happens in all types of behavior correction. Humans are as guilty of that as cats, so the best thing to do is to examine what happened that created the setback, make necessary adjustments, and move on.

REBUILDING TRUST

You and your cat may not be the best of friends due to whatever behavior problem has been occurring, but you have to work on regaining her trust. Don't just go through the motions of behavior modification without also working on reestablishing that bond. If you've used inappropriate correction techniques previously, there's a good chance your relationship could use a little repair. If you've physically punished your cat, she may flinch when you extend your hand toward her, or she may just run away out of fear. You have to work on helping her see that your hands are not meant to inflict pain, but rather are for petting, holding, and showing affection. Use the techniques described in the previous chapter on play therapy so she can stay within her comfort zone while being near you. As you engage in more and more play sessions, she'll start to associate you with positive experiences, not negative ones.

Even if you haven't issued physical reprimands, your cat may still be afraid of you, or at least somewhat cautious, if you've chased, yelled, or squirted her with water. As a cat owner, you should be a source of security for your cat. That can start with your voice. Pay attention to the tone of your voice when you talk to your cat now that you're trying to regain her trust. Your voice should be calm, soothing, and friendly. Even if you aren't yet feeling the love, call your cat's name in the most inviting tone you can. Don't use baby talk or high-pitched tones because that's not soothing or reassuring. Use your voice in a way that conveys softness. Regardless of the problem you're trying to correct, you need to be a source of comfort to your cat. Her behavioral issue isn't rooted in spitefulness or meanness and shouldn't elicit those feelings from you.

CORRECTING THOSE LITTLE ANNOYING PROBLEMS

For most people, these are not deal breakers when it comes to life with a cat, but some cat owners find these behaviors increasingly harder to accept day after day and year after year. Some cats display these behaviors in very subtle ways, while others' little annoying behavior quirks result in a grand-scale war between cat and human. Little annoyances may be something you thought you had to resign yourself to if you were going to live with a cat, but they are often easy to correct. As with large problems, you have to understand what the underlying cause is or why the cat feels the need to exhibit the particular behavior. You can then apply appropriate behavior modification to ease the kitty away from that behavior and toward a more beneficial one. Even if a particular little annoying habit is acceptable to you and has become a normal way of life at this point, it may not be a healthy behavior for your cat, either physically or mentally. Some little behaviors need to be modified for the cat's sake, some need it for your sake, and some need modifying for both of you. It's never too late to retrain unwanted behaviors into acceptable ones. Even if you can accomplish an improvement only by degrees, the retraining makes life better for everyone.

Counter hopping

Have you battled in vain for years to keep your cat off the kitchen counters? Have you given up and surrendered them to her, or do you continue to shoo and chase several times a day? I know many people who have kept spray bottles on the counter and, time and time again, grab one, aim, and squirt. All too often, the only thing that has been accomplished is that a wet cat leaps from the counter and dashes out of sight, frustrated but determined to try again later when the human isn't around.

Perhaps having a cat on the counter didn't bother you before but the situation changed due to the addition of a new family member who doesn't agree with your choices or has allergies, or because you've moved to a new home. Perhaps the battle heats up only when there's food present, or maybe you allow your cat on the counter when you're alone but would prefer not to when there are dinner guests. If you've allowed her there under certain conditions, such as when there isn't food present, then you've sent her a mixed message. The training has to be consistent; the cat is either allowed or not allowed, period. If you'd prefer that she not be allowed up there, then it's time to do some proper retraining.

You may have tried multiple methods only to have your cat continue to leap up on your freshly cleaned counter. The problem with many of the methods used—whether it's chasing, yelling, or even gently shooing her off—is that your smart kitty knows that all she has to do is wait until you aren't around to get right back up there.

Since you'll be taking a preferred area from her, you'll need to replace it with a more acceptable option. That's an important part of the retraining process. She hasn't been jumping on the counter all these years simply because she enjoys being scolded. The counter has been an appealing place, or even a very needed place, and now you're going to take that away. You have to give her something just as good or, hopefully, even better.

First, try to figure out what it is about the counter that appeals to your cat. For many cats it's because of all the delicious food prepared there, whether it's her own cat food in the process of being served or the roasted chicken you just took out of the oven for the family. In addition to the retraining process I'll provide in a little bit, you'll need to make sure she's not having to wait too long to get her meals. If you schedule-feed, she may need the portion divided up into smaller meals fed more frequently. If she's underweight, she may be due for a checkup by the veterinarian to make sure there isn't an underlying medical problem. Some medical conditions such as hyperthyroidism can cause a cat to have a large appetite even though, at the same time, she is unable to keep weight on her body. If your cat is overweight, the issue may be that there isn't enough stimulation for her and all she thinks about is her next meal. A veterinary checkup is needed so your cat can be put on an appropriate nutritional plan.

Your cat may be the picture of health, her meal schedule appropriate, and yet she still attempts to steal a chicken leg or the meat out of your sandwich before you've taken the first bite. Many cats just can't resist the opportunity to check out the interesting aromas that come from the food on the counter. While you're doing the retraining, reduce temptation as best as you can. Cover foods that must be left out on the counter as soon as possible. Don't leave dirty dishes with leftover food on the counter or in the sink. I know I probably sound like your mother right now, reminding you to clean up, but the less temptation for your cat, the faster the retraining will progress.

Your cat may not have any interest in the food on the counter; she may simply enjoy the fact that it's an elevated area that's very open and overlooks a wide space. Perhaps there's a window in the kitchen and the counter provides her with a conveniently large perch for bird watching or napping in the sun. It's a natural part of a cat's life to seek elevated areas and to climb, leap, and explore. Your living space may not have enough comfortable elevated areas for your cat and she may have decided that the kitchen counter was the most appealing. Maybe she just enjoys being with you and sitting on the kitchen counter while you're preparing meals is an easy way to get close. Your cat may have decided a long time ago that the counter was a fun place to leap on and off and provided an opportunity for exploration during her day. If you've come to the conclusion that your cat just enjoys being up there for the sake of being up there, provide her with an acceptable alternative when you begin retraining. If you don't have a cat tree or a couple of window perches, it might be time to do some shopping. If you've had a cat tree for a number of years and your cat ignores it, the problem might be the location of the tree, its height (or lack of height), or its stability. Place a sturdy tree near a window or at least in a room where you spend most of your time.

Some cats use the counter for safety purposes. This is seen more often in a multicat home, but it can also be due to a companion dog in the home or if there are children present. The counter is elevated and provides the cat with a wide visual field. If the kitchen is small and closed in, the cat may feel more protected up there in case someone suddenly comes in. If she's fed in the kitchen and has been the victim of a surprise while distracted with her meal, she may be on the counter to see who might be coming. In a multicat situation in which there's some tension, she may be on the counter ready to chase another cat out of the feeding area, or maybe she's afraid she's going to be the one chased away. Sometimes in a hostile multicat environment, a kitty may resort to urinating on the counter because she feels safer in an elevated area. Other times a cat may urine-spray against the backsplash because it's one area of the home that no other cat has claimed. If you think your cat prefers the counter due to a safety issue, you'll need to do some retraining work on her relationship with others in the home. If it's a multicat issue, incorporate the behavior modification techniques described in other chapters to help everyone feel as if they have adequate personal space. Environmental modifications may need to be done to make sure the litter box is secure and the feeding station is safe. If she's fearful of a child or a dog, work on improving those relationships (see chapter 9).

What I've listed above are some of the most common reasons why a cat tends to gravitate toward the kitchen counter, but I may not have hit on why your cat has chosen to be there. Do your cat detective work and, if necessary, make some environmental changes to offer her an alternative. Then begin the retraining.

The method you're going to use will be sort of remote-controlled, but you won't need any batteries or to point any devices at your kitty. This will be a very low-tech but highly effective version of remote control.

The reason I refer to it as remote control is because you won't have to be present for it to work. That's an important part of successful behavior modification when you're using any form of deterrent. The cat must think this is a mysterious change in the object itself and not something coming from you. This protects the relationship between the two of you and allows the retraining to continue even when no one is at home.

Here are a couple of the methods I use to help clients retrain their cats. Get a plastic carpet runner that has the little nubs on the underside. Cut the runner so the pieces will fit the entire counter surface area. Place the runner *nubby side up*. This creates a very unappealing surface for the cat to land on or spend any amount of time on. If the runner slides on the counter, secure it at the corners with tape. Put the carpet runner on the counter every time you don't need to use it. By cutting pieces, you can remove only some sections so the vacant area of the counters will still be protected if you're working on part of it. Before you leave the kitchen, replace the runner. I know it'll be inconvenient for a while, but it's an effective way for your cat to come to the conclusion herself that the counter isn't the fun place it used to be. You'll remain the innocent party in all of this. After a couple of weeks, you should be able to remove the runners. I recommend that you cut a few long, thin strips to place on the edges of the counter during the last part of the retraining phase. Let the runner hang off the edge just a bit to serve as a visual reminder.

There's an outstanding product called *X-Mat* that's made specifically to keep cats off particular areas. It's based on the same principle as the upside-down plastic carpet protector. The *X-Mat* has raised bumps your cat will find uncomfortable to walk or lounge on. It is hinged and folds for easy storage. The hinges enable you to drape it over a round object, such as the back of a particular chair that you don't want your cat on. This product or the carpet protector can be used on any piece of furniture where you don't want your cat to be. The *X-Mat* is available at some retail stores and online.

If you have the most hard-core counter-loving kitty on the planet, and neither the carpet runner nor the *X-Mat* worked, you still have one last trick up your sleeve. Take some empty soda cans and/or plastic bottles, put a few pennies in them, and line them up along the edge of the counter, in front of the carpet protector or *X-Mat*. If you use cans, securely tape over the openings, and for bottles, tightly twist the caps back on. With these homemade shake cans and bottles, it won't take but a couple of times before your cat realizes this isn't a fun place to be. Don't use the cans or bottles in a multicat home, though, because the sound can startle an unsuspecting cat who isn't doing anything wrong. One cat may be eating at the feeding station when another cat jumps on the counter and knocks a can or two to the floor. Sound-generating deterrents are to be used only in single-cat environments and only for cats who aren't normally skittish or frightened. Always choose the minimally aversive method, and remember to always provide a better option, such as a cat tree or window perch.

I have heard of people doing some pretty drastic things to keep their cats off the counters, and, sadly, I have had to do consultations for cats who had developed behavior problems due to the frightening methods used. Don't use upside-down mousetraps, don't coat the counters with sticky gels, don't use harsh-smelling chemicals, don't use electronic pet alarms, and don't use training mats that create low-voltage shocks to your cat. These types of products may create too much fear, especially if your cat is skittish or fearful to begin with. All behavior modification should be humane. Use the LIMA approach: **L**east **I**nvasive, **M**inimally **A**versive.

Door dashing

Do you have to literally squeeze out the door in the morning to prevent your cat from escaping? Whenever someone comes in or goes out the front door, can you be heard yelling from another room, *"Don't let the cat out!"*? After years of forcing guests to inch sideways through the door opening, you may have had enough. Perhaps a recent scare, in which your cat actually did dart outside and was lost for a while, might have made you decide that things had to change. An outdoor cat who is now living indoors exclusively may still be a little confused about the change and might make a break for the door every chance she gets. When you're going through the transition phase of turning an outdoor cat into an indoor one, door dashing is one of the most common problems that continues to linger on, even after the cat seems to have accepted her new living arrangements.

Door dashing is dangerous for the cat and scary for both cat and owner. Even if you do allow your cat to go outdoors, dashing through the door is just plain bad training. You don't have time to decide if the conditions are acceptable for your cat to go outside if she just races out the door whenever she sees it open. An added twist to door dashing is when the cat has actually trained you to open the door to let her out whenever she cries, yowls, scratches at the door, paces, or even bites you to get your attention. So whether she bolts out the door whenever she can, or whether you've become an accomplice by opening the door in order to stop her incessant meowing, it's time to get things under control.

The first step is to create an "official" greeting place in the room other than right inside the front door. When you're leaving the house and returning home, don't do your hellos and good-byes right at the door. Establish another place in the room for greetings, be it on a chair, by the window, or on her cat tree. It doesn't matter, as long as it's consistent. It can even be in the middle of the room, just as long as it isn't at the door.

To get your cat accustomed to this new greeting place, make it a commonly used affection area. When you want to pet her, call her over to that spot. If she loves being groomed, brush her in that spot, but only if she *loves* it. This is a great clicker-training opportunity. When she responds to your call by going to that spot, click and reward. For specifics on clicker training, see chapter 3.

When you're getting ready to leave, call your cat over to the greeting spot, give her the usual amount of affection, then offer her a piece of a treat or leave a toy there with her so you can walk away. If she runs to the door, call her back to the greeting spot. Keep your tone of voice very casual and calm. Don't get all excited or make a big deal out of the fact that you're leaving. You don't want her to think you might not be coming back. If you establish a calm routine, she'll very likely follow right along.

When you return home, don't acknowledge your cat if she's standing there with her nose at the door opening. Walk over to the greeting place and call her over. There you can give her the type of greeting she enjoys. No matter how hard it is to ignore your cat when you first walk through the door, you have to be consistent in your re-training. Use a verbal cue if you'd like, calmly instructing her with *"Greeting place"* or whatever phrase or word cue you choose. Again, if you want to clicker-train, this is another ideal time. Assign a verbal cue or hand signal to that specific place and instruct her to go there.

If your cat refuses to cooperate in any way and insists on dashing out the door whenever it's opened, you'll have to go to plan B. Keep a spray bottle of plain water outside the door. Stand outside and open the door just a crack. If your cat is right there, ready to escape, give her a quick squirt of water. I specifically want you to open the door just a crack because that'll be enough for her to get a startling water spritz, but not so much that she associates this episode with your arrival. The water squirting has to be something she connects only with the door itself. After you've given the squirt, close the door, wait a few minutes, then open it again just a crack. If she's there, give another quick squirt, then close the door. Do this method whenever you come home and she's right there, but don't go inside the house immediately after squirting her. Wait several minutes so she'll have time to regain her composure and be ready to greet you. If you spray the water and then walk right in, she'll know it was you, even if she didn't see you. Cats are smart.

If you do need to resort to plan B, incorporate a positive into the retraining as well. Make sure she's greeted warmly at the greeting place. If you come through the door and find that your cat is sitting quietly by the door and no longer making any attempt to dart through it, then come inside and completely close the door before praising her. I had one client who got so excited that her cat had learned to sit on the mat just inside the door, she started greeting and praising the cat *as she was opening* the door. The retraining soon deteriorated because the cat started walking toward the open door as the owner was calling her name.

The other behavior that's often the companion to door dashing is the demanding meowing, yowling, pacing, scratching at the door, or whatever else the cat can do to get you to recognize that she wants *out*. Very often, this undesirable behavior actually gets rewarded by the cat owner, who can no longer stand the noise and opens the door in exasperation. While the persistent meowing or scratching noise may have stopped temporarily, opening the door guaranteed repeat performances. If you're hiding your head behind the pages of this book because you know you're guilty of this, it's time for retraining.

Use distraction as a method to change your cat's focus from the door to something more exciting and fun. When she sees that her indoor world has everything (and more) that she enjoyed about outdoor life, she'll start to cooperate, but this method won't work if you haven't created a stimulating and cat-friendly environment.

Distraction must occur while the behavior is still beginning to formulate in your cat's brain, before she actually exhibits it. For example, if she always sits at the door and meows, distract her as she's walking to the door. Use an interactive toy or just toss an interesting little toy in her direction but away from the door. Create an interesting sound. For example, keep a *Play-N-Squeak* mouse handy and shake it to make that squeaking-mouse noise. Another irresistible sound for many cats is when you run your fingernails down a nearby scratching post. I kept a scratching post near the door just for that purpose when I was working with my two feral cats. They couldn't resist scratching the post whenever they heard the sound. After they were done scratching, I continued the distraction by having an interactive toy ready to go, or by setting up a solo activity toy. An open paper bag with a toy inside or a Mylar ball whizzing by on the floor was often impossible for them to ignore. All the toys and games were set up on the opposite side of the room from the door.

Timing is important. You have to do the distraction before the actual behavior takes place, or you'll be rewarding the very behavior you don't want. If your cat is predictable in terms of when she typically heads toward the door, use that knowledge and be ready to distract her. The more often you successfully divert her away from the door for something positive, the better your chances of permanently breaking that behavior pattern.

Very often, the cat is crying at the door because there's nothing to do inside and she knows all the fun stuff is outdoors. Refer to chapter 2 to evaluate whether your indoor environment could use a little improvement. Another part of creating a stimulating environment is through regular interactive play therapy sessions. If your cat wants to go outside to hunt, offer her "hunting" opportunities right inside your living room. Play therapy is covered in chapter 3.

If you missed your opportunity for distraction or your cat started meowing at the door while you were in another room, ignore her. I know it can get hard to take—it's amazing how such a tiny animal can create such a loud sound—but you have to break the pattern. Even if you yell or chase her away, you're acknowledging the behavior and that will reinforce it. Ignore it instead.

If you allow your cat outdoors to eliminate because she doesn't have an indoor litter box, then you have to let her out when she meows or sits by the door. If you don't want her to meow at the door, you'll have to provide her with an indoor litter box (something an indoor/outdoor cat should have anyway). I hope you'll reconsider turning her into an exclusively indoor cat, though, for her own safety.

Plant nibbling

Cats seem to enjoy doing their own version of indoor hedge trimming by chewing on many types of indoor plants. It's actually a very dangerous activity for a cat, and in many cases can prove to be deadly. Most houseplants are toxic to cats. Some are just toxic enough to cause illness, but others can kill. It's not only the exotic plants; most of the common plants found in just about every home are actually toxic to cats.

In the wild, cats enjoy chewing on green grass. Experts have tried to pinpoint exactly what it is about grass that's attractive to cats. Though it has been determined that it's not the chlorophyll, no one knows precisely what benefit the cat receives from eating grass. If a cat eats enough grass she'll vomit, so many people seem to think this is the cat's way of ridding herself of something unpleasant in her digestive system that is causing her illness or pain. Since cats can feel the desire to chew on some greenery, their only option is usually one of your houseplants. There are so many plants that are toxic to cats that it's best to assume none of the plants in your home should be within your cat's reach if she's a chewer. For a list of poisonous plants, go to the ASPCA's Web site at www.aspca.org.

The way to deal with a plant nibbler is to set up deterrents on the plants. Keep only plants that are safe around cats, but even so, set them up so they aren't tempting.

There's a bitter antichew spray that can be used on the plants to make them very unappetizing to your cat. Called *Grannick's Bitter Apple for Indoor Plants*, the spray is widely available at pet supply stores and online. Place newspaper around the base of the plants to catch any overspray, so you don't ruin your carpet or flooring. Spray the tops and bottoms of the leaves with the product. Wear disposable gloves when you're doing this so that the hand touching and moving the leaves doesn't get saturated with the product. Wash your hands after applying the product because you certainly don't want to taste this stuff yourself—it's very unpleasant.

Bitter Apple may have to be reapplied every few days, depending upon how determined a plant nibbler you have. Even after the nibbling has ceased, reapply the product periodically. Using the deterrent intermittently will help reinforce the training, just as intermittent rewards work to reinforce positive behaviors during clicker training.

Provide your little plant nibbler with an acceptable alternative to unsafe houseplants by purchasing a kitty-greens kit at your local pet supply store. With a little water and a few days' time, you'll have a pot of fresh grass. After the blades are long enough, put the container in a sunny spot for kitty's munching pleasure.

You may also want to consider creating your kitty's own personal indoor garden. If there's a sunny spot in the house where your cat enjoys spending time, grow kitty grass there in a large, flat container so she can nibble, lounge, and play in the grass. Use rye, wheat, or oat seeds to grow an indoor garden. You can also grow a catnip plant to put in your kitty's indoor garden. Packets of catnip seeds can be found at your local gardening center.

When you set up the indoor garden, place a couple of comfortable lounging areas there as well. If you really want to create the ultimate indoor garden, add a pet water fountain nearby.

Curtain climbing

If you thought you could never have curtains on your windows as long as you lived with a cat, you can now relax and get ready to dress those windows the way you've always wanted to. Cats love and need to be able to climb, but they don't have to do it on your curtains. Once you provide your cat with a better and safer alternative, such as a cat tree or scratching post, you can create a deterrent on the curtains. Place the tree or scratching post near the curtains to serve as a reminder of where she should climb and scratch.

X-Mat is a hinged training mat with uncomfortable bumps on it that can be used to prevent your cat from climbing the curtains by placing it on the floor in front of them. You can also use the extra-large size of *Sticky Paws* (a double-faced tape made especially for training purposes) by taping strips of it to the bottom of the curtains, high enough to prevent your cat from reaching over them. *Sticky Paws* is safe for many fabrics because it doesn't leave a residue, but if you're unsure, do a test on an inconspicuous area or contact the manufacturer of *Sticky Paws* before using.

Computer crashing, cat-style

If you don't have a keyboard drawer, you have probably experienced the many fun things your cat can do to a computer. Even if you do have a keyboard drawer, if you've neglected to push it in before leaving the desk, your cat may have made some editing changes to your work.

Cats love computers mainly because they love being close to us. Your cat may sit on the monitor or on the desk or even on your lap as you work away. That may be wonderful and very welcomed by you, but what your cat may do at the computer when you aren't around isn't so wonderful.

Your cat may innocently walk on the keys, or she may stand on the keyboard as she tries to bat at the moving cursor. Either can cause information to be lost and create a lot of extra work as you try to figure out which planet she just sent your files to.

There are a couple of low-tech solutions and one high-tech solution to this. The most basic way to control keyboard strokes from Fluffy is to invest in a keyboard drawer for your desktop computer if your desk doesn't currently come equipped with one. There are drawers that you can install under the desk as well as portable models that sit on top of the desk. Another alternative is a keyboard cover.

Then there's the really cool high-tech solution to kitty on the keys. Called *Pawsense*, it's a software program that detects random keystrokes based on timing and combinations. The software boots up when you start your computer and runs in the background regardless of what other software you're currently using. Your cat can get in only a couple of keystrokes before the program is alerted and prevents further input. There's also an optional sound deterrent you can use as well to get your cat to leave the keyboard altogether. Use the sound deterrent only if your cat isn't timid. Currently, it can be a harmonica sound or a hissing sound. I don't recommend using the hissing sound, though, because you don't want your cat to start worrying that there's a hostile cat in the house. The software can be ordered from their Web site. Check the appendix for contact information.

 CATWISE CLUE

If your cat jumps onto your desk when you aren't around and rearranges papers or plays with pens, place a couple of *X-Mats* on your desk before you leave. Reduce temptation as well by not leaving pens and small loose objects on the desk.

Interior decorating with toilet paper

Cats aren't the only ones who love to show off their decorating skills. Dogs and kids also possess this gene. I think it must be part of the owner initiation ritual to have at least one complete roll of toilet paper unraveled, shredded, and strewn throughout the house in the form of confetti.

You no longer have to keep the roll of toilet paper high atop a shelf in the bathroom. There are ways to keep it in its proper and more convenient location and still have it remain intact.

There are a couple of products available that prevent pets or children from unrolling the paper. *TP Saver* consists of a band that can be locked in place over the toilet paper roll. *Toilet Paper Guard* has a spring-loaded cover that keeps the roll in place. Both *TP Saver* and *Toilet Paper Guard* can be quickly installed and are easy for adults and older children to access.

Until you get those products, or if you prefer a homemade solution, there are a couple of things you can do to make it more difficult for a cat to unroll the paper. Put the paper roll on the holder so it unrolls from underneath rather than up over the top. Having a cat in the house can then end the age-old debate as to which is the proper way for toilet paper to unroll. The other modification you can make is to gently press the roll of paper before putting it on the holder so the cardboard center is no longer perfectly round. I actually used the latter method with my children during potty training to prevent them from unrolling an excessively large amount of paper.

Toilet water fascination

It isn't a pleasant sight to walk into the bathroom and find your cat standing at the toilet with her front paws on the rim and her head near the water. As you hear the sound of lapping water, you cringe at the realization of what is occurring. Perhaps your cat also enjoys pawing at the water as she watches her rippling reflection. What fun! Then there are the cats who enjoy taking some of their toys to the toilet for a little swim.

If your cat enjoys quenching her thirst with water from the toilet, the most obvious solution, of course, would be to keep the lid closed so she doesn't have access to it. That's fine in theory, but how many family members will comply with that rule on a regular basis? In addition to establishing a "keep lid closed" rule, there are some ways you can help your cat find healthier and safer places to drink. The reason some cats choose the toilet water is because it's often cooler than the water that has been sitting in their bowl. Also, believe it or not, it can taste fresher because it contains more oxygen from the flushing. The water in your cat's water bowl may have been sitting there for days and tastes about as stale as can be. It can also be a location preference. If you have the water and food in a double dish or individual dishes that are too close together, your cat may not like food particles getting into her water.

To correct the toilet drinking problem, make sure that her current water bowl is being kept clean and that you're changing the water daily. Even if it looks as though your cat hasn't taken one sip from the bowl since you last changed it, replace the water every day. Wash the bowl out, make sure there are no traces of dish detergent left on it, and then fill it with fresh water. If you use a double dish for food and water, get two individual dishes and don't place them next to each other; put them a foot or two apart. Also, look at the size and type of bowl you use. It should be appropriate for the size of your cat.

Faucet fixation

I can't even count the times people have told me about how much their cats love to drink from either the kitchen or the bathroom faucet or simply enjoy pawing at the water. In many cases, the cats have actually trained their owners to turn on the faucet whenever they jump on the counter or meow at the sink. While it may have been cute the first few times you watched your cat lapping at the water trickling from the faucet, you might have unintentionally started a behavior pattern that you wish you hadn't. This faucet fixation can become so bad that some cats may then refuse to drink from their bowls.

You can put an end to this behavior by creating an alternative to the faucet that's more appropriate for your cat. There are pet water fountains available at pet supply stores and online that will provide your cat with the running water she enjoys. The fountain also keeps the water more oxygenated, which adds to the taste appeal. Diabetic cats, ones in chronic renal failure, or those who have urinary problems need to drink more water, and the pet fountain can actually be a good way to encourage that.

If your cat doesn't take to the fountain at first and still sits by the sink, place the fountain on the counter. Then, as she starts to use it, you can move it to the location you prefer.

Be sure you keep the fountain and all its parts clean. Don't rely on the filter to do the work for you. The fountain requires more cleaning than a regular water dish, but it's worth it to break the faucet fixation and to encourage your cat to drink more.

Nightly noises and crack-of-dawn wake-ups

That cats are nocturnal is a common misconception. They're *crepuscular*, which means they're more active at dawn and dusk. Since much of the prey a cat would normally hunt in the wild is also more active at those times, this is a natural time for your kitty's system to start revving up.

Much of the reason why your cat may be driving you nuts during those late-night hours when you're trying to sleep may be that she isn't getting enough stimulation during the day and the earlier part of the evening. Think about how our schedules tend to work versus how a cat's does. Most of us get up in the morning, go off to work, then, when we come home, start to unwind from the day. As the evening wears on, we get more relaxed. Our cats, on the other hand, are spending most of the day napping, so when we come home, they're ready for activity and interaction. For many cats, though, that interaction involves sitting on the cat owner's lap or beside the cat owner while dinner is eaten, mail is read, and TV is watched. Lots of petting and affection may take place, which is wonderful for the bonding process, don't get me wrong, but where's the stimulation? When your system is winding down, your cat's system is revving up. When you get into bed, your cat may hang around for a while, but at some point her normal cat energy may be too hard to hold back. Her keen senses are picking up on those interesting nightly noises or shadows. She may hear or see the insects just outside the window. It can be too much for a cat to resist.

In the past, the methods you used to try to correct the behavior may have failed because you were coming at it from the wrong angle. Locking the cat out of the room, shouting, or tossing a pillow won't change her natural cat rhythms. All those methods succeed in doing is making your relationship with her deteriorate. There's a much better approach.

CATWISE CAUTION

If your cat has started vocalizing more at night, have her checked by the veterinarian just to be sure there isn't something else going on that needs attention. If your cat's night-time activity or increased vocalization is not typical for her, then there might be an underlying medical problem. In an older cat, increased vocalization at night can be a sign of a medical condition, declining senses, or the start of age-related cognitive dysfunction.

Let's start with the nighttime activity. Since the end of the day means winding down for you but revving up for your cat, you can do a little behavior modification to help reset her internal clock, so to speak. If you play with your cat during the early part of the evening, that's wonderful; keep that up. Now, though, I want you to add an extra interactive play session right before bed. There's a good reason for this. In the wild, there's a behavior cycle that repeats over and over again as the cat hunts. If you follow that cycle, you'll have better success at getting her to let you have a good night's sleep. The cycle basically consists of four things: *hunt, feast, groom, sleep.* The cat goes through the physical activity of hunting her prey. After the capture, she eats her prey, and then she grooms herself. This grooming behavior is important for the cat because it removes traces of the just-eaten prey so that other prey won't be alerted to her presence and she doesn't put herself at risk of larger predators. When the grooming is completed and her stomach is full, she'll be ready for a nap.

This four-part cycle can be applied to your indoor cat and here's the way to do it. If you schedule-feed your cat, divide up her portions so you can save one last meal for just before bed. If you free-feed, take up her food in the early evening. Right before bed, engage in an interactive play session with her (*hunt*) so she can work off the energy. When playtime is coming to an end, wind the action down just as you do during your normal interactive play therapy sessions so she can have one final grand capture and be left relaxed. Next, offer her the last portion of her meal (*feast*). If you free-feed, put the food down and top it off with some fresh food. After eating, she'll most likely spend a little time on hygiene (*groom*), and then you stand a much better chance of having her curl up in bed beside you or stroll off into another room for a nap (*sleep*).

In order for this method to be successful, you must do the last play therapy session right before bed, not one or two hours before. I know it means you might be postponing your bedtime by fifteen to twenty minutes, but it'll be worth it to get an uninterrupted night's rest.

For a really active cat, or if your cat tends to rev up again a few hours later, set up some activity toys to keep her occupied while you sleep. You can have a special supply of toys that you put out only at night and strategically place them in areas that your cat frequents in the wee hours of the morning. If you have enough privacy, try leaving the curtains or blinds open just a bit on one window and place a window perch or cat tree there so your kitty can enjoy watching outdoor nighttime activity.

Now, what about those five AM wake-up calls? Have you endured the feline alarm clock for years, thinking there was nothing you could do about it? The standard feline alarm consists of your cat sitting on your chest and staring at you until you feel her eyes piercing through your closed eyelids. Of course, once you make eye contact with her, you're as good as done. Normally, a cat sitting on your chest may not be at all uncomfortable, but when she's in alarm mode, she's all pointy bones that sit precisely on your most sensitive areas. She also manages to magically gain an extra ten pounds during the night.

Then again, you may have one of the vocal feline alarms that sits on the nightstand, waiting until you've rolled over just enough so your ear is directly facing her, and then meows and meows and meows. Maybe you're one of the lucky ones who has the deluxe model, so you get both the chest sitting and the meowing.

The first rule with a feline alarm clock is to not reinforce the behavior by getting out of bed to give her some food in order to stop the behavior. This short-term fix will cement the technique in her brain and she'll use it again and again. Whether you get up the second she meows or wait until you just can't tolerate it anymore, you'll still be reinforcing the very behavior you don't want. You must ignore her behavior. I fully recognize how difficult that's going to be in the beginning. It may even cause her to ramp up her technique a bit (just as children do), so be prepared.

The behavior modification isn't all about ignoring her, though. It's about creating other options that are positive and rewarding. Start by doing the same prebedtime interactive play session that was discussed earlier in this section. That late-night meal may be especially helpful in the case of a feline alarm clock. For her playtime/eating enjoyment later on, leave a few puzzle feeders out, either homemade ones or *Play-N-Treat* balls or the *Peek-a-Prize*. If you use the *Play-N-Treat* balls, make sure they're out of earshot if you don't have carpeting.

If your early riser is fed on a schedule, part of her problem may be the weekday/weekend inconsistency. If you're up early on weekdays, she may be used to getting fed at that time and doesn't understand why Saturday and Sunday are different, especially if you like to sleep late. A cat is a creature of habit, and predictability provides comfort for her. If her alarm-clock routines are occurring on weekends, you can use a timed food dish that opens at the precise time you set it for. Some dishes have a cooling compartment so you can feed wet food without worrying about its spoiling. Some owners who schedule-feed wet food will leave some dry food out in the bowl for free-feeding. If you do this, just make sure her overall caloric intake is appropriate for her weight, age, health, and activity level. You don't want to solve one problem only to create a secondary problem of obesity.

Oliver Twist syndrome

A.k.a. begging. Whether your cat learned the behavior through observation of the family dog or you or another family member contributed to this behavior by feeding her from the table, it shouldn't continue. Your cat should not be fed table scraps. They're not nutritionally appropriate, and the actual behavior itself can end up being deadly should she be unwittingly given something poisonous to cats. Feed your cat a nutritionally balanced cat food that's formulated for her stage of life and for any health condition she has. If you're feeding a good-quality food, there's no need to supplement it with food from your table. A good-quality cat food is created to provide the precise balance of protein, fats, carbohydrates, vitamins, and minerals that your cat needs. If you throw that out of balance with the addition of table scraps or other goodies meant for humans, you can create health problems. Some foods, such as chocolate, can be fatal for a cat. Garlic and onions are also not safe.

Aside from the health risks, feeding your cat from the table, or while you're in the kitchen preparing dinner, will turn her into a cat who begs. Begging, while it may be cute the first few times, gets annoying very quickly. It's also not a pleasant behavior for your cat to display when you have guests for dinner.

Begging can also be a symptom of a dietary or medical problem. Make sure your cat is on the appropriate nutritional program. If she's overweight or underweight, seek the advice of your veterinarian in order to get her started eating the right food. Even if your cat is the correct weight, if she isn't satisfied with the type and amount of food you are offering, discuss the situation with your veterinarian.

In order to correct this behavior, everyone in the family has to be on the same page. It won't do any good if there's inconsistency in the retraining because of one family member who is a softy. The first order of business is a family meeting to make sure everyone understands the new rules.

Remember that your cat learns to repeat behaviors that you reinforce and acknowledge. Pay attention to little things you may be doing without being aware of the mixed message they're sending. When you're standing at the kitchen counter and your cat is sitting on the floor meowing, or maybe even pawing at your leg, are you guilty of giving her a little piece of food to quiet her? If you've done this, you've reinforced the very behavior you are trying to stop.

If you feed your cat on a schedule, portion her food so that one meal can be served at the same time as the family dinner, or just before, so her stomach won't be empty should she wander around the dining table. If you free-feed but supplement her dry food with some wet food, offer it at or before your dinnertime. If you free-feed only and your cat begs, set up activities for her while the family is eating. If you have a toy like the *Panic Mouse*, you can turn that on in another room for her to play with, or maybe your cat enjoys the cat entertainment DVDs. For some cats, even a crinkly ball in a paper bag can occupy her long enough for you to eat dinner in peace.

There are very few times when I'll tell you to keep a squirt bottle handy, but this is one of them. Keep it on the table next to you, and if your cat jumps on the table, give her a quick squirt. DO NOT squirt her for begging; squirt only if she jumps on the table or reaches up to paw at a dish or some food. For the begging, your technique will involve ignoring her. It may take days or even a week for her to get the message, but eventually she'll see that her begging behavior isn't getting her anywhere. The lack of reinforcement will naturally show her the behavior isn't resulting in any kind of payoff.

CORRECTING MORE SERIOUS PROBLEMS

Boredom

When your cat was a kitten, she was probably stimulated to play by just about anything in her environment. Whether it was a ray of sunshine dancing on the floor or the curtains gently moving in the breeze, your kitten was sitting on ready. Some of the behavior problems you may be experiencing with your adult cat now may be as a result of boredom. She needs stimulation in her life and she needs to exercise her talents as a hunter. Depending on her age and health, the degree to which she moves will vary, but she still needs some spark in her life. If you don't provide her with stimulation, discovery, and fun, she may look for it in ways that aren't acceptable to you. She may also develop behaviors that start out innocent enough and end up becoming compulsive, as you'll learn later in this chapter. Boredom can also lead to obesity, as the only activity becomes the walk to the food bowl. Finally, boredom can lead to depression. Tackle boredom before it has a domino effect by improving your cat's environment and customizing her playtime routine as described in chapters 2 and 3. A bored cat is a terrific candidate for clicker training. She'll be learning how to learn, and that creates opportunities for you to shape her behavior.

 CATWISE CLUE

Signs of boredom:
- Weight gain
- Change in activity level
- Destructive behavior
- Self-directed overgrooming
- Lack of grooming
- Change in sleep habits
- Change in interaction with family

If you have already modified the environment and you play with your cat on a regular basis and yet she still seems bored, consider adding a second cat to the family. This may be very beneficial if you think your cat is bored and lonely due to your long absences from home. However, adding another cat requires some finesse, so before you run out and bring home a friend for kitty, learn the proper introduction technique described in chapter 9.

Depression

Depression can be a difficult problem to notice because it creeps up rather than arriving with a bang. It's very easy to miss those subtle signs along the way that indicate things are going downhill for your cat.

Depression can occur for many reasons. It may be due to a physical or medical trauma in a cat's life, such as recovering from an injury or illness. It can also happen due to emotional trauma from a move to a new home or the loss of a family member. Even a change in your work schedule can create depression. The problem is that your cat may seem so stoic, you aren't aware of what's happening to her internally. Her behavior may change so gradually that by the time you're aware of it, you have a major problem on your hands.

Signs of depression can include a change in appetite, lack of interest in self-grooming, change in litter box habits, hiding, increased sleeping, or a lack of interest in play. You may notice that your cat is losing weight or that her coat doesn't seem as healthy. Perhaps your cat, who normally would meet you at the door, now prefers staying curled up on a chair or even under the bed.

The signs of depression may also indicate underlying medical conditions, so a veterinary examination is needed. Don't assume your cat is depressed without having appropriate diagnostic tests done to rule out other potential problems.

Depression is serious, and since each cat is an individual, what triggers one cat may not be a trigger for another. This requires detective work on your part to figure out what has changed in your environment or in your life that might be negatively affecting your cat. If your cat has changed her behavior, that's a red flag that something is probably wrong. Once you pinpoint the cause of her depression, you then have to work on helping her to overcome it.

The environmental and external changes you'll need to make will depend on the actual cause of the depression. For example, if your cat is depressed because she has been forced to stay in a certain part of the home due to another cat in the home who chases her, then your first order of business is to improve the relationship between the two. Figure out what the underlying cause could be so you can do your best to create more security and enrichment.

The next stage involves helping your cat find that spark in life again. The spark will come from you. Use interactive play therapy to build your cat's confidence and fire up that prey-drive. The play therapy will also help strengthen the bond between the two of you. Initially, your cat may not offer much of a response to the sessions, but don't give up. If you get even the faintest glimmer in her eyes, then you're making progress. If your cat responds favorably to catnip, kick-start a play session with it. Go shopping for some new toys because it may take "new prey" to get her interested.

If she starts to respond to the play therapy, do several short sessions a day. Stay within her comfort zone, so if she feels most secure doing the playtime in a certain room, don't venture out yet. Let her set the pace of when she is ready to expand her playing field.

CATWISE REMINDER

Work closely with your veterinarian when dealing with a depressed cat. Health and weight need to be monitored. In some cases, psychopharmacological intervention may be needed. Your veterinarian may refer you to a certified behavior expert.

The grieving cat

So many people are surprised to discover that their cats grieve when there's a loss of a family member or companion pet. It's important to recognize that your cat will grieve over a loss. How you interact with her and decisions you make concerning what's best for her must take into consideration the grieving period.

When a cat loses a family member or companion pet, she has the added confusion of not knowing what happened. When we lose a family member, we're devastated, but at least we know the person has passed away and won't be returning. With your cat, she has no idea where her family member has gone and is completely confused over the sudden disappearance.

As if the confusion and loneliness aren't enough, your cat also doesn't understand why the remaining members of her family are acting so strangely. Keep in mind that your cat takes comfort in familiarity, and when you're in mourning over a loss, your behavior changes. You may be crying, you'll be stressed, you might not be at home as much as usual. Perhaps you're trying to comfort your cat by doing lots of extra cuddling and showing an excessive amount of affection, or you may be so lost in your own grief that you're unable to show your cat as much attention as she's used to. All of this behavior, although perfectly understandable in our human world, is very unsettling for your cat. From her point of view, her entire world has just collapsed. No one is acting the way they should and someone very important in her life is no longer around.

If a companion cat was the one who passed away and that cat didn't have a good relationship with your surviving kitty, there will still be a grieving process and lots of confusion. Because your cat doesn't know where the other cat has gone, she'll be unsure about whether she should risk venturing into areas that the other cat had claimed. If you have more than one surviving cat, then at some point those cats have to renegotiate the turf and adjust their social rankings. If your cat had a close relationship with the cat who passed away, then part of her grief and confusion may involve going to the places where that cat liked to sleep. She may cry for her companion or search through the house.

It doesn't have to be a death that causes mourning. A child going off to college or moving away from home creates that same deep loss. A divorce is another situation in which the bottom may fall out of the cat's world. In the case of a divorce, one spouse may also take one of the companion pets, which creates a double whammy of grief for the cat. It also creates an unbelievable amount of stress for the other cat, who not only loses a feline companion and a human companion but her familiar territory as well.

It's important to recognize that your cat will grieve so you can help her through it. One thing you shouldn't do is overdo the affection and cuddling. Don't send the message to her that, yes, this is truly the end of the world. Provide comfort and affection, but also do your best to maintain as normal a schedule as possible. She needs the rest of her world to stay intact.

Follow the instructions in the previous section on depression. Provide regular play sessions for your cat and set out solo toys so she'll have distractions when you aren't at home. If you must be away from home longer than usual, perhaps there's a neighbor or friend who can visit with the cat. Just make sure it's someone the cat enjoys being around.

Watch your cat's appetite because it's not unusual for grieving cats to stop eating. While it's certainly understandable that she wouldn't want to eat as much as she usually does, if she stops eating for more than two days, contact your veterinarian right away. It's extremely dangerous for a cat to go without food for longer than that. Your veterinarian may prescribe an appetite stimulant.

Take time to groom your cat because she may not be up to the task herself. If she normally enjoys being brushed, this can be a time of quiet and calm that may help to reassure her.

Use *Feliway Comfort Zone* in the environment to help her recognize those friendly pheromones. It may help create some calm if she thinks she has facially rubbed there recently.

One very common mistake that many cat owners make when a cat has lost a companion pet is to rush out and get another pet. The cat owners feel as if the grieving cat is lonely, and so a new companion seems to be the perfect choice. Unfortunately, this decision usually has disastrous results. Your cat needs time to grieve and will view the sudden appearance of an unfamiliar pet as an intrusion. She'll be far too stressed to be able to handle the introduction. It's also not fair to the newcomer to bring him in under such stressful circumstances. You'll end up setting him up to be the victim of lots of aggression—much more than might normally occur during the introduction of a new companion pet.

The addition of another companion pet may be a wonderful idea later on, but it isn't the healthy decision to make during the grieving process. Allow your cat adequate time to accept the loss and create a new routine for herself in the home. In cases in which the cat who passed away was a constant source of stress for the surviving cat, you may find that after the grieving process, the surviving kitty is happier and more at peace. She may now enjoy being the only cat in the home. You won't be able to make a wise decision about that until after your cat has had time to mourn.

The fearful cat

This can range from a cat who fears a particular object to one who fears everything. There are certain things that cats generally fear, such as going to the veterinarian, but some cats have fear within their own homes, and that's the one place they should feel safe and secure.

As a general rule, to eliminate or at least reduce fear, introduce any change into a cat's life in the most gradual, nonthreatening way. Even if you're pretty sure your cat won't be frightened of something, play it safe and don't spring it on her. Prevention is much easier than damage control.

The two general behavior modification techniques for helping a fearful cat are desensitization and counterconditioning. Desensitization involves the gradual exposure of something that the cat fears so she has time to get used to it without it overwhelming her. Counterconditioning refers to having the cat do something she wouldn't ordinarily do in the presence of what frightens her in order to focus her attention on something positive and help her realize that the cause of her fear isn't such a bad thing.

One thing many cats fear, and something I'm asked about quite often, is the vacuum cleaner. If you look at it from a cat's point of view, it's understandable why she would be frightened of it. The vacuum is extremely noisy and it moves around the house like a predator, sticking its nose under chairs and behind sofas. Some people even escalate their cats' fears by using it to chase their kitties out of the way if they need to vacuum in certain spots. There has also been absolutely horrible advice given by some so-called experts recommending the use of a vacuum cleaner to chase the cat away from the bed when she disturbs you early in the morning. This creates a cruelly unnecessary amount of fear.

To help your cat overcome her fear of the vacuum, first get on a good schedule of doing interactive play therapy so you know which toys are irresistible to her. Once you have that established, place the vacuum in the corner of the room and then do a play session. Don't turn the vacuum cleaner on; just let it sit silently in the corner. If your cat is fine with that, move the vacuum out a bit for your next session. Get to the point where your cat can get close to and around the vacuum without fear. If you're using clicker training, click and reward any positive behavior throughout the desensitization and counterconditioning process. Regardless of how brief the calm and relaxed behavior is, click and reward at the precise moment. These are the baby steps of progress that'll lead your cat in the right direction.

Now it's time to put the vacuum in another room and turn it on. If there's another family member at home, he or she can vacuum in the other room while you do a play therapy session with your cat. If you're alone, just turn the vacuum cleaner on, but be sure it isn't sitting on a surface that'll get damaged or burned and don't run it for too long. Keep the door to the room closed so that your cat is faintly hearing the machine but it's not creating too much of a distraction. If the room you're in is too close to the sound and she seems fearful, move farther away. Find her comfort zone and work within that for now. The next session can move a little closer to the room where vacuuming is going on. How gradual this phase has to be will depend on your particular cat. If her fear is intense or has been going on for a long time, be prepared to move at a snail's pace. Ease up to where you can have the door to the room where the vacuum is running open. You may have to go farther away than you were with the door closed, but you'll still be making progress.

The final phase involves having the cat and the vacuum in the same room while the vacuum is running. Set it in a corner again and turn it on. If it's very loud you may have to buffer the sound by putting pillows around it. Do a play session with your cat at whatever distance she is most comfortable. If she runs from the room, that's okay; just casually go to her and reassure her through playtime. Hopefully, you can ease your way closer to the vacuum.

In addition to play therapy, you can use food or treats as a way to help your cat get more comfortable. I often use clicker training with fearful cats so that I can mark the exact behavior I'm looking for from them. For example, if you've been clicker training your cat, you can click and reward when she walks calmly past the vacuum or sits on one side of the room while the vacuum is running.

The vacuum is often an over-the-top object of fear for many cats, so you may not get your cat to be comfortable enough to stay in the room while you're doing your cleaning, but she shouldn't run in terror and hide under the bed whenever it's in sight. Use behavior modification to find a balance that allows your cat to remain as comfortable as possible.

Maybe your cat's fear doesn't involve the vacuum, but something else in the house sends her running in fear of her life. You can still use the above method to help her expand her comfort zone.

Fear of people

This is a very common fear, especially when you consider that for most of your cat's life, the only people she comes in contact with regularly are her human family members. Throw in the occasional veterinarian visit, which strikes fear in the heart of almost every cat, and you have very little reason for her to welcome visitors to your home with open paws.

If your cat hides in fear when visitors come to the house, look at what might have been the trigger for that. Let's start with the fact that a cat is territorial and her home is her major source of security. When guests enter the home, although they're welcomed by you, they're often a surprise for your cat. She may have walked into the room after hearing the doorbell and was surprised to find strangers there. The combination of the sight of unfamiliar people with their unfamiliar scents and sounds can create anything from mild concern to outright panic in a cat. This is especially the case if you don't tend to have visitors very often, because your cat never really had a chance to learn to adjust to that way of life. Cats that were socialized well grow up to be comfortable and confident whenever people visit. For others, though, every stranger in the home is perceived as a possible threat. In your home, things might have gotten to the point at which the cat has been conditioned to hide the second she hears the doorbell.

Often, a kitty owner can inadvertently create more fear in the cat by trying too hard to show her that the guest isn't a threat. If you've picked up your cat and held her up to a guest as a way to show her that the person means no harm, you've probably ended up with a scratch or two as your cat frantically struggled to get out of your grasp. Or maybe your cat tried to hide in your arms or defensively hissed at the visitor. Physically forcing a cat to get to know your guest only creates a greater sense of fear. The next time the doorbell rings, your cat will make sure she's nowhere in sight. Force never works with cats, and ends up causing more of a problem for everyone.

Guests also can make the situation worse by attempting to befriend your cat too quickly. If your cat is inching her way closer in order to investigate, a guest may interpret that as a sign to interact and respond by reaching down to pet the cat or pick her up, which panics the kitty and sends her bolting from the room.

People often wonder why cats always seem to gravitate toward the one visitor in the home who is allergic to or who dislikes cats. There's really no mystery if you think about it. That person makes no overtures toward the cat and usually doesn't even make eye contact. From the cat's point of view, that person immediately comes across as nonthreatening. The cat feels it's safe to come closer and investigate the individual, much to that person's dismay. It's the cat lover who makes too much eye contact, reaches too quickly, or even bends down to pick the kitty up who doesn't give the cat any time to make the determination of whether she has anything to fear.

We all want our cats to be friendly and sociable, but you have to remember that the survival instinct is very strong in animals, even in a pampered indoor setting. In the cat's world, unfamiliar cats who don't want to appear threatening either stay on the perimeter of the territory or enter in a way that follows official kitty protocol. The cat who barges right in, making direct eye contact, will be perceived as a threat.

For fearful cats, visitors to the home are frightening, but in many cases, their presence is limited to a few rooms. Overnight guests can be truly frightening because in addition to spending a longer amount of time in the home, they move throughout more rooms in the home. In some cases, a guest room that has been the cat's little sanctuary ends up being off-limits to her during a guest's stay. Imagine the extra confusion if the empty guest room was where you were keeping your cat's litter box, forcing you to suddenly move it to another location.

Another trigger for fearful cats is the presence of visitors who do not limit themselves to just certain common areas of the home. Think of the times you've had a plumber, electrician, house-keeper, exterminator, carpet cleaner, or some other type of repair person into your home. Imagine how stressful that must be for a fearful cat to see a total stranger entering all the "private" areas of the home. If you're not at home and have a neighbor or apartment superintendent let the repair person in, yikes! That can really put kitty over the edge.

Is there hope for your fearful cat who panics at the sound of the doorbell? Yes, although you have to be realistic about how sociable she'll become. If her fear turns into total panic, you may have to be happy with simply getting her to stop trembling under the bed. She may never happily trot out to personally greet each and every visitor. The end result we want from this retraining process is to create a sense of comfort for your cat so she can decide how much closer she wants to come. You may want a cat who will sit on your guest's lap, but you have to be realistic about the personality of your kitty, how she was socialized as a kitten, and the dynamics of your home. Taking all of that into consideration, there's a behavior modification technique you can use to ease your kitty through this and help increase her comfort zone.

As always, the process starts with the environment itself. Make sure there are plenty of escape options for your cat so she can go where she feels most comfortable. Don't ever close off rooms in order to keep her in an area. The first rule here is that if she wants to dive under the bed, let her.

There should be areas in the room where you host your guests that are specifically cat-friendly. It can be a cat tree, window perch, hideaway, or even a paper bag on its side with a towel inside. The more safe areas you create in that room, the greater the chance that your cat will find a safe spot there and not run to another room.

Set up the *Feliway Comfort Zone* diffuser to help send out some positive feline facial pheromones (see chapter 2 for information on this product). You'll also need to have established a schedule of interactive play therapy with your cat so she's conditioned to the fact that the sight of the toy means safety and fun. Pay attention to the specific interactive toy she likes the best because that will be important later in this process.

Now comes the actual behavior modification. This part requires an accomplice. The person you pick should be a friend or neighbor who has a calm demeanor. The accomplice should come for a visit with the understanding that this is a retraining session. Have your guest come in and stand just inside the door for a few minutes. If your cat is in the room, this gives her time to adjust to the unfamiliar sight, sound, and scent of that person. The body language and positioning of the guest also indicate that he's not threatening because he isn't barging right into the house. Have your clicker and treats handy so you can click and reward any calm or relaxed behavior displayed by your cat.

Instruct your guest not to make eye contact with your cat or attempt to pet her. If any interaction is to take place between your cat and your guest, you'll give specific instructions when the time is right.

Once your guest has been with you at the front door for a few minutes, casually walk to the seating area. If your cat has long since bolted from the room, don't worry about it. Especially during the first couple of retraining sessions, it's totally understandable if she reacts in her usual way. So even if your cat is out of sight, spend about ten minutes chatting with your guest while seated. Remember that it's important for both of you to keep your tones calm and casual. I don't mean you have to whisper; in fact, whispering is definitely not what you want to do. You just don't want to be using tones that are extreme (such as sudden, high-pitched laughter or shouts). That's why it's important to pick the right person for this retraining process, because your best friend, although very willing, may have too loud a voice.

After ten minutes, excuse yourself from your guest and go find your cat. Bring along an interactive toy and casually move it around. If your cat is hiding under the bed, don't try to pull her out and don't even dangle the toy in front of her. Instead, move the toy in a very light and low-key way just beyond the bed so she can see it. She may still be too frightened to paw at it, but any degree of interest that is sparked is that much less that she's focusing on her fear. Use your voice by talking to her in your typical way to let her know that all is okay with her world. The message you should send through your voice and toy movements is that even though there's a visitor in the home, there's nothing to worry about. Cats are little emotional sponges, and they pick up on our level of anxiety, so you want to make sure you're sending calming messages.

If your cat ventures out from under the bed, even just a little, engage in a little play session to help calm her and then offer her a treat as a reward. If you use clicker training, this is a good opportunity to click and reward when she paws at the toy. If you have used a target stick during clicker training, you can also display that for her to either nose, paw at, or reach up for. The sight of the target stick can be a calming factor for many clicker-trained cats because it puts them into training focus. Click and reward any step in the right direction to encourage her.

Whether or not your cat has braved coming out from under the bed, after about ten minutes, go back to your guest. Your cat might come out on her own at that point and may even appear in the doorway. If she doesn't, then ten minutes later, excuse yourself again and do the play therapy again. The first few sessions may not produce much, but the more you show your cat that all is normal in her home, the less anxious she'll be.

If your cat does happen to make an appearance in the room where your guest is, casually greet her with your voice and go back to talking with your guest. Remind your guest not to make eye contact. Your cat may venture closer and eventually sniff at the guest's shoes. Just keep up as if nothing earth-shattering is happening. Even if the cat jumps up next to the guest, let her do her investigation. It may take several sessions before your particular cat ever gets to that point, if at all, but it's important to always let her set the pace of her progress. If the cat's actions are calm and she doesn't display any hissing, click and reward positive steps she makes toward the guest. If you find that the click-and-reward process is distracting her and it seems as if she wants to approach without any sort of interruption (even a positive one), then let her proceed while you act as if nothing is happening. Your cat will set the pace at which she's most comfortable.

If your kitty sits in the doorway and doesn't enter the room, or even if she enters the room but doesn't move much, you can slide off the couch, sit on the carpet, and casually conduct a play session with her and/or click and reward steps in the right direction. You may even have to very casually move closer to where your cat is sitting. Keep the game very low-key so she can split her focus between the toy and the guest. She will be too anxious to focus totally on the toy in the beginning, so it's important that it not make wild and fast movements initially.

If you're clicker training, click and reward when she responds to any of your cues or reaches for the target stick. Click and reward even the smallest attempt she makes. Make sure you're far enough away from the guest so your cat can stay within her comfort zone.

By doing the play therapy in the same room that the guest is in, your cat will be getting the message that the guest isn't threatening and that she can start to relax. Subsequent retraining sessions with the guest present will continue the process, and you may eventually get to the point at which the cat will send a signal to the guest that it's okay to interact. That's when you'll give the verbal okay to your guest to quietly extend his index finger to the cat. This is the same as nose-to-nose sniffing in the cat world. The cat will probably walk over and sniff the guest's finger. If she wants more interaction, she will either rub against the finger or walk closer to the guest. If she doesn't want interaction, she'll stop sniffing, stand still, and look at the guest or just walk away. Even if she does walk away, don't consider that a failure. The fact that your fearful cat even came that close is a huge step.

CATWISE REMINDER

Direct eye contact can be viewed as a challenge. Be sure to instruct your guest not to look directly at your cat.

If kitty never ventures into the room, end the visit after about forty-five minutes and go back to your cat in that same calm and casual manner. Do another play session or just sit there and talk to her for a few minutes, then go about your day as usual. The overall theme throughout is *casual.* If she finally comes out from under the bed an hour later, don't make a big deal out of it. Just casually greet her and offer to play or pet her. Do not, under any circumstances, cuddle her in a way that reinforces her fear. Some people cuddle and comfort in a manner that tells the cat that, yes, this was a terrible experience and what a poor baby the kitty is to have had to endure it. Don't reward your cat for displaying fearful behavior. She may pick up the message that in future similar circumstances she should exhibit this same nervous behavior again. Don't reinforce unwanted behavior but *do* reinforce even the smallest positive steps.

Do these retraining sessions as often as you can so your cat gets used to the process. Start with the calmest friend. You can then gradually introduce others. Always let your cat set the pace. You may be able to get to the point at which you can hand off the interactive toy to your guest and he can continue the play therapy session with your cat. That's the best way for your cat to see that visitors to the house can be a good thing. Your cat may get to this point quickly or not all, but don't rush to get there.

If the guests your cat fears are overnight visitors, then you have to do a little preparation work before they come. If your cat currently sets up camp in the guest room, and especially if there's a litter box in there, adjustments need to be made while the house is quiet, before the company arrives. If the litter box is in there, gradually move it to another location a few inches a day, so it isn't a shocking change for your cat. Don't just put it outside the guest room if your cat is fearful of guests, because eliminating anywhere near the source of her fear will be the last thing she wants to do. Set up the litter box in a place where she'll feel safe and secure. The farther away you plan on having the box, the further in advance you'll have to prepare for it. Make sure your cat is comfortable with the change well before the company arrives. Another option is to have two litter boxes, so she can have a choice as to how close to the company she feels she's willing to be.

Make sure she has extra hideaways and areas of sanctuary while company is visiting. If she's normally fed in the kitchen and it's currently a very noisy place due to the company, either set up a time when she can be in the kitchen in peace for meals or feed her in another part of the house. The places where she eats, sleeps, and eliminates are the areas where she'll need the most security.

Even though you may be extremely busy with your visitors, it'll be important to find time for regular interactive play therapy sessions during their visit. Since play therapy helps build confidence and reduce anxiety, it's an important part of helping her deal with this major change in her life.

When it comes to repair personnel in your home, put your cat in a safe room, away from the stranger. Since his presence is very temporary, don't expose your cat to him. While the plumber is unclogging the kitchen sink, let her enjoy a nap on your bed with a cat entertainment DVD playing in the background, or give her a little catnip in another room.

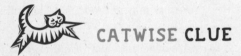 **CATWISE CLUE**

No matter what it is that causes your cat to be nervous, it's the repeated, low-intensity, gradual, nonthreatening exposure that helps her gain more confidence. Too much too soon will only magnify her fear. Gradual desensitization and counterconditioning work very well together.

Separation anxiety

You probably think of dogs suffering from separation anxiety more than cats, but cats do experience it as well, and the effects can be devastating. Separation anxiety can happen to a cat when the cat owner makes a drastic schedule change and goes from being home a lot to being away from home for long periods. I had one client who decided to end his home-based business and take a full-time job.

His cat had known life only with her human companion at home practically twenty-four hours a day. Suddenly, he was gone. The cat, already one who needed to be physically close to her owner most of the time, was beside herself when she was left alone.

Symptoms of separation anxiety can include excessive vocalization, elimination outside the litter box, vomiting, change in appetite and water consumption (a typical example is that the cat doesn't eat when the owner isn't at home), restlessness, uncharacteristic clinging when the owner returns home, destructive behavior, and excessive self-grooming.

The treatment for separation anxiety involves creating more confidence in the cat when you're at home and also providing activities for when you're gone. Start by getting on a schedule of doing interactive play therapy. Although you want your cat to be affectionate and enjoy being close to you, it's also an important part of the cat's life to be confident and secure on her own. The play therapy helps her be "with" you without having to be physically on your lap or in your arms at all times. It also triggers the prey-drive, and that stimulates her to focus and use mental energy to plan and capture her prey. The interactive play therapy done on a regular basis keeps her active, and that helps to reduce the stress. Do an extra play session before you leave in the morning and when you come home at night. Keep your hellos and good-byes casual so she doesn't think it's the end of the world.

Environmental enrichment also plays a huge role in helping a cat with separation anxiety. While you're gone, there has to be enough mental and physical stimulation for your cat so she doesn't keep focusing on your absence. Use the ideas listed in chapter 2 to create a more interesting environment. Puzzle feeders can help keep a cat active and using her brain in a way that focuses more on accomplishing a task than falling victim to frustration and anxiety. I have several clients who feed their cats only by way of puzzle feeders during the day.

When you set up toys, choose ones that will stimulate and occupy your cat's brain. Even something as simple as a ball inside an empty tissue box can create a fun challenge during the day.

Simple modifications such as leaving a radio on and having the lights on timers can help as well. Think of it as creating signs of life inside your home.

If your cat enjoys TV or even the cat entertainment DVDs, leave the TV on with the sleep timer so she can enjoy a little viewing while you're gone.

Sometimes it helps just to have someone visit your cat during the day to ease separation anxiety. If your cat enjoys the company of one of your neighbors, perhaps he or she can pop over for a quick visit once a day as you ease your kitty through separation anxiety. Another option is to hire a pet sitter to visit once a day for an interactive play session. Several of my clients have hired responsible older children in the neighborhood to visit for a play session. One of my clients hired an older retired lady in the neighborhood who loved the opportunity to make a little extra money by visiting the cat. Another one of my clients found an elderly neighbor who walked every day as part of her exercise routine. She was more than willing to stop by halfway through her walk for a little cat visiting. All of the above examples were successful because my clients made sure the cats enjoyed the company of other guests and were very comfortable with interacting with the specific people involved. If you choose this option, have the person meet and interact with your cat while you're there so you can make sure there is a positive connection. You'll also need to show the person how your cat enjoys doing her interactive play therapy. In some cases, it may just be petting or affection that the cat enjoys from the visitor. I know that my mother's cat loves curling up on someone's lap, so when I cat-sit for her, I spend a little time watching TV or reading so she can have her much-loved lap time.

If the separation anxiety is so extreme that this behavior modification alone isn't providing enough relief, talk to your veterinarian about a referral to a certified behavior expert. Medication may also need to be prescribed by your veterinarian, but that should be done only after the behavior expert has seen your cat and received the full behavioral history. That way, if medication is needed, your veterinarian will be able to make the decision on what specific prescription is best. Keep in mind that medication must be accompanied by appropriate behavior modification. Putting your cat on antianxiety medication is NOT to be used as a shortcut.

COMPULSIVE BEHAVIORS

When a cat seems conflicted between running away and engaging in a confrontation, she may start to develop behaviors that can become compulsive. Overgrooming is a common example of this, as are wool sucking and wool chewing. If the cat is routinely put in the position of being torn between escape and confrontation, her tolerance to conflict may lower. This can cause the compulsive behavior to be triggered much more quickly and by a lower degree of stress. In time, this may become the cat's routine response to tension and anxiety. The behavior may also be exhibited even when there's no anxiety-provoking trigger present. Compulsive behaviors often crop up as a result of ongoing exposure to stress.

Before determining that your cat is exhibiting a compulsive behavior, a precise diagnosis must be made by your veterinarian. Your cat's general health must be evaluated and appropriate diagnostic tests need to be performed. There may be an underlying medical cause for the behavior and it's important to rule that out before labeling the behavior as compulsive. Don't discipline a cat who is displaying a compulsive behavior because that only adds to her stress and you risk having the behavior show up in other forms.

CATWISE CAUTION

Treating compulsive behavior is best left to a certified professional. Certain disorders that cause seizures can be misdiagnosed as compulsive behavior.

Sometimes what starts out as an innocent enough behavior can turn into a compulsive one. For example, your cat may enjoy chasing a flashlight beam, a penlight, or a laser light. In some cases, this may turn into a compulsion to go after other flickering lights and light reflections.

Tail chasing is a behavior that can become compulsive. It's not unusual to see kittens chasing their tails in play because kittens will chase almost anything that moves, but if the tail chasing becomes habitual, your veterinarian should be seen so an evaluation can be done. With tail chasing or tail chewing you also need to first rule out causes such as back pain, tail injury, parasites, skin conditions, or anal gland problems. Injuries to tails can lead to compulsive tail chewing, especially if there's any loss of sensation due to the injury. Tail chasing can turn into tail biting, despite any pain the cat may be inflicting upon herself by the behavior.

Although tail chasing, whether in a kitten or an adult cat, may look funny, don't ever encourage the behavior by using the cat's tail as a way to entice her to play. What starts out as an innocent game can develop into a problem down the road. Interrupt tail-chasing behavior as soon as you see it.

The treatment for tail chasing, after the veterinarian has ruled out any underlying physiological cause, is to reduce the cat's exposure to stress and eliminate or modify the provoking triggers. That means you have to try to identify the trigger. It might be a companion cat or a child or perhaps tension in your home between family members. Is there a neighborhood cat outside who literally sends your cat into a tailspin? Did the cat suffer an emotional or physical trauma recently? If you can't identify the cause of the stress, you still need to create an environment that's as stress-free as possible for your cat.

Use environmental enrichment techniques and plenty of play therapy. Distract your cat with positive things that lower her stress level and redirect her away from the compulsive behavior. In some cases, this can't be done without the help of psychopharmacology, so seek your veterinarian's advice. You may also need a referral to a certified behavior expert.

Psychogenic alopecia

This is a compulsive behavior in which the cat overgrooms, usually to the point of creating bald patches. Grooming, within normal limits, is a cat's typical response to stress or indecision, but taken to the extreme, a cat may develop a grooming habit that she can't control. Some cats become more aggressive in their overgrooming and actually bite and chew at themselves. Because overgrooming can also have an underlying medical condition, it's important to have your cat checked by the veterinarian. For example, a common sign of hyperthyroidism is overgrooming. Grooming to the extreme can also be caused by skin conditions, allergies, or parasites.

With overgrooming, the areas of the body affected are places the cat can reach, such as the flanks, legs, tail, and abdomen. Because of the barbs on the tongue, persistent licking of an area creates bald spots and possibly lesions.

As with the previous section on tail chasing, you must find the cause of the cat's anxiety and create an environment with lower stress triggers. Create diversions for your cat and other confidence-building activities as described throughout this book. Simply putting an Elizabethan collar on the cat won't solve the problem because you haven't dealt with the source of the stress.

Very often with psychogenic alopecia, psychopharmacological intervention is needed in addition to behavior modification. If you're unable to identify what might be creating so much anxiety for your cat, ask your veterinarian for a referral to a behavior expert.

Compulsive licking

A cat may engage in compulsive licking that is not self-directed. She may lick a companion pet or an object. Some cats engage in compulsive plastic licking, which may progress to ingestion of the plastic—something that's extremely dangerous.

If you suspect compulsive licking, consult your veterinarian immediately so that possible underlying medical causes can be ruled out before you attempt to tackle this from a behavioral standpoint.

The treatment, as in the previous sections, centers around identifying the stressors and cues. Careful evaluation of the environment must be done to create more secure surroundings. Use confidence-building play therapy on a regular basis, as well as for distraction if you think the cat is about to engage in the behavior. Use puzzle feeders and set up solo activity toys to keep your cat's mind occupied when she is alone.

Psychoactive medication may be needed as an adjunct to behavior modification. Consult your veterinarian for a referral to a certified behavior expert.

Wool sucking, chewing, and pica behavior

This is the repetitive sucking of fabric, and although it's referred to as *wool* sucking, the target can be whatever a particular cat prefers—cotton, synthetic, and so forth. The most common targets are sweaters and blankets, but some cats may suck on carpet or even plastic bags.

Wool sucking seems to be a holdover behavior from nursing and is usually first seen before the cat reaches adulthood. Many things may trigger wool sucking, including early or abrupt weaning, lack of environmental stimulation, or separation anxiety. There may also be a genetic factor to wool sucking since it's more commonly seen in Oriental breeds.

Wool sucking can sometimes transition into pica behavior (eating nonfood objects). It's not uncommon for people to find holes in sweaters, socks, or blankets when the sucking escalates into chewing.

If you have a chronic wool sucker, use the same methods previously described to increase environmental stimulation and keep your cat's mind active and confident. If you have a young cat who has started wool sucking, divert her attention to a toy or start petting her under the chin to disengage her from the object in a positive way.

Since prevention is your best tool, if you see your cat starting to get into a position that indicates she's about to wool-suck, or if she's eyeing an object that looks like a potential target, redirect her toward a toy. With many wool suckers, as they develop more confidence and find other forms of stimulation and comfort, the behavior becomes less frequent.

CATWISE REMINDER

When treating a wool sucker, don't underestimate the influence of your cat's surroundings. Identify possible environmental stressors so you can do your best to decrease or eliminate them.

Once again, create a more stimulating environment to keep your cat's mind active. Engage in regularly scheduled interactive play therapy and set up solo activities for her to enjoy. Scatter puzzle feeders around so she gets the opportunity for hunting and discovery. If she doesn't take to puzzle feeders even after you've shown her how they work, then place small bowls of dry food in several locations for her to discover. Any degree of hunting for food will help keep her mind engaged.

With pica behavior, you may have to take some other measures in addition to the ones mentioned above. First, make sure there isn't an underlying medical cause for the need to chew on the fabric. If your cat is chewing on hard nonfabric objects, you have the added risk of injury to her teeth. Have your veterinarian do a thorough workup to make sure there isn't a nutritional deficiency or other underlying cause.

Even though wool chewing isn't diagnosed officially as a need for increased fiber, it seems to help in many cases, along with behavior modification. Consult your veterinarian before making *any* nutritional changes, but often adding a little canned pumpkin to wet food helps. Pumpkin is high in fiber, cats don't mind the taste, and it's easy to mix into wet food. Ask your veterinarian how much to add based on your specific cat's size and health, but generally about ¼ to ½ teaspoon is a good start. You don't want to add too much too quickly because a large increase in fiber can have some very unpleasant intestinal repercussions. After your cat gets used to the initial amount, you can then increase or decrease based on your veterinarian's recommendations.

CATWISE CLUE

Chewing on wool and other fabrics may have a genetic connection for some cats. The behavior is seen most often in Siamese and Burmese cats.

If you feed your cat only wet food, sometimes leaving some dry food out as well may help. If you already feed dry food, talk to your veterinarian about possibly switching to a higher-fiber formula. If you feed on a schedule and are feeding only twice a day, increase the number of meals (not the size of the total portion) so that she gets several small meals a day. You can use a timed food dispenser if you aren't at home to feed. Set up a couple to go off at various intervals so your cat can enjoy the correct portion of her food at the times you specify. Puzzle feeders can be used as well.

Whether your cat is wool sucking or chewing, keep temptation out of sight as much as possible. If you know she goes for blankets, tuck them tightly around the bed and then cover with a comforter that's not appealing to her appetite, or remove the blankets during the day. If the room isn't one she cares to be in during the day, close it off. Don't leave socks and sweaters around where she can get to them. I had a client who accidentally left her dresser drawer slightly open because she was in a hurry to get to work. When she returned at night, she found that her cat had spent quite a bit of time munching away. Almost every sock in her drawer contained holes.

You can also set up a few deterrents during the retraining process if your cat consistently targets specific objects. If she's a sock chewer, take a couple of socks, coat them with a bitter antichew product, and leave them around for your cat to find. If you use this method, make sure it's in combination with environmental enrichment and interactive play therapy. Remember, whenever you do anything negative, make sure you offer a positive alternative. Also, if you don't combine the use of a deterrent with appropriate behavior modification, your little wool chewer may just move on to another fabric.

For many wool chewers and pica kitties, the opportunity to munch on safe, edible kitty greens aids in solving the problem as well. You can find kitty greens in any pet supply store.

CATWISE REMINDERS

- Deter with a bitter antichew product.
- Distract your cat when she looks as if she's about to engage in the behavior.
- Increase confidence through play therapy and environmental enrichment.
- Reduce stress and create maximum security where your cat eats, sleeps, eliminates, and plays.
- Modify your cat's diet as directed by your veterinarian.
- Provide safe edibles such as kitty greens.

Feline hyperesthesia

I included this under "Compulsive Behaviors," but not all cases can be labeled as compulsive or anxiety-driven. Physiological or neurological problems may also result in this syndrome. Feline hyperesthesia is still a mysterious syndrome to experts.

This is also referred to as rolling skin disease. With this condition, the cat becomes extremely sensitive to sensory input. Sounds, touch, sight—anything can trigger it. Hyperesthesia commonly presents as excessive overgrooming accompanied by seemingly unprovoked aggression. In the extreme, it can even lead to seizures.

Symptoms can include skin twitching, pupil dilation, excessive grooming that can often appear self-aggressive, and excessive vocalization. The cat may also suddenly seem frightened for no reason at all and bolt from the room. She may also become afraid of her own tail. Restlessness and pacing are also common symptoms.

The cat usually experiences an extreme sensitivity to touch and may suddenly exhibit aggression when stroked or petted. Stroking down the back seems to be the most common touch trigger.

After an episode, the cat usually looks as if she's confused and often seeks out the cat owner's attention for comfort. This makes it confusing for the cat owner as well because there's often reluctance at that point to physically touch the cat for fear of setting off another aggressive episode.

Some Common Triggers of Hyperesthesia

- Loud noises
- Petting the cat along the back
- Early or abrupt weaning
- Being placed in a new home
- Addition of a new pet or person in the home
- Separation from the human family
- Ongoing stress in the environment

Treatment for hyperesthesia requires the elimination or reduction of anxiety-provoking triggers, if possible. It needs to be diagnosed by your veterinarian to make sure there isn't another underlying cause for the excessive grooming and aggressive behavior. Pharmacological intervention is also usually needed for the cat. The environment is key in dealing with hyperesthesia, so you have to carefully reexamine what might be going on in your household. Everyone in the family needs to be on the same page to avoid setting off triggers, whether it's a teenager being more aware of not playing loud music, or the family needing to backtrack and help the cat make a more secure adjustment to the new home, or having to separate hostile companion cats in order to do a less stressful reintroduction. Be alert to your cat's body language so you can see whether she's heading toward overstimulation.

Hyperesthesia is scary for everyone in the family, and the accompanying aggression can be dangerous. Don't try to diagnose and treat this yourself. After an accurate diagnosis, your veterinarian will guide you as to what is needed specifically, and may also refer you to a veterinary behaviorist. Your cat hasn't gone crazy, and she doesn't need to be isolated from the family, but the family does need to be educated on how to work on this safely.

MEDICATING A CAT WHO DOESN'T WANT TO BE MEDICATED

How many times has your veterinarian given you a prescription medication to give to your cat and you've either laughed at the notion or felt your stomach jump into your throat at the thought of trying to get a pill into the Jaws of Death.

Many times a veterinarian will prescribe an antianxiety medication for a cat with an aggression problem, but it doesn't get administered because the cat owners are terrified to stick their fingers anywhere near their crocodile in cat's clothing.

Part of the problem you may be having in medicating your cat is that your technique may be too forceful. Your body language beforehand may also be alerting the cat that something bad is about to happen.

Know your options

When your cat is prescribed medication, you may have a choice of what form to get it in. Some medication can be prescribed in either pill or liquid form. If you know from previous experience that your cat handles one better than the other, ask your veterinarian if there are prescription options.

Some liquid medications can be flavored. If you have young children, you're probably familiar with this benefit. Popular cat flavorings include chicken, beef, and malt. Ask your veterinarian about this option. Some veterinarians have the ability to do this in their clinics and many pharmacists can do it. Certain medications can be reformulated into liquids, gels, or chewable forms and flavored. This is done by a compounding pharmacist. Not all medications can be reformulated, but if a particular prescription can be, it may make it more palatable for your cat.

There's also another option that may be available to you that could make medicating your cat much easier. Certain oral medications can be reformulated into a transdermal form. With this method, the medication is absorbed through the skin. The way you medicate your cat transdermally is to rub the prescribed medication amount onto the skin at the inside of the ear tip. The medication will be in a paste or gel form and you'll need to cover your finger with a finger cot or wear a disposable rubber glove. This is to ensure that the cat gets all of the prescribed amount and that none is absorbed into your own skin.

Some transdermal medication is administered in patch form, such as with the pain medication fentanyl. This works well because the pain medication can be absorbed slowly over time. For a skin-patch administration, your veterinarian will shave a section of fur in order to place the patch directly against the skin on an area of the body where the cat cannot lick or chew it off.

Pilling

Let's start with what *not* to do. A common mistake cat owners make is to try to sneak the pill into some food in the hope that the cat will gobble everything down without realizing he has been medicated. I wish it were that easy, but unfortunately it isn't. Your cat has an incredible sense of smell and can usually detect that there's something foreign in his food. Even if he doesn't detect the scent of the pill, he'll detect the bitter taste once he takes his first bite. If he doesn't continue eating, that means he won't get the entire prescribed amount needed. It can also cause him to start to reject his food even if it doesn't contain any meds.

Crushing pills and mixing them into food is also not a good idea. In addition to the reasons above, some pills have a coating on them to ensure they'll get through the stomach acid and into the intestines for proper absorption. The coating can also prevent the cat from tasting the bitterness of the pill.

If you have a cat who eats first and analyzes later, then you might be one of the lucky ones who can hide a pill in food. If that's the case, do not put it in his regular food because even if he accepts it now, he may catch on later and start to reject that brand of food. Use something special like a bit of cream cheese that's been blended with chicken or sardines.

There's a terrific product available called *Pill Pockets*, and for many of my clients it has made pilling a cat a much easier event. The product is available as a meat- or salmon-based treat that has a pocket for concealing the pill that can be pinched closed. I have seen a number of cats who wouldn't normally be fooled into eating food that contains a pill willingly eat a *Pill Pocket*. The product is available at many pet supply stores, veterinarian clinics, and online. Before using *Pill Pockets*, find out from your veterinarian whether the pill can be given with food, as some medications need to be administered between meals.

If your cat bites and you're afraid to have your fingers close to his mouth, the *Pill Pockets* may be the safest way for you to pill your cat. Another option is to use a pill gun. This is a plastic syringe device that grasps the pill on one end and has a plunger on the other.

If you have to pill your cat manually, there are a couple of techniques to know about before trying to force a pill into the mouth of an animal who is fighting you every step of the way.

If you feel more comfortable with your cat elevated, put him on a table for pilling. Place the palm of your hand over the cat's head and gently tilt his head up. Don't tilt it too much, because it'll make it difficult for him to swallow. Next, apply gentle pressure with your thumb on one side of his mouth and your index or middle finger on the other side. The position of your thumb and finger should be behind your cat's canine teeth (the fang teeth) and that's where you'll apply gentle pressure. With your other hand, hold the pill between your thumb and index finger. Still with me? Now, with one of the other fingers of the hand that's holding the pill, gently pry the lower jaw open and drop the pill on the back of the tongue. Don't try to shoot the pill all the way down the throat. You just want it to go on the back of the tongue. If you try to overshoot, you risk having your cat inhale the pill. Stop tilting your cat's head back now so he can swallow. Don't force his mouth closed because he won't be able to swallow the pill. You can gently hold his mouth (not clamped shut) and massage the pill down his throat. If his tongue comes out to lick his nose, that's a good sign that the pill has gone where it was supposed to go.

Have a small bowl of water on hand because you need to make sure the pill doesn't stay lodged in the esophagus where it could cause irritation. Humans don't swallow pills without water and animals shouldn't either. If your cat doesn't want to drink water and the veterinarian says the pill can be given at mealtime, offer your cat some wet food after being medicated. If he doesn't want cat food and he happens to like yogurt, offer a few drops of that to help ensure the pill gets a smooth ride down to the stomach.

Some cat owners find it easier to pill their cats by coating the pill with butter to help it slide down the throat. This method can make it a little difficult to release from your fingers, though, so don't use too much if you decide to try this. Another trick is to get some *Nutri-Cal*, which is a vitamin supplement paste for cats, and use that for enticement and coating the pill. The technique I use is to first offer a little *Nutri-Cal* to the cat (no pill). I then pill the cat with the pill that I've coated with the *Nutri-Cal* and follow up with another drop of plain *Nutri-Cal*. If your cat likes the taste of the *Nutri-Cal*, it can make the whole procedure a little more pleasant. As with the butter, though, the paste can make the pill harder to release from your fingers, so don't use too much. When you do use a pill that you've coated, you have to slide it off your finger onto the cat's tongue rather than attempt to pop it into his mouth. *Nutri-Cal* is available at many pet supply stores, through veterinarians, and online.

Whatever method you use to pill your cat, your demeanor is important. Be relaxed, casual, and quick in order to send a calm message to your cat. If you're tense and nervous or attempt to be forceful, you'll turn this into an experience he definitely won't want to repeat. Don't allow yourself to get frustrated or angry or you'll set up yourself and your cat for this to be a nightmare every time in the future.

You can also use the pilling procedure as a training opportunity for future medication needs. Have your clicker handy (if you have an assistant with you, that person can be in charge of the clicker) and click when the cat takes the pill. Remember to immediately reward him with a bit of wet food. Only do the clicker training if the veterinarian says the pill can be given during mealtime.

If you think you're going to have a hard time pilling your cat, use the clicker training to ease him into it in stages. If you need to get him used to having your hand over his head and/or prying open his mouth, click and reward when he stays still as you place your hand over his head. Once he's comfortable with that, you'll now wait to click and reward when you use your other hand to open his mouth. He's now learning there are two parts to this behavior. Once the behavior is learned, you'll be ready to pop the pill into his mouth, click, and reward.

If putting your cat on the table to pill him doesn't work for you, there's an alternate position to try. Kneel on the floor, sit back on your heels, and open your legs wide enough to form a V. Place your cat between your legs but have him face away from you so he'll have nowhere to go if he tries to back away from the pill. Then place your hands in the positions previously described in order to administer the pill.

CATWISE CLUE

If you use the V pilling position, wear jeans, or at least don't wear shorts, to prevent any injuries to your lap if the cat struggles and scratches.

After the procedure, engage your cat in a little play session if he wants, so you can end the whole thing on a positive note.

Be sure to wash your hands after handling the pill because if it has a strong smell, you don't want your cat to detect it on your fingers when you go to pet him later.

Alternate Method for Desperate Cat Owners

If your cat is very aggressive and you're in danger of being seriously scratched, wrap him in a towel for the medication procedure. Use a large enough towel so you can securely wrap it around his body, leaving only his head and neck exposed. Lay him down to wrap him so you can wrap the towel tightly enough. If the towel is just draped over him, he'll be able to squirm out from under it easily. Offer him a reward afterward and/or engage in a little interactive play session so you can leave the experience on a positive note.

Administering liquid medication

If the liquid medication can be flavored, that might make it much easier for your cat to accept.

The position to use is either to put your cat on a table or to use the V position previously described.

Liquid medication is best administered with a plastic dropper or plastic syringe that usually comes with your prescription. If not, you can ask your veterinarian for a few extra or get some at your local pharmacy. Don't use a glass dropper because it could break if your cat bites down on it. Don't administer liquid medication with a spoon either, because it's just about impossible to do without spilling some on the cat's fur or on you. If the medicine is very sticky, then you'll really have a mess if it ends up all over the cat's face and neck. That will also only add to your cat's stress level. The syringe or plastic dropper is the safest way to guarantee that all of the prescribed amount of medication will end up in the cat's mouth.

There's a space in the cat's mouth between the cheek and the molars that's referred to as the cheek pouch. It is the easiest place to dispense the liquid. This way, you don't have to pry open the cat's mouth; just slip the syringe into the cheek pouch and administer the liquid. Do this in small amounts to allow your cat time to swallow. If you try to do too much at once, your cat is at risk of inhaling the medication. Too much medication at once may also result in his spitting out most or all of it.

In addition to the syringe or dropper of medicine, have a damp cloth nearby so you can quickly and easily wipe your cat's fur if some is spilled.

As with the previous section on pilling, your demeanor is a huge factor in your success. Be calm, quick, and casual, and show your cat that this procedure will be over before he even knows what happened.

Applying ointment or cream

For me, the easiest way to do this is as an extension of petting and affection. Have your ointment or cream ready and sit in a chair with the cat on your lap. If he doesn't like to be on your lap, sit next to him. You can also use the other positions of placing your cat on a table or in the V position. Pet him in the spots he enjoys the most and then quickly and casually apply the prescription to the affected area. Once that's done, go back to petting him where he enjoys it. If the prescription has a strong odor, have a damp cloth nearby so you can wipe your hand before continuing to pet your cat. If he doesn't want to be petted, engage in a little interactive play therapy session so he stays distracted for a while. This will give the medication extra time to get absorbed into the skin.

Eye medication

This can be a tricky procedure for a cat owner even if the cat is being very cooperative. You have to be extremely careful when you're applying medication to the eye area. If your cat is difficult to handle, enlist the help of an assistant if possible so one person can hold the cat while the other person medicates. You can also use the towel-wrapping technique if your cat becomes very agitated during medicating. If the towel method doesn't work for you, there are cat medicating sacks available at pet supply stores and online, but honestly, I find a thick towel to be easier and less stressful than trying to get the sack around the cat and then get it Velcroed, snapped, or zippered up. Still, the sack is an option that may work better for you.

Place your cat on a table or on your lap, or use the V position. Tilt his head up slightly and hold it with one hand. If you're administering ointment, rest the hand holding the tube gently against your cat's cheek so you don't end up poking him in the eye in case he suddenly jerks forward or back. Very gently pull the lower lid down just enough so you can place a small strip of ointment there. You don't have to place the ointment on the eye itself because it'll spread as soon as the cat blinks. Don't touch the applicator itself to the eye or eyelid and do not close the cat's eyelid and try to rub his eye. The ointment will spread on its own and you don't want to cause irritation.

If the medication is in liquid form, you'll use the same positioning technique and then drop the prescribed amount into your cat's eye without touching the applicator to the eye itself. Allow the cat to blink on his own and don't attempt to rub his eye.

Ear medication

If your cat's ear needs medicating, it's probably very sensitive, so be very gentle. Place the cat on a table or your lap, or use the V position. Wrap him in a towel if you think he'll put up a fight.

Hold the ear at the base or at the midway point. Don't hold the ear tip because you risk pulling the ear up too much and that'll be painful for the cat.

Most ear medications come with a long applicator tip, which is designed to fit right down into the ear canal. Don't force it down there. Instead, gently insert it into the ear and squeeze out the pre-scribed amount. If the ear isn't irritated, you can gently massage the base to help spread the medication. If the ear is sensitive, as is the case with ear mites (which make the ear irritated), don't massage.

Immediately after administering the medication, hold your cat's head gently to prevent him from shaking it in an effort to get the ointment out of his ears. In many cases, the cat feels much relief when the soothing medication is in the ears, but it does feel funny and often causes an immediate head-shake.

After the medication has been administered, your cat may walk around with his ears in a T position for a while, or he may use his paw to groom the ear area. To help distract him, offer a portion of his meal, a treat, or engage in an interactive play session.

5

Tired of Those Out-of-Box Experiences?

Retraining to the Litter Box

Cats and their litter boxes. Oh, what complicated relationships they truly are. How can a concept that initially seems so simple—*get box, fill with litter, cat uses box*—go so wrong? Perhaps the fact that a cat uses a litter box is one of the reasons you chose a cat over a dog in the first place. Cats don't have to be walked, and having a litter box tucked away in the corner is so convenient. So why did your cat long ago decide that the dining room carpet was going to be his new litter box?

I wish the answer to the above question were a simple one. For some of you, the answer will be relatively simple, but for others, you may have to do some serious detective work and be patient as you apply the recommended behavior modification techniques. If your cat just started eliminating outside the box yesterday, it'll be easier to solve than a problem that has been ongoing for months or even years. If you're dealing with a long-term problem, though, don't lose heart. I'll guide you through the process step-by-step and help you try to unravel the mystery.

The majority of calls my office receives are litter box related. Some concern problems that are easily fixable by making some adjustments to the litter box setup itself. Some are complex and require reading between the lines of the cat's behavioral history and creating a comprehensive behavior modification plan for the entire family. Then there are the cases in which a problem has been ongoing for years and either the owner or the owner's spouse is at the breaking point. Those cases require not only an emergency house call but also a realistic total family behavior modification plan. Communication becomes key because all family members need to express their frustrations. How can that innocent-looking litter box tucked away in the corner cause so many problems?

Before we delve into the heart of this chapter, there are two extremely important points that need to be made. First, no matter how convinced you are that your cat's problem is behavioral, you must have him examined by the veterinarian to rule out any possible underlying medical cause. If your cat is urinating outside the box, this examination must also include a urinalysis, along with any other diagnostic tests your veterinarian recommends. You'd be surprised to learn how many so-called behavior problems are actually due to a medical condition. A cat who is experiencing urinary discomfort due to stones or a bladder infection often urinates in small amounts due to the pain. He may associate the litter box itself with his pain, so he tries going in other places, thus you may find small amounts of urine in various locations around the house. In other cases, a cat who experiences pain upon urination may retain his urine as long as he can until finally he can't even make it to the box and must void wherever he is.

There are many medical conditions that can contribute to litter box problems, such as chronic renal failure, diabetes, and hyperthyroidism, to name just a few. Medically related litter box issues are not restricted to urinary problems, either. Your cat may be defecating outside the litter box due to constipation, diarrhea, parasites, inflammatory bowel disease, megacolon, and a list of other possibilities. Don't treat an out-of-box experience as a behavioral problem without first having your cat receive a veterinary checkup. If your veterinarian determines that your cat does have a medical condition, you may still need to do some behavior modification as well. If your cat has developed a negative association with the litter box due to pain, it may be necessary to make some setup adjustments. If your cat has diabetes or chronic renal failure, it may be necessary to create some additional litter box locations for his convenience.

The second important point I need to stress concerns time and expectations. You probably want this problem resolved yesterday, but behavior modification takes time because you're changing the way your cat is thinking. If you're living with a cat who has been eliminating outside the box off and on for four years, it isn't going to be resolved by the end of the day. You have to be willing to put in the work and be patient as your cat takes baby steps in the right direction. What's important to keep in mind is that you both *will* be moving in the right direction. The biggest mistakes I see when I do house calls are that (1) cat owners aren't compliant—they start out strong and then don't stick with the plan—and (2) cat owners rush through the steps, expecting too much too soon.

Hang in there when it comes to dealing with a litter box problem. If you have a cat who tosses litter over the side, you can solve that quickly, but for those cats who are struggling with litter box problems resulting from layers of underlying issues, you'll need to take things one step at a time. I'll do my best to help you help your cat find his way back to the box.

REEVALUATE THE CURRENT SETUP

What we assume cats want

When it comes to the litter box, we often think too much like a human, and that gets our cats in trouble. When you think of a bathroom, you think of the need for privacy and cleanliness, right? Those two factors are pretty important to us, especially those who travel a great deal and have endured more than their share of dirty restrooms.

When it comes to cats, some people go way overboard on the privacy factor, so much so that it takes quite an effort even to track down the box. You may tell yourself that you're creating all this privacy for your modest cat, but let's face it, you've seen cats eliminate in the neighbor's front yard with a line of traffic driving by. True, a degree of privacy is important for cats, but some people use that belief as a reason to create an out-of-sight-out-of-mind setup. More often than not, cat owners hide the litter box in an out-of-the-way location because they don't want to see, smell, or be reminded of the fact that it's in the house in the first place.

There are other reasons why you might want to have the litter box in a remote location. You may have young children or a dog, and your strategy was to locate the box in a place where they couldn't get to it. Perhaps you located the box out of the way due to a family member's allergy. Maybe you just put the box in the only room without carpet to make cleanup easier.

For the most part, though, I find cat owners just take the privacy issue too far and it ends up backfiring. Your first step in figuring out the cause of a litter box problem is to remember where the heck the box is in the first place. Is it too private? Too remote? If so, we'll work on location strategies later in this chapter.

 CATWISE **CLUE**

Give your cat a comfortable level of privacy by placing the litter box in a quiet, low-traffic area, but not so remote that both the cat and you forget where it's located.

What your cat really wants you to know

Now that I have you feeling anxious about whether you've hidden the litter box too much, I'll add to that anxiety by bringing up the issue of cleanliness. Whereas I find cat owners are often over-the-top on privacy, they tend to drop the ball when it comes to keeping the box clean. You may think you're keeping the litter box adequately clean, but as you read through this chapter, I promise you'll get some eye-opening reality checks. Here's one for starters. If *you* can smell the litter box, then it's not clean enough. I'm not talking about the odor from very recently deposited feces. I'm referring to the general odor that comes from the box as a matter of course. If someone can walk into your home and locate the litter box blindfolded, then we need to talk. A litter box shouldn't smell like an unflushed toilet.

Why problems occur

Once an underlying medical condition has been ruled out, you'll need to examine two general areas for litter box problems. One is the litter box itself. The other is environmental factors. By the litter box itself, I'm referring to the cleanliness (or lack of), litter type, location, number of boxes, and so forth. By environmental factors, I mean the household dynamics. That covers anything that could create stress, from tension between companion cats to a new family member or a move.

When you try to uncover the cause of the behavior problem, remember that it's not the cat's fault. Let me repeat that: *it's not the cat's fault*. If you convinced yourself that your cat knows he's doing wrong or is deliberately misbehaving in order to be spiteful or defiant, banish that thought from your head for good. Your cat doesn't plan a behavior to be spiteful toward you. His so-called misbehavior is actually a normal response to a problem. Since your cat is a naturally fastidious animal with a strong sense of survival, he *wants* to use the litter box, but *something* or *someone* is making that difficult. If you've been living with a litter box problem for a while, it's not unusual for you and your cat to have developed a tense coexistence, especially if you've been viewing his behavior as deliberate. That means that not only will you have to find the true underlying cause for the behavior and work to correct it, but you'll also have some repair work to do to reestablish that strong bond.

Spraying and indiscriminate urination

Spraying and indiscriminate urination are not the same. If you've been unsuccessful in solving your cat's problem, it may be because you didn't know there was a difference between the two.

Spraying is usually performed against vertical objects. Indiscriminate urination is usually done on a horizontal surface. Just because you now know they aren't the same doesn't mean you can quickly and easily determine which one your cat has been displaying. In some cases, you may have come across a puddle on the carpet, unaware that the urine was actually sprayed on the wall and then dribbled down to the carpet. In addition, not all cats spray against something. A cat may spray on the cat owner's bed, or spray an object such as an article of clothing lying on the floor. A clue you can use is that sprayed urine usually looks like a line or stream whereas indiscriminate urination tends to look more like a puddle.

It's important to know the difference because they tend to have different causes.

Causes That May Lead to Indiscriminate Urination

- a medically related problem
- inadequate cleaning of the litter box
- aversion to the location of the litter box
- aversion to the type of litter used
- scented litter additives
- use of plastic liners that catch on the cat's claws during cover-up
- dislike of the box type
- litter box too small—overcrowding of cats
- change in household
- change in routine or cat owner's schedule
- abrupt changes in the litter box setup
- abrupt changes in food
- punishment

Causes That May Lead to Spraying

- entering unfamiliar territory
- sexual announcement
- information gathering regarding another cat
- a threat or a response to a threat
- marking
- competition with another cat
- victory display

BACK TO THE BOX

Products you'll need

Before we get into the detective work and the behavior modification, you'll need to be armed with the appropriate type of cleaning products for abolishing urine stain and odor. You can do all kinds of terrific behavior modification, but if you don't get rid of the urine odor, it may trigger the unwanted behavior again. A cat's nose is much more sensitive than a human's, so it takes specialized products made especially for pet urine to clean and neutralize urine odor.

Don't use ordinary household cleaners on urine stains. While they may eliminate the stain, they don't effectively eliminate the odor. You need a product that specifically states it neutralizes urine odor. There are several enzymatic products that are designed to clean and neutralize pet-related stains and odors. Some are better than others. You may have to do some trial and error to find the product that works best for you. Different products have different instructions, so make sure you read labels carefully to ensure an effective outcome. For cat urine, a product I especially like is *Urine-Off*. I have found it to be effective on virtually any surface. It's available through veterinarians and on the manufacturer's Web site (see the appendix for the manufacturer's information). Other good products include *Nature's Miracle* and *Folex*, but these are just a few of the many available. Just make sure that whatever you use claims to neutralize urine odor through enzymatic action. Older stains and areas of repeated soiling will need a deeper cleaning, and in some cases you may need to rip out soiled carpet and start fresh.

You'll also need a black light to help locate all the urine stains. This is a special light that causes the urine to fluoresce, or glow. You can find these lights at pet supply stores, in mail-order catalogs, and online. They come in several sizes and are extremely helpful in pinpointing exactly where you need to clean. *Urine-Off* sells a black light by itself and also in a set with the stain/odor remover. *Nature's Miracle* and *Stink-Finder* are two other good ones.

When you shop for the black light and cleaner, get a roll of painter's tape as well. This will be used to outline where you have to clean. Darken the room, shine the black light, and outline the fluorescing urine stain with the tape. When you turn the room light on again and the urine stain is no longer visible, you'll know exactly how much of the area needs to be treated. The reason I use painter's tape instead of other tape is because it won't leave a residue and removes easily.

Prepare yourself for a shock when you first start using the black light, especially if your cat has been a sprayer for quite a while. Go through the whole house and don't overlook furniture, walls, cabinets, or clothing in closets.

Another product that I've found very useful is *Feliway* spray and *Feliway Comfort Zone* diffuser. You can read more specifically about *Feliway* in chapter 2. It was originally created to aid in behavior modification for spraying problems. After the urine-mark is cleaned with plain water, *Feliway* covers the urine smell with cat-friendly facial pheromones. You can use the spray version on vertical objects that have been urine-sprayed. If you're going to use it on these areas, don't clean the area with anything other than plain water. Other products, including enzymatic cleaners, will deactivate the pheromones. Use your enzymatic cleaner on carpets, floors, and other horizontal surfaces, and use *Feliway* on vertical objects. *Feliway* has specific instructions, so follow them carefully in terms of how much to use and how often.

The *Feliway Comfort Zone* diffuser can be used in place of or in addition to the spray. I tell clients to use the diffuser if the urine-spraying is happening in many areas of a room.

Spraying

If your cat is intact, his hormones are driving him to spray. Neutering an intact cat will, in almost all cases, correct the problem. If your intact cat has been spraying for a long time, you may still have to incorporate behavior modification because this has become a long-standing habit. Once an intact cat is neutered, it takes about a month for the hormone levels to decline. Some undesirable behavior may still occur in the meantime.

Depending on how long this has been going on, you may be feeling optimistic or extremely skeptical. The key here will be to create a more secure environment from your cat's point of view. If your previous approach involved cleaning up the urine and adding a litter box to the spot, then you missed a major need that the cat has. For him to spray, it means something or someone is triggering a reaction, and you have to create an atmosphere in which that is no longer happening. That takes good sleuthing.

Spraying is so misunderstood by people. All too often, the cat owner assumes the cat is merely marking territory. It also surprises people to learn that spraying is not just limited to males. Females will also display this not-so-pleasant behavior. Spraying, as you saw from the above list, can have many causes. A high-ranking cat in a multicat home may spray various areas around the house to remind everyone of how far-reaching his domain goes. A cat may spray when a new cat is brought into the home as a way of seeing what kind of response he gets to that covertly placed threat. A new cat may spray when entering a new territory as a way to show he isn't someone to mess with, or he'll spray as a way of seeing how much of an opponent he'll have to deal with. He may be trying to see if he gets a counterspray in response. The urine-mark tells the sniffing cat much about the spraying cat. He can tell how recent or old the mark is, the general status of the cat, and the sex of the cat. This is a way for cats to safely learn about each other without risking a physical confrontation. So even though having a cat spray is certainly not an enjoyable experience from the cat owner's point of view, it's important for you to put in perspective how and why it's important for cat-to-cat communication. A better understanding of what *your* cat may be reacting to will shed light on how to solve the problem.

Start by looking at where your cat has sprayed. The location itself will provide very valuable clues. If the spraying is done under or against a window, there's a good chance your cat is feeling threatened by the appearance of a cat in the yard or on the street. If the sprayed area is confined to just one window or a series of windows that overlook the same area, that means there's an excellent chance that uninvited feline guests have been showing up. If you put an outside bird feeder by the window for your cat's viewing pleasure, it may, unfortunately, also be attracting the neighbor's outdoor cat.

Spraying can be a result of something new in the environment or even the environment itself being unfamiliar. Your cat may have a history of reacting strongly to unfamiliarity by spraying when new items are brought into the home, such as a new piece of furniture.

If your cat is spraying due to a move to a new home, he's probably completely overwhelmed by the loss of his comfortable, familiar surroundings. Keep in mind that spraying is a normal behavior for a cat who feels threatened or is trying to find out more information. Even though it's very upsetting to have your cat spraying in your brand-new home, he's not doing it to be bad—he's trying to figure things out.

Spraying is more often a problem when more than one cat share a single environment. It can be something that happens from the moment they're first aware of each other's presence or it can be something that suddenly happens after years of living together. It's especially frustrating when cats who have always gotten along suddenly begin spraying.

It can be tricky just to figure out which cat is the sprayer. If you've tried to catch a cat in the act but have been unsuccessful and feel clueless as to who might be behind the behavior, there's a method you can use. Ask your veterinarian to make up some fluorescein capsules. This harmless ophthalmic dye will cause the urine to fluoresce brightly under black light in some cats. Fluorescein is normally used to check for abrasions on the surface of the eye or blocked tear ducts, but it sometimes works in this secondary function and is harmless for your cat to swallow. There can also be a large difference in how much a specific cat's urine may fluoresce. The pH of the urine as well as the concentration can affect the degree of fluorescence. This method isn't foolproof. Your veterinarian can create the right-sized capsule with the appropriate amount for your cat. You give the fluorescein to the cat you most suspect is the sprayer. After a few days, if there's no evidence of the fluorescein-treated urine, you can then give it to the next likely cat. Any urine will normally fluoresce, but the fluorescein-treated urine often is a very bright yellow-green. It's important to be able to tell the difference between the treated urine and normal, untreated urine. Check multiple areas because you'll come across at least one old urine spot for comparison. Become familiar with the difference, but if you're still unsure, ask your veterinarian for guidance.

A more reliable method of determining which cat is spraying is to set up a video camera, or "nanny cam." This will not only identify the cat, it will help you see the precise circumstances under which the event occurred. Nanny cams are widely available and relatively inexpensive.

You may find yourself in a situation in which more than one cat is doing the spraying. That's when feline communication takes human frustration to a whole new level. A mistake some people make is to quickly assume they know which cat is doing the spraying and why. Don't be in a rush to cut short your detective work in a multicat household unless you've witnessed the cat in the act or have used the fluorescein. And even that doesn't mean the other cat isn't spraying as well. It isn't correct to assume that only a high-ranking cat will spray to mark territory. Both confident and nonconfident cats can spray. As you saw in the list on causes for spraying, it can be anything from a victory display by a high-ranking cat to an attempt at covert aggression by a low-ranking, nonconfident cat.

When you get into detective mode, you'll find yourself picking up on things you previously didn't pay attention to. Here's an example: a spraying episode may happen after a stare-down or posturing by two cats. The less confident cat may then spray after the two have separated. The less confident cat may even spray *horizontally* instead of vertically because a vertical spray mark appears to be more of a challenge. The less confident cat may know he doesn't have what it takes to back up his threat, so he sprays horizontally. The behavior modification needed will work on elevating his confidence and creating enough security in his environment. The confidence boosting doesn't mean trying to raise his status over the other, more confident cat. You don't want to interfere in any ranking the cats have developed naturally. You just want all cats to feel comfortable where they are so that no one feels threatened.

Another relatively common example of spraying is when a new person moves into the house, such as a new spouse. Suddenly the cat is faced with a truckload of items in his territory that contain this person's scent, as well as the person, who may have taken the cat's favorite spot—sleeping next to his cat owner. This is not a good way to start out a marriage. The spraying may also occur with the arrival of a new baby. The behavior may begin long before the baby even makes an appearance. Spraying could happen during the preparation of the nursery. It's not based on jealousy, as some people mistakenly assume, but rather on confusion over the changes in his territory. The cat doesn't understand the abrupt changes taking place in his environment.

Again, look at where the cat is spraying because clues will be found in the choice of location. For example, a cat may be spraying in a hallway that leads to the litter box or a coveted area of the home, such as the cat owner's bedroom. That may be one cat's communication to another that this part of the home is off-limits.

A cat who is both indoor and outdoor may spray upon returning inside. The outdoor environment isn't one he can control as easily as his indoor home, and he's faced with many unfamiliar and ever-changing animal scents. He may encounter a rougher, tougher cat in the outdoors and is afraid of a confrontation. Upon returning indoors he may spray as his form of covert aggression or as a way of marking the perimeter of his well-established territory. A more confident cat may spray upon returning inside as the exclamation point to his confrontation victory or to further mark the line at which the unfamiliar cat had better not cross.

When you're faced with a cat who sprays, as hard as it might seem, look beyond the act itself. Pay attention to the environment, other pets or people in the home, what took place before the incident, and, most important, look at it from *your cat's point of view.*

CATWISE CAUTION

- **N**ever rub your cat's nose in his urine or feces. This method, which, sadly, is used by too many people, is completely counterproductive. Your attempt at showing your cat that his location choice was inappropriate actually sends the message that elimination in itself is bad. He'll be so confused by your actions that he may actually be too frightened to return to the litter box for fear of being reprimanded again. Rubbing a cat's nose in his waste is inhumane and cruel.

- **D**elayed reprimands also are completely counterproductive. If you come home and find a wet spot on the floor, don't bring your cat over to it for punishment. He'll have no idea what you're trying to communicate other than the fact that he'll now be afraid of you. Some people justify that ineffective form of reprimand by saying the cat "looks" guilty when brought to the spot. That is a misinterpretation, though, because what the cat is actually feeling is confusion and fear.

Retraining a sprayer

First, clean and neutralize the area(s). If you decide to use *Feliway*, remember not to use the enzymatic cleaner where you plan on using the pheromone spray product. Otherwise, use the *Feliway Comfort Zone* diffuser.

Determine who is doing the spraying and the possible cause of it. If you still feel clueless as to why this is happening, or if it has been going on for so long you think it has become a cemented habit, consult your veterinarian. He/she may be able to help you figure out the original cause. If not, you have the option of consulting a certified behavior expert. See the appendix for more information on getting professional help.

If the problem is due to the appearance of an outdoor cat, you'll find the retraining technique in chapter 8.

If your cat is spraying when new items are brought into the home, such as furniture, follow these steps. If his history indicates that he tends to react by spraying new objects, use that knowledge to prevent it from happening again. Your cat is a territorial creature of habit, so create a comforting familiarity to a new item. If you bring in a new sofa, for example, cover it for a few days with bed sheets that contain your scent. Spray the corners of the sofa with *Feliway*. An alternative to *Feliway* is to put a clean sock over your hand and then gently stroke your cat around the face to gather some of his facial pheromones. Then rub the scent-filled sock on the corners of the new sofa. Rub this at the same height as your cat's nose so he'll conveniently come across the pheromones when he comes to investigate the new object. If you have more than one cat, you'll have to use the sock technique with each one. Place the scent from each cat at a slightly different location on the corners of the sofa—don't go over the same spot. If you "assist" the sofa in taking on the scent of the home, it may help to prevent it from triggering the spraying behavior from your cat.

If the new object is a carpet, gently rub it down with towels or sheets that contain your scent. Also use towels that contain your cat's scent. In hard-core spraying cases, leave a few scented towels down on the carpet for several days, even up to a week if necessary.

If the cat is spraying your new spouse's clothing or belongings, you can intermingle his/her clothing with yours in the closet temporarily. Instead of having separate sides, mix the clothes together so that the new person's clothing takes on a more familiar scent. Shoes and other items normally left at the bottom of the closet should be temporarily put on shelves for now. During the retraining process, be extra mindful to keep closet doors closed and clothes off the floor. Here's a perfect excuse to tell your partner that he/she has to tidy up more. The relationship between your cat and your new spouse or partner needs improvement in other areas as well if there's a spraying problem. You'll find the retraining behavior modification technique for that in chapter 9.

Spraying due to the arrival of a baby requires lots of TLC for both the baby and the cat. A little retraining now will go a long way toward creating a loving relationship between the two that can last a lifetime. Refer to chapter 9 for the technique.

If your cat is spraying due to a move to a new home, there's an excellent chance he's totally overwhelmed by the loss of his surroundings. Take a few steps back and reintroduce him to the environment in a less overwhelming manner. Use the information in chapter 2 to create a more secure and inviting environment. Use the interactive play techniques in chapter 3 to distract him and to help ease anxiety. Close off some areas of the home if your cat seems overwhelmed by the enormity of his new environment. Ease him through the transition gradually. If the situation is really bad, take a few steps back and *start from scratch*. Set up one sanctuary room for him so he can get his bearings and take time to get comfortable with a more realistic amount of space. Then, as he seems more confident, you can gradually reintroduce him to a little more of the home. When he's in the sanctuary room, go in there often to comfort and play with him. A sanctuary room is not a prison. It should be a space in which your cat can feel safe, secure, and comfortable. Your presence is a valuable part of that security, so take time out to play and interact with your cat.

No matter what the cause of the spraying is, a very important component in retraining is to change the cat's association with the targeted area. You can do this in several ways. One of the easiest is through playtime. Conduct your interactive play sessions in areas where your cat has sprayed. If it's an area he has sprayed due to feeling threatened, it may help change his mind-set by having positive experiences there. If you're dealing with a less confident cat, the use of interactive play sessions in those areas may help boost his confidence. He'll start to build up a more recent history of fun, hunting, and success in a now nonthreatening environment. In a multicat home, place other cats in another part of the house during these play sessions so nothing triggers the spraying kitty's negative reactions. If there are multiple targeted areas, do a play session in each area if practical. You don't have to be in each area every day if there are numerous spots; just set up a schedule of rotation so that every location gets hit—with play, not spray—on a regular basis.

Place a scratching post or corrugated scratching pad in the area where he's spraying. In combination with the other behavior modification, this may address his need to mark. As you work to lower his stress level, he may be satisfied with marking via scratching instead of spraying. You can also encourage him to mark by rubbing. If there's a corner nearby, attach a plastic cat self-grooming aid. They act as little plastic combs so the cat can rub, have a little massage, and get rid of some loose hair all in one shot. These cat-corner products are widely available at pet supply stores.

Another common retraining technique involves food. Cats typically don't eat where they eliminate. They also don't eat in areas that appear dangerous or threatening. If you free-feed, divide up your cat's regular daily portion and place a small bowl of dry food in front of each of the targeted areas. If you feed on a schedule, keep feeding your cat where you normally do, but feed a smaller amount. Reserve some food for clicker-training purposes to use in the targeted areas. If you free-feed, you can also do clicker training, but the cat has to be hungry enough to respond to the training, so timing will be important. Follow the directions in chapter 3 to learn clicker-training basics and to get an understanding of why operant conditioning works. Then start doing your clicker-training sessions in the targeted areas. Once you and your cat get the hang of clicker training and you know he's responsive to it, use it to remind him of the behavior you *do* want and to keep his mind focused and positive. Once he has learned to respond to a cue from you such as calling his name or issuing the cue of "Come" along with his name, be ready to exercise that when he walks near a previously targeted area and looks as if he may want to spray again. Give the cue calmly and issue it before he backs up to the target. You want to shift his focus before he gets it into his mind that he needs to spray. Issue the cue and, if he responds, immediately click and then reward. This won't work unless you've done the groundwork and your cat has consistently responded to the cues given during training sessions. You can also use the clicker if he goes near a previously targeted area, sniffs, and walks away on his own. When he walks away without spraying, click and reward. Don't click while he's sniffing the spot. Click only when he clearly leaves the spot.

CATWISE CAUTION

Never call your cat to come to you for punishment or a reprimand. If you suspect he's about to spray, don't yell out his name; instead, use a positive method of distraction such as gently tossing a small toy across his visual field. If you're too late to distract him and he has already engaged in the behavior, don't reprimand him—just clean up the spot. He's already stressed enough, so he doesn't need you adding more anxiety to the current situation.

If you aren't using the clicker training, use distraction to refocus your cat if you notice he is approaching a previously sprayed area. If you even suspect he might be considering spraying, calmly distract him by using something positive. Toss a toy so he can hear and see it, but don't toss it *at* him. Keep a stash of irresistibly interesting-sounding toys that will cause his focus to shift from negative to positive. Whenever you can trigger the prey-drive or, at the very least, create any amount of curiosity, you'll get his mind away from what he was originally planning to do. Use the distraction method *before* the actual spraying begins. If you wait until he starts to spray, you'll be rewarding the very behavior you don't want. Timing is everything.

If there are numerous sprayed areas, keep your supply of distracting toys stashed all around. Always put them back in their handy hiding places so they'll be ready next time. These toys shouldn't be the same ones you leave out for your cat's solo playtime. These toys get limited use because they have to remain irresistible to the cat.

In a multicat home, the behavior modification process for spraying also involves retraining how the cats coexist. Refer to chapter 8 for the correct intervention techniques to get your cats to better tolerate one another. You'll also have to rethink litter box placement. Make sure there are litter boxes scattered throughout the home to accommodate all individually claimed areas. If a cat no longer has to pass into another cat's area to use the only available litter box, then the sprayer may not feel the need to spray.

CATWISE CAUTION

When a cat sprays, he backs up to the object and sends out a urine stream at a height of approximately eight inches from the ground. Protect all outlets by covering them with the type of outlet covers used for baby-proofing. Any power strips and surge protectors should be concealed inside baby-proofing covers as well or hidden behind furniture. If you have surge protectors or outlets that have large transformers plugged into them, you can find baby-proofing outlet covers specifically made to fit over those large items.

If your indoor/outdoor cat is spraying, I urge you to consider transitioning him to be exclusively indoors. This will reduce the potentially threatening aspects of his environment. He needs the familiarity and security of knowing he's safe and his territory is his. Indoor transitions aren't as scary as you may think. Refer to chapter 2 for ways to help your cat enjoy the indoors more than the outdoors.

Sometimes, no matter how hard you work at behavior modification, some target areas are just too hard to resist. If you have a truly hard-core sprayer, you'll have to use some deterrents along with behavior modification. If the sprayed target isn't something you can physically remove, then you have a few options to modify it. A plastic carpet runner works well to cover horizontally sprayed areas and even baseboards. Place the carpet runner with the nubby side up to make it less comfortable on the cat's paws. Use a wide carpet runner so you can bend it to go up over the baseboard of the wall as well as cover the floor or carpet. Painter's tape can help to hold the carpet runner in place over the baseboard. You can also use a product called *Catpaper*. It comes in rolls or packs, so you can customize the size you need. *Catpaper* is an absorbent paper with a nontoxic polyethylene backing. What I like about this product is that urine will be absorbed and won't soak into carpet or furniture. If you use plain plastic, the urine will just puddle. You can also use *Catpaper* under the litter box if your cat sometimes overshoots. The product is available at some retail stores and also on the manufacturer's Web site (refer to the appendix).

Indiscriminate urination

Retraining a cat who urinates outside the litter box involves the same type of detective skills used for retraining a sprayer. You have to get to the true underlying cause.

As mentioned in the beginning of this chapter, have your veterinarian check your cat, including urinalysis and possibly other diagnostic tests as well. You must make sure the behavior problem isn't the result of a medical condition. The reason I stress this so much is that I have had calls and e-mails from so many people who were absolutely convinced their cats' litter box problems were completely behavioral. It was only when I insisted that the cats be seen by veterinarians before I would agree to a house call that many cat owners learned the problems were, in fact, medical. Some cats had bladder infections, some had stones, several were hyperthyroid, and a number of the older cats were in chronic renal failure. I had two people call me recently who had grumbled and complained about my insistence on their cats' getting veterinary exams. One cat owner accused me of getting a kickback from the veterinarian. Both people then called back to apologize and inform me that their cats did have medical conditions. One cat was diagnosed as diabetic; the other was diagnosed with a kidney infection.

Never assume a problem is behavioral until your cat gets a clean bill of health from the veterinarian. To do otherwise can cause your cat tremendous discomfort and may even put his life at risk.

Usually, the first visible sign a cat displays to indicate a possible urinary tract problem is that he'll eliminate away from the box. This can occur for several reasons. He may experience immediate discomfort as soon as there's the slightest amount of urine in his bladder, forcing him to void wherever he happens to be at the moment. In such a case, you may notice small drops of urine around. A cat may also try to retain his urine as long as possible due to the pain of urination. Finally, when his bladder can't hold any more, he urinates before he can make it to the box. In this case, you may find large puddles of urine around the house.

Some cats associate the litter box itself with their pain. They think that if they eliminate somewhere else it won't hurt. Some avoid the box only for urination, but some cats will develop a total negative association and start refusing to use the box for defecation as well.

Some Signs of Potential Urinary Tract Problems

- more frequent trips in and out of the box
- staying in the litter box for longer than usual
- voiding small amounts of urine
- blood in the urine
- crying or vocalizing during urination
- straining to urinate
- urinating outside the litter box
- frequent licking of genitals
- appearing to be in pain when touched or picked up
- change in disposition
- decrease in appetite
- change in water consumption
- change in appearance

When you're faced with a litter box problem, you have to, like it or not, go to the source, the litter box. If you've been dealing with a long-term problem, you may have *thought* you had created a perfectly adequate litter box setup, but have you *really* looked at the box lately? I know it's a place you probably don't want to spend much time, but your cat's relationship with his litter box is a very important part of his life, so it needs to be an important part of yours.

How clean do you keep the box? Second question, how clean do you *really* keep the box? A very common reason for litter box rejection is that it's just too dirty to use. Your fastidious feline doesn't want to have to step over mounds of dried feces and clumps of old urine in order to find one tiny granule of clean litter.

Overcrowding is another common cause of litter box rejection. Too many cats having to share too few boxes leads to dirty box conditions as well as potential territorial disputes.

Substrate aversion can lead to litter box rejection. Cats are tactile, and the texture of the litter on their paw pads can drive a cat away from the box if he finds the feel uncomfortable or unfamiliar. This is often seen when a cat owner makes an abrupt change in litter brands and/or types. The substrate aversion can also be due to heavily perfumed litter, dustiness of litter, or litter additives.

The box itself can be the culprit in creating aversion problems. Consider size and type when evaluating the possible cause of your cat's litter box problem. The box you bought when your cat was a kitten may no longer be comfortable now that he's an adult, especially if he's a large or overweight cat. How tall the sides are is a concern for an older cat who may have trouble with arthritis. Type comes into play because it's not just about a plastic box filled with litter. There are many types of boxes on the market, and the one you thought would be the answer to your dreams may actually have ended up as a nightmare for your cat.

A covered box may seem, in theory, to provide privacy for the cat and convenience for you in terms of litter-scatter reduction and odor control. Actually, it's often the culprit behind behavior problems because it holds the odor in the box and the litter takes longer to dry. Imagine how distasteful it must be to enter a dirty, dark, damp litter box. The covered box can also be too confining for a big cat. You may have even noticed your cat sticking his head and shoulders out of the box opening while attempting to eliminate. A covered box also makes it more inconvenient for the cat owner to do routine scooping. A cat owner may even forget that the box is in need of scooping since the contents are out of sight, making the box even less desirable to the cat.

The biggest drawback of the covered litter box is that it greatly reduces the cat's ability to escape. This is most important in multi-cat homes, but even in a single-cat household your kitty may need more options for a quick escape. The idea of escape from a litter box may sound odd from a human perspective, but this is where your problem-solving success depends on looking at the environment from the cat's point of view. When your cat is in the process of eliminating, he's in a very vulnerable position. If ambushed or even just surprised while in the box, a covered box allows for only one way out, right into the face of the opponent. The cover also reduces the cat's visual field while in the box. Some people have even contributed further to the lack of escape potential by going overboard on privacy. I have seen many covered boxes turned so the entrance faces the wall. Yikes! Not only is the cat trapped in the box, he has zero warning time before a potential ambush. This can even create anxiety or hostility in the approaching cat if he was innocently going toward the litter box and ends up surprised to find it already occupied. The approaching cat may feel backed against the wall—literally.

Other types of boxes than can be unpleasant for the cat are the self-cleaning models and electronic types. The motor on the electronic model may be frightening to a cat approaching the box or one just in the general vicinity. Even though the motor is timed by sensors to clean ten minutes after the cat leaves the box, it can't detect an approaching cat or one close enough to the box to be affected by the sudden sound. Another downside is that the actual surface area for the litter in the electronic box is not that big. The housing for the motor and the soiled-litter containment compartment make the box look much larger than it actually is. If you have an electronic model and your cat is experiencing a litter box problem, you have to consider that this type of box may not have been a good option for your kitty.

Manual self-cleaning models may be objectionable due to the type of substrate some require or the feel of the plastic grates on the bottom of the box.

Plastic liners, another convenience that is human-oriented, may also be litter box deterrents. A cat digging in the litter may get his claws stuck on the liner. If the liner has holes in it from the cat's claws, urine can seep underneath instead of being absorbed by the litter. Also, an ill-fitting liner can create folds where urine can pool.

Litter additives intended to mask or absorb litter box odors can be objectionable to cats due to their strong scent or the increased dust they add to the box.

Location aversion is another relatively common cause for litter box rejection. The right litter box in the wrong place will still create anxiety and could result in your cat choosing another elimination location. A litter box too close to the feeding station can drive a cat away due to his survival instincts. Cats eliminate away from the nest and cover their waste to prevent predators from finding them. A litter box close to the feeding station creates all kinds of anxiety and confusion. The cat has no choice but to eat at the feeding station, so he's forced to choose an alternate elimination area.

Litter boxes in closets, under desks, or wedged into small spaces can trigger anxiety over a lack of not having escape potential, just as with covered boxes. Basements may be too damp, resulting in odor problems. Basement locations also bring into focus the potential problem of stairs. Some cats don't want to go up and down stairs or have trouble doing so. In a multicat home, stairs can be a site of face-offs and challenges. A lower-ranking cat may not feel confident enough to pass another cat on the stairway.

How cats divide up their turf in the home can influence whether a litter box location is good or bad. If a box is situated in an area that one cat has clearly claimed, another cat may be too intimidated to enter that space.

In an effort to put the litter box as far away from the family living quarters as possible, some people put it in the garage, or maybe the screened-in porch. The garage holds too many dangers for a cat, even if you aren't using it to house your car. Tools, paint, antifreeze, and other poisonous chemicals are usually stored in there and pose a danger to a curious kitty. If you do go in and out with your car, then it's over-the-top dangerous because of the risk of hitting your kitty or having a garage door mishap. A screened-in porch puts the cat in a vulnerable position from his perspective because he's exposed to the unfamiliar scents, sounds, and sights of other animals. Weather and temperature changes can also be deterrents.

Sudden changes in a cat's life can cause enough stress to translate into litter box problems. Stress is a cat's big enemy. A stressful situation that may seem minor to a human might be major to a cat. Major life changes, such as a move to a new home, a new marriage, a new baby, death of a family member, divorce, or home renovation are only some of the larger events that can send a cat reeling. Even if the major event occurred a while ago, if your cat has a litter box problem, he could still be struggling with whatever happened. He may have been borderline okay with the new marriage and the sudden permanent addition to his human family, but the move to a new house soon after may have put him over the edge. You may not have been aware that anything was wrong because your cat seemed as affectionate and playful as ever, but the stress showed up somewhere in this cat's life. Some cats may deal with an overload of stress by overgrooming, hiding, or exhibiting personality or appetite changes. Other cats react by developing an issue with the litter box. You've read in this chapter about how important the relationship to the litter box is. You've also learned throughout this book how reactive cats can be to change. So it isn't surprising that stress can easily translate into a feline elimination problem.

Abrupt changes in a cat's life don't have to be huge to cause a level of stress that can lead to a litter box problem. A cat can become confused and stressed by an owner's change in schedule, holiday commotion, an owner's absence due to a vacation, seemingly minor changes in home decor (carpet, furniture), loud visitors, or changes in food or in litter, among other things. You know your cat and you know if he has had a history of being reactive to events that seem minor to you. That history is your clue that one or more so-

called minor events created enough stress to make him feel the litter box was no longer an acceptable place for elimination. You have
to do a thoughtful evaluation of how and why particular events may
be affecting your cat. I'll give you a typical example. Your cat may
have had an initially bad reaction when you first brought your new
baby home. In time, though, he got used to the infant, so you
thought everything would be okay. Things may have gone well for
many months, but then your child started becoming more mobile.
The sight of a crawling baby coming toward your cat may have created renewed stress. A litter box issue may not have occurred at that
point, but the stress was building. The litter box issue may have
started when the baby became a toddler and found his way to the
cat's box. This goes back to that concept of escape potential. Once
the baby was on the move, the issue of escape became front and
center in the cat's mind.

The relationship between companion cats in the home has a
huge influence on whether the litter box gets used without incident or not. There may be more going on between your cats than
you realize. What looks like play may actually be intimidation. You
read about litter box location and the danger of creating a litter box
setup that sits right smack in the middle of one cat's claimed area.
One cat casually lounging in the hallway in front of the room leading to the litter box may, in reality, be guarding. What looks to be a
relaxed posture to us may send a completely different message to
the other cat in the household. Think about how you refer to your
cats' behavior toward each other. Do you always refer to one being
the bully or the one who rules the roost? Do you often refer to one
as merely *tolerating* the other? Does one consistently chase the
other? These could be clues to the source of the litter box aversion
problem.

Retraining an indiscriminater
If lack of cleanliness in the litter box is the issue (be honest with
yourself), it's time to don your rubber gloves and get to work. Even

if you're pretty sure the box is clean, it'll improve your chances of successfully solving this problem if the box is extremely inviting.

You may be scooping the box every day, but guess what? That's not enough. If you use scoopable litter, you should be scooping the box a minimum of twice daily. Get on a schedule of scooping morning and night. Even better, do an extra check midday as well, especially if you know your cat has just visited the box. Because litter scooping is not one of the more pleasant aspects of life with a cat, some people put it off or forget about it until the cats remind them by eliminating on the carpet in the dining room.

If you made the commitment of acquiring a cat, that commitment includes providing for that cat's needs, pleasant or otherwise. Your cat needs a clean and inviting litter box. I can't tell you how many cat owners would have saved themselves the cost of my services if they had only been more diligent about cleaning the litter box. If you scoop at least twice a day, the job won't be so unpleasant because you won't be facing mounds of waste. Twice-daily scooping is also a valuable diagnostic tool for you. Evidence of diarrhea, constipation, changes in urination amounts, and possible blood in urine may be found more quickly. You'll also become more familiar with your cat's normal litter box patterns and habits, so you'll be more quickly alerted if something doesn't seem right. If you scoop the litter box only every other day, your cat might have been straining to urinate without success, a potentially fatal problem, and you may have wasted precious time.

CATWISE CAUTION

Don't place air fresheners or other scented products near the litter box area.

If you use traditional clay litter or a type that doesn't clump, you still need to check the box and remove soiled litter at least twice a day. Use a large plastic spoon or an unslotted shovel to remove wet litter or solid waste. The more often you keep the litter dry, the less odor you and your cat will have to deal with. It's also unpleasant for the cat to have to walk over wet litter substrate. It can create enough stress to drive the cat to seek another location for elimination. If you're using traditional nonclumping clay litter, put a little baking soda in the bottom of the box before putting the litter in to help absorb odor. Don't overdo the baking soda, though; just a sprinkling in the bottom of the box is all it takes.

When you scoop regularly, you also have to maintain a consistent litter level. Every few days check the level and top the box off with some fresh litter, if necessary. I've seen many litter boxes in my time and I'd have to say many people simply don't put enough litter in the box. Spread a good three-inch layer of litter in there so your cat will have enough to dig and cover a few times during the day. If you can see the bottom of the box, that means urine will just sit there and that puddle will dry to a sticky, smelly mess. Don't go overboard, though, and put so much litter in the box that your cat thinks he's eliminating on sand dunes. Establish a comfortable level based on how often your cat goes and how enthusiastic he is about digging and covering.

A cat's rejection of the box due to lack of cleanliness isn't limited to the litter. Even though you may faithfully scoop twice a way, the box itself needs to be scrubbed regularly. If you use scoopable litter, a twice monthly washing is probably sufficient. If you don't use scoopable, you should wash the box weekly.

Scrub the box with a diluted bleach solution. Don't use ordinary household cleansers. Diluted bleach will work best for killing germs and bacteria. Household cleansers have too much of a lingering scent. When you scrub the box, use the time to check it over for scratches that might harbor bacteria and odor. If the box is badly scratched, it's time for a replacement. After scrubbing the box, rinse it thoroughly to remove all traces of bleach.

If you think the cause of the litter box rejection could be substrate aversion, think back to when the problem began. Did you switch brands or types of litter? In addition to avoidance of the box altogether, there are some other signs that a cat may not like the substrate in the box. These include perching over the edge of the box while eliminating; keeping the front paws on the lip of the box; refusal to dig and/or cover litter; eliminating near the box but not actually in it. If you can pinpoint the start of the behavior problem to the day the box was filled with a new type or brand of litter or you suspect substrate aversion, there's a relatively easy way to check your cat's preferences. Get another litter box and fill it with another brand or type of litter. Set it out near the original box. If your cat chooses the new litter, you'll have your answer. Some cats may try the new litter initially, but then not use it again, so don't be too quick to determine his preference based on a one-time usage. Never switch brands by merely putting the new brand into the original box. Even if you think your cat will like it, you don't want to make such a drastic change. Set out the second box so the choice can be left to the cat.

If you aren't using scoopable litter, I'd suggest you try it first when setting out your alternate litter box. The scoopable has a soft, sandy texture, which most cats find very comfortable. It resembles the sandy soil they would naturally choose in an outdoor setting, but with better odor control than ordinary outdoor soil or sand. The urine will form a clump that can be scooped up with a litter shovel for disposal. Most scoopable litters can't be flushed down the toilet, so make sure you read the directions on the package to avoid damaging your plumbing.

If scoopable is what you currently use, try another brand, preferably unscented. You can even put out a third litter box with another type of litter. There are many types of substrates. If you have gone through a few brands of scoopable, try the crystals or the other alternative types. There's a litter available called *Cat Attract* that contains certain herbs to attract the cat to use the box. It's a little more expensive than regular litter, but many of my clients have had terrific success with it. The litter is available at most pet supply stores as well as online. If it's a substrate issue, your cat will let you know when you've found the right litter.

Once you find the substrate your cat prefers, you can discontinue use of the litter from the original box. Do this only if your cat is now using the new litter exclusively. If he's mostly using the new litter, but occasionally goes in the original box, then do a gradual transition. Start adding a little of the new litter to the old, increasing the ratio of new to old daily so that the changeover is completed in about five days.

For a cat who dislikes any substrate, even *Cat Attract*, and has eliminated only on flooring, put out a low-sided litter box, lined with a sheet of *Catpaper*, in the location where he's currently urinating. If you can't find a litter box with low enough sides, buy a low plastic storage container, a baking sheet, or a plastic tray. If your cat begins to urinate in it, gradually introduce the smallest amount of litter. Use soft, scoopable litter or *Cat Attract*. If he accepts that small amount, you can slowly add a little more every so often, and then eventually stop using the *Catpaper*. When you have worked up to a fair amount of litter, introduce a regular litter box if the low-sided one causes too much litter scatter.

If your cat urinates on throw rugs only and dislikes all brands and types of litter, and even the *Catpaper*-lined box doesn't work, get a few cheap throw rugs, cut them up, and place a piece in an empty litter box. Put the box in the targeted location. Remove the piece of rug as it gets soiled and replace it with a fresh one while your cat gets used to being in the litter box. Gradually start to add small amounts of litter onto the rug in the box. It'll look messy, but you're doing a slow transition for your cat. Eventually, the litter will cover the rug and you can throw the scrap rug pieces away for good.

Sometimes a cat will eliminate in the soil of indoor potted plants, especially the large floor planters. This can be out of desperation because the litter box is too dirty, or it could be a location issue because the current litter box isn't in a place where the cat feels comfortable. It can also be a substrate issue because the cat prefers the soft texture of the soil. If your cat has been urinating in the soil, you'll have to thoroughly replace the old soil with clean soil. Then lay strips of *Sticky Paws for Plants* across the planter in a tic-tac-toe pattern. This product is available at pet supply stores and online. The *Sticky Paws* will prevent the cat from being able to walk around on the soil. Another option, if you have very large floor planters and you DO NOT have any children in the home, is to lay large river rocks across the top of the soil. The rocks have to be large enough so that the cat or any dog in the home could not get them in their mouths. The rocks also have to be heavy enough that the cat can't move them with her paw. Don't use this method if you have children, though, because of the risk of swallowing small rocks or dropping large ones on fragile toes.

To prevent substrate aversion in the future, don't make abrupt changes in litter brands or types. Even a subtle change in scent or texture can be enough to upset some cats. Once you find a litter your cat likes, stick with it. If you absolutely have to change brands, do a gradual transition. Add a little of the new litter into the old, slowly increasing the amount. The transition should take place over the course of five days. If your cat is extremely sensitive to any minor change in his life, extend the transition period to seven days.

An outdoor cat who has eliminated only in sand or soil probably won't care for highly scented litters. Use an unscented scoopable formula if you're doing a transition to indoor living or if you just want to provide an indoor litter box option for him. If you have an in-and-out cat and you don't even have a litter box for him, there's a good chance that's the cause of any inappropriate elimination issues. It may be more convenient to have him eliminate outdoors, but he needs an indoor option. Inclement weather may make it less than desirable to go outdoors to take care of business. Altercations with other animals may inhibit him as well, as he might dart back indoors while he still has a full bladder. He also needs an indoor box because there are times when he won't feel well enough to go outdoors. As he ages, being outdoors will be less safe for him, so it's good to acclimate him to the litter box now.

The box itself may need some modification. If it has a cover, bite the bullet and remove the lid. Let that box see the light! If you're worried about litter scatter, use a higher-sided box. In our house we use *Sterilite* plastic storage containers. They come in all sizes and you can find one with higher sides than the traditional litter box. If you have an electronic box or a manual self-cleaning model and you think your cat may be unhappy with it, offer a regular open litter box and see which one your cat prefers.

Check the size of the box to make sure your cat is comfortable in it. A box that's suitable for a little Cornish Rex may be too tight a squeeze for a large Maine Coon. Again, if a traditional litter box is too small, look for a plastic storage container. Just don't get one so large that it becomes impossible for you to lift for cleaning.

Location strategies

To address litter box location issues, look at where your cat is currently going for clues about what might be bothering him. This is often how escape potential can be evaluated. I've been on many house calls because the cats in question were urinating in the dining room. In many cases, the dining room was relatively unused by the family other than for holidays or family get-togethers. The cat owners were so stumped as to why their cat would choose the dining room, of all places. To me, it was very easy to see the appeal of the dining room. When it comes to not feeling trapped while in the vulnerable position of elimination, a dining room is usually ideal. Much of it has to do with the availability of escape. The dining room is typically an open room with easy visibility for the cat. The cat can see around the legs of the dining table and chairs with ease, whereas other rooms in the house contain view-blocking furniture such as sofas and upholstered chairs. The cat can feel somewhat protected and hidden behind or beneath the dining table yet have a good visual field. This gives the cat more warning time. If he can see his opponent from way down the hall, the less tense he'll be because he knows he has enough time to escape. Many dining rooms also have more than one entrance. This can be crucial to a cat's sense of safety in a multicat home in which there's tension, or in a home with a cat-intimidating dog or child. The cat can more easily watch for his opponent and, should that opponent appear in one doorway, escape out the other doorway.

Of course, inappropriate elimination doesn't happen only in dining rooms. It can happen anywhere in your home. Consider the example of the dining room, though, and maybe you'll see a similarity to the area your own cat has chosen. Is he seeking more escape potential? In a particular room, he may be eliminating on the side opposite the entrance. That position may give him more warning time to watch for an opponent. Perhaps he's eliminating in a family room that has more than one entrance. He might have chosen a spot in the middle of the upstairs hallway so he can dart in either direction or duck into one of the bedrooms for escape. Even if your cat doesn't live with other pets, he may still feel the need for escape potential. This issue can be addressed simply by making some modifications to the current litter box setup.

First, remove lids from covered boxes. If you don't currently have a covered box, you may still be reducing escape potential if the box is in a closet, under a desk, or tucked tightly into a corner. In the bathroom, a popular human-chosen litter box location is usually wedged between the toilet and the wall. Bathrooms are the most popular location for litter boxes, but take a second look to be sure your cat isn't telling you he'd prefer another spot. In some cases, it may just require that you slide the box out from the corner to give the cat more visual warning time. If the box is in a room on the same wall as the entrance, move it to the opposite side so he can see across the room and into the hallway leading to the entrance. Do the move gradually, though, a few inches a day, especially if the room is large. Similarly, boxes that are under desks or in closets should be pulled out a couple of feet. For some cats, just sliding the box twelve inches away from the wall might increase his security level enough.

Escape potential is also a concern for many cats who must pass through a pet door to gain access to the litter box. The cat must commit himself to sticking his head through the flap, and that may mean he's suddenly met with a paw swipe from another cat lying in wait.

Pet doors are popular with many people who put litter boxes in basements or garages. I have even been on house calls where clients installed pet doors in laundry rooms or (gasp) closets. Bad idea. If you've installed the pet door as a way to keep the litter box out of sight, you may have done a big disservice to your cat. If the laundry room is the only acceptable place for the litter box, keep the door open. If that's absolutely not possible, at the very least permanently attach the pet-door flap in the open position so that the cat can clearly see the room he must walk into. If you have a timid or easily startled cat, keep in mind that the laundry room may not be an ideal location in the first place. The sudden noise of the spin cycle may be too much. If the litter box is currently in a closet with a pet door, it's time for it to see the light. Think *escape* and *visual warning time.*

In order to find out if the pet door and/or the box location is unsatisfactory to your kitty, place another litter box in a more open, escape-friendly location. Keep the original litter box where it is so you won't be confusing the cat with a disappearing box. If the cat starts using the new box, you'll have your answer.

Even if you've decided that the litter box location is totally wrong, if your idea for a better location is in another room, it's better to get a second box and put it in the new spot rather than abruptly reposition the original one. An alternative way to do this, if you absolutely don't want to get an extra box, is to move the current one a couple of inches a day until you reach the ultimate destination. This allows the cat to ease through the transition, and he won't be frantically searching for the box when his bladder is full. In the case of the original box located too close to the feeding station, put the second box in its new location *and* slide the original box several feet away from the food at the same time. The sooner you move the box away from the food, the better. You just have to make sure the cat knows where the new box is located.

Turf claims and overcrowding

One of the fastest ways to create a litter box problem is to ask multiple cats to share one box. The double whammy you create here is that the box gets overcrowded and dirty, and one higher-ranking cat may claim the area containing the box as his turf. Many of my new clients are quick to tell me that the current litter box problems can't possibly be due to overcrowding because they have more litter boxes than cats. Unfortunately, they soon learn that lining up the boxes in one room can negate the advantages of multiple boxes. In a multicat home, you need the same number of boxes as cats *and* you need to locate them in various spots throughout the house. Consider which areas are most used by each cat to be sure the lower-ranking cats have safe options that don't require them to cross over into hostile territory. I even advise my clients that when there's a litter box problem, have *more* litter boxes than cats. It may seem to be more work at first, but when you really think about it, cleaning an extra box is easier than cleaning urine from your carpet.

If your cat has developed a negative association with the box due to either a medical condition, previous ambushes from other pets, trauma while in the box, or past unclean box conditions, add another box with a different brand and/or type of litter substrate. Sometimes just putting out another box with a different brand of litter is all it takes. Just the fact that it's not *that* box may relax your cat enough to venture in.

For a household with young children or dogs, a big part of why you had your original litter box setup may have been to prevent ambushes and to keep curious toddlers or dogs from investigating the contents of the box. Unfortunately, while you may have kept the kids and the dog out, you may have also made it less desirable for the cat.

Instead of using covered boxes or hiding them in the most remote and forgotten locations, try an easier solution. Get a baby gate with the plastic crisscross mesh inserts. Size the gate to fit snugly in the doorway. Cut a cat-sized opening in the plastic mesh and then frame the opening with wood or plastic. This creates a permanent opening in the gate similar to a pet door (without the flap). The gate will keep larger creatures out but allow your cat to go in and out with ease and to plainly see anyone on the other side of the gate, so there won't be any surprises, as there would be with a regular pet door. The gate allows the cat to have his own secure place for the litter box. If you have a medium- or large-sized dog, make the opening in the gate much smaller than the dog's head so you won't risk having him get his head stuck in the gate. If your dog is smaller than the cat and will fit through the opening, or if he's very large and can jump the gate, you have a canine training issue in front of you. Rather than hide the litter box, train the dog. Dogs are very intelligent and they want to please you. Take the time to train the dog that what is beyond the gate is off-limits. Training will help create a better relationship between the cat and dog that's more relaxed and positive. Clicker training would work very well in helping your dog understand the boundaries. There are several excellent books on clicker training for dogs. If you don't feel comfortable doing the training yourself or would like personal guidance, consult a qualified dog trainer or certified dog behavior consultant.

Other deposits that occur outside the box

It isn't always a urination or spraying problem that cat owners face when it comes to litter box issues. Sometimes the deposit consists of solid waste. As with the previous sections on urination and spraying, you must first rule out any underlying medical cause for the behavior. There are numerous medical conditions that can create a bowel movement–related litter box problem, ranging from parasites to serious illnesses. Just because the cat's stool looks normal doesn't mean there isn't something going on internally.

If you have a long-haired cat, he may be having a problem with feces that stick to the fur on his anus or on his bloomers, only to drop off outside the box. If the fecal balls don't fall off on their own outside the box, the cat may groom to remove them, and they may be found on the carpet or floor near you. Long-haired cats need daily grooming, and the hair on their hindquarters and back legs may need to be trimmed on a regular basis to reduce the risk of having fecal matter tangled or stuck there.

Throughout my years of doing house calls, I have come across many cases in which the problem was due to discomfort or pain during elimination. Constipation is not unusual in cats because of the accumulation of hair ingested during grooming. That discomfort can create a negative association with the box. Diarrhea can also develop into a litter box problem because of pain or the sense of urgency.

When you take your cat to the veterinarian, bring along a fresh stool sample, if available, for analysis. Defecation outside the litter box may be due to internal parasites. By evaluating the stool sample, your veterinarian will be able to determine whether your cat has worms. You may have thought only kittens get worms, but if your cat goes outdoors and hunts, he is still at risk of worms. If he has fleas, there's also a good chance he has tapeworms. But even if you see worm segments on your cat or in your cat's stool, don't use an over-the-counter dewormer. Your veterinarian will prescribe a safe and effective deworming product.

Once the medical possibilities are ruled out, you can start looking at this behaviorally. As with the previous sections, cleanliness plays a big part in whether the box is acceptable. This becomes an even bigger issue for many cats when it comes to bowel movements because of the longer amount of time spent in the box. If you haven't been keeping up with your cleaning duties, or if you've asked too many cats to share too few boxes, it's time to step up your efforts.

Covered boxes can be very uncomfortable and unpleasant for cats attempting to defecate. Look at the posture for defecation versus urination and you'll see your cat position himself more upright for BM elimination. This means that any feeling of confinement from the covered box is magnified. That confinement, coupled with the longer length of time the cat must occupy the box, puts him more at risk for a potential ambush or startle. That could be the reason he defecates in other areas. Create an open, safe, clean litter box environment and address location issues as discussed in previous sections.

There are some cats who, no matter how clean you keep the box, won't defecate in the same box used for urination. Even in a single-cat household, this can be the issue. If you know you've been good about scooping and cleaning and have placed the box in the most ideal spot, but your cat is still defecating elsewhere, add a second box near but not too close to the original one. If you give the cat the option of dedicating one box to urination and another to bowel movements, it may just do the trick. How far apart the boxes need to be will depend on your cat's preference. A few feet apart may do, or they might have to be on opposite sides of the room. In the case of our friend Mr. Grumpypaws, he preferred to have separate boxes for each personal bodily function and the boxes needed to be in separate rooms. If your cat has the same preference, he'll let you know when you've created an acceptable distance. Just keep increasing the distance daily until you notice that he's using both.

In multicat homes, there are situations in which a cat will mark with feces. This behavior, called middening, is usually seen in an outdoor setting. A cat will leave a pile of feces in the center of a pathway. Fecal marking provides the advantage of being seen at a distance. If one of your cats in your multicat home seems to be leaving feces on display in hallways or in front of the litter box, it may be a case of middening, especially if there's tension among the companion cats. A fecal deposit in front of the litter box may simply be due to lack of box cleanliness or it could be due to a medical problem, so don't assume middening without checking off the other issues first.

In the case of middening, you'll have to work on the relationships between your cats. More litter boxes are needed, more environmental security needs to be created, and lots of behavior modification must be started as described in previous chapters in this book. Has there been a new cat added to the household? Is there a stray cat visible outside? Are two companion cats displaying a new hostility toward each other? Perhaps an upstart cat is vying for the top cat position. It's time to be a detective again.

If you have no clue as to which cat is doing the marking with feces, there's a technique some veterinarians suggest. You may be able to do an identification by putting a small amount of shavings from a *nontoxic* crayon into the food of the most likely suspect. DO NOT do this without checking with your veterinarian first. If he/she advises this method, you'll be instructed on how much to use.

Toilet training cautions

You may have seen ads for toilet training your cat. They make it sound easy and very appealing. You may even know someone who successfully toilet-trained their cat. Don't be fooled—it's a behavior problem waiting to happen.

It's instinctual in a cat to seek a sandy substrate, dig a hole, eliminate, and then cover waste. Perching on a toilet seat is not a normal behavior for a feline and it has many disadvantages.

First of all, it can be very stressful to put the cat through the training process. You also have to dedicate one toilet for the cat's use. That means the door must stay open and the toilet lid must remain up—always.

If the cat is constipated or has diarrhea, it can be uncomfortable for him to stay perched on the toilet seat.

I have known of many cats who have slipped and fallen into the toilet. For a healthy adult cat it isn't fatal (though it is very stressful), but for a young kitty or an old, weak one, it can be. If the fall takes place after the cat has eliminated, you will have a very dirty, stressed-out cat. Are you then going to try to bathe this cat?

If a toilet-related trauma does occur, you stand a very good chance of having the cat become extremely reluctant to want to try perching on that thing again.

If the toilet used by the cat is one that other family members or guests use, they have to comply with keeping the lid up and leaving the door open when they're through. One slipup can mean trouble for your cat.

If your cat is ever hospitalized or boarded, he'll be required to use a traditional litter box. This could be confusing for him when he returns back home.

If you're considering toilet training your cat to bypass current issues with the litter box, it won't work. You have to solve whatever it is that's causing the problem. For the time you'll spend trying to train your cat to use the toilet, you could retrain him back to the litter box with less effort and less stress.

6

Tattered and Shredded
Retraining Inappropriate Scratching

Confetti. If that's a word you'd use to describe the current state of your furniture, then you truly have a hard-core shredder. Some people give up and surrender their sofas, chairs, and curtains to the cat. After years of trying to keep the cats away from the furniture, those owners raise the tattered and shredded white flag. Others refuse to give in and continue to battle with the cats on a daily basis. They booby-trap the furniture, squirt water at their cats, yell, spank, chase, squirt more water, and yell louder until, eventually, neither the humans nor the cats want anything to do with the other.

Life with a hard-core shredder can lead a person to desperate measures—the decision to declaw. You may be considering this in your cat's situation because despite your having tried everything you can think of, she continues to scratch the furniture. Maybe you're at this point because you're about to purchase new furniture and there's no way you're going to allow your hard-core shredder to ruin the new and expensive pieces.

A cat's scratching behavior can test the limits of your patience, but only if you don't understand *why* she needs to do it and *how* to create ideal places for her to do it. I know you're probably thinking that you already know the reason why she scratches—to sharpen her claws. That simple assumption is part of the reason you're having this problem with your cat. You don't know enough about the cat's needs and motivation. You also might be pretty frustrated by the fact that you supplied her with what you thought was an acceptable scratching post, yet she repeatedly ignores it. Well, buying a scratching post is like buying a car—only much less expensive, thankfully. It needs to be safe, sturdy, reliable, and appealing, and the features need to make sense. Don't be fooled by all the bells and whistles. You want to buy something you can count on. I believe the reason your cat has become a hard-core shredder is because you didn't receive the right information in order to supply her with exactly what she needed. Just as with other purchases we may make for the cat, we often look at a scratching post's human appeal and get fooled into thinking our cats want what *we* would want.

THE NEED TO SCRATCH

It's not just about sharpening claws, and it's not at all about being destructive. It's also not a behavior you can *untrain* in a cat, nor should you ever attempt to do that. Your cat didn't just look at your beautiful sofa one day and decide to claw it to shreds. She also doesn't continue to scratch defiantly in spite of your repeated reprimands. She isn't trying to create a problem between the two of you. Believe it or not, she's just following through on an innate behavior that has underlying motivations—all of which are normal and natural aspects of being a cat. The fact that she's performing this normal and natural behavior on your *sofa* is the part we can modify. Ceasing the scratching behavior altogether is the part we shouldn't modify. You'll understand why as I give you a brief rundown on the basics of why cats scratch, but before we get to that, if you're thinking of declawing your cat to cure her scratching behavior, you need to understand what declawing really means.

DECLAWING

Sadly, too many people rush into this decision without understanding what it involves for the cat. Too many times when someone gets a kitten, one of the first considerations is how soon the little kitty can be declawed. Some veterinarians offer discounts if declaw surgery is done at the same time as the spay or neuter surgery. I understand the concern people have about keeping furniture free from damage. With a young kitten, those sharp little claws always seem to be out, but *training* is the way to go, not *declawing*. Even after being declawed, a cat may continue to exhibit scratching-type behavior against objects. Some people attempt training but fail because they don't understand what their cats actually need. Other cat owners don't even attempt training—they go straight for the surgery option and the kitten never gets a chance to learn.

Declawing is not a more extreme form of a nail trim, as so many people mistakenly believe. It's literally the amputation of a joint. The nail can't be removed on its own—the entire first joint must be severed. Think of having the first joint of all your fingers amputated. That's the equivalent of declaw surgery. The thought of that is shocking, yet people rush to have their cats declawed every day.

After declaw surgery, the cat's feet are tightly bandaged and she's kept overnight at the hospital. Shockingly, many cats aren't even given post-op pain medication.

The bandages are removed the next morning and, unless there are complications, the cat is sent home after that. The cat owner is given special litter, usually pelletized newspaper, or instructed to use plain shredded newspaper in the litter box for about ten days. This is important during the healing process to prevent litter granules from getting into the wounds. Newspaper is also much easier on the very tender paws of the newly declawed cat. Thus, in addition to the pain of being declawed, the poor kitty has the added confusion of such an abrupt change in her litter.

I was a veterinary technician for many years and watched cats trying to recover from declaw surgery. They were in pain as they tried to stand, walk, and maneuver on their tender feet. There were even some people who had both the front and back feet of their cats declawed. To watch those cats attempt to move after surgery brought me to tears.

In theory, the healing period for declaw surgery is about ten days. At that point, the cat can usually return to her normal litter. Some cats don't recover as well and their toes remain sensitive much longer. Some kitties' toes remain tender for the rest of their lives. I've seen cats who would no longer accept being touched or petted on the paws after being declawed. If you have an adult cat and are considering declawing, it can be even more physically and emotionally traumatic for her.

Not all declaw surgeries are done well. For some cats the nightmare continues as one or more claws grow back, usually incorrectly and causing more pain.

Once declawed, the cat must never be allowed outdoors. Even if she has her back claws, she's too vulnerable without front claws. She lacks her first line of defense against an attacker. Her ability to escape by climbing is also reduced.

For so many reasons, declaw surgery is not a decision to make without being informed and carefully thinking it through. You want what's best for your cat, I know that. That's why you bought this book—to try to figure out ways to solve your cat's behavior problem. Proper training and providing your cat with the right equipment are what's best for her, and it's never too late to do both. Now that you know more about what it means to declaw your cat, I hope you'll make the decision never to do that to her.

NAIL CAPS

A much more humane alternative to declawing is to use vinyl nail caps on the claws. Although this is a much better option than the mutilation of declawing, try to retrain your cat using the technique in this chapter before giving up and using nail caps. I would much rather see you and your cat happy because you both get what you want. By using my techniques you get undamaged furniture and your cat gets to enjoy scratching.

Nail caps, which are made of a nontoxic vinyl, are attached to the nails with glue. As with declawing, usually just the front claws are done since they're the ones that cause the damage, though some people choose to have all the nails capped.

Your veterinarian will apply the first set and show you how to do it for at-home application later on. Keep in mind that the nails have to be trimmed in order to fit the nail caps, so if you're unable to trim or handle your cat's nails, you won't be able to do at-home application.

The nail caps last about a month. Some cats don't take well to them and try to chew them off. If one comes off, the cat can still do damage while scratching. That's why proper training is the best option. But if you're seriously considering declawing, at least discuss the option of nail caps with your veterinarian before you put your cat through an irreversible surgery.

REFRESHER COURSE ON SCRATCHING

As with everything else we've talked about in this book, the key to solving a so-called behavior problem is to understand why your cat feels the need to do something. Scratching is no exception.

Stop looking at scratching as a "bad" behavior. I know that's hard to do if you're staring at an expensive chair that's now shredded, but try to stick with me here. Where your cat has chosen to scratch is not *acceptable*, but it's certainly not a *bad* behavior. Your job will be to create a better option for her. I'll guide you through that a little later in this chapter.

First you have to get inside that furry little head of hers and gain some insight into her desire and need to scratch.

Scratching is a multifaceted behavior in that it serves several functions. Some seem obvious, but others are more subtle.

Scratching conditions the cat's claws. As she rakes them down a rough-textured surface, the outer dead sheath of the claw is removed, exposing the new part of the nail. These dead sheaths are thin and crescent-shaped. Look at where your cat currently scratches and you'll probably find two or three of these sheaths.

Scratching is also a marking behavior. When a cat rakes her claws down an object, she leaves a visual mark (much to your dismay, I'm sure, if that object is a piece of furniture). The visual marking behavior is a survival instinct. In an outdoor setting, a cat may visually mark a tree. That mark can be seen at a distance, giving a visiting cat enough warning to avoid a potential confrontation. The visual mark also serves as a familiar landmark to the cat who did the scratching.

In addition to the visual mark, scratching enables a cat to leave an olfactory mark through scent glands in the paw pads. As the cat presses her paws against the tree to scratch, the scent glands release pheromones, which contain valuable information about her. If a visiting cat chooses to approach the scratch-marked tree, she'll receive more information regarding the cat who left the scratches. Since cats prefer not to have actual physical confrontations if at all possible, the combination of visual and olfactory marking is important. Your indoor cat has the same need to scratch for visual marking. Even if she doesn't share her home with another cat, the need to scratch remains. She wants those signs around her territory as familiar signposts. It adds a level of comfort whenever she visits those spots and sees/smells only her own marks.

Physically, scratching has additional benefits beyond claw maintenance. When she hooks her claws on the object and leans into it, your cat can give her back and shoulder muscles a good stretch. Cats are extremely flexible and can curl into the tightest balls for sleeping or stay curled in one spot for stalking. The ability to fully stretch those amazing muscles is valuable.

There is also an emotional component to scratching behavior that many people aren't aware of. For a cat, a buildup of emotion often needs to be displaced somewhere. Grooming is one way a cat may displace anxiety, excitement, anticipation, or frustration. Scratching is another way. Your cat may head to her scratching location after she greets you at the door when you return from work. She may also feel the need to scratch after the frustration of sitting still during grooming or when she's anticipating a meal or a play session.

There are many reasons each individual cat may choose to scratch emotionally. What's important is that your cat has the opportunity to use this form of expression.

Now that you have a better understanding of why your cat scratches, you can understand the confusion and frustration she may have felt if you've reprimanded her for this normal, natural behavior. It may even have escalated into a deterioration of the bond between the two of you. If that's the case, it's time to get you both back on track so you can be happy, your cat can scratch, and your furniture can stay safe.

RETHINK THE CURRENT SCRATCHING POST SETUP

If you've read this far into the chapter and you've never even had a scratching post for your cat in the first place, then your furniture has more than likely paid the price. Don't worry. It's not too late to re-train so that future furniture purchases can be kept untouched. You can wear your dark glasses when you go to the pet supply store so no one has to know you've never purchased a scratching post before.

You may be reading this and thinking you did the right thing long ago by purchasing a scratching post, but your cat never even used it. She may have sauntered over to check it out the first time, then, after one quick pass with her claws, ignored it.

In chapter 5, I talked about how important the cat's relationship is to the litter box. You learned there was so much more to it than just a plastic box filled with litter. Your cat's relationship with her scratching post is important as well. These two areas of a cat's life are driven by instinct. If you don't provide what she needs, her instincts will force her to find other options. It's not willful misbehavior—it's the need to be a cat.

It's time to take a second look at the scratching post setup your cat currently has. Right off the bat, if the post is covered by carpet, that's one big reason why it's being ignored. Soft, carpet-covered posts are basically useless from your cat's point of view. She needs something she can really sink her nails into that'll help slough off the dead sheaths. The soft texture of the carpet fails miserably. Additionally, it's easy for a cat to get one of her claws entangled in the loop of the carpet. That can be painful and dangerous. At the very least, it can create a negative association with the scratching post.

I believe manufacturers create carpet-covered posts to appeal more to the human eye than to the cat's claws. There's a better chance an uninformed consumer will purchase a particular scratching post if it fits in aesthetically with the decor. Sadly, that strategy backfires on the consumer because if the pretty, carpet-covered post isn't being used by the cat, it means the furniture is. Pretty post, shredded furniture. That's not a good trade-off. Look at where your cat is currently scratching for clues as to the type of texture she prefers. Perhaps it's the rough texture of the sofa fabric. Maybe she's even scratching a welcome mat or the carpet in your home. The texture of the carpet or mat may be very rough, unlike the soft covering of her scratching post.

The height of the post is also a major factor in whether it gets used. If the post in your home is too short, the cat can't reach up and get a full stretch. A short post forces your cat to crouch to get into scratching position. Your cat would prefer to be able to get a full stretch so she can unkink those back muscles while scratching.

Sturdiness is important no matter what size the post is. When your cat leans her weight against it to scratch, does it wobble, tip, or move in any way? Is the post itself coming loose from the base? These are things that can drive a cat to seek another option. She knows that if she leans against the sofa to scratch, it'll be sturdy enough to withstand her weight.

Now we come to location. Just as with other things in a cat's life, such as the litter box and the food bowl, the right product in the wrong location still equals failure. Have you hidden the scratching post? If your cat has the desire to scratch, does she have to go on an indoor hike to get to it? I've come across many people who tuck the post in a remote corner because it's not an attractive addition to the decor. If you've done that, your cat has probably resorted to scratching on whatever is nearby.

The training techniques you may have used may also have ended up working against you. How did you train your cat to the post and what do you do when she scratches the furniture? If you placed her paws on the post, I can pretty much guarantee that she ended up struggling to get away. Did you reprimand her for scratching furniture? If so, it probably resulted in her immediate departure from the area. But while that may have gotten you an immediate stop to the scratching, it was only temporary. The desire and need to scratch still exist, only now you've added confusion and fear into the mix. She's being reprimanded for a normal behavior and hasn't been given an acceptable alternative place to scratch. Reprimands may also create a fear of you. She'll continue to scratch, but she'll just do it when you aren't around. When she does scratch, she'll be anxious because she'll be anticipating you coming into the room to chase her.

Finally, compare the number of posts to the number of cats. Since part of scratching is a marking behavior, each cat should have her own post. Marking is one way of identifying familiar surroundings, and each cat needs to have her own post to claim. Cats who don't have the best relationship with each other will appreciate not having to share an object used for marking.

THE RETRAINING PROCESS: OPERATION VELVET PAWS

It's never too late to retrain a hard-core shredder. Based on the analysis you just did of your current setup, you may have only one or several modifications to make. That's the first step. When all the pieces of the puzzle are put together, you'll create an option for your cat that surpasses the sofa, chair, table leg, or anything else previously claimed by her claws. Let's get started.

Furniture armor: Set the stage for retraining

If you've used verbal and/or physical reprimands in the past, leave those methods there—in the past. You've now seen how ineffective and counterproductive they are. You are going to use deterrents, but they won't be directly connected to you. The deterrent method you'll create will make the once appealing scratching surface suddenly become unappealing. And as far as kitty's concerned, you had nothing to do with it.

The deterrent phase of the retraining is just one part of the behavior modification. It must be done in combination with creating the right scratching setup and retraining your cat to use it.

If the object scratched is an upholstered sofa or chair, the easiest deterrent is double-sided tape. *Sticky Paws* is a double-sided tape made especially for this purpose. As opposed to regular double-sided tape, *Sticky Paws* doesn't leave any residue when removed from the fabric. The product comes in two sizes, regular and extra wide. It can be used on a variety of surfaces, so if your cat is scratching an area other than a sofa or chair, check the manufacturer's label on the package of the tape.

Apply *Sticky Paws* to the areas your cat is likely to scratch. If she has scratched on only one corner of the sofa, you should still cover all corners with *Sticky Paws* to make the whole piece seem unappealing. Otherwise she'll just switch to an uncovered corner. When you use *Sticky Paws*, make sure everyone in the family knows where you put it so no one leans against the tape.

If your cat scratches everywhere on the sofa or chair, cover the entire object with a sheet. Don't just drape the sheet loosely over the sofa, because your cat will easily get underneath in order to gain access to her favorite scratching surface. Tightly fit the sheet over the furniture and tape it around the legs. Depending on the size of the piece of furniture, you may need more than one sheet. A trick I learned from a friend, designer Frank Bielec, is to fit narrow PVC pipe around the cushions of the sofa to hold the sheet tightly in place. Stuff the PVC pipes down around the back and sides of the cushions.

Once the sheet is in place, put some strips of double-sided tape or *Sticky Paws* on the corners, just to further add to the furniture's lack of appeal. I know the furniture won't look very attractive, but this is temporary as you retrain your cat.

You may have to get creative in setting up the deterrent, depending upon where your cat chooses to scratch. As a general guideline, think *slick* or *sticky*. If you can't use the double-sided tape, use something such as a slick plastic placemat, shelf paper, or a plastic carpet runner. For example, the carpet runner would work well if your cat horizontally scratches a section of carpet. Another alternative to the carpet protector is to use an *X-Mat* over the horizontal place your cat is scratching.

Don't use balloons as a deterrent. This is a method some misinformed experts may have recommended, but it's way too aversive. That form of deterrent is extreme and cruel. Balloons taped to furniture are terrifying for a cat. I don't like sound-generating deterrents if there are other animals in the home. The sudden pop of a balloon could frighten an unsuspecting cat nearby. If you use a deterrent that creates fear, it can backfire because the cat might be afraid to scratch on *anything*, even her scratching post. That'll result in secondary behavior problems if she has no way to displace her emotions constructively.

 CATWISE **CLUE**

If you plan on shopping for a new sofa or chair to replace the old cat-shredded one, choose a smooth fabric that's less claw-tempting. Stay away from rough-textured, nubby material. For a long-term, hard-core shredder, the less temptation during retraining, the better.

The right post

Think of a nail file's texture. It needs to be rough, not dull or smooth, in order to get the job done. *Texture* can make or break a scratching post's appeal. Remember, your cat needs something that'll effectively remove the outer dead sheaths when she rakes her claws down the post. The material most cats can't resist is sisal, which has a rough, ropelike texture. Sisal-covered posts are easy to find no matter where you live. Between your local pet supply store and the Internet, you should be able to track one down. Sisal is rough and ideal for sinking in those claws for sheath removal. Just the sound of a cat scratching on the sisal post can spark a companion cat to start scratching as well.

An alternative to sisal is the rope-wrapped post. This is another material most cats find hard to pass by without indulging in a little scratching. Rope-wrapped posts are widely available, and you can even wrap the post you currently have. Just be sure to wear gloves so that you can wrap it very tightly without getting a rope burn on your hands.

Carpet can be acceptable if it's tightly woven with a rough texture. For the most part, though, your best bets are sisal or rope. If you do decide to use carpet because you know your particular cat prefers it, don't use leftover pieces from your own carpet in the home. That would send a mixed message by allowing your cat to scratch the carpet-covered post but forbidding her to scratch the matching wall-to-wall carpet. Keep the retraining process consistent—make sure the post is not the same material as anything else in the home.

You may have a cat who prefers scratching on bare wood and has put scratch marks on your wooden furniture rather than your uphol-stered pieces. You can create a plain post yourself by securely attaching a tall piece of four-by-four wood to a heavy wooden base. Sturdiness is vital, so make sure you create a post that doesn't wobble or tip over. The taller the post, the heavier and wider you must make the base.

There are several companies that manufacture tall, sturdy, sisal-covered posts. Two excellent companies are *TopCat Products* and *SmartCat*. We have several *TopCat* posts in our home as well as a couple of *SmartCat* posts, and my cats use them multiple times a day.

TopCat posts can be ordered through the manufacturer's Web site (see the appendix). *SmartCat* posts are available at pet supply stores and online. If you feel sticker shock when you first go shopping for good-quality posts, remember that a good sisal post will last your cat a long time and will save you money in the long run because you won't be replacing damaged furniture. It's such a nice feeling to hear your cat scratching and know you don't have to worry because you recognize the familiar sound of the scratching post.

A cat tree is another option to consider. Cat trees serve double duty as elevated perches and scratching posts. Just as with regular scratching posts, though, there are good ones and useless ones. Choose a good-quality, sturdy tree with wide U-shaped perches. You can find specifics on what to look for in a cat tree in chapter 2. If you're looking for a tree to serve as a scratching post, look for rope-wrapped or sisal-covered support posts on the tree. The support posts must also be tall enough for the cat to get a full stretch without hitting her head on the lowest perch. If the tree has bare wood posts, you can wrap them with sisal or rope, unless your cat is a wood scratcher, in which case they're perfect as they are.

Not every cat scratches vertically. You may have a cat who prefers horizontal scratching. She may scratch on carpeting or mats. She may sit on the back of the sofa and scratch horizontally across the top. For a horizontal scratcher, choose a corrugated cardboard scratching pad. The pads are inexpensive and cats generally enjoy scratching cardboard. These pads come in various sizes from regular to extra wide. You can get incline scratching pads for even more fun for the cat. Once the cardboard gets totally shredded, just flip the insert over to reveal the new side. Corrugated cardboard scratching pads can be found in just about any pet supply store. Many cats enjoy both vertical and horizontal scratching. Since the cardboard pads are inexpensive, you can supply both options for your kitty without breaking the bank.

Some companies, such as *TopCat Products*, make sisal-covered scratching pads. If your cat prefers sisal over any other texture, these pads are a great option.

The right location

If you have the ideal post, you can still have a problem if it's placed in the wrong location. Posts should be placed where the cat spends most of her time, and they should be where she likes to scratch. This applies to cat trees and cardboard pads as well. When you look at where your cat is currently scratching, her choice is usually based on the texture/sturdiness of that object, but it's also due to its location. If your cat enjoys scratching after she wakes from her naps, she may be scratching on a particular piece of furniture because it's convenient. If your cat loves to scratch to express her joy and excitement when you come home from work, she may be scratching a particular object because it's close to the door. A cat who feels the need to scratch-mark near front or back doors might be scratching on the door casings. It's not unusual for a cat to feel the need to scratch near the entrance to her territory.

Look at where your cat prefers scratching and put the post there. Make it convenient for her to succeed at retraining by having the post in sight. Don't tuck it in a corner just because you may not like the look of it. If you want to save your furniture, the scratching post has to come out of hiding.

If you have a cat tree, place it by a window, if possible, in the room where the cat enjoys being. Generally, most cats want to be in the room where the family spends most of their time. Don't put the tree in a far-off location that no one frequents, especially the cat.

Retraining

You can't do this by force—you can't place your cat's paws on the post. If this is one of the methods you've tried in the past, it has only made your cat fear the post and possibly fear you as well. You can't force a cat to do anything.

The easiest way to retrain is to set the stage so your cat thinks this is all her own idea. Do this by placing the great new scratching post right next to the spot where she was scratching. You have already set up the deterrent on the old object, which makes it no longer appealing when your cat attempts to scratch. At that point, when she sees her old spot looking unscratchable, she'll notice this terrific new option. How lucky can a cat get! Her curiosity will kick in and she'll step closer to investigate. She'll sink her claws in and, ahhhh, scratching ecstasy!

Some posts come with catnip inside to entice cats to scratch. If your know your adult cat responds to catnip, take this a step further and rub the post with a little extra catnip. If the sight of the new post doesn't spark her interest, the scent of catnip surely will.

With my cats, the sound of scratching gets them interested. All I have to do is give one of the sisal posts a little scratch with my nails. The sound is usually too irresistible. At least one of my two cats will have to come join in.

You can also use interactive play to help in the retraining process. Use a fishing-pole toy, or even just a long feather, and move it in an enticing manner across the post. When your cat pounces, she'll realize what an amazing scratching surface she just discovered.

If you're still having trouble enticing your cat, place the post on its side and move the toy around it. When your cat hops on the sideways post or goes underneath it to grab the toy, she may scratch and realize she really likes it. When you feel she has accepted the post, place it upright again.

For horizontal scratchers, use the same location strategies for retraining. Place the scratching pad right over or next to the currently scratched object. If you made the object less appealing through the use of double-sided tape or some other covering, the cat will see the cardboard pad as a much better option.

Once your cat is consistently using her scratching post, you can begin to remove the deterrents. Do this step gradually—don't rush. Make sure your cat is completely happy with her new post before removing the deterrents.

If you have more than one cat, provide enough scratching posts for everyone. If one cat has established a clearly defined area, place a post there for her and place another post in the area your second cat prefers. It's also a good idea to place a post or two in the main living area that the cats and the family use most. This way, if any tension results from commingling, a cat may choose that opportunity to scratch in order to displace anxiety. You won't be able to control whether or not one cat scratches on another cat's post, nor should you. What's important is that you are giving your cats more *choices*, and that's a great way to reduce anxiety.

Bonus retraining tips

I have two very important pieces of advice that many people overlook. Even if you sailed through the previous aspects of scratching-post retraining, following these two tips may save you heartache down the road.

Tip #1: Don't try to take the easy way out of retraining by deciding to surrender a scratched piece of furniture to the cat. Even if the cat is scratching her new scratching post, if she continues to scratch the furniture, you must set up the deterrent. I have also known many cat owners who have thrown in the towel and decided to let their cats shred the sofa. These cat owners thought they had the ideal plan because they decided to eventually purchase a new sofa. Even if these owners booby-trap the new sofa to within an inch of its life, the plan won't work. Don't surrender the furniture over to the cat. There's no shortcut when it comes to proper training. It's extremely unfair to allow a cat to scratch a sofa, then discard the shredded sofa, purchase a new one, and reprimand her for doing the same behavior. It's confusing to the cat who is trying to perform a normal cat behavior, especially when she hasn't been given a better option. Don't send mixed messages. Be consistent in your retraining.

Tip #2: After your cat has been successfully scratching on her post for years, it may eventually start to look a bit ragged. You may decide to purchase a brand-new one for her and toss out that nasty-looking old one. Big mistake! She loves that old post because it confirms her familiar surroundings. That post contains *her* scratch marks and *her* scent. She doesn't want to wake up one morning to discover that it's missing. Sure, it may no longer have enough fibers left for an effective scratch, but an abrupt disappearance isn't the way to help your cat. Instead, purchase the new post and place it next to the old one. Once your cat has accepted the new one, then and only then can you quietly put the old one into retirement.

7

Mealtime

I Want What I Want When I Want It!

In theory, it seems as if it should be simple: cat owner buys food, cat eats food, cat is happy. However, if you've been dealing with a mealtime-related behavior problem, you know this is far from the truth. Whether your cat eats too much, too little, wants a different food every day, wants the same food every day, eats too fast, chases companions away from the bowl, wants to be hand-fed, or insists on eating what you eat, mealtime can turn into an anxiety-provoking event.

If your cat has mealtime issues, regardless of what they are, the first place to start is by taking him to the veterinarian. Mealtime behavior problems may have an underlying medical cause, so an examination, along with appropriate diagnostic tests, needs to be done. Even if you simply aren't sure whether you're offering the right kind of food for your cat's stage of life, your veterinarian will be able to guide you. There are so many food choices out there, and if you've strolled down the pet-food aisle recently, you know it can be a bit overwhelming. Based on your cat's health, age, and activity level, your veterinarian can help you decide which food would be most appropriate and how much to feed.

CATWISE CLUE

The instructions found on the cat food labels regarding amounts to feed are to be viewed as general guidelines. These instructions don't take into consideration specifics such as the cat's physical health and activity level. Use the instructions regarding the amount to feed as a starting point. Your veterinarian can help you determine whether it's correct for your particular cat.

MAYBE THE BOWL IS THE PROBLEM
AND NOT THE FOOD

It's worth reevaluating what you put your cat's food and water into if you're dealing with some food-related behavior issues. For example, some cats paw at the dish and scoop the food out onto the floor. Some cats drink water by dipping their paws in and then licking the water from their fur. In many cases, it's just a playful habit or something the cat learned by observing another cat use that technique. Cats learn through observation, so if your cat had this habit as a kitten, he may have learned it from his mother or another companion cat in your household.

For some kitties, though, this behavior is based on necessity due to the size and/or shape of the bowl itself. If the bowl is narrow and deep, your cat may be uncomfortable pushing his face into it because his whiskers get forced against his face. In a multipet household, your cat may not feel comfortable putting his face in the bowl because he won't be able to see if anyone is approaching. For a Peke-faced (flat-faced) cat, such as a Persian or Himalayan, it may be difficult for him to get his face into the bowl without getting his fur filled with food. If the bowl is very narrow and deep, he may not even be able to reach all of his food at the bottom. The solution many of these cats come up with, for both safety and comfort, is to use their paws as scoops.

Then there's the *bucket o' food* that some cat owners use as a way of ensuring the cat never runs out. The large bowl is filled with dry food and there it sits, day after day after day, allowing the food to get stale. I have seen a number of homes in which the bowl containing the dry food is constantly topped off but never emptied and washed. Cats have very sensitive noses that are used to help determine a food's safety and palatability. This is a survival instinct because in the wild, a cat who comes across already dead prey would depend on scent to determine whether it is safe to eat. In your home, a food bowl that contains old, dried-out food signals to the cat's nose that it's not palatable, and maybe not even safe.

Speaking of stale, are you guilty of leaving the bowl of wet food out so long that it turns into rock-hard cement? That's not the way to encourage a healthy eating pattern.

The bowl may be the right size and shape, but what it's made of may be the problem. There are so many choices out there—glass, plastic, ceramic, stainless steel. The one you chose may not be what your cat prefers. Glass, which is easy to keep clean, may get chipped, and that could be uncomfortable on your cat's tongue. It may even cause an injury. If you're using a glass dish, inspect it regularly to make sure there are no cracks and the edges aren't chipped. The same applies to ceramic. Some ceramic bowls are rougher than others and that can be uncomfortable, so run your fingers over the bowl to make sure it's smooth enough.

Plastic, probably the most popular choice for cat food bowls, has lots of negatives associated with it that can make it less desirable for your cat. Plastic tends to retain the smell of food, and even after washing, your cat might be able to detect the scent of the previous meal. Plastic is easily scratched and can harbor bacteria in those little lacerations. Plastic bowls are also extremely light, and your cat may not enjoy having to follow his bowl around the floor as he eats. There's also an important health concern when it comes to plastic food bowls. Some cats have an allergy to the plastic, which shows up as hair loss on the chin or even feline acne. This acne looks like black specks on the chin and, if untreated, can become infected and painful. If your cat has feline acne, the plastic food bowl may be the culprit.

Stainless steel food bowls are virtually indestructible and easy to keep clean. Some cats, though, don't like the way the stainless steel may change the taste of some foods. Additionally, if the stainless steel bowl has a rubber ring around the edge to keep it in place on the floor, you must remove that regularly so you can thoroughly wash the bowl. Food, saliva, and all kinds of bacteria can hang out between the rubber and the steel and create a very unpleasant odor. Make sure the bowl and the rubber ring are thoroughly dry before you reassemble.

These concerns apply to water bowls as well. There are even a couple of extra concerns when it comes to water. While the size and shape of the food bowl may be appropriate for your cat, you may have gone overboard on the water bowl. Maybe you're expecting your cat and dog to share a water bowl so you're using one that would more appropriately be considered a bathtub for a cat. One thing I commonly see when I do house calls is that while clients may be diligent about washing the food bowls, they just keep refilling the water bowls without cleaning them first.

If your cat dips his paw in the water bowl rather than using his tongue, it may be because of an ever-changing water level. If you're inconsistent in how often you fill the bowl or how much or how little you fill it, it might be easier for him to just dip his paw in rather than use his face. With some bowls, it's more difficult to see the water level, and that's another reason why a cat may use his paw. If you think this is the case with your cat, be consistent in how high you fill the bowl and consider using a bowl with a design on the bottom as that makes it easier to see the water level.

Double bowls may seem like a great idea because they conveniently house food and water together, but they can actually be deterrents when it comes to mealtime. Some cats don't like their food and water close together. They don't want their water to smell like the food, and when they want to get a drink in the middle of the day, they don't want the scent of food right there if they aren't hungry. With a double bowl, it's very easy for pieces of food to fall into the water and contaminate it. This can make the water unpleasant for the cat.

Even if you aren't using a double bowl but have the food and water right next to each other, separate them a bit to see if that makes a difference for your cat.

THE BOTTOMLESS BOWL: PROS AND CONS OF FREE-FEEDING

For many cats, this method works well because they can nibble at will throughout the day or night. This method is also most convenient for owners because they can leave their cats for longer periods without having to worry about getting home in time for dinner. Another benefit of this feeding method is that, in a multicat home, cats who have appetites at different times can satisfy themselves conveniently. If there's tension in the multicat home, this can also allow one cat to come in and feed when another cat isn't around.

However, free-feeding works well only if your cat self-regulates his amount and is able to maintain a healthy weight. Unfortunately, based on the fact that there's an epidemic of obesity in cats, I would say that free-feeding isn't working well for many of them.

Free-feeding in a multicat household makes it difficult for a cat owner to monitor how much or little each cat is getting. It also prevents you from using food as an effective behavior modification tool. The use of food in a controlled way can become a strong motivator for your cat to change undesirable behavior. With free-feeding, he's usually not hungry enough to be enticed.

PROS AND CONS OF SCHEDULED FEEDING

When you have a set amount that you feed your cat each day, you're better able to monitor his weight and make sure he's eating all that he should. In a multicat environment, it's also an easier way to make sure each one gets his fair share. If your cat eats wet food, scheduled feeding is the only way to go because it should be left out for a maximum of a half hour. If you try to free-feed wet food, it becomes extremely unappetizing as it dries rock-hard in the dish. Scheduled feeding gives you the added benefit of being able to use food as a behavior modification tool because it isn't always readily available for the cat.

The downside of scheduled feeding is that it's more inconvenient for the cat owner. You have to be at home at the right times in order to provide the meals unless you use a timed food dispenser. With some cats, if you're just a few minutes late, you hear about it as kitty vocalizes his displeasure from the moment you walk through the door.

The problem I see many cat owners make with scheduled feeding, though, is that they feed their cats only once or twice a day. Once a day is never appropriate for a cat. Cats have small stomachs and should not have to wait twenty-four hours between meals. Twice-daily feedings are okay for some cats, but for most kitties more frequent meals of smaller amounts is more natural. If your cat is gobbling his dinner at ninety miles per hour and then having it reappear shortly afterward right next to the bowl, it may be due to the fact that he's getting too hungry. This may also be due to an underlying medical problem. If your cat vomits shortly after eating, make sure he's seen by the veterinarian.

FINICKY EATING SYNDROME AND FIXED FOOD PREFERENCE

If your cat loves a certain food one day but rejects it the next, you've probably resigned yourself to living with a finicky eater. For some people, the finicky part rears its ugly head when the cat owner dares to serve food from a previously opened can. For others, the rejection occurs when you attempt to serve a canned variety with gravy when the cat is expecting the chunk variety without gravy. Maybe you fed one kind of food for years and then attempted to try a new brand, only to be met with the sight of the back end of your cat as he walked disgustedly out of the kitchen.

Finicky eaters are created, not born, although the process can start at a very young age. Kittens who are fed only one kind or type of food are more likely to have a fixed food preference later in life. The behavior usually appears when the food is abruptly changed. Cats don't like sudden changes. If you've been feeding your cat the same food for quite a while, and have abruptly placed a new brand, flavor, or texture in his bowl, you may have inadvertently set this ball into motion. If your cat has eaten only dry food and now must eat canned food due to a medical problem, the abrupt change can cause rejection.

Cats react first to the aroma of their food. If an unfamiliar scent is suddenly detected in their food bowl, they may not even attempt to take the first bite. If the aroma is appealing, the next hurdle is taste. Along with taste, many cats have texture preferences. There's a reason why wet food comes in many different textures and dry food comes in various sizes and shapes. It's because cats can have strong preferences concerning mouth feel. A cat who was used to eating a round kibble may not like the feel of a star shape or a triangular one. Pet food companies spend lots of money researching the appeal of aroma, taste, and texture.

In an effort to please your finicky eater, you may have run yourself ragged trying to find just the right food. Cat owners open several different brands of food at one time in a desperate attempt to hit on the right one. Unfortunately, when you have a cat with finicky eater syndrome, the more you keep changing the food from meal to meal out of desperation, the more confusing it gets for the kitty.

Some experts will contend that cats do very well eating the same food every day for life (age-appropriate food, of course). If you're feeding a good-quality food, that may indeed be true. The problem is that events may occur that are out of your control. The particular formula of that food may change, or the company may stop making it altogether. If your cat has developed a fixed food preference, making the change can be difficult. The other important consideration is that if your cat develops a particular health problem, he may need to go on a prescription formula food. If he has eaten only one kind of food his whole life, it may be very difficult to convince him that this new food is better for him.

Many experts and veterinarians recommend that cats be fed a variety of foods of different flavors and brands to prevent fixation. If you do this from the start, you may be able to prevent finicky eater syndrome or a fixed food preference altogether. There's a proper way to do it, though, and that's *gradually*. If your cat is eating one brand or flavor of food and you now want to include another kind, add a little of the new food into the old food over the course of five to seven days. Eventually you'll be increasing the amount of new food and decreasing the old. (Note: This transition is to be done only when trying to switch to the same type of food. Don't mix canned into dry food or vice versa.) This enables your cat to make a gradual transition, reducing the chances of rejection. It's also better for his digestive system not to have abrupt changes. The cat's system needs an adequate amount of time to adjust to the unfamiliar ingredients. If the change is too abrupt, the cat is at risk of having anything from mild upset stomach or gas to mild or severe diarrhea.

CATWISE CAUTION

Finicky eater syndrome can be dangerous because cats can't safely go more than two days without eating. If they do, they run the risk of developing a disease called *hepatic lipidosis*, which results in fatty deposits in the liver. This condition can develop in as little as two days of not eating, so it's crucial to get immediate veterinary help if your cat has totally stopped eating for any reason.

RETRAINING THE FINICKY EATER

First, make sure there isn't an underlying medical cause for the behavior.

Usually, the easiest way to retrain finicky eating if you currently free-feed your cat is to switch to scheduled meals in order to increase his appetite at mealtime. Don't go from free-feeding to once or twice daily meals, though. Do several small meals a day in order to make the transition more gradual and appealing.

If you're feeding canned food, warm it slightly for a few seconds in the microwave to release the aroma. Stir it before serving it to your cat to make sure there are no pockets of excessive heat in there. If serving refrigerated leftover canned food, never put it down for your cat straight from the refrigerator. Let it come to room temperature, or warm it a bit in the microwave. If serving dry food and your cat rejects it, you can moisten it just a bit and then warm that as well in the microwave. Do not overheat! Stir the food and test the temperature with your little finger before serving. It should be room temperature or slightly warmer, but not hot.

If you're trying to transition from one type of food to another, such as canned to dry or dry to canned, don't mix the two together. Cats usually dislike their dry food being contaminated with canned food. Soggy dry food is never appealing. Instead, crush the dry food and place it on top of the canned food. This way, the cat has the familiar aroma of the dry food and most of the taste, but will start to get a taste of the canned food as well.

If your veterinarian says it's okay and your cat doesn't have any health concerns, you can also pour a small amount of tuna water on top of canned food. The water from the tuna can be strong enough to entice an appetite, but tuna has a very strong taste and smell and can become addictive to cats, so you have to use this sparingly. Sometimes it helps to smear a drop of baby food on top of the canned food. If you do this, make sure it's a food that doesn't contain onion powder or garlic powder, as they can pose a health risk to cats.

If your cat is still rejecting his food, talk to your veterinarian about whether the use of an appetite stimulant is appropriate.

CATWISE CAUTION

A common cause of finicky eating is an excessive amount of treats being offered. Treats should not amount to more than 10 percent of your cat's diet. Use treats as behavior modification tools and break them into small pieces so you can offer a piece of one as a reward instead of an entire treat. Remember, it's a *treat* and not a *meal*.

BOWL BULLIES

Sometimes when there's more than one cat in the household, one may try to take charge of the feeding station. It can be related to status in that a higher-ranking cat may intimidate the lower-ranking one into backing off until he has eaten. If there's a hostile relationship between cats, the victim kitty may feel too frightened to approach the bowl until the intimidator has left the area. The intimidation can seem subtle to you but very obvious to the targeted cats. The intimidator may guard the entrance to the kitchen by appearing to lounge in the doorway. He may also not bother with any degree of subtlety and choose to growl and challenge any other approaching kitty with direct stares and intimidating forward-facing posture.

If you feed your cats in their own separate bowls, there can still be a problem if the intimidator noses other cats out of their bowls so he can eat their food first before finishing his own. This can also happen when you have a cat who is on a special diet and knows the food in the other bowls is more appetizing.

Even if your cats get along in other areas of the home, problems can show up at the feeding station. The cats may eat in the same room together, but one may be very nervous while in the presence of the more intimidating cat. Mealtime should be safe, quiet, and relaxing for your cat. This isn't the time when he should have to worry about being ambushed or nosed away from his food bowl.

If you have a bowl bully, there are a number of ways to handle the situation. If you're currently feeding out of a community bowl, everyone needs to have his own dish. If you feed on a schedule, place the dishes far enough apart so that everyone gets to stay well within his comfort zone. You also will have to play security guard during mealtime to make sure the bully doesn't start wandering over toward the other cat's bowl. If the cats stop eating and watch each other, then you haven't set the bowls far enough apart. Once you've achieved sufficient distance between the bowls, make sure you place the bowls in the same location every time so that each cat starts to identify which bowl location belongs to him.

If the cats are not comfortable in the same room, or if you can't keep the bully away from the other cat's bowl, feed the cats in separate areas. The bully can't be everywhere at one time, so setting up multiple feeding stations can help everyone feel more comfortable. The bully won't see the other cat, so he'll be able to relax and eat, and the intimidated cat will soon realize that his new feeding station is secure, so he'll relax as well.

For cats who free-feed, set up multiple feeding stations around the house so the more subordinate cats can choose the safest spots to eat. This also allows them to find food even if an intimidator is lounging at the entrance to one of the feeding stations. If you schedule-feed, it's a good idea to feed smaller meals more often so that the intimidator doesn't get very hungry at mealtime.

In multicat homes, use vertical spacing as well when setting up the feeding stations. You may have a cat who feels more secure on an elevated surface when eating, either as a status display or just because he's frightened and it gives him a better visual field to check for approaching opponents.

CATS ON DIFFERENT DIETS

"Will everyone please just eat your own food!" is the cat owners' plea heard around the world. How do you handle it when you have multiple cats on multiple foods? The solution I've seen many cat owners use if there's one cat in the family on a special diet is to simply put all the cats on the same food. Depending on the particular food and the ages, activity levels, and health of the other cats, this may not be the wisest choice. For example, a young, healthy cat doesn't need to be eating a diet meant for your elderly kitty who is in chronic renal failure. A cat who is active and the correct weight shouldn't be eating the restricted-calorie diet of your overweight, inactive feline. This is a common problem in two-cat households in which one cat is an adult and the other is a kitten. The adult shouldn't eat the kitten formula because it is too high in fat and protein, and the kitten shouldn't be eating the adult's food because he won't be getting the adequate amounts of fat and protein that he needs at his life stage.

So just how do you manage it when the cats aren't on the same diet? This is where scheduled feeding works better than free-feeding because you can set out the proper food for each cat and monitor mealtime to make sure everyone eats what she is supposed to. If one cat's food is simply too irresistible for another cat and feeding in the same room is too much of a temptation, then feed in separate areas.

In some cases, such as when you have a very overweight or elderly cat, you may be able to elevate the other cat's food. If the cat who needs to be on a special diet is unable to jump or climb, the younger/healthier cat's food can be placed high enough to make it inaccessible to anyone who shouldn't be eating it. Just make sure the younger cat has no problem getting to that spot. If you choose this option, make sure the elevated spot is one where you'll consistently allow this cat so you don't send mixed retraining messages. If you've been retraining your cats to stay off the kitchen counter, don't place a feeding station there.

TUBBY TABBIES: SAFE MEALTIME RETRAINING

Being overweight is not healthy for a cat at any age, but it can have even more serious implications in an older kitty. Overweight cats are more at risk for heart disease, diabetes, and arthritis. There seems to be an epidemic of feline obesity, as veterinarians are seeing more and more overweight cats in their clinics. I think people have become so used to the image of cats with fat pads on their haunches that when they actually see a cat of the appropriate weight, they think that kitty must be starving. If the image of a football comes to mind when you think of your cat's body shape, then he's probably carrying around more weight than he should. He also shouldn't have a large fat pad dangling from his stomach that could double as a floor mop.

Different breeds have different body types. It's important to know what your cat's ideal weight should be for his age, health, activity level, and breed. For example, the Siamese body is very different from the cobby (stocky, short-legged) body of the Persian. The Maine Coon is a big cat, but not a fat cat. There's a difference between being big and being overweight.

I couldn't even begin to tell you how many consultations I've done in which my clients have been totally shocked by my observation of their cats as overweight. When I question these clients, they don't even know how much their cats weigh or how much they *should* weigh. In many cases, the veterinarians have recommended putting the cats on weight-reduction programs, but the clients haven't followed through.

For many cats, the answer is simply a need for increased activity. Too many indoor cats have absolutely nothing to do but eat and sleep. People have created warm, soft, loving environments with endless access to food but have neglected that very important aspect of cat life: *activity*. Cats are hunters who were born to work for food.

To begin a healthy weight-reduction plan, you have to start by getting your cat examined by the veterinarian, including appropriate diagnostic tests to make sure there isn't any underlying medical problem causing the weight gain or that has developed as a result of the increased pounds. Your veterinarian will be able to tell you what your cat should weigh and how to safely get your cat to that point in terms of how slowly to change his diet. You can't drastically reduce your cat's food because it can have disastrous effects. If a cat loses weight too quickly, he'll be at risk for liver disease as fatty deposits form in the liver. This is very serious, so no matter how motivated you may be to get your cat svelte again, it can't be done quickly. The other danger of putting your cat on a drastic diet is that it can create additional behavior problems such as eating too fast and vomiting the food right back up, stealing food, constant meowing, begging behavior, and anxiety-related overgrooming.

Your veterinarian will tell you how much weight your cat should lose on a weekly or monthly basis and he or she will give you some starting guidelines on how much food to feed. In some cases you may be instructed to continue feeding the current brand of food, slightly reducing the amount. In other cases you may be instructed to use a reduced-calorie over-the-counter food or a prescription food. If you're instructed to use a new food, gradually mix it into your cat's current brand in order to ease through the transition. This should take about five to seven days.

One of the best tricks for helping a cat adjust to a diet is to feed smaller meals more often. Measure the daily amount and then divide it up into several meals. Your cat will think he's getting more food than he actually is and his stomach won't get uncomfortably empty for long periods of time. With a weight-reduction plan, scheduled meals are better than free-feeding to prevent your cat from gorging himself early in the day with no other food to eat later on.

 CATWISE **CLUE**

If you want to monitor your cat's weight loss accurately, invest in a baby scale that measures ounces.

A common mistake I see is that cat owners will switch the cat to a reduced-calorie food but free-feed it in endless supply. You can't do a successful weight-loss program if you have no idea how much your cat is eating. You have to have a measured amount each day to control his caloric intake.

If eating has become the only activity in your cat's life, it's time for some exercise. Fortunately for your cat, that'll come in the form of fun playtime rather than having to get on the treadmill or go to the gym. You're going to use what comes naturally to a cat: *hunting*. In your cat's case, that skill may be very rusty or even seemingly forgotten, but trust me, it's still there. Start a schedule of doing interactive play therapy sessions with your cat at least twice a day (see chapter 3). You'll have to customize the technique to fit your cat's physical ability, but any amount of movement will be beneficial. If your cat is extremely obese, then don't expect him to do backflips and move at incredible speed to chase a toy. Initially, he may only bat at the toy with his paw as he continues to lounge on the sofa. That's a start, and it's probably more activity than he has had in years. As your cat gets more comfortable, he'll be able to move more during the game as instinct kicks in to remind him that he was born to be a mighty hunter.

With an overweight cat, it's better to do several low-intensity play therapy sessions a day so as not to overtax him. Don't attempt a half-hour nonstop session, even if your cat seems up for it. If he isn't used to activity, ease him into the routine gradually. Follow the playtime techniques described in chapter 3 to learn how to stimulate the prey-drive.

Use play therapy as a way to distract your cat away from the kitchen if he tends to sit in front of the empty feeding station. Additionally, set up some activity toys and challenges to keep him busy between play therapy sessions. Look around your environment and see what can be done to improve the feline stimulation factor. Refer to chapter 2 for specifics.

For some clients who have overweight cats, I recommend that

they use puzzle feeders such as the *Play-N-Treat* balls for feeding. The balls can be used in one of two ways. You can either set them out for your cat to enjoy during the day while you're at work, so he doesn't have to go all day without a meal, or if your cat really takes to the ball technique, you can use them exclusively for meal feeding. The *Play-N-Treat* dispenses only one or two pieces of kibble at a time, so it forces your cat to eat slowly, plus your cat has to actually *move* in order to get the food reward. Working for food is a natural behavior for a cat. But don't use the balls for exclusive feeding unless you're sure your cat completely gets the concept of how to roll the ball to get the food reward. Also, if you do use them exclusively for feeding, place them in rooms in which they won't be able to roll into areas where your cat won't be able to retrieve them. You can also make homemade puzzle feeders by cutting paw-sized holes in a sturdy cardboard box and placing dry food inside. Cardboard toilet-paper or paper-towel roll inserts make good puzzle feeders as well. Punch holes in the cardboard roll that are larger than the kibble. Seal each end with a circle of paper. Tape the ends smoothly so the cardboard rolls easily. Test out the homemade puzzle feeder by rolling it on the floor to make sure the kibble falls out easily before you give it your cat. You now have a very cheap and fun puzzle feeder.

The timing of playtime and activity is also an important part of successful weight control. In the wild, cats go through physical activity before they can enjoy the food feast of their capture. Do your play therapy sessions before your cat's meals to mimic that pattern.

CATWISE REMINDER

Don't leave dirty food bowls on the floor after your cat has eaten. The smell of the food residue or the sight of the empty bowl can continue to trigger his hunger.

STICK TO THE PLAN

Overfeeding is not love. Getting your cat on a healthy nutritional plan is love. That extra piece of chicken you sneak him or that table-spoon of tuna you always save for him when you make a sandwich aren't doing him any favors. He may look at you with those big beau-tiful eyes and guilt may try to overtake you, but don't weaken and sneak him extra food. If you stick to the plan of providing the right amount of food at the right times while providing an increase in ac-tivity and a more stimulating environment, your cat will soon start to enjoy life in a way he never was able to previously.

8

Spits and Spats

Aggression, Biting, and Fighting

In the animal world, aggression is a natural part of life. In one form or another, it is how cats establish colonies, find mates, determine territory, protect their nests, and capture their food for survival. In the home, aggressive behavior, whether it is directed toward a companion cat or a human family member, is always scary. It is one of the top two reasons cats are relinquished to shelters, abandoned, rehomed, put outdoors, or euthanized. The other top reason is elimination outside the litter box.

Aggression can be difficult to correct because it is often misunderstood. A cat may display aggression only under certain circumstances, or she may seem unpredictable in whether or not she's going to lash out. It's important to understand that aggression can be either offensive or defensive. Cats use posturing to display their intent, often in the hope that they can avoid an actual physical confrontation. Urine marking may also be used as covert aggression if cats are trying to determine how much of an opponent they may have to deal with. Many owners fail to recognize such behaviors as aggressive. They may assume their cats are getting along because they never see any overt displays of battle. They may often misinterpret a urine-marking problem as simply a *litter box issue* when it's actually due to aggression.

Aggressive behavior can have an underlying medical cause, so you should never tackle it as simply a behavior problem until your cat has had a thorough evaluation by your veterinarian. The aggression could be due to a previously unseen injury or illness. Don't bypass this step even if you're sure the problem is behavioral.

As with any other behavior problem, it's important to try to find the cause of your cat's aggression because there are several types. If you can figure out what might be setting it off, you can hopefully eliminate or at least modify the trigger. In so many cases, a cat owner will tell me that his cat's aggression is *unprovoked*, but in reality it rarely is. There's usually something consistent that triggers it, and in many cases the cats give some warning signals beforehand.

THE BITER

Your cat may be a mild biter during play or she may be one who means business when she chomps down, inflicting pain and drawing blood. In either case, biting behavior must be corrected.

First, figure out the trigger. Does she bite your hand when you're playing with her? One of the most common mistakes people make is to use their fingers as toys to entice cats to play. This may have seemed harmless enough when your cat was a kitten, but as she grew and developed adult teeth, those bites probably started to hurt more. Unfortunately, if you used your fingers as toys, you sent a message to her that biting flesh was acceptable. In her mind, if biting flesh is okay during play, then it's also okay for her to bite when she needs to communicate other things as well. Some cats bite to solicit playtime. From previous experience, they learned that biting gets a response from the cat owners and a toy is tossed for them. Unfortunately, that just reinforces the biting behavior. In this way, *she* has trained *you*.

If you use your fingers as toys, even if protected under a blanket or other fabric, it's time to stop. No more mixed messages are to be sent to your cat. From now on, all playtime that involves you should be done with an interactive toy. The typical fishing pole–type toy puts a safe distance between your fingers and your cat's teeth. Don't even use a small toy when playing with her. Little fuzzy mice and other small toys are meant for her solo play. Even if you've never used your fingers as toys, if you've tried to hold a small solo toy for interactive play, your cat may have bitten you accidentally because she couldn't distinguish where the toy ended and your fingers began. Her prey-drive was in gear and she was focused on capturing her prey, and that experience during playtime should be set up so that you don't have to worry about where your fingers are.

Your cat may bite moving hands or feet because that's the only stimulation she receives that satisfies her desire to play. If there are no other outlets for her, it's not surprising that she's resorted to biting anything that moves, even if it's your bare feet.

Your biting cat may also be communicating that she wants you to stop doing something. A bite to the hand that's been stroking her often gets you to stop doing what you're doing. She may have been giving other signals to let you know she was no longer enjoying the interaction, but if you missed them, she may have felt her only option was to bite. If your cat seems to bite during petting, see the section on *petting-induced aggression* later in this chapter.

Biting may have become a very effective means of communication for your cat. She may bite you when she wants to take your spot on the couch or to be fed, let outside, given attention, left alone, and so forth.

Don't use any physical reprimands when trying to get your cat to stop biting. Hitting your cat will only confuse her, and if she bit you as a defensive reaction, that'll only heighten her feeling of being threatened.

If your cat bites during play, stop the game and ignore her for a minute. Let her see that biting doesn't produce desired results. Then direct her back toward the appropriate interactive toy. If she bites to elicit playtime, don't reward her with play. Instead, tell her "No bite" and then ignore her for a few moments. Offer playtime when she's well behaved and doesn't bite.

If your cat has your hand in her teeth, it may seem natural to pull away. Instead, gently push *toward* her. If you pull away, it often triggers her to bite harder because struggling to get away is what prey does. If you push toward her mouth, you'll momentarily confuse her and she'll disengage. If she isn't biting hard, you can add a freeze motion before pushing forward to show her that the play has stopped due to her biting. You can also add a verbal "No bite."

Many people are under the false impression that thumping the cat on the nose is a good way to correct a cat for biting (or any misbehavior). These cat owners have been led to believe that the thumping action mimics the way a mother cat corrects her kittens for misbehaving. While a mother cat may thump her kitten, that correction is also accompanied by specific vocalizations and other body-language signals that humans can't replicate. Don't follow the advice of nose thumping because all forms of physical reprimands are inhumane and counterproductive.

AGGRESSION

There are multiple types of aggression that cats may exhibit. In order to apply the appropriate behavior modification technique, you have to identify the one you're trying to correct. In many cases, a cat offers some warning signals before engaging in actual aggression. If you become more familiar with how your cat communicates, you may be able to avoid or interrupt some instances of impending aggression. Refer to chapter 1 for a refresher on interpreting your cat's signals.

Fear aggression

Many people are familiar with this behavior in a cat, most especially when trying to get kitty out of the carrier at the veterinarian's office. It can come as quite a surprise to find your docile, sweet-tempered cat suddenly channeling her inner crocodile.

In general, your cat would prefer avoiding confrontation if at all possible. All of the posturing that cats go through when faced with an opponent is either to look big and intimidating to scare the enemy away or to communicate that no threat is intended. When a cat exhibits fear aggression, it's because she feels backed into a corner with no means of escape.

Fear aggression is a defensive behavior, which means the cat is reacting to a potential threat. Her posture indicates that she doesn't want you to continue approaching, but if you do, she'll defend herself.

This type of aggression, which is most commonly seen at the veterinarian's office, usually consists of the cat tucking her paws under her body and backing up against a wall, if available. If she's in her carrier, she'll be against the back wall of it, letting you know that she doesn't want any interaction. Although her head and front paws may be facing her opponent, her back paws are not. This conflicting posture indicates that should an escape possibility arise, she'll take it. Her hind feet stay in position to propel her out of harm's way.

 **CATWISE CLUE**

The cat displaying fear aggression will try to avoid direct eye contact, since that's viewed as a challenge or threat.

The cat's pupils are usually dilated, her whiskers are flattened back against her cheeks, and her ears are rotated and flattened against her head. Initially, her ears may be in a T position, resembling airplane wings, but as the perceived threat increases, the ears will rotate back.

Vocally, the cat hisses and often growls. She usually doesn't move to strike until someone or something continues to advance. That's when a paw lashes out with lightning speed.

The cat may also display piloerection of the hair on her back and tail to appear bigger and more threatening, or she may curl up as tightly as she can to appear as invisible as possible. Either way, if the opponent continues advancing, the cat might roll over into the ultimate defensive position to be able to utilize all of her claws as weapons as well as her teeth.

If your cat displays fear aggression while at the veterinarian's office, there's a way to reduce her stress before and during the visit. Follow the instructions in chapter 10.

A cat who didn't receive adequate socialization at an early age, or who was gradually and gently exposed to various experiences, sounds, and sights, is more likely to display fear aggression. As an adult cat, if changes are presented to her abruptly, such as the addition of another pet or person in the home, she may also exhibit this behavior.

If your cat exhibits fear aggression on a regular basis, it's time to evaluate what might be triggering the repeated episodes. Are there small children in the home who corner the cat? Is there another pet in the home with whom your cat has a hostile relationship? Is there a particular person in the home or a guest who visits regularly who might be the trigger? Once you're able to figure out what causes it—and there may be multiple causes—you can try to modify the situation to help your cat feel less threatened.

When your cat is displaying fear aggression, don't attempt to comfort her. In most cases, any attempt at interaction will only heighten her reactivity. When she's feeling backed into a corner, the best thing you can do for her is to either provide a means of escape or remove the aggressive trigger. She needs time to calm down and feel secure again. Let her stay in a quiet area so she can settle down. Reduce auditory and visual stimuli by turning off the TV or radio and darken the room if it's brightly lit. Then leave her alone to settle down. After she has had a chance to relax, you can approach her at a distance using a soothing tone of voice. If she seems as if she's open for more interaction, you can let her out of the room (if she's sequestered) and open the drapes or turn lights on again. If she approaches you and wants to be petted or held, don't overdo the affection or tone of voice at the risk of reinforcing and rewarding her fear. If you cuddle and comfort too much, it can send a signal that her fear was justified and that will increase the chance that she'll show fear aggression in the same situation in the future. Never reward an unwanted behavior. That's also one reason why you don't want to try to touch and cuddle your cat while she's in the middle of exhibiting fear aggression, but the most important reason not to reach out to a cat under those circumstances is that you'll undoubtedly get injured. For many people it's hard not to reach out and try to soothe their cat during these times, but trust me, when your cat is showing fear aggression, especially if she's extremely reactive, she isn't going to take the time to figure out if it's your hand coming toward her or an opponent. She'll react first and think later.

In the case of a cat who routinely shows fear aggression in the home, there are some likely environmental modifications that need to be made in addition to the behavior modification, depending on the specific dynamics in your house. If you have young children, your cat needs adequate areas of sanctuary and avenues of escape. With a cat who routinely displays fear aggression, these areas need to exist in every room she occupies. She needs hiding places, safe elevated areas, and clear paths to her litter box and feeding station. You can also use the *Feliway Comfort Zone* plug-in diffuser in the areas where your cat and your children must coexist. If your children are old enough, they should be taught about "hands-off" areas and when not to approach kitty.

If the fear aggression is routinely triggered by a particular person in the home, use techniques to help the cat gradually become more accepting and less fearful. Start by having that person on the opposite side of the room while you either conduct a gentle interactive play session, feed your cat a meal, offer a treat, or do a clicker training session. The person must be far enough away that your cat doesn't show fear. She has to be comfortable enough to focus on the game, the food, or the clicker training. After a few sessions, the person may be able to inch closer. More specifics on this type of retraining can be found in chapter 9.

Fear aggression caused by a dog in the home requires the same type of behavior modification mentioned above. One technique is to feed the animals in the same room but far enough apart so that the fearful cat is within her comfort zone. If the dog is a legitimate threat to the cat in terms of chasing, even if in play, then additional training must be done to teach the dog how to act around the cat. Additional information on dog-cat relationships can be found in chapter 9.

If the trigger is another cat in the home, see the section on *inter-cat aggression* later in this chapter.

Petting-induced aggression

This one usually takes people by surprise because it occurs when the cat owner and cat seem to be enjoying closeness. What happens is that at some point while the cat is being petted, she suddenly whips around and bites or scratches the very hand that's showing her affection. It's scary and it seems to come out of nowhere, but there are usually several warning signs that are exhibited before the cat reaches the point of having to bite.

Specifically why and when petting-induced aggression occurs can vary from cat to cat. It can happen as the cat starts to get very relaxed during a petting session, maybe even to the point of starting to doze. Suddenly, she becomes aware of being touched and her survival instinct takes over and she reacts defensively to whatever is touching her. In other cases, and this is what I see most often, the cat initially enjoys the physical contact, but then it gets to be too much. That's where the warning signs start to be displayed, because what was previously pleasurable is now crossing the line into over-stimulation. It might be due to the particular way an owner is petting, or it might be due to the length of time the petting has been going on. When warning signs are ignored, the cat feels she has no other option but to bite. After biting, the cat may jump down and start self-grooming or just look confused. Although you may think your cat is being bad for having bitten, she's actually anxious due to the fact that she gave "official" warnings that went unheeded.

To avoid being the target of petting-induced aggression, your best plan is to become more aware of the warning signs your cat gives while being stroked. Some typical ones include skin twitching, tail lashing or thumping, meowing, cessation of purring, ears going into a T position or rotating back, and shifting of body position. If the cat is facing away from you, she may glance back in your direction. If she's facing you, she may glance over at the hand doing the petting. Although these may seem like warnings that you wouldn't miss, it's easy to overlook them if you're petting while watching TV, talking on the phone, reading, or conversing with another person in the room. If your cat is prone to petting-induced aggression, you can't absentmindedly pet her anymore. During your petting sessions, you have to watch for warning signs so you can stop petting at the first signal.

Some cats will be able to handle only a certain amount of petting, while others enjoy lots of it depending upon whether the timing is right. Your cat may jump up to sit on your lap, but it may not be because she wants a cuddle session. She may want the security of being on your lap as she surveys the room. In a multicat home, she may want to be on your lap or close to you because she feels safest there; however, her mood while in your lap may not be one of contentment.

If your cat is predictable in terms of how long she generally enjoys being petted, use that knowledge to avoid even getting to that first warning signal. For instance, if your cat usually lets you pet her for ten minutes before biting, then stop after five minutes. This way you leave her in a contented state or even wanting more rather than reaching the overstimulation point. If you stop petting before the warning signal or, at the very latest, at the nanosecond you see the first sign, then she'll probably relax again and remain on your lap. After several minutes, you might be able to pet her again for several strokes. If you aren't sure whether she wants more petting, then be content with just having her on your lap or sitting beside you. The more sessions you do in which she sees you have understood her body language, the more she'll enjoy being near you. With some cats, you can gradually work to increase the number of strokes over the course of numerous sessions. Watch her body language and pay attention to timing.

CATWISE CAUTION

No matter how relaxed your cat may initially seem when she's being petted, if there's a history of petting-induced aggression, you must pay attention to subtle changes in body language.

Reevaluate your petting style as well. If you're doing fast short strokes, your cat may prefer long and slow ones. Maybe she doesn't like it when you go near the base of her tail. In a dry environment, static electricity may bother her every time you reach to pet her. You may notice that when you stroke down her back she seems tense, but if you switch to just petting her behind the head or under the chin she relaxes again. She's letting you know what she prefers, and if you pay attention you can both enjoy this time together.

Redirected aggression

This is often misdiagnosed as unprovoked aggression because it appears as if the cat is lashing out for no reason at all. You might be walking by, not even looking at your cat, when suddenly you're the target of her aggression. Redirected aggression can also be directed at other companion cats or dogs in the home.

Redirected aggression occurs when a cat is unable to gain access to the primary source of her agitation, so she lashes out at whoever is nearest. The cat is in such a highly reactive state that she doesn't realize she has just attacked her closest companion or her loving cat owner. Her anxiety takes over and her good kitty judgment takes a backseat.

The most common occurrences of redirected aggression take place when an indoor cat is sitting at a window and spots an unfamiliar cat in the yard. She becomes highly aroused and frustrated that she's unable to get to her target. As luck would have it, a companion cat just happens to jump up to that area, or maybe even just walks by, and is immediately attacked. The interaction just elevates the original cat's agitation. The victim cat either fights back in defense or runs for cover. Either way, it's an extremely stressful and dangerous situation for both cats.

Usually, a cat calms down soon after displaying redirected aggression, but some kitties can stay aroused and confused. The reason aggression is so often misdiagnosed as unprovoked is because you may not have seen the original cause of the agitation. The cat in the yard may have been visible only momentarily before disappearing, but after seeing that outdoor cat, your kitty can stay agitated for a long period, so you or another pet could be the victim of the attack hours afterward. If the cat redirected the aggression toward a companion cat, then it can take a while for the two of them to get their relationship back to normal, depending upon the severity of the episode. The attacked cat may start to posture differently around the original cat. She may start to show more defensive body language, and that can cause the original cat to continue to connect her with the cause of her agitation. In some cases, the sight of each other can cause the aggression to continue, repeating the cycle again and again.

When your cat shows redirected aggression toward another cat, the best course of action is to keep them separated until both cats are calm and back to normal. DO NOT try to break up a fight by sticking your hand between the cats or attempting to pick one up—you'll surely get injured that way. Instead, bang a pan on the counter, clap your hands, or make some kind of noise to startle the cats into separating. If you use the technique of throwing a blanket, towel, or jacket over them, make sure you cover only one cat so the other can get away. If you throw something that covers both cats, you lock them in closer together and cause more panic, which could increase the intensity of the aggression.

Once they're separated, one will probably run into another room. If not, try to usher one into another area (don't handle an aggressive cat) where you can close the door. The sooner you separate the cats after an episode of redirected aggression, the better your chances of having them get back to a normal relationship. Many of the cases I've seen in which cats have seriously damaged their relationships due to redirected aggression have occurred because cat owners didn't separate them soon enough.

When the cats have been separated long enough (the time can vary from a few hours to several days, or even weeks, depending on the severity and your cats' personalities), reintroduce them gradually. Don't attempt this until each cat appears to be back to normal behavior, such as displaying normal posture when walking, eating, using the litter box, playing, and so forth. If the aggressive episode was severe, or the event occurred awhile ago and the cats' aggression toward each other has escalated, then the separation should be long enough to give them adequate time to settle down. See the section on doing a reintroduction later in this chapter for how to gradually ease the cats back together again. Depending on how mild or severe the aggression was, you can modify some of the reintroduction process. If the aggression was mild and the cats seem just slightly tense around each other, then you won't have to take it as slowly as you would if the episode was traumatic. Don't rush the process if the cats aren't ready. If the reintroduction isn't done properly, the cats may remain opponents indefinitely.

If your cat appears agitated at something, or you've been the victim of redirected aggression, leave the kitty alone so she can calm down. If the cause was the sight of another cat outside, close the drapes or blinds, darken the room, and let your cat recover. Watch for signs that she has returned to normal behavior, such as eating, grooming (not displacement grooming, though), using the litter box, or sleeping. Look for signs of your cat's typical patterns returning. With grooming, your cat should be returning to the length and pattern of grooming that was done before the redirected aggression episode. If she typically self-groomed after eating or being petted and you now notice she's grooming her stomach or flanks for long periods, or seems nervous while grooming, it probably means she's still dealing with the anxiety from the recent event. If she normally would eliminate in the litter box, cover her waste, and then hop right out to go on with her activities and now you notice she's sleeping in the box or jumping out before she has even finished taking care of business, that's another indication that her stress level is still elevated.

Once you know your cat is susceptible to redirected aggression, you can plan accordingly to avoid future episodes. At the first sign of agitation, make sure children and pets are safely in another room. If you suspect that a certain event—such as having a repair person in the home—might trigger an episode, put the susceptible cat in another area so she isn't exposed to the trigger.

If the cause is the sight of other cats or animals in the yard, make some environmental modifications to reduce your cat's chances of exposure to the trigger. If there are one or two windows in particular through which the unfamiliar outdoor cat is usually visible, cover the bottom part of those windows with an opaque material or white poster paper. The paper has to be strong enough not to be easily ripped by cat claws. You have to cover only as much of the window as is needed to prevent your cat from seeing out. That way, you can still leave the top of the window uncovered to get adequate light.

If your cat's favorite cat tree or window perch is at the trigger window, move it to a neutral one. Use lots of playtime and treats around the tree in its new location to help your cat realize this is a positive and not a negative move.

Keep the covering on the windows for a week or more, depending upon how serious the incident was. In some cases, you may have to create some kind of permanent (and more attractive) blockage if the outdoor cat is routinely visible there, as in the case of a neighbor cat in his own yard.

Keep a long-range water pistol handy in case you have to chase the outdoor cat away from your yard. If the cat doesn't have a home and you don't feel comfortable attempting to capture him in order to take him to your local humane organization, contact your veterinarian or shelter to find out if there's a feline rescue group in your area. They may be able to help you trap this kitty and find it a safe home. If the cat belongs to a neighbor, perhaps you can gently inform him or her that the presence of the cat in your yard is creating aggression problems for your indoor kitty. I know it can be a touchy subject for some people when you even hint that their outdoor pets are becoming a nuisance, but if done gently and without getting emotional, you may have success. Show your concern for the neighbor's cat as well as your own and your message may be received less defensively. You might find that the neighbor would like to keep the cat indoors as well but didn't know how to do the transition.

If your yard has become a favorite hangout for the neighborhood cats or dogs or other animals who trigger your cat's aggression, look into installing the *ScareCrow*, a water sprinkler that's motion-activated. If you do this, make sure you set it up so it doesn't go off when people walk up your driveway or sidewalk. For more information on the *ScareCrow*, see the appendix.

If the outdoor cat is coming around to use your garden soil as a litter box, place garden netting over the soil and then cover it with a light layer of additional soil or mulch. You can also place large stones on the soil if it fits with your landscape design so that the cat can't find enough room to dig and eliminate.

Pain-induced aggression

This can be caused by an underlying medical condition, an injury, or if the cat is handled in a painful way. Pain-induced aggression may occur when the cat's tail is pulled or when she is petted aggressively by a child.

A cat who is allowed outdoors may come home with an unseen injury that can cause pain when touched. It's common for bite wounds to turn into abscesses due to the very sharp canine teeth that harbor bacteria. The wound seals over and the infection grows beneath the skin.

An older cat may experience pain due to arthritis when petted, groomed, or handled. Some cats with kidney infections are sensitive when touched along the back.

If your cat displays aggression when touched, the first step is to have him examined by the veterinarian because there may be an underlying medical cause. If a cat who normally enjoys affection has suddenly started showing aggression when handled, don't assume it's a behavioral problem. There's a very good chance that something is hurting her. In the case of an elderly cat, many people explain away the aggression as senility or old-age grumpiness when the cause really is medical.

Territorial aggression

This behavior can be exhibited toward another animal or toward a human. Since a cat is a territorial creature, there are certain times when you can count on territorial aggression rearing its head. A common example is when a new cat comes into the household and the existing cat displays aggression because she feels her territory is in danger. Territorial aggression can also be displayed toward a person who comes to visit the home. It is also not uncommon to see it displayed toward one person or cat and not toward another.

Territorial aggression can even occur between companion cats who have previously gotten along well if one of them oversteps her bounds. Cats who are going through social maturity (between two and four years of age) may start showing more territorial aggression toward companion cats.

This type of aggression isn't always obvious to the human family because cats are masters at posturing and subtle forms of communication. A higher-ranking cat may lounge in the hallway in front of the room where the litter box is located as a way of guarding her side of the house. Even though it may appear as if she's merely relaxing, a companion cat may be intimidated enough to know not to try to pass by. This can lead to an inappropriate elimination problem if the companion cat has to find a safer place than the litter box.

Many cats who share an environment work out their time-sharing of the space and create a peaceful coexistence. Others, though, remain in conflict, either through subtle ongoing communication that manages to stay just below the surface or through outright day-to-day battle.

In a multicat household, when one cat goes to the veterinarian but the companion cat doesn't, sometimes the cat left at home displays territorial aggression toward the returning kitty. The cat returning from the veterinarian doesn't smell familiar and, in fact, smells threatening, since vet-clinic scents aren't viewed by cats as very comforting.

If the territorial aggression is between two cats in your home and one is a relative newcomer, then the proper introduction may not have been done. When you do a proper introduction, it prevents the resident cat from feeling as if her entire territory is up for grabs. It also prevents the newcomer from feeling as if she has been dropped behind enemy lines. Don't let the two cats "work it out themselves." Take a few steps back and start the introduction over again. It doesn't matter that they've already met. Separate them and let them calm down and then do the whole process over, only this time do it the *starting from scratch* way. The proper introduction method can be found in chapter 9.

Even if the aggression is between longtime companion cats, you can still start over again. Yes, even if they've been together for years, there's a good chance you can improve the relationship by doing a *reintroduction*. Details can be found later in this chapter.

If the behavior between the cats isn't consistently aggressive, or if the territorial aggression seems to just sit under the surface, you may not need to reintroduce them, but you'll need to make sure there's adequate space for each cat. That doesn't mean you have to add on a room—just make more use of vertical space, which will automatically increase the size of the territory. Increase the number of litter boxes in the home so that there's one for each cat and don't put them all in the same room. Place the litter boxes so that one cat doesn't have to cross over into another cat's area. This applies to the feeding station as well.

For a cat who displays aggression toward a companion cat returning from the veterinarian's office, place the returning cat in a separate room until she has time to groom herself and take on the familiar scents of the home. You can also rub the returning cat down gently with a towel that has first been rubbed on the cat who stayed home. Don't do this in the reverse order, because you don't want to spread the threatening scent. After the returning cat has had time to groom and get adjusted, you can reintroduce the cats by offering a meal or a treat.

Never leave cats alone to fight it out. There's a high risk of injury and the stress level that'll be created in the home can have a lasting effect that's devastating to everyone. The cats may never become friends if their first encounters with each other have been hostile. One cat may end up living in fear of the other and spend most of her days under the bed. Even the intimidating cat will live under stress with the constant worry of having to guard her territory.

Play aggression

You may be playing with your cat and suddenly notice that her behavior seems more aggressive than playful. She may bite or use her claws on your skin. This is often seen in cats who were taken away from their litter too early, robbing them of the lessons learned during social play with littermates. This behavior can also be unknowingly taught to the cat by a person through improper play techniques. If you use your fingers as toys, allow your cat to bite you, or wrestle with her, you're sending the message that *you* can treated as a toy or as prey. These inappropriate techniques may have seemed fine when the cat was a kitten, but now that she is an adult, she gets carried away and crosses over into aggression. Play aggression can also be brought on if your play technique is too energetic and you frustrate your cat by teasing her with a toy or waving it in her face. Although she wants to play, the movements of the toy may have her crossing in and out of aggression.

It's never too late to correct the way you play with your cat and teach her that biting is unacceptable. Reevaluate your play technique. If you've been using your fingers as toys or playing too aggressively with her, start using the interactive play techniques described in chapter 3. Keep a safe distance between her teeth and your hands by always using interactive toys. Do several play sessions a day to prevent her energy from building up over the course of the day to the point at which she gets too over-the-top when playtime finally does come around.

CATWISE REMINDER

Don't send mixed messages to your cat. Educate all members of the family not to use fingers, feet, or clothing as toys when playing with kitty.

If she does bite, use the technique previously described in this chapter by pushing toward her mouth rather than pulling away. Stop the game when she gets aggressive, let her calm down, and then restart at a more low-key level. If you're consistent, she'll learn the difference between the behavior that gets her what she wants and the behavior that ends the fun.

Predatory aggression

When a cat displays predatory behavior toward actual prey or a toy, it's normal. When she displays that behavior toward you, it's unacceptable. With predatory aggression, the cat displays stalking behavior toward you, attacks your feet as you walk, or pounces on your hands as they move. She'll display typical stalking behavior by hiding behind objects and then advancing with low-to-the-ground stalking motions. Her head remains still and her eyes are fixated on her target as she walks. There's nothing fun about this behavior, and in many cases the cat draws blood and causes painful injury. Being afraid of your cat isn't the type of relationship you want to have.

Cats who display predatory aggression need more appropriate outlets for their prey-drive. They need at least two interactive play sessions per day. With this type of cat, it's absolutely crucial that you wind the action down toward the end of the game to allow her to relax. Follow the game with a portion of her meal or a treat to show her that predatory behavior toward the appropriate object is filled with rewards.

Carry a squirt bottle with you during the initial retraining period, because there will probably be a few slipups that result in her reverting back to inappropriate predatory aggression. You can find small squirt bottles in the beauty-supply section of the discount store, and they're more convenient to carry around. Some of my clients even attach them to their belts with coiled stretch cords. When you notice your cat stalking you, give a quick squirt. If there are no other pets in the household, you can also use a small bicycle horn. Don't use a sound-generating aversive when there are other animals present. The sound could easily startle an unsuspecting pet who is doing nothing inappropriate.

To help your cat engage her normal predatory behavior between interactive play sessions, use puzzle feeders and tunnels, or hide toys in boxes and paper bags.

Put a bell on your cat's collar so you'll be more aware of her location during retraining.

Intercat aggression

This is a big one and it can have many causes. If you have an intact male, I can pretty much guarantee that you're dealing with some intercat aggression. He's either fighting with other cats in the home or, if you let him outdoors, engaging in battles with other males. Once your cat has reached sexual maturity, his main goals are to find females for mating and to fiercely defend his territory. Before any behavior modification can be put into place, the cat needs to be neutered.

Intercat aggression can rear its ugly head when you least expect it. You may have a multicat home in which everyone has gotten along well. Then suddenly things turn upside down. Social maturity, which happens between two and four years of age, can create conflict as cats become more concerned with their place in the pecking order.

Intercat aggression can be obvious, with lots of growling, fur flying, and fighting, or it can be less obvious, with lots of posturing and intimidation. If you notice a change in the relationship between your cats, it means more detective work needs to be done to figure out the cause so that you can apply appropriate behavior modification.

Confused About Whether Two Cats Are Playing or Fighting?

- When playing, there should be no growling, hissing, spitting, or screaming.
- Companion cats usually take turns being the mock aggressor in playtime.
- With aggression, ears are rotated back and flattened against the head.
- If companion cats who don't get along are wrestling, it's not play.
- Unfamiliar cats do not play together.
- Swatting with extended claws is a sign of aggression.
- Tufts of fur on the floor indicate the wrestling was aggressive.
- If the cats avoid each other after the encounter, it was aggressive.
- If one cat routinely chases the other away, it's not play.
- Any sign of injury or blood indicates aggression.

If you allow your cat outdoors, just because you don't see her engaging in intercat aggression doesn't mean it isn't happening. It's not unusual for an owner to be unaware of any conflict until the cat develops an abscess.

In a multicat home, be aware of the dynamics and don't disregard changes in relationships. Guarding, intimidation, stalking, hiding—these are just some of the clues that all isn't harmonious. Litter box problems can develop as a result of one cat intimidating another.

Make sure that there's adequate territory for the cats and that it's set up in a way that limits competition and intimidation. There should be multiple litter boxes spread throughout the home. Make use of vertical space and include multiperched cat trees to allow the cats to share space while maintaining their status. Watch for intimidation at the feeding station and set up multiple stations if needed.

Clicker training works well with intercat aggression problems. Once your cats have learned what the click sound means through individual training (see chapter 3), you can use it to mark good behavior as you retrain them to share space peacefully. Click and reward any positive behavior they display toward each other. For example, if the cats pass each other in the hallway without incident, you can click and reward. These baby steps that move them in the right direction keep reminding them that there's a benefit to good behavior. They'll eventually start displaying more positive behavior in the hope of hearing that click. In time, they'll likely move beyond whatever was creating tension in the relationship. They may never become the best of friends, but even if you get them only to the point of peaceful coexistence, that's a huge relief.

If one cat is consistently being the aggressor, put a bell on her collar to give the other cat advance warning of her presence.

CATWISE CAUTION

The assumption that feuding cats will "work it out" on their own often proves dangerous and counterproductive. You

risk injury to one or both cats and you may cause the relationship to continue to deteriorate instead of improve. Both
cats end up living under unnecessary stress.

Use *Feliway Comfort Zone* diffuser in the environment to help
each cat identify with the space in a more relaxed way. Locate the
diffuser in the part of the house where the cats spend the most time
together.

If the aggression is serious or if the cats are even unable to be in
the same room without tension, then the *starting from scratch* technique is needed in the form of a total reintroduction. Instructions
can be found later in this chapter.

Status-related aggression

A cat may display this aggression toward a specific person but not others in the home. This type of aggression also doesn't influence the
cat's own status within the multicat environment. Just because a cat
displays status-related aggression toward a human doesn't mean the
behavior will cause her companion cats to view her as higher-ranking.

Behavior can include stalking, direct stares, blocking a person's
path, and growling. The cat may accept affection from the person,
but only when it has been initiated by the cat. If the person attempts
to pet her first, the cat will bite or swat with her paw.

To retrain a cat displaying this behavior, get familiar with her
body language so you're more aware of when you're being stared at,
challenged, or blocked. If she's blocking your path to another room,
walk past her but have your squirt bottle ready. Don't let her win the
challenge by intimidating you away from the area. If she jumps onto
your lap and gives you a challenging direct stare, stand up so she'll
be released (gently) back down to the ground. Don't lift her off with
your hands, because that physical contact may trigger her to bite.
Your motion of removing her from your lap lets her know that she
can't successfully intimidate you.

If you free-feed her, switch to scheduled feeding. She's about to learn that nothing in life is free and that YOU are the source of her food and comfort. When you switch to scheduled meals, you can incorporate clicker training to give her a mission and help her focus on the good behavior you want. Make the clicker-training sessions fun and keep them short so she doesn't get frustrated. As she learns the connection between behavior and consequences, you'll see a change for the better.

Once she understands the clicker-training concept, you can use it to initiate petting and touching. Click and reward her when she accepts touching that you've initiated.

If the cat displays aggression toward another family member, you can do training sessions with your cat on a leash and harness. Don't use the leash and harness to yank your cat. You and your cat should be far enough away from the targeted family member so that the cat is within her comfort zone. The leash and harness are just to be used as an extra safety precaution. Provide your cat with treats or a portion of her meal when she's calm and relaxed in the presence of the family member. If using clicker training, click and reward any positive behavior. Work up to the point at which the family member (if old enough) is the one offering the treats or food. This may have to be at a distance, with the family member tossing a treat at the cat or placing a drop of wet food on a small plate in front of the cat. The family member shouldn't attempt to hand-feed the cat.

Incorporate twice-daily interactive play therapy sessions to help her work off her built-up energy, but also to continue the process of letting her see that you're the source of her fun. If another family member is the target, he or she should be the one conducting the play sessions. In some cases, you may have to work up to this by starting the game yourself and then handing off the toy.

Maternal aggression

This can be directed at humans or other animals if the queen feels her kittens are being threatened. Even a cat who was normally very gentle before giving birth can show aggression to protect her nest.

Make sure she has a quiet, safe place for herself and her kittens. Don't let other cats near the nest, especially males.

If the queen feels her nest isn't safe, she'll start moving her kittens, and the new location she chooses may not be where you'd prefer. Set up an area where she has a comfortable nest, a litter box, and her food and water. For specific information on preparations needed when a cat is due to give birth and how to do kitten training, refer to my book *Think Like a Cat* (published by Penguin). You should also seek the advice of your veterinarian.

Idiopathic aggression

This aggressive behavior is totally unprovoked and seems to have no identifiable cause. Idiopathic aggression is rare because if there isn't a behavioral cause for the aggression, there's usually an underlying medical cause. As previously mentioned, redirected aggression is often misidentified as idiopathic aggression because the source of the agitation isn't always visible to the owner.

Before labeling a cat as exhibiting idiopathic aggression, your veterinarian needs to do a complete workup, including more extensive diagnostic tests beyond routine blood tests. If the cause still can't be identified, you should seek the advice of a behavior expert.

THE *STARTING FROM SCRATCH* REINTRODUCTION TECHNIQUE

If you have feuding felines, it doesn't matter how long they've been fighting; it's time to stop going down the same dead end. Whether it has been just a few weeks or years, they've established a negative pattern that keeps feeding the tension. Stop what you're doing, let everyone take a breather, and then *start from scratch*—yes, even if they've known each other for years.

To start the reintroduction, you need to temporarily separate the cats who are fighting. This is an important step because it allows each cat to calm down and develop a sense of security within her environment again. It also stops the destructive cycle of aggression that has become the pattern.

How they should be separated takes careful consideration. If one cat is routinely displaying offensive aggression, then that cat should be separated into the less-premium area of the home. The intimidated cat should be given the run of the house or separated in the preferable area. If you put the offensive aggressor into the choice area, then she'll assume her bullying tactics worked when she no longer sees her victim around. The intimidated cat also needs to build up some confidence and establish a feeling of safety and comfort in the house. She'll start to do that as she realizes that she can walk around without fear of being ambushed.

If, however, the intimidated cat is too overwhelmed and frightened in the main part of the home, then she needs to be sequestered in a smaller room. The offensive aggressor still needs to be separated in a less-than-prime area, though. It may be inconvenient to have two cats sequestered in two different rooms, but this is the best way to do the reintroduction when one cat is terrified and the other is a bully.

The separation period is not a prison sentence, even though you may feel as if it should be for the aggressor. It is to let each cat calm down and regain a sense of security. Even though you may be frustrated with the aggressor, her behavior is due to feeling threatened, and that's very stressful. Both cats need loving behavior modification and in no way are deserving of any punishment. The cat who is separated is put into a "sanctuary" room. This room has all the necessary items, such as a litter box, food, water, toys, and a scratching post, but also hideaways and a perching area, if practical. Family members should go in to visit the cat regularly so she doesn't feel as if this is a punishment.

If the intimidated cat is in the choice area, it may take her a while to realize that her opponent isn't waiting around the corner to attack her. Encourage her with interactive play therapy, starting in the areas she's most comfortable and working up to the spots in the home where she may be more nervous. Eventually, you should see her begin to relax. She may start walking more in the center of the room than around the perimeter. Don't rush; let her enjoy this sense of freedom and comfort before you move on to the next step of the reintroduction.

Use the *Feliway Comfort Zone* diffuser in the main part of the house. In addition, some environmental modifications may need to be made before the actual reintroduction. Make sure there are plenty of escape options for when the two cats start sharing space again. You may need to move the sofa out from the wall a bit to create a tunnel behind it. If you currently have a cat tree, reevaluate its location to be sure it's in a common area that all the cats share. This way, the higher-ranking cat can go up there when she feels the need to show everyone who's boss without resorting to aggression. It can also allow the cats (when they're getting along better) to share a closer space while maintaining their pecking order. Make sure there are adequate hideaways so that a cat doesn't feel totally left out in the open when she enters the room. This can be as basic as using a tablecloth on the dining room table so it flows over the sides to create some degree of cover for a cat sleeping on one of the chairs. If you purchase cat beds, choose both semicovered and open ones so the cat can decide where she feels safest. She needs the security of not being ambushed as she naps. Some cats want to feel hidden in a covered bed while others prefer the option of multiple escape routes. Having *choices* gives cats much more security.

When the intimidated cat is feeling more confident, you can start the next phase of the reintroduction. Place her in another room temporarily and let the other kitty out for a brief tour of the house. Use the time to engage her in some interactive playtime so she doesn't just walk around the house looking for her victim. The interactive play therapy sessions will also help her change her association with these areas. Previously, just as with the intimidated cat, the main part of the house was essentially a battlefield. Through the interactive playtime and the fact that the other cat isn't there as a trigger, the area starts becoming one of fun and security.

After a good play session and some time to sniff around and deposit her scent, place the cat back in her sanctuary room and then bring the intimidated cat back out again. This brief outing for the aggressive cat is important because she's leaving a fresh scent in the area in addition to smelling the fresh scent of the victim cat. It's important for each cat to know the other one is still around but without the direct confrontation. Repeat this exercise several times a day to help the cats through the scent-recognition phase.

If each cat is handling that stage well, you can move on to the next step. Treat this stage as if the cats have never met each other before. The key is for them to see each other at a safe distance and for a very brief period. Use diversion to keep them only semifocused on each other. If there's another family member in the home, this will make the reintroduction process much easier because you can each concentrate on one cat. Open the door to the sanctuary room, armed with a small amount of delicious food for each cat. Let them eat their treats in sight of each other, but make sure they're far enough apart that they're within their comfort zones. Also, keep them far enough apart so that you have time to close the door if the situation gets tense. You can also have the more aggressive cat, or both cats, on a leash. Don't use a leash with a cat who hasn't been previously trained to one and isn't completely comfortable with it. To do so would heighten the cat's level of reactivity and make the situation worse. If one cat growls or stops eating and stares at the other cat, then they're too close together or just not ready for this phase yet. Close the door or lead one of the cats out of the area. Don't handle an aggressive cat or you'll risk injury to yourself.

Close the door to the sanctuary room as soon as the meal is over. Always try to end the session on a positive note. Do this step several times so they see that whenever they are in each other's presence, they get fed or they get extra treats. Use the clicker to click and reward any sign of positive behavior. If this stage is going well, you can gradually move the bowls closer together. This can be tricky, though, because you want to keep them in their individual comfort zones. Don't get daring and try to put the bowls close together right away. What you're trying to accomplish right now is for them to not shift into aggressive mode when they see each other. By feeding them small meals several times a day and incorporating clicker training, they're getting used to each other, and they're learning that if they don't display intimidating or challenging postures, there's a payoff—food!

When the feeding routines are going smoothly, you can move on to group-play therapy. In chapter 3, I talked about how group play involves the use of two toys. This is especially important when doing a reintroduction. If there's another family member, he or she should be on one side of the room with one cat and you on the other with the second kitty. If you're alone, don't move to this step unless you're sure the cats are comfortable being that close together. Keep the session short and positive. Don't try to stretch it out if things are going well. You'll risk one cat losing interest in the toy and locking the other cat into a stare-down.

As the cats get more comfortable in each other's presence, you can start to let them stay out together after their meal or the play session. Keep an eye on them, but do it in a casual way so it doesn't appear as if you're following them around; otherwise, they'll pick up on your anxiety and that can make them anxious as well.

When they're out and about, keep some interactive toys stashed in various rooms so you can be ready to distract them from each other if necessary. You can even keep a few furry mice or Ping-Pong balls in your pocket in case you have to toss one out as a distraction. Keep your clicker and treats ready as well so you can click and reward if they do something positive, such as pass closely by each other without showing any aggression or lie down on chairs in the same room.

You'll gradually build up the amount of time they spend together. Just because they get along for fifteen minutes doesn't mean they'll get along for an hour, so increase the time gradually over several subsequent sessions.

Distraction and redirection will be your main tools when your cats start spending greater amounts of time together. During retraining, you'll need to keep a supply of toys in various rooms so you can easily get to them if needed. I like using the *Cat Dancer* because it's easy to curl up and stash in a drawer or under a sofa cushion. It's also a very inexpensive toy, so you can keep one in each room the cats tend to occupy. When you need to distract and redirect, you don't want to be running down the hall trying to locate a toy.

Here's how the distraction-and-redirection method works. When the cats are out together in the main part of the house and you notice that one seems to be starting to stalk or stare at the other, distract her with the toy and redirect her away from her intended victim. A typical example is when one cat is sleeping on a chair and the other cat is walking toward her with the body posture of a kitty about to pounce. If you distract her with the toy, you'll trigger her prey-drive, which shifts her out of that aggressive mode and into the positive one of a hunter. Even though she may have been planning to attack her companion, she'd much rather go after the prey. Conduct an impromptu little interactive play session, moving her away from the other cat and allowing her to work out her tension in a positive, rather than aggressive, way. The victim cat remains safe and the aggressor gets to release all that anxiety. Everyone wins.

The good thing about the distraction-and-redirection method is that it's a positive way of retraining. Your previous method may have involved reprimanding the cats and separating them after one attacked the other. Even though that stops the fight for the moment, it doesn't give them a reason to like each other. This new method breaks the negative behavior pattern they've set up and gives them a reason to like each other because they're getting treats, meals, playtime, and lots of positive attention when the other cat is present. Use the clicker to accelerate the process by specifically marking and acknowledging the good behavior. The other good thing about this method is that if you were wrong in your assumption that one cat was about to stalk the other, the worst that happened is that she got a bonus play session. If you were using a negative method and you reprimanded the cat because you thought she was about to pounce and she really wasn't, then you've increased her anxiety and confusion.

There's one important caution with this method and it involves timing. You must use distraction and redirection *before* the aggressor starts the attack. If you use it to redirect her toward the toy after she has made contact with the other cat, you'll actually be reinforcing the very behavior you don't want. The earlier you can catch the behavior, the better. You know your cat, and if you really tune in to her body language and her patterns, I'll bet you can tell she's about to stalk the other cat as soon as the thought enters her head.

If you didn't get the chance to distract the cat in time and she makes contact with the other kitty, interrupt the fight by making a noise. Don't reach in there to physically separate them or you'll get injured. Clap your hands, bang two pans together—create some kind of a disruption so that they go their separate ways. Then, once they're apart, let them calm down in separate areas. If the fight was very bad, you'll have to take a few steps backward in the reintroduction process and maybe keep them separated again, bringing them together for meals or playtime only. Gauge this based on how well they were doing, what triggered the attack (you may have had them together for too long), and the severity of the fight.

The main reason for failure during the reintroduction process is that many people rush through it. If the cats have been feuding for years, the reintroduction will need to be very gradual. You aren't going to undo years of fighting in just a week of reintroduction. Think of the reintroduction process as wiping the slate clean and starting all over again. Although it requires more time, effort, and inconvenience on your part, you're giving your cats the wonderful gift of a second chance at their relationship. The time invested in doing so will help ensure a lifetime of peaceful coexistence.

OTHER USES AND VARIATIONS ON THE REINTRODUCTION TECHNIQUE

Once you know the basics of reintroduction and become more alert to the body language of your cats, you can use variations on it in other situations. A common example is when one cat goes to the veterinarian and the other cat stays at home. In the section on *territorial aggression* I described how to temporarily separate the cats and use scent to familiarize them with each other again. If the aggression is more severe and they don't seem to be back to their old selves, do a minireintroduction. It may not take weeks to reintroduce them, as it might if there are long-term aggression problems, but it might take a few days. In the case of redirected aggression, you can use the reintroduction technique to help them get beyond that traumatic episode.

Sometimes, when cats are extremely aggressive toward each other and you can't even get to the stage of having them see each other in the same room without fear of serious injury, you have to create a buffer zone. This will also keep the cats physically safe at this point. You can install a temporary screen door on the room where one cat is sequestered. This will allow the cats to see each other safely. A less expensive but more inconvenient method is to install three sturdy baby gates up the doorway, one on top of the other. If you do this, you can't just let the cat outside the room sit and stare at the sequestered kitty twenty-four hours a day. You still have to do the behavior modification where they're in each other's sight while eating, and you and a family member can still conduct group play sessions with one in the room and one outside the room. The cats still need that help in finding a reason to like each other. This interim step simply eliminates the risk of injury.

WHEN PROFESSIONAL HELP IS NEEDED

Aggression is scary. Whether it's directed at you or at another cat, it's frightening to see your cat displaying the behavior. It's especially frightening when you have no idea what caused it. There's professional help available to assist you if the aggression is severe or if you're unsure what type of behavior modification to use. You certainly don't want to get injured, nor do you want your cat to sink deeper into this behavior pattern. If you have children or elderly people at home with you, then you also have their safety to consider. A certified expert can help find the cause of your cat's aggression and work out an effective behavior modification plan.

There are many people out there who call themselves experts, but they can do more harm than good if they aren't professional and ethical. The way to start on the path toward getting professional help is to talk with your veterinarian. After your veterinarian gets an in-depth behavioral history from you, he or she may be able to refer you to a certified behavior expert. If your veterinarian doesn't know of a behavior expert in your area, you have several options. You can contact the behavior department of the veterinary university closest to you. You can also contact the International Association of Animal Behavior Consultants to see if there's a certified cat consultant near you. Through the Animal Behavior Society, you can find a certified applied animal behaviorist. Through the American College of Veterinary Behaviorists, you can find a veterinary behaviorist. Depending on the area in which you live, the behavior expert will either do a house call or have you bring your cat in for a clinic visit. If there are no certified experts close enough to you, there are many who do telephone consultations.

The idea of consulting with a certified behavior expert may seem strange or even intimidating to you. Many people don't even know that cat-behavior consulting is available. After all, who ever heard of training a cat, right? Well, it does exist, and with the help of a qualified professional who is *certified* in animal behavior, it can save the life of your cat. More information on finding professional help can be found in the appendix.

PSYCHOPHARMACOLOGICAL INTERVENTION

Nowadays, it seems as if you can't go a couple of days without hearing about a neighbor's or relative's pet being on Prozac or some other psychoactive medication. Whether it's the dog with separation anxiety or the cat who eliminates outside the litter box, it seems as if the answer is as quick as filling a prescription.

We have come a long way in behavior modification, and the use of psychopharmacology has been a tremendous help when prescribed and used appropriately. There are times when it takes the use of a particular drug to get a cat calm enough to be able to do effective behavior modification. The problem is that drugs get prescribed too quickly, without the veterinarian getting a thorough behavioral history, and some people just give their cats the medication and totally bypass behavior modification. I've seen so many cat owners who don't even know what type of psychoactive drug they're giving their cats, nor do they know what the potential side effects are, what the drug is supposed to do, or whether the cat must be weaned off the medication slowly. These are all things you should be informed of before you ever give medication to your cat.

If your cat is prescribed medication for a behavior problem, you need to stay in contact with your veterinarian and your certified behavior expert as you go through the behavior modification. Psychopharmacological intervention is a serious step to take, and your responsibility as a cat owner is to be informed and follow through on behavior modification. Otherwise, you're merely temporarily suppressing the unwanted behavior and potentially putting your cat's health at risk.

9

Why Can't We All Just Get Along?

Your Cat and Other Family Members

Relationships can be difficult. When you add multiple species into the mix, they can become downright overwhelming. There's so much to learn—you have to understand how your spouse communicates, how your cat communicates, and how your dog communicates. Not to mention ferrets, birds, hamsters, snakes, and all the other interesting family members we acquire. Then there are children—just when you think you understand *them*, they grow a year older and enter an entirely different phase—but that's a whole other book in itself.

Although I can't help you through the challenges of getting human family members to get along, I can help you ease your cat through some of those stressful family transitions. As much as you may try to create a low-stress environment for your cat, at some point in life, changes will probably occur in the family if they haven't already. Perhaps you've added a second cat and now there's a turf war going on, or maybe a new baby came into the family. You may even have had a whole new family come into your life in the form of a new spouse with children from a previous marriage. Regardless of whether the change happened quite a while ago or is just on the horizon, the proper behavior modification can ease much of the resulting stress and improve relationships between your cat and his new family members.

IS YOUR CAT MEANT TO BE THE ONLY CAT IN THE HOME?

Although companionship is wonderful for most cats, some are better off being the only cat in the home. If your cat is exceptionally territorial, aggressive, or terribly frightened of most things, he may not adjust well to sharing his turf with another feline.

The introduction of a second cat will initially be viewed negatively by just about any cat, but if your cat has had trouble adjusting to other changes in his life, regardless of how gradually you've introduced them, then he may not be a candidate for a companion. Think carefully about what's best for your cat before deciding to add to your feline family.

The decision to add a second cat shouldn't be made impulsively. A bad match may set both cats up for a lifetime of stress and behavior problems. If your cat currently has a behavior problem such as elimination outside the box, fear of strangers, or biting, you should work on correcting those issues before adding to his stress by introducing another kitty.

If you're concerned that your cat is lonely or bored but feel he wouldn't do well with a companion cat, use the behavior modification techniques described in this book to create a more stimulating environment, increase playtime opportunities, and recruit family members to take part in helping the cat stay active and occupied.

DISLIKE OR FEAR OF THE NEW CAT IN THE HOME

Starting from scratch with a proper introduction

Your intentions were the best when you decided to get a companion cat for your resident kitty. You thought he was lonely and would enjoy having a playmate to romp around with. Based on his reaction to the newcomer, though, you may be seriously doubting your decision. Maybe you haven't gotten the new cat yet but are dreading the moment when you bring him home because of the horror stories your friends have told about the times they added a cat to the household.

Even if the cats have been together for some time and you have only now realized that you incorrectly introduced the new cat, it's not too late. Just *start from scratch* and go back to the beginning as if they never met. It's much better to wipe the slate clean and begin the right way than to continue down the wrong road. Whether the cats have yet to see each other or have been in a standoff for a few hours, days, weeks, or months, if there's stress in the relationship, start over again.

How you introduce the new cat lays the groundwork for how the cats will view each other. If you just put the newcomer into the home, you're setting them both up to feel threatened, stressed, frightened, and hostile. Even if your resident cat was best buddies with a previous cat in the home, the introduction of an unfamiliar kitty must be done with finesse and sensitivity.

Cats are territorial and you have to understand their need for territorial security in order to do a successful introduction. Even at that, the introduction will have its ups and downs and your resident cat will have his doubts about the new situation or new family member. If introduced properly, however, those fears will be kept to a minimum.

CATWISE CAUTION

Before bringing a newcomer into the home, make sure he has been tested for contagious diseases, vaccinated, dewormed, and is otherwise in good health. If he isn't healthy, keep him separated until he is before exposing him to your resident cat. The newcomer also needs time to recuperate without the stress of dealing with an unfamiliar and hostile cat. Make sure your resident cat is also up-to-date on appropriate vaccinations and in good health before attempting an introduction.

The introduction must be gradual and positive in order to address the needs of both cats. The resident cat has a well-established turf, and if you just dump a newcomer into the room, your kitty will feel as if his home is being invaded. He'll view the newcomer as an intruder and will either run the stranger out or hide in panic now that his territory is no longer safe. The newcomer needs a gradual and positive introduction because he's being placed into a totally unfamiliar environment, which from his perspective is probably hostile, since there is already another cat there. If you put him in the middle of your home with no preparation, he has the overwhelming task of finding his way around, determining how hostile his opponent is, and attempting to find some unclaimed turf in which to remain safe. Failing that, he's likely to issue a preemptive strike and be the first one to show hostility. For both cats, abrupt introductions will cause them to go into survival mode, and they'll start out their relationship being hostile toward each other. While in some cases that hostility may ease as time goes on, it more often sets the tone for the relationship from that point on. The two cats often don't become comfortable with each other because every encounter they have is hostile. It's unfair to put either cat through such an unnecessarily stressful experience. There's a much easier way, and it's not too late to do it, even if both cats have already declared war.

Start by setting up a sanctuary room for the newcomer. Ideally, this should be done before the new cat even comes into the home. Have his litter box on one side of the room and his food and water bowls on the other. The litter and food should not be close together. This room should also contain a scratching post. Even if you already have a scratching post for your resident cat, you'll need another one for the newcomer. After the introduction is done, the cats may still prefer to scratch on separate posts. You can also put a corrugated cardboard scratching pad in the sanctuary room in case the new kitty enjoys horizontal scratching.

Place a *Feliway Comfort Zone* plug-in diffuser in the room or spray

Feliway spray on the corners of objects to help the newcomer feel at ease with the unfamiliar environment more quickly.

Provide elevated areas and hideaways for the new kitty. This way, if he feels more secure being up high, or if he's relaxed enough to perch somewhere to look out the window, he can do that. The hideaways are in case he feels totally overwhelmed and prefers being hidden. You can create hideaways by putting boxes on their sides and lining them with towels. You can even turn the boxes upside down and cut out an opening so the cat can feel totally hidden.

If the sanctuary room is a bedroom, it's very important to provide additional hideaways so the kitty doesn't spend all his time hiding under the bed. If he's very nervous, create a couple of tunnels in the middle of the room so he can more comfortably go from one side of the room to the other. This way, he may feel more at ease when walking to the litter box or food bowl. You can create tunnels by connecting paper bags or boxes, or you can buy soft-sided cat tunnels.

Don't forget the toys! Although the newcomer may not feel comfortable enough to bat a fuzzy mouse around the room initially, there should still be some irresistible toys placed in there for him.

If you have a radio in the room, play some soft music just to serve as a buffer from the unsettling noises he may hear outside the door. If your cat meows outside the door he'll still hear it, but the radio may ease the sound just a bit.

When you bring the newcomer home, bring him directly into the sanctuary room without stopping to show him to your resident cat or letting the family greet him in the hallway. Just casually come into the house and bring the kitty into the room. He should be in a carrier and not loose in your arms to avoid any risk of having him leap from your arms on the way to the room.

Once inside the room, close the door behind you and place the carrier down. Open the carrier door, but don't pull the cat out or turn the carrier upside down to force him to come out. If he's afraid, let him stay in the carrier with the door open. He'll come out when he feels comfortable. He may need time to get his bearings, and that's usually best done within the safety of the carrier.

If the cat is very frightened, leave him alone in the room so he can start to venture out of the carrier without having to worry about your being there. Depending on how frightened he is, he may stay in the carrier for the rest of the day, or he may come out the minute you leave the room. Give him that time to check out his new surroundings, use the litter box in private, and maybe nibble on some food. If he's not frightened at all, he may walk right out of the carrier. In that case, spend a few minutes with him, but then leave him alone to check out his sanctuary room.

CATWISE CLUE

If you're bringing in an adult cat who was in a previous home or a shelter, initially use the same type of litter that he's used to in order to avoid overwhelming him with too many changes at once. You can then gradually switch him to the litter you prefer by adding a little at a time to his current brand.

The same applies to his food. If he was used to a certain type of food, start with that and make any transition gradual to avoid upsetting his stomach or increasing his stress.

It's not cruel to leave the newcomer in the room alone right now because he has a whole new environment to get familiar with in there. He'll be busy for a while. During that time, you need to check on what's happening on the other side of that door, where your resident cat may be sitting and wondering what the heck is going on.

Even though you can't totally remove the scent of the newcomer, wash your hands before greeting your resident cat. If you held the newcomer in your arms, change your shirt. One tip I always give my clients is to keep a bathrobe in the sanctuary room so you can slip that on over your clothes when you're in there holding the new cat. You'll still have the scent of the newcomer on you, but it won't be so over-whelming to your resident cat. This tip is most important if your resident cat reacts aggressively toward the slightest scent of an unfamiliar cat on you. Use *Feliway* in the diffuser or spray form in your resident cat's environment, especially near the door to the sanctuary room.

When you greet your resident cat, keep it light and casual. Don't cuddle him and show an unusual amount of affection toward him. Greet him as you normally would if you had walked into the house without a new kitty.

Be aware that your cat may show redirected aggression toward you if he's very agitated by the sound or scent of the new cat in the environment. Look for the signs and don't reach down to pet him or attempt to pick him up if he's growling, hissing, or displaying an aggressive body posture. In that situation, the best thing you can do is to walk away from him and let him calm down. If he's just mildly agitated, you can go into the kitchen and prepare a meal for him, or distract him away from the sanctuary room door with a low-key interactive play therapy session.

Depending upon how agitated your resident cat is and/or how reactive the newcomer is, you may have to stay at this sequestered stage for a while. Every cat is different, so don't be discouraged if your cat is much more reactive at this early phase than the cat of a friend who did an introduction.

After both cats get over the initial shock of knowing there's *something* on the other side of the sanctuary room door, you can move on to the next step. Since scent communication is extremely important to cats, you're now going to let them gather some information about each other in a safe, controlled way. Take a clean sock, gently rub the newcomer around the mouth and head, then give the sock a quick spritz with *Feliway*. Take *another* sock (make sure you aren't using the same sock), rub your resident cat in the same way, and give it a spritz of *Feliway* as well. Deposit the sock containing the new-comer's scent in your resident cat's space. Don't place the sock in a much-cherished area, such as where your cat sleeps or where the litter box is located, but rather in an area that's relatively neutral. Place the sock with your resident cat's scent in the newcomer's sanctuary room in a similarly neutral area. One or both of the cats may react with only mild curiosity or may show aggression or fear while sniffing the socks. This is an important step because it allows them to gather information while avoiding the risk of an actual confrontation. In addition, the pheromones that you gathered on the socks by rubbing the cats around the mouth are the friendly, non-threatening ones (made all the more so by the addition of *Feliway*), so the cats are not gathering indications of hostility from each other, as they might have if they came across the other cat's urine-mark.

The scented socks also give you valuable information because you'll be able to get an idea of how slowly or quickly to progress with the introduction. If one of the cats goes ballistic, then you know you'll be doing the snail's pace version of a new-cat introduction.

Continue with the scented-sock stage until the cats seem more comfortable. Then take a tiny bit of soiled litter from your resident cat's litter box and place it in the newcomer's box. Only do this once he's relatively comfortable with the scented sock. Do the same with the resident cat, but make sure you're using a very small amount of soiled litter. You don't want to create a litter box aversion problem by putting too much in there.

When everyone seems ready for the next step, place your resident cat in a separate room so you can start to introduce the newcomer to the house. You need to do this in a controlled way so he feels comfortable. That's why your resident cat must be sequestered somewhere.

Once the resident cat is safely secluded, open the door to the sanctuary room and let the newcomer start to investigate the rest of the house. He may want to take only a few steps beyond the threshold, or he may be confident enough to explore everything. In a large home, keep several doors closed so you can control where he goes. This will keep him from being overwhelmed or hiding under a bed.

If he's nervous, confine the exploration to the area immediately outside the sanctuary room and use an interactive toy to keep him distracted, or if he doesn't want to play, offer some food or a treat. Keep the atmosphere calm and casual. If he seems too nervous or starts to get too stressed, cut the session short. It's better to do short sessions that end calmly rather than try to get him to check out the entire home at once, which could cause him to become panicky or agitated.

This exploration is important for the newcomer because he can check things out in safety, but it also serves other valuable functions. As the newcomer explores, he's gathering more information from the scents of your resident cat and he's depositing his own scent around the house.

If the newcomer doesn't do much facial rubbing on objects as he ventures around, you can help him the next time. When he's in his sanctuary room, gently rub him on the cheeks and along the sides of the mouth with a soft sock. Then, with the sock on your hand, rub the corners of objects in the main part of the house. Rub at the approximate nose height of the cats to make it easy for them to come across the scents. Rub just a few objects and pick ones that are close to his sanctuary room. Even if you're using *Feliway* spray, you should do the pheromone sock rub if the newcomer isn't rubbing on his own. This will deposit scents that will allow your resident cat to gather information and get used to the fact that the newcomer is starting to expand his area.

You'll have to judge how often to do this before moving on to the next step, depending on how the newcomer and your resident cat handle the exploration. Again, each cat is an individual, so don't be concerned with a specific time frame. This step may last a day, several days, a week, a month, or more. The specifics of your situation, the personalities of the cats, their level of socialization, and what, if any, trauma the newcomer endured before being adopted by you must all be factored in.

After the scent stage, move on to the visual phase. Food is a great motivator, so use it as one of your behavior modification tools in this process. Open the door to the sanctuary room a crack and let the cats see each other as you offer them each a meal. If there's another family member in the home, one person can be in the sanctuary room while the other stays outside the room with the resident cat. If you're alone, situate yourself between the resident cat and the sanctuary door so you can close it quickly if necessary. The cats need to be far enough apart so they each stay within their comfort zones and so you'll have time to close the door before they make contact with each other. As soon as the meal is over, close the door again. Do this exercise for every meal. This is where scheduled feeding works to your advantage because the cats will be hungry whenever you do the training session. You can even divide up the food into smaller portions so you can increase the number of daily sessions. You can also use treats when the cats see each other.

As the cats get more comfortable with each other, you can open the door more during the meals and move the bowls closer together. Be conservative in how close you put the bowls, though. A common mistake people make is to put them too close too soon, prompting the cats to become aggressive. If you put the bowls closer to each other and the cats stopped eating, then you went a little too fast.

Having the cats eat while in sight of each other teaches them that good things happen when the other cat is around. This positive association is the start of helping them find a reason to like each other.

 CATWISE **CLUE**

When the newcomer is out of his sanctuary room, never close the door behind him. He needs the security of knowing he can dash back in there at any time.

After you've had success with the food phase, you'll be able to add the toy phase. Open the sanctuary room door so the cats see each other. Have an interactive toy in your hand so you can be ready to distract someone if tensions start to build. During introductions I also keep a couple of Ping-Pong balls handy so I can roll one in a certain direction to divert one cat's attention away from the other kitty. I especially like using a Ping-Pong ball if the cats are on a hard surface such as a hardwood or tile floor because it makes an interesting sound. You can also use a crinkly Mylar ball for distraction. Scrunch it between your fingers to make an enticing sound before tossing it. Use an interactive toy as well, as a way to keep each cat in a more positive focus. If the cats are handling the sight of each other well, you can have a toy in each hand and conduct a group play session—a very short one—or you can have another family member play with one cat while you play with the other. Each session in this toy phase needs to be short and positive. It's always better to end it sooner than you think you really need to. Always be armed with treats as well, so that you can toss those to the cats if things are going well. I wear a trainer's treat bag (or fanny pack) when doing introductions so that I have treats and small toys conveniently ready for my use. If you planned ahead and clicker-trained your resident cat, click and reward any positive behavior.

Keep a toy handy for distraction as the cats start spending more time out in the main part of the house together. Don't panic if there's a little hissing or if one cat gets a little too close and the other cat retreats. They do eventually have to start to get to know each other. You just want to keep the interaction calm. Eventually, as they learn that the appearance of the other cat means food and/or playtime, they'll start to develop a more positive association. It may start out as mere tolerance at first, but that's a tremendously successful step when you consider that they didn't pick this pairing—*you* did. We ask so much of cats when we decide who will be their companions and how small or large a space they must share. They have much to work out in terms of negotiating who will claim certain pieces of furniture or rooms in the house, how they'll

share time with you, how close they want to be to each other, and so
forth.

Until you are absolutely sure the cats are comfortable with each
other, you should always be there to supervise when the newcomer
is out of his sanctuary room. As they start spending more time together, you may need to watch them only casually in case too much
tension mounts. At that point, they may not need to be separated;
they may just need a little distraction. This is something you can
do by keeping interactive toys stashed in every room so you can
easily grab one. Refer to chapter 8 for specific information on how
to use distraction and redirection on an as-needed basis when the
cats are together for longer periods. Strike a healthy balance between helping them find reasons to like each other and letting
them handle some negotiations according to proper cat etiquette.
You may find yourself confused about whether your two cats are
engaging in play or are being aggressive with each other. Sometimes playtime wrestling can look aggressive or can start out
friendly and turn aggressive. Refer to chapter 8 for a general list of
indications.

Even after you get to the point at which the cats are together 24/7,
keep the sanctuary room set up for a while until you're sure the newcomer no longer feels the need for it. Even after the cats have been
sharing space, the newcomer may still enjoy the security of having a
room that has been clearly designated as his. The litter box in the
sanctuary room should also remain there as long as the cat continues to use it. Even after you get to the point at which you don't feel
the need for the sanctuary room, the cats will still need to have two
litter boxes (or more if you have more than two cats). Don't put the
litter boxes in the same room—make sure you place one in an area
where the newcomer is clearly comfortable. That may end up being
the room where his sanctuary was originally set up or just outside it.
If you do end up moving it away from the sanctuary room, make the
move gradual by doing it a few inches a day so he doesn't lose track
of it or cease to identify it as his.

DOG PANIC

I hate the saying "fighting like cats and dogs," because it leads so many people to believe the two species are born to be enemies. Cats and dogs can have wonderful relationships with each other if they're introduced properly and trained correctly. That being said, if you didn't do individual training and a proper introduction, you may have inadvertently turned your home into a battlefield. An untrained animal, regardless of whether it's the cat or the dog, will create stress for himself and others around him and is at risk of being injured or causing injury.

Whether you're dealing with aggression or fear or both, the first step is to stop allowing the behavior that's causing the deterioration of the cat-dog relationship. Separate the cat and the dog so you can do some individual evaluation and training.

If you're dealing with a cat who absolutely panics at the sight of the dog, but also panics at the sight of just about everything else in his environment, then you need to do some work with him individually to build his sense of security and confidence. You can't expect him to coexist peacefully with a dog if he's too distracted by his overall fear of numerous other things. Refer to chapter 4 for retraining tips for dealing with fearful cats.

Does the cat have problems with aggression? Does he growl or hiss at anyone who comes near him? Then some work has to be done to help him feel less threatened overall so that he can be open to the idea of life with a dog companion. Use the information in chapter 8 to figure out what the underlying cause of his aggression is so that you can do the necessary behavior modification.

The same thing applies to the dog. He can't be expected to respond favorably to the cat if he's a bundle of nerves or if he has a short fuse. This is why individual training is crucial prior to the reintroduction of the two animals.

Use the time that both animals are separated to reevaluate their individual personalities and needs and determine if there have been gaps in their training, or no training at all. Is your dog trained to respond to voice commands? Does he know "Come," "Sit," "Stay," "Down," "Leave it," or any other basic commands that are necessary to have a well-trained dog who is a pleasure to live with? Does he walk nicely on a leash or does he pull and tug? Are you unable to physically restrain your large-breed dog? You absolutely must have him trained to obey voice commands. Is your little dog a bundle of energy that barks, runs around, and is in everyone's face (especially the cat's) twenty-four hours a day? You must look at what improvements need to be made to your pets' behavior on an individual basis before you can ever expect them to get along together.

Part of the reason why your cat and dog aren't getting along may be the fact that they don't really speak the same language and misread each other's cues. Cats often need more personal space, and your dog may be unaware that he has crossed the line. Dogs and cats also don't share the same play techniques, and they can be misinterpreted. Dogs play by chasing and wrestling. If your cat runs away in fear, that may be interpreted by the dog as a play signal. The more the cat runs, the more the dog chases.

Maybe your dog is frightened of the cat because every time he ventures close he is met with a swipe across the nose. It can be confusing for both animals if certain ground rules aren't set and proper training implemented.

Start by doing basic training with your dog. Whether you take him to a class, have a training expert come into your home, or do it yourself by following instructions in a book, this needs to be done. It doesn't matter whether you're dealing with a puppy or an adult dog, it's not too late to make corrections in unwanted behavior. Your dog wants to please you, and he's very smart, so if the training is done correctly and with lots of love and patience, he'll be receptive.

Just as with cats, dogs respond to pheromones, and there's a product that can be used in the home to help a dog who is nervous or anxious. *D.A.P.* is the canine version of *Feliway*. It stands for dog-appeasing pheromone and contains a synthetic version of the pheromones of a lactating female. It was created to help dogs with separation anxiety. The product is available at pet supply stores, through veterinarians, and online. If your dog is frightened of the cat or even just nervous in general, you may find that using *D.A.P.* helps his sense of security and makes the introduction process a little less stressful. It is available as a plug-in diffuser. Use *D.A.P.* in the room where you're doing the dog-cat introduction as well as in the area where your dog spends most of his time.

When reintroducing a dog and cat, I like to use clicker training. The idea behind the session is to show the dog that he gets rewarded when he relaxes and doesn't pay attention to the cat. Use the clicker and treats every time he displays a positive behavior. The message you want to send is that there are benefits to good behavior. Even if the attention he wants to give the cat is playful from his point of view, if it isn't welcomed by the cat, then the dog has to learn *proper cat protocol*. It may not seem fair that the dog has to learn the cat's language, but since most cats have a greater need for personal space, it makes life much easier for everyone if the dog adjusts to that.

The message the cat receives during these retraining sessions is that he doesn't have to be terrified when the dog is in the room. Over subsequent sessions, he'll see that the dog doesn't intrude into his space, bark at him, or seem to be a threat in any way. As a result, he doesn't have to show defensive behavior toward the dog. Soon your dog and cat will start to see each other in a new light. The tools you'll need are lots of tasty dog treats and cat treats, toys, and your trusty clicker.

Before the session, make sure the nails of both the cat and the dog have been recently trimmed. Take the dog outside to play so he can work off his excess energy and be more relaxed for the retraining session. Once you've tired the dog out a bit, take him into the room where the cat is located. Have the dog on a leash and take him to the side of the room opposite where the cat is. Get your dog relaxed and focused on you and not the cat. Having the dog on a leash gives you more control. Have the cat loose in the room. In most cases, the cat will just stay on the other side of the room. If the cat is absolutely terrified and won't stay in the room or if he's so aggressive that he attacks the dog the second he sees him, then place him in a carrier. Make the determination on whether to have your cat in the carrier based on your individual kitty. Some cats will feel more secure in the carrier while others may feel trapped. If he's loose, make sure he has a safe place, such as a cat tree or box or bag turned on its side, where he can feel somewhat protected. If there's another family member available, have him or her concentrate on one animal while you concentrate on the other.

Cue the dog to sit or put him in a down stay. Have him face the cat slightly sideways so the kitty doesn't feel he's being stared at directly. As your dog relaxes and doesn't focus on the cat, reward him with a treat and praise. If he lunges toward the cat, pulls on the leash, or growls, give a mild correction and get his focus back on you. When he responds to your cue, click and reward if you're using clicker training. Click and reward anytime your dog shows relaxation, is quiet, or comes to you when called. If you have a chew toy, you can use that if he enjoys curling up next to you with his toy. Use this method only if he relaxes with the chew toy and doesn't become hyper, possessive, or aggressive. If you have a dog who is absolutely out of control with barking, yapping, or tugging at the leash, he should be kept in a dog crate for the initial sessions. Click and reward any moments of calm and quiet.

If the dog isn't the problem and sits perfectly still, but the cat is the aggressive one, use the above technique toward the cat. Put the dog and cat far enough apart so your cat is able to relax. Start him off in a carrier and click and reward any quiet or calm behavior. In future sessions you can gradually decrease the distance between them. If your cat is leash-trained, you can also have him on the far side of the room on a leash in subsequent sessions.

If the cat is so terrified that he has to be in a carrier, after a few sessions you can try opening the door to the carrier. If you're clicker training, use a target stick to entice your cat to stick his nose out at it.

Otherwise, place a treat at the threshold of the carrier or offer him a portion of his meal. Don't ask him to step too far out of the carrier if he prefers to remain inside. This process must be very gradual and you have to move at the pace of the most frightened of the two animals.

CATWISE CAUTION

It is easy to revert to incorrect training methods when you feel nervous during the introduction. You may be tempted to bribe the dog or cat by offering a treat when one displays aggression or shows fear. *Don't reinforce unwanted behavior.* Identify the behavior you want, create an environment that encourages success, and then reward positive steps.

Your midway goal is to get to the point at which the animals can be in the same room without focusing on each other. They can look at each other, but they shouldn't be staring or concentrating on each other. Use an interactive toy to distract the cat, and use clicker training and/or a toy to distract the dog.

CATWISE CAUTION

Never leave a cat and dog together unsupervised until you've done all the necessary training and are sure they get along. In some cases, despite proper training, the dog and cat may never be able to be left alone together. If you're unsure, consult a certified trainer or behavior expert for an evaluation.

Some environmental modifications may need to be made in order to help ensure a peaceful coexistence. The litter box setup must be completely off-limits to the dog because the last thing your cat needs is to be surprised by a canine face as he's trying to take care of business. Even if the dog's intentions are friendly, they won't be appreciated during that time. Some dogs develop a taste for the solid cat waste (strange, but true) and have been known to visit the litter box for between-meal snacks. It is not only extremely unpleasant for the cat to come to the box and find his waste strewn all over the place, including the floor, but it's also not healthy for your dog. If the cat has covered his feces with litter, then your dog is ingesting that as well, which isn't good for him. So for many reasons, the cat's litter box is just not a dog-friendly place. Part of your retraining process with your dog should involve training him to stay away from the litter box. Don't take the shortcut route and use a covered box as a way of bypassing training. The covered box is not a good idea for the cat (refer to chapter 5), and I have seen many large dogs get their heads stuck in the box entrance, knock the lid off, or simply take their paws and scoop the litter onto the floor until they get to the buried *treasure*.

If your dog doesn't get that close to the box but still sits too close for the cat's comfort, create a no-dogs-allowed room for the cat where the litter box can be kept. Train the dog that he isn't allowed to cross the threshold into the room. You can also use a baby gate in the doorway. Place a medium-sized heavy box or other object on the other side of the gate so the cat has a landing pad when he jumps the gate. Even if you have a large dog who could easily hop the gate, use it in combination with training so he knows that it is off-limits. The presence of the gate may also provide some added security for the cat when he sees the dog on the other side rather than just in the open doorway.

If you have a dog who is larger than your cat, put the baby gate in the doorway with a cat-sized square opening cut out in the middle or at the bottom of the gate. The opening size must be much smaller than the size of the dog's head to prevent him from getting his head stuck there. Instructions for this can be found in chapter 5. This way, the cat can go in and out and still have lots of visual warning time, and yet the dog can't get through the opening if you did your measurements correctly.

Mealtime may be another stumbling block in the relationship between your cat and dog. Cat food is higher in fat and protein than dog food, and some dogs find it much more appetizing than what's in their own food bowls. It won't help the relationship if the dog is pushing the cat out of his own bowl. If you feed on a schedule, use this as a training opportunity. Stay in the room with the cat and dog so you can keep everyone at their own locations. Mealtime can also be used to help them continue to form positive associations with each other. If the cat is frightened, elevate his food bowl so he has a safe location to eat, but be certain he can access it easily, or feed the animals in separate areas. If you free-feed, make sure the dog isn't getting into the cat's food. Elevate the cat's feeding station or keep his food in a room off-limits to the dog. If you set up a no-dogs-allowed room for the cat's litter box and you want to put his food in there as well, it needs to be far away from the litter. Place the food and water on the opposite side of the room. If it's a very small room, elevate the feeding station to create more distance, but make sure it's easy for the cat to get to, especially if he's older, overweight, or less mobile for any other reason.

BIRDS, HAMSTERS, AND OTHER SMALL PETS

A cat is a hunter, and his instincts tell him that a bird, hamster, small rabbit, or other tiny pet is potential prey. Your cat isn't being vicious or jealous, he's being a cat. It isn't fair to expect predator and prey to coexist together peacefully. Even if your cat can't reach the birdcage or hamster cage, it's stressful for those little creatures to live with the constant threat of a nearby predator. Don't cause unnecessary stress to either your cat or your other little pets by trying to get them to live together. A tragedy could happen in the blink of an eye.

If you share your home with pets who could be viewed as potential cat prey, keep them in a totally separate room that your cat can't access. Make sure everyone in the family understands the importance of keeping these pets apart.

WHEN THE NEW BABY CREATES KITTY CRISIS

Adding a precious new baby to the family can be one of the happiest times of your life, but it is also a time when you're exhausted and stressed. The last thing you need is for your cat to go into crisis mode and react negatively to the newest family member.

If the baby isn't home yet

If you're fortunate enough to have some time before your cat and your baby meet for the first time, then there are some advance preparations you can make to help ensure an easier adjustment. Start by doing the nursery decorating and furniture purchasing gradually so your cat has time to get used to each change. This is especially important if the room that'll become the nursery is currently the room the cat considers his own. I have had many clients who planned on turning their extra guest room into a nursery, but had previously been keeping the cat's litter box in there. If that's the case with you, place a second litter box in another location well before you start the nursery decorating. Then start moving the original litter box toward the new litter box location a few inches a day. When the original box is in the new location next to the second box, you can get rid of one of them. If your kitty also loves napping in the guest room, set up an inviting location somewhere else in the home. A cat tree by a sunny window or a padded window perch is usually hard for a cat to resist. Once the cat is totally comfortable with the new litter box location and cozy napping area, you can start the nursery preparation.

Don't do everything at once. If you're painting or wallpapering, don't do that the same weekend that you rip up or install the carpet. Let your cat adjust to one change at a time. Take several breaks during the decorating process to do interactive play sessions with your cat as well.

If your cat has trouble adjusting to new furniture in the home, spray the corners of the crib or other baby furniture with *Feliway*. You can also put a clean sock over your hand, gently rub your cat

around the mouth, and then rub the sock on the corners of the furniture at cat height.

Large baby equipment that moves or makes noise, such as swings
or exersaucers, can be unsettling for some cats. If you think your cat
might be skittish around these objects, set some of them up at least a
couple of weeks in advance of the baby's arrival so your cat can
calmly investigate them. Turn the swing on so it's gently swaying
back and forth while you conduct an interactive play session with the
cat on the other side of the room. For something like an exersaucer
or another toy, touch the object gently so it makes noise. Your touch
should be much lighter than the baby's will eventually be so that you
can ease your cat into feeling comfortable with the sound.

The sound of a crying baby can be very scary for a cat. If you have
a neighbor or friend who has a baby, ask if she'll record the crying
sound so you can play it softly in the background for your cat as you
conduct interactive play sessions. Also, invite a friend over who has
an infant so your cat can get used to the sight, sound, and smell of a
baby. It's preferable to do this at a time when the baby is happily
sleeping or otherwise quiet, so that your cat's experience is positive
and not negative.

Another trick to help a cat adjust to the upcoming changes in his
life is to have the expectant mother start wearing baby powder and
baby lotion. If you start wearing the scents that your baby will soon
have, it may help your cat more quickly identify the newcomer as a
member of the family.

Once you've set up the crib, your cat may decide to use it as a
place to nap. There are techniques you can use to retrain this behavior well before the baby arrives. Get some empty soda cans and plastic bottles and place a few pennies in each one. Securely tape over
the openings of the cans and tightly replace the caps on the bottles.
Place the cans and bottles in the crib so that your cat can't really find
a comfortable spot to curl up in without disturbing them and making
noise. Use enough bottles and cans so that he can't move them aside
to find a place to curl up. Keep the crib this way until right before you

bring home your baby. As an alternative to the cans and bottles, you can also place an *X-Mat* in the crib. This flexible mat is covered with uncomfortable bumps that'll make it too unpleasant for your cat to want to lounge on the crib's mattress. Another option is to use a crib tent, which I think is a good idea for many reasons. The *Cozy Crib Tent* is one that's very well made and will come in handy later on when your baby starts trying to climb out of the crib. With my son, who showed the ability to climb in and out of just about anything at a very early age, the crib tent gave me tremendous peace of mind. The product is widely available at stores and online.

Another age-old trick for helping your cat adjust to a newborn is to have a family member bring home a blanket or piece of clothing with the baby's scent on it from the hospital. This may be hard to re-member to do amid the excitement over your new arrival, but if you remember to do this, it can be very helpful. If you do remember, don't force the blanket in the cat's face. Just place it on the carpet in the nursery or just outside the nursery. When the cat goes up to sniff it, if he reacts calmly, reward him with a treat. Have your clicker with you so you can click and reward if he sniffs and stays calm.

CATWISE CAUTION

Many people make the mistake of showing their cats an overabundance of attention during the mother's pregnancy but are unable to maintain that schedule after the arrival of the baby. This is extremely confusing and stressful to the cat. Maintain a schedule of affection, attention, and playtime that your family will be able to continue once the baby is home.

After the bundle of joy arrives

Even if you tried to prepare your cat well in advance of the baby's ar-rival, he may not be as receptive as you'd hoped when he realizes the little baby isn't just visiting—he's *staying*. If you didn't do any advance preparation, then your cat has been completely blind-sided by this event.

Cats don't like abrupt changes, and the addition of a new baby involves many major changes. The new little person sounds and smells totally unfamiliar, and if the cat isn't used to the sound of a wailing baby, it can be very unsettling. This new arrival also usually marks a total shift in the cat's normal routine. Time that was previously devoted to the cat is now devoted to the baby. If you made the well-intentioned mistake of giving your cat an overabundance of affection and attention during the pregnancy, then you're probably now dealing with a cat who is confused by your sudden lack of interest.

Playtime, an important part of the cat's daily routine and a time the two of you spent together, might now be cut severely or even cut out altogether. Due to the baby's schedule, your cat might also be getting his meals late or having his litter box cleaned less often.

Because of the fears associated with cats and babies, your cat might find himself shut out of your life in drastic ways. Some people believe their cats are no longer clean enough to have around their babies, so they banish them from rooms they're used to being in, confine them to unappealing areas such as the basement or garage, or even turn them into exclusively outdoor cats. Even if you haven't banished your cat, if you've reprimanded him out of fear when he approached the baby or the crib, you can't blame him for being anxious and unhappy about this latest arrival.

Your cat may be naturally curious about that warm, cuddly sleeping baby in the crib. He might even enjoy curling up next to the infant. When that results in panic and anger from the parents, it only creates confusion in the cat. You don't want your cat to feel as if he's misbehaving by wanting to check out the baby. You do, however, need to keep the baby safe in the crib. Common sense should prevail. You should keep the cat out of the crib because the newborn may not be able to roll over if the cat is in the way. You also don't want your infant to risk being scratched unintentionally. Many cats, when in a warm, soft environment, begin to knead with their paws, and their claws can extend just enough to prick the delicate skin of the baby. A sudden move from the baby could also startle the cat and he might unintentionally scratch.

Your cat isn't the only thing that shouldn't be in the crib; because of the risk of suffocation, there shouldn't be anything in there—not even a blanket, pillow, or toy. If the problem is that the cat won't stay out of the crib, it's easy to install a crib tent over the top. In my house the ear-splitting sound of a baby crying was the most effective deterrent of all for keeping the cats out of the crib.

It isn't just the arrival of the baby that creates anxiety in the cat, there are other stress-producing events that go along with the appearance of that noisy, hairless being. Think of all the stuff you have to go along with the baby. If you didn't prepare your cat for the transition by easing him through the changes, then his anxiety may have started several months before the baby even showed up. You may not have even been aware of it because of your own stress or excitement in preparing for the baby. If you kept the cat out of the nursery altogether or weren't aware of signs that he was becoming slightly anxious about all the changes, then by the time the baby came along, your cat may have been ready for a kitty meltdown.

If your cat tends to be sensitive or skittish around sudden noises and you didn't prepare him for life with an exersaucer or sound-generating toy, life might have become pretty unsettling for him. Imagine how startling it must be for him to walk by just as the baby in the bouncy seat kicks the swinging noisemaker or tosses his noisy rattle to the floor. In his previous life with you, your cat never had to deal with such things. Now he never knows what's going to happen from one moment to the next.

Another thing that accompanies the arrival of a newborn baby is a sudden onslaught of visitors to the home. If you were already dealing with a cat who was afraid of company or was aggressive toward visitors, this really puts his patience to the test. If your cat is skittish or nervous, set him up in a quiet room away from the company during those visits. Since there may be numerous visits from family and friends in the coming days or weeks, have a cozy and inviting room prepared for your cat. If he likes to nap in the sun, set up a window perch or place a soft cat bed on an elevated area for him to enjoy the warmth of the afternoon sun. Play the radio softly so he isn't hearing the excited voices coming from your visitors down the hall. Have some activity toys set up for him or maybe even throw a little catnip party. Bring out a couple of new toys (or ones that were put away as part of the normal toy rotation) for him to enjoy while being sequestered. If there's a television in the room, turn on a cat entertainment DVD so he can watch the mice and squirrels. When the visitors have gone, you or your spouse should spend a little time with the cat, even if it's just a few moments, to praise and pet him.

If you are fearful about your cat being too close to or hurting your baby, your body language or tone may be creating anxiety in him. If he attempted to get close in order to check out the baby or to get close to you and has been shooed away or pushed off the sofa, then that's another reason for him to view the appearance of this new-comer as a negative change in his life.

Allow your cat to share in the time you spend with your baby. If you're holding the baby and your cat wants to be close, let him curl up next to you. If that's not possible, at least talk to him, using his name to make some kind of connection with him. Interactive play therapy sessions with the cat when the baby is in the room are an important way to help build a positive association. If the baby is in the swing, use that time to entertain your infant with the numerous antics of your cat during playtime.

Make sure your cat is getting his regular schedule of interactive play sessions on a daily basis. Even though you're exhausted, this isn't the time to shortchange your cat when it comes to the routine he de-pends on. At the very least, set up a toy such as the *Panic Mouse* so he can enjoy a little playtime while you're busy with the baby. If your cat likes cat entertainment DVDs, pop one in so he can watch the mice and birds as you head off to the nursery with the baby. If there are other family members in the house, this may be a good opportunity for them to pitch in and dedicate some time to interactive play therapy. Your cat also needs some one-on-one time with you, so seek him out for cuddling and playtime when your baby is napping. He needs to know that not everything in his life has been turned upside down.

If your cat is showing any signs of aggression toward the baby, make sure the only time they're in the same room together is when you're either doing an interactive play session with the cat, feeding him, or petting him at a very safe distance from your child. This should show your cat that good things happen when he's in the room with the baby—he gets playtime, meals, treats, and affection. Stay well within the cat's comfort zone so he reacts positively. Do these sessions when the baby is quiet or sleeping so the cat isn't agitated by crying or noisy toys. It's also important for you to be calm and relaxed. Your cat needs to get the signal from you that there's nothing to be threatened by. Use clicker training so you can click and reward any signs of calm or positive behavior on your cat's part.

If your cat has started spraying as a result of the arrival of the baby, conduct play sessions in the nursery (without the baby being present at first) so your cat can begin to feel more comfortable surrounded by the scents associated with that room. Conduct play sessions in the areas where he's spraying, use *Feliway* in those areas, and follow the instructions outlined in chapter 5. Make sure he has areas of his own in rooms that are filled with baby equipment. If there are lots of playthings and baby stuff in the family room, that might be a place to put the cat tree so your cat can safely watch the activities from high above. If the cat's litter box is located in a spot that requires him to walk past the giant toy that your infant is seated in at the moment, rethink toy and litter box locations and make sure your cat has a clear, safe, and quiet path to his litter box. Add an extra litter box, or even two, in other areas of the home to give him more options if he doesn't want to have to pass too close to the baby.

Pay attention to where you have the feeding station for your cat and whether it's causing him anxiety if he's at his food bowl when your baby is in the high chair. My son loved to pound on his high-chair tray and was so enthusiastic when it was time for dinner that the kitchen became an extremely noisy room. It was too noisy for my cats to enjoy having their meals or a drink of water. I set up two additional feeding stations in other areas of the home that allowed them to have peace and quiet for their meals. This became even more of an issue when my son got older and I began to teach him to feed himself. Sippy cups and spoons were always hitting the floor, and those sudden noises certainly would've startled an unsuspecting cat who was trying to eat at his food bowl.

As a baby becomes more mobile, it can create more anxiety for your cat. Suddenly this strange little creature is able to move on his own, and he usually seems to be headed in the direction of the cat. Always make sure that in the rooms where the baby is crawling, there are plenty of elevated escape options for the cat. It's also never too early to start teaching the baby not to chase the cat. The baby probably wants nothing more than to touch the cat, but that must be done only under your direction. Show your baby how to pet with an open hand and how to be gentle. Your baby will watch how you interact with your cat, so make sure he sees you petting the cat only in the way you want him to do it as well. Pet only in the direction the hair grows and stay away from the tail, tummy, and whiskers.

KIDS AND CATS

Children and cats can have wonderful relationships, but they require teaching from you. Pay attention to the type of personality and temperament your cat has so you can teach your child to respect how much interaction your cat wants and will tolerate.

To a child, a cat may look like a moving toy, so it's important to explain how delicate and sensitive a cat's body is from the very start. A moving tail is enticing but should never be pulled. Even how a child picks up and handles the cat can make the kitty begin to fear the very sight of the youngster. I have seen cats dragged around by children holding them by the middle—the cats could barely catch their breath. If your child is old enough to hold the cat, he's old enough to learn the proper technique that involves supporting the hind quarters. With toddlers, an exuberant hug can squeeze kitty too tightly.

Some cats don't like to be held by anyone, yet alone a child. Know your cat's preferences so you can instruct your child on how to approach kitty and what he does and doesn't enjoy. If your cat loves being gently scratched under the chin or behind the head, show that to your child. If your cat likes sitting on your lap, that can be a secure place for him when your child begins to learn how to pet and touch him. With the kitty on your lap, have your child sit next to you, and then demonstrate how to pet with an open hand. You'll be able to feel if your cat starts to get tense or impatient.

A cat will, for the most part, choose escape over confrontation, so if your cat scratches or bites, it may be because he was cornered with no way out. Your child needs to learn how to read basic cat body language. He should know that ears in a T position or flattened means the cat isn't happy at the moment.

A cat needs "leave me alone" areas in the house, and the children should know where they are. Cat trees and perches or favorite napping areas should be off-limits to children. Where the cat eats and eliminates are also places that need to be left alone. A sleeping cat, no matter where he is, shouldn't be disturbed by a child.

High-pitched voices, quick footsteps, and all the other fun commotion that go along with being a child can be unsettling for a cat. Teach your child that the cat is to be approached quietly and gently. If your child has friends over, it might be best for the cat to be in another room.

Many parents use the cat's presence as an opportunity to teach responsibility to children. Your cat's health and well-being are too important to place that task on a child. If you give your child any cat-related duties, make sure that they're age-appropriate and that you monitor the situation so the cat never suffers due to a child's neglect. For example, if your child is responsible for filling the cat's water bowl, you still need to check it every day. Don't ask a child younger than a teenager to be responsible for scooping the litter box. A child may not practice adequate hygiene afterward. Besides, litter box scooping is an important way for you to monitor your cat's health. The person who does it has to be old enough to be aware of potential problems such as diarrhea, constipation, and an increase or decrease in urination.

If you have an older cat or one with health problems, an adult needs to be the one who handles water, food, and litter box responsibilities, or an adult needs to supervise the duties. How much a cat eats, drinks, and eliminates is valuable information when it comes to monitoring his health.

If a child is responsible for feeding the cat, make sure he or she uses a premeasured amount so you can be sure the kitty isn't getting too much or too little food. Water can be given from a prefilled plastic bottle so you can monitor how much is being consumed.

The front and back doors open and close on an almost revolving-door basis in many homes with children. That's an easy way for a cat to slip outside without detection. If your cat is strictly an indoor one, your child must learn not to hold the door wide open or stand in the open doorway. Explain how frightening it would be for the cat and tragically sad for the family if the kitty escaped outside. As a reminder, place a picture or sign on the door in case your child has trouble remembering the rule.

Injury to the cat can occur accidentally, such as a tail being stepped on or shut in a door. A trauma like that can leave the cat feeling fearful of the child or even start a pattern of fear aggression. Such behavior can compound the guilt and sadness your child already feels over the original accident if he or she doesn't understand why the cat is still afraid long after the injury has healed. In this case, you have to take a few steps back and almost begin an reintroduction so your kitty can start to associate your child with positive experiences again. Have your child on one side of the room reading, watching TV, or playing quietly (key word: *quietly*), while you feed, offer treats, or conduct a low-key interactive play session with your kitty. Over subsequent sessions, you can start to gradually move closer, and eventually have your child be the one who offers the food, treats, or playtime. Move at the pace of the cat, though. Don't be in rush. Also, when your child gives treats to the cat, demonstrate how to place it in an open hand and not hold it between the fingers. The last thing anyone needs is for the cat to make a mistake and nip the tip of a finger instead of the treat.

If your cat had been doing fine with your child but now displays fear or aggression, there may be something going on such as rough play, rough handling, or even abuse. I worked with one client whose young daughter created a fear problem when she forced the cat (a very shy declawed cat) into doll clothes and tried to take her for a walk in a stroller. The cat panicked and ran through the house, trying to get out of the clothing. I have also had some clients for whom the fear or aggression toward the child was due to secretive abusive behavior by the child toward the animal. Seemingly unexplainable or unprovoked aggression is rarely truly unexplainable or unprovoked.

Help your child, in an age-appropriate way, to see life from the cat's point of view. Some children may not fully understand that an animal feels pain, fear, sadness, and so forth.

When your child is old enough to participate in interactive playtime with your cat, it can be a wonderful way to build trust and help the two of them bond. Your child needs you to demonstrate how to conduct the play session in a way that will be fun and rewarding for the cat. You must supervise and make sure your cat isn't at risk of being poked in the eye with the wand of the fishing-pole toy. You may want to start with toys that have shorter wands and longer strings or toys so your cat can stay farther away from the end of the pole. The *Cat Charmer* is a good toy for children to start training on because it has a shorter wand and a long, thin fleece "snake." The movement is usually easy for a child to coordinate in the beginning. As he or she gets older or gets more comfortable, you can move on to other fishing-pole toys.

Parents' Checklist

- Teach how to pick up and hold the cat.
- Show how to pet with an open hand.
- Make sure your child is aware of the cat's "leave me alone" areas.
- Give your child only age-appropriate responsibilities for caring for kitty and be sure to monitor their tasks.
- Teach how to read the cat's body language.
- Warn your child never to use fingers as toys.
- Teach your child not to share food with the cat.
- Make sure your cat has areas of escape.
- Keep the litter box and feeding station off-limits to children.
- Continue to monitor the relationship.

FIXING BLENDED-FAMILY CAT-ASTROPHES

Does *your* cat hate *his* cat? Does *his* cat bully *your* two cats? Is *her* dog afraid of *your* cat? Does *everyone* hate *everyone else*? Blended families face many challenges as people try to transition smoothly from two households to one. It can be hard enough trying to get the children to coexist peacefully, let alone the cats, who look like two gunfighters at high noon.

If you haven't made the big move yet, here are some basic guidelines. If you're moving into your new spouse's home, then your cat is the one who needs to be in the sanctuary room and viewed as the newcomer. If your spouse is moving into your home, then your cat gets the run of the house while the other cat starts out in the sanctuary room. You will then follow the instructions mapped out in the first part of this chapter. One extra point to keep in mind is that the resident cat will be dealing with not only the addition of an unfamiliar cat but also the addition of at least one other unfamiliar person and all the belongings of that person. If there are children involved, then kitty has lots to get used to, so you have to take the necessary behavior modification steps for each individual issue. Your cat might be afraid of a child as well as concerned about your spouse's cat or dog. Even if your cat was comfortable with your spouse previously, it can be a whole different ball game when the spouse doesn't go home anymore and all of that person's belongings are now part of the household.

Combining households is overwhelming for both the cat in the current home and the cat entering the new environment. While you're making adjustments to this new life, remember to do the appropriate behavior modification to ease all the animals through this change. During the excitement and chaos of the beginnings of the blended family, it can be easy to overlook the anxiety a cat may be experiencing. Have a game plan beforehand and make sure everyone knows what to do. If there's a dog involved who has never been around cats or who has been allowed to chase cats, then some dog training sessions must be done before the introduction. If you have an older cat and now a very young cat is going to be joining the household, you'll have to do some kitty-proofing of the home beforehand. Just because your cat no longer has an interest in the electrical cords or the houseplants doesn't mean your spouse's young kitty won't want to investigate those dangerous items. This is a big move for everyone, so plan ahead. Get the house ready, set up whatever sanctuary rooms are needed, and make sure everyone is on the same page in terms of the behavior modification plan.

If you're dealing with a multipet situation in which one spouse has a single cat and the other spouse has two or more, don't overwhelm the single cat with having to get to know everyone at once. Do one-on-one introductions, starting with the animal who seems the most agreeable.

If the move has already taken place and things have gone from bad to worse, stop what you're presently doing, separate the animals, and *start from scratch*. Reintroduction after a period of calming down is the best way to stop the continuing deterioration and start building positive associations.

If the new companions are feline, environmental modifications need to be done once they're officially introduced in order to ensure that everyone has adequate space. The cat tree that's used by the resident cat may not be something he wants to share with the new cat, so a second tree may be needed. More than one litter box will be needed. More than one feeding station may be needed as well. It's important to offer them more options in the environment so they can choose if they want to share something or maintain their own space. Environmental modifications may also have to be made if the companions are a dog and cat. A baby gate, preventing access to the litter box, monitoring the feeding station, and other modifications described in an earlier section of this chapter may be required.

THE CAT-AVOIDING SPOUSE

How do you deal with the fact that the person you love the most in this world hates the cat you love the most in this world? What if the cat you cherish so much hisses and growls at the very sight of the love of your life? Some people have been forced to choose one over the other (you might be surprised how often people choose the cat). In other cases, the families grit their teeth and live in tension, with the spouse and the cat existing more as sparring partners than as members of the same household.

If you're in a relationship and you're at the point at which you're considering taking that giant leap toward marriage or living together, one of the discussions you should have is how this will or won't change the way your cat is used to living. If the person in your life strongly dislikes your cat, don't just assume things will improve once he or she gets to know him. That wouldn't be fair to your spouse or your cat. You need to sit down and talk about the concerns, expectations, and feelings your spouse has, and he or she needs to listen to yours. If your soon-to-be spouse absolutely hates your cat and wants you to get rid of him, but your cat means everything to you, you need to resolve that issue *before* you alter your living arrangements. At the risk of venturing into Dr. Phil territory, if you and your soon-to-be spouse disagree over something like this, is there a chance this isn't the right person for you? Not everyone has to like cats, just as not everyone likes dogs, or fish, or birds, but if you're sharing your life with someone, he or she should understand that your cat is a big part of your life. Is this person willing to work with you on a plan to try to get to know your cat, or at least willing to live in peace with kitty because he means so much to you? Or is he or she demanding that your cat be rehomed? Don't wait until after you have moved in together to have this discussion. Your cat's life may depend on it.

It's harder to dislike a well-trained cat than it is a poorly trained one. Take a look at the behaviors your cat exhibits that you've learned to live with but that may not be appropriate or in the cat's best interests. If your cat has litter box issues, work on them now, because chances are they'll only get worse once the new spouse is on the scene full-time. Inappropriate behaviors such as food stealing, scratching furniture, and so forth need to be worked on now.

In addition to training issues, there may be health and hygiene issues with your cat that may make him less appealing to your spouse—things that should be addressed anyway but you might have neglected. For example, does your cat have fleas? Do you groom your cat regularly or does he look like a knotted mop? Is there cat hair everywhere? Do you keep his nails trimmed regularly? Does he have an ongoing problem with hairballs? How clean do you keep his litter box? While these are issues that should be addressed immediately, and not solely to make your cat more appealing to your spouse, they're some of the common points cat avoiders focus on.

When you have your discussion with your spouse or soon-to-be spouse, pick a time when you are both in the right mood for openly and calmly talking about what he or she specifically dislikes about cats. Information is power, and you can use this opportunity to enlighten him or her about misconceptions. I have found that in many cases people who dislike cats don't really know anything about them, or their previous experiences were with a poorly trained cat. During one of my consultations, I found out that the reason my client's husband hated cats was because as a child his house always smelled like cat urine. As we talked more, it became obvious that his parents had an intact indoor/outdoor male cat. The other thing this man disliked was the fact that the cat was not friendly and had scratched him several times. As a result, the view of cats that he carried throughout this life was that houses with cats smelled like urine and cats scratch. The fact that his parents neglected to neuter the cat and didn't do any proper training gave this gentleman an inaccurate impression of cats.

Listen to your spouse's concerns and don't dismiss them or respond to them defensively. He or she may have some valid issues regarding your particular cat, and this will require both of you to be willing to do the work necessary to create a household in which everyone can be happy.

If your spouse is willing to live with your cat but doesn't want to get too close or have your cat sleep in the bed, you both need to make some compromises. Life for your cat will obviously have to change, but the bottom shouldn't fall out of his world. You and your cat have a relationship that needs to be maintained and nurtured. Don't try to make your cat's presence less intrusive by ignoring him when your spouse is around or, worse, locking him in a room, putting him outside, or forcing him to live in the garage or basement. Decide beforehand what compromises will need to be met and begin doing appropriate and humane behavior modification to gradually ease your cat into the transition. For example, if you decide that your cat will no longer be able to sleep in bed with you, then create a very appealing alternative spot for him and start having him sleep there before your spouse moves in so the cat doesn't associate the spouse with the altered sleeping arrangements. I usually suggest that cat owners trying to get kitty to sleep elsewhere start keeping their bedroom doors closed all the time, even when they're not at home, so the cat doesn't keep getting reminders of where he'd rather be napping. Set up a cozy cat tree and/or a couple of cozy hideaways for your cat to choose for sleeping. If the weather is turning colder, consider installing a heated window perch. If your cat enjoys sleeping on a chair by the fireplace or on a pillow on the sofa, play up those areas by placing a shirt or towel there that contains your scent.

When you set up a few new sleeping options, make those special places where you offer treats and affection to your cat. Call your cat over to those spots for a little scratching under the chin or petting in the areas he loves the most. If the location is a cat tree, you can also do some playtime there.

In addition to your regular interactive play therapy sessions, do a bonus play session right before bedtime, wind the action down at the end of the game, and then offer your cat a portion of his meal or a treat. This way, he'll have fun with you, work off his energy, and be left relaxed and satisfied.

It's also important not to make a big deal about the fact that you're going to leave him out of the room when you go to bed. Don't make the good-night ritual into a dramatic scene that makes it seem as if you're going away for a month. Give a casual farewell greeting. Remember, your cat is a little emotional sponge who can easily pick up on your level of anxiety.

Your spouse may have issues with other aspects of your cat's routine or behavior. Some or all of them may be valid and need behavior modification. For example, if your spouse doesn't want your cat on the kitchen counters and you have previously allowed that, then part of your compromise may be the need to retrain your cat in order to correct that behavior. Other aspects may require compromise on his or her part. If your spouse doesn't like the location of the litter box and would prefer it to be in a more remote location, you have to explain to him or her the importance of keeping the box where it's convenient for your cat and that a change to a remote location could create litter box aversion problems. Keep the box clean so your spouse doesn't have more reason to object to its presence.

If you are moving into your spouse's home and he or she isn't happy with the fact that you'll be bringing your cat along, this will require lots of discussion beforehand. Your kitty is going to be faced with an unfamiliar territory *and* a hostile new roommate. Explain to your spouse that your cat will have to be eased into the environment by using a sanctuary room. If your spouse is concerned about potential damage from scratching, prepare the house in advance by setting up scratching posts in areas where you think your cat would most likely want to scratch. This is a great time to use corrugated cardboard scratching pads for extra insurance because they're inexpensive and you can scatter them throughout the home. If there are pieces of furniture that your spouse is particularly worried about, set them up with deterrents such as *Sticky Paws* or cover them completely and place a scratching post right beside them. If your spouse is a true cat avoider, he or she probably doesn't even understand the need for a scratching post, so make sure you offer an explanation so that there's an awareness of how crucial this is to your cat's daily life.

Look around your spouse's home and cat-proof as necessary. If you have a very active cat and your spouse has some delicate and/or valuable items that you know will create bad feelings if damaged, then secure them out of your cat's reach, and don't underestimate your cat's reach. You want to give your cat and your spouse every reason to like each other, and a big part of that is creating an environment in which they can coexist happily.

One problem I see quite often when a cat owner moves into a cat avoider's residence is the battle over the paraphernalia that goes along with living with cats. We already discussed the litter box and scratching post, but perhaps you also have a giant cat tree or a huge basket of cat toys. Maybe your spouse doesn't want the clutter of cat toys all over or the presence of a big cat tree to ruin the decor of the living room. This can be an especially difficult hurdle for your spouse to get over because a cat tree in the living room isn't an easy thing to hide. Your spouse may want the tree in a little-used room down the hall and you may want it front and center. What matters most is putting the tree where it'll be the most useful to the cat—that's the purpose of the tree. You know your cat, and if he wants to be in the room with the family, then the tree should be where you spend the most time. If your cat loves watching the outdoor wildlife and there's a great spot for it at the big window in the den, then maybe that's the best place. One good negotiation point to use with your spouse is that the more time your cat spends on the cat tree, the less time he spends on the furniture. The cat tree is also an important security place for your cat in this unfamiliar environment because it contains all of his comforting scents and will be an elevated spot where he can go when he feels anxious. The more secure your cat can feel in this new environment, the more "attractive" he will be to your cat-avoiding spouse.

Don't force your cat on your cat-avoiding spouse, but do show him off! If your spouse has been focusing on the negatives about life with a cat, show him or her the positives. If your cat is clicker-trained, demonstrate some fun behaviors or tricks. Many people don't think a cat can be trained, so if you have secretly worked on training your cat to jump through an embroidery hoop, go through a homemade obstacle course, or even just roll over, it'll be very impressive. If you haven't worked on any special behaviors, just conduct a fun interactive play session. It's hard not to be fascinated or even chuckle at how intense a cat can be as he stalks and pounces on his pretend prey. Show off how athletic your cat is and how lightning-fast his reflexes are. One of the things I do in consultations when I'm dealing with a cat avoider in the family is to talk about how incredible the feline senses are and how cats beautifully walk the line of being so graceful and yet so powerful. I also do an initial clicker training demonstration to show the cat avoider how smart the cat is and how easy it'll be to train him.

If you see that the cat avoider is intrigued by the play session, casually hand the toy off to him or her. You may find that this is the icebreaker you needed.

THE SPOUSE-AVOIDING CAT

I see this quite often in my consultations, but there's much that can be done to improve the situation. If you're facing this problem right now, don't panic. You have lots of behavior modification tools.

First, let's go over what NOT to do. Don't force your spouse on your cat. Don't put the cat in your spouse's lap or hold him so your spouse can pet him. That will only drive more of a wedge between them. Also, don't punish the cat for hissing, spraying, or any negative behavior displayed. If you want your cat to like your spouse, you have to give him a reason to think this is a good addition to his life, not the reason he's always getting reprimanded.

Instruct your spouse not to look directly at the cat or approach him. If your cat wants to close the gap between them, let him be the one to initiate that.

Some cats who have lived only with women may find the heavier footsteps or deeper voice of a man to be a bit unsettling at first. Cats who are used to men may have some trouble with the higher female voices, and so forth. Your spouse should be aware of how he or she walks into a room or talks. I had one client whose cat was terrified of her boyfriend, and much of it centered around the fact that he had an over-the-top personality and a very loud voice. He was a delightful man, but my client's cat was skittish to begin with and was used to living in a very calm and quiet setting. The client and her boyfriend truly represented a case of opposites attracting. It took awareness on the part of the boyfriend in order to ease the cat out of her shell.

You know the expression "The way to a man's heart is through his stomach." The route to your cat's heart is similar. Have your spouse be the one who serves the cat all his meals. If you schedule-feed, this is even better because your cat is seeing for himself where the chow is coming from. If you free-feed, still have your spouse be responsible for the duties because your cat will see it happen often enough and the scent of your spouse will be on the dishes he handles. The spouse-avoiding cat may not appreciate having your spouse stand right next to the bowl during mealtime, so once dinner is served, he or she should step out of the way. If your cat is comfortable, the spouse can stay in the room; he or she should otherwise serve and leave.

Speaking of feeding, if you know beforehand that your cat will not take it well when the new spouse becomes a permanent fixture, make a gradual transition to schedule feeding. Do this well in advance of the spouse's arrival. This way your spouse can be the main provider of the meals once he or she arrives. You'll also be able to use clicker training to identify and mark any positive behavior on your cat's part.

At any point, if your cat attempts to come closer to investigate your spouse, let him do so without interruption. Your spouse shouldn't reach down to pet or view this as an invitation to hold the cat. Direct eye contact should still be avoided. The cat needs the freedom to do a scent investigation and start to build trust.

After the trust building has started, your spouse can extend his index finger for your cat to sniff. This is similar to the nose-to-nose sniffing that cats often do when they first greet each other. The cat will either approach closer to sniff or he'll back away. If he approaches, then he's making progress in the trust department. He may then sniff and back away, which means he isn't ready to take this any further right now. On the other hand, he may sniff and then rub his cheek along your spouse's finger or approach even closer. This is a great sign that things are improving. After a couple of those sessions, if the cat sniffs, rubs, leans against your spouse's hand, or comes closer, then he's probably saying it's okay to pet.

You know where your cat likes to be petted and where he doesn't, but your spouse doesn't know that. He or she may not know much at all about cats, so a little education is in order. During the early stages of trust building, the spouse-avoiding cat should be petted briefly in the most guaranteed-to-get-a-good-response place. That's usually on the back of the head or maybe under the chin. Stick to the tried-and-true places that you're sure of. Instruct your spouse to end the petting session well before he or she thinks it's necessary so things can end on a positive note.

Play therapy is an important tool in helping the spouse avoider. Start by doing interactive play therapy sessions with your cat while your spouse is within sight but still far enough away that kitty is well within his comfort zone. During subsequent sessions, your spouse can inch closer, but make sure he or she appears focused on something else, such as reading or watching TV. This distracted presence will help your cat get comfortable while seeing that having him or her in the vicinity isn't posing a threat.

You want to work up to the point at which you and your spouse can be sitting side by side during the interactive play therapy session. Provided your cat is clearly comfortable with every step up to this point, you can eventually hand the toy off to your spouse. Before you attempt this, though, make sure you have given lessons to your spouse on how to conduct the game. If things go well, the next play session can be started by you and then your spouse can take over the majority of it. Following that, your spouse will be the one to do all of the play sessions. Hopefully, you'll get to the point at which you don't even have to be in the room. Get to this point gradually, though, because your presence is a source of security for your cat.

What if your cat is lounging on a chair that your spouse wants to sit on or sitting on a pile of papers that the person needs at that moment? If you're at home, you should be the one to move the cat. If your spouse is alone with the cat, then he or she shouldn't attempt to lift the cat off or shoo him away. Instead, your spouse should get out a toy or a treat to entice the cat off the spot. Keep everything positive.

One trick I often recommend to clients with spouse-avoiding cats is to use *Feliway* spray in a rather unconventional way. Have your spouse give a quick spritz of *Feliway* to the bottoms of his or her pants. If your spouse is wearing shoes, he or she can opt to spritz the tips of the shoes instead of the clothing. *Feliway* was not intended for this purpose, but I have found that the presence of those friendly synthetic feline facial pheromones often aids in helping the spouse avoider start to make positive associations.

10

Travel Retraining
On the Road with Your Own
Mr. or Miss Grumpypaws

LOOK AT TRAVEL FROM YOUR CAT'S POINT OF VIEW

Throughout this book I've talked about engaging your cat in activities and creating more stimulation for her. Thus far that has centered around the security of her familiar home environment. There's a reason for this—cats are territorial and they take great comfort in the security of their environment. Your cat is perfectly happy staying within the perimeters of her comfort zone. Even outdoor cats establish a familiar home range in which they hunt and socialize. It's usually only the intact male in search of a female who goes off into unknown areas.

For a territorial animal, an unfamiliar surrounding can be a very scary place. The cat doesn't know where the safe hiding places are or if she's at risk of being attacked by someone. The sights, sounds, smells, and textures are all unfamiliar. These concerns are compounded by the fact that the travel destination for most cats is usually stressful in and of itself, whether it's the veterinarian's office, the boarding kennel, a move to a new home, being rehomed to a new family, or a stay at a relative's house while the family goes on vacation. The concept of traveling is never the cat's idea. Unfortunately, she has to go along for the ride whether she likes it or not. Even if she's not the one doing the traveling, the concept still involves stress because her family will be gone and she'll be left home alone or in the care of others whom she isn't that familiar with or maybe doesn't even like.

For us, travel usually involves excitement, fun, and adventure, or business advancement. Even though vacations can contain stress (especially during the packing-and-getting-there stage), we generally look forward to the time when we get to *travel*. Now take out all the excitement, adventure, and fun and replace them with confusion, fear, stress, and the unknown. That's how your cat views travel.

If you exposed your cat to travel at an early age and used behavior modification techniques to help her adjust to changes and view travel as something positive, then you probably have it much easier when it comes time for vacations, moves, or trips to the veterinarian's office. However, not many people think to do that when their cat is a kitten. Besides, if you acquired your cat when she was an adult, you may not have had the chance to do it even if you wanted to. Is it too late? Absolutely not. Granted, you'll have a little work ahead of you to help counteract her previous experiences of life on the road, but you certainly can reduce the anxiety associated with travel.

RETRAIN YOUR CAT TO THE CARRIER

If the thought of having to transport your cat somewhere causes beads of sweat to appear on your forehead, you're not alone. It doesn't have to be that way, though. You can retrain your cat to tolerate travel without the stress she currently feels. Notice I said *tolerate* and not *look forward to* or *joyfully embrace*. If your cat has spent years associating travel with trips to the veterinarian or getting anxious or sick in the car, then getting her to tolerate travel will be a huge step. If she had been exposed to various travel experiences, most of them positive and short, when she was just a youngster, then you wouldn't be in the situation you're currently in. Regardless of how you and your cat got to this point, it's not too late to make life easier for her and, as a result, for you. It won't happen overnight, though, so prepare yourself for a gentle and gradual behavior modification process.

Whether you have never transported your cat in a carrier or you have and she hated it, you'll need a carrier from this point forward. It's dangerous to try to travel with a cat who is loose in the car. She can easily cause an accident, and being loose causes most cats' anxiety levels to rise. Additionally, if your car breaks down on the road, you'll have no safe way to remove your cat. Carriers are a must.

There are all sorts of carriers out there, but if you're dealing with a travel-hating kitty, your best bet is a plastic kennel-type carrier. With this type of carrier, the top and bottom can be taken apart. The entrance is a metal or plastic grille door with a secure locking mechanism. The kennel carrier is virtually indestructible, easy to clean if your cat has an accident, and it provides a good level of security for a nervous cat. There are good-quality carriers and cheap ones, so make sure the carrier you choose is well made and sturdy.

For the cat's feeling of security, this carrier is good because she's hidden and protected while inside and can back herself away from the entrance. If she's really nervous, you can put a light towel over the top during travel so she feels totally hidden. The carrier's hard shell also gives her a feeling of stability amid all the shifting that occurs when you are handling it. Soft-sided carriers, while fine for some cats, don't provide that same level of stability. Cardboard carriers are not sturdy enough for long-term use and have to be thrown out if the cat has an accident.

The carrier needs to be the right size. The carrier you had for your cat when she was a kitten may be too small now that she's an overweight adult. If so, it's time to upgrade, but don't overdo it. Cats feel more secure if the carrier isn't so big that they end up being jostled all over the place while in transit. Many times I have seen cat owners purchase carriers that are way too big for their cats. This ends up creating more fear in the cat. It's also extremely difficult for the cat owner to handle an oversize carrier. If the carrier you have is way too large, then put it away for use if you ever do long-distance car travel (during which your cat will appreciate the extra leg room), and purchase a carrier that's a better size for general day-to-day use. Plastic kennel carriers come in many sizes, so you should be able to find the one that's a perfect fit for your cat. She should be able to settle comfortably without feeling squished or cramped. When reclining, she needs enough room to be able to shift her weight from one side to the other. She doesn't need to be able to stand up completely, but she should be able to fully raise her head.

A very important feature of the plastic kennel carrier is that when you do have your cat on the veterinarian's examination table, you can detach the top portion and allow her to remain in the bottom section. Being able to remain in that familiar part of the carrier often helps a cat's stress level remain a little lower. This is also an easier way for the veterinarian to gain access to the unhappy cat rather than trying to reach into the carrier and extract a hissing, growling patient.

The *starting from scratch* retraining process

Whether you already have the carrier at home or you have to go out and purchase one, give it a good scrubbing to remove any residue of previous trips to the veterinarian or other unfamiliar and potentially unpleasant scents.

Detach the top of the carrier from the bottom so you can remove the door. Then put the carrier back together. The first part of the behavior modification process involves the carrier itself without your cat having to worry about the door being shut on her should she venture in there.

Place the carrier in a room where you and your cat spend much of your time, such as the living room or family room. Set it down somewhere in the room as if you were creating a cozy little sleeping hideaway for your cat. Don't place it in too remote an area of the room, but don't stick it front and center either. The first part of this exercise will be to change your cat's association with the carrier, transforming it from a dreaded traveling prison cell into a benign object in the room. Right now, the very sight of the carrier might send her diving under the bed. Much of that comes from the fact that in most homes, the carrier gets brought out of the closet only when it's time to go to the veterinarian. If you leave the carrier out all the time, it will lose some of that association.

To make the appearance of the carrier friendlier and less intimidating, line the inside with a towel. Also, give a quick spray of *Feliway* to each inside corner.

Initially, your cat may do everything she can to avoid walking near the carrier when she's in the room, but that's okay. Just let the carrier sit there, minding its own business, until your cat gets used to its presence.

For the next step, you'll use treats or a portion of her meal. Place a treat near, but not too near, the carrier. How far away the treat needs to be will be determined by how reactive your cat has been to the presence of the carrier. If she has no problem going near the carrier, then you can place it a foot in front of it. If she still eyes the carrier with suspicion, then the treat needs to be several feet away.

If you're using a portion of her meal, give her a couple of pieces of dry kibble in the area near the carrier or place her food bowl there with a tiny amount of wet food. If she doesn't eat, then you've placed the food too close to the carrier. You need to be far enough away so that the cat is still in her comfort zone, but close enough so that the carrier is still in view.

Do this exercise a couple of times a day until your cat is clearly comfortable with this step. Next, place the treat or the food bowl closer to the carrier. When your cat is comfortable, place a treat right at the entrance to it. Don't make a big production out of the fact that you've placed the treat there, just let your cat discover it. Eventually work up to tossing a treat inside the carrier. You may have to inch your way from the entrance to the middle and then to the back, but you want to get to the point at which your cat freely walks into the carrier to retrieve the treat. If you're using a portion of her meal, place the food bowl in there. It's important to move at her pace. If she's nervous, return to the previous step until she's ready to venture into the carrier.

When your cat is comfortable going in and out of the carrier, you can put the door back on, but keep it in the open position. Once the door has been on for a while and your cat is comfortable with that, you can toss a treat in and then shut the door (but don't latch it) when your cat goes in to retrieve it. Open the door again immediately and praise your cat in a calm and low-key way.

 CATWISE CLUE

If you've been using a clicker, here's a good opportunity to expand the training. Create a cue to use when you want the cat to go into the carrier. You can use any word, for example, *kennel*. As she steps into the carrier, say "Kennel" so that she starts making the association, and then click and reward her.

The next step is to close and latch the door, count to ten, and then open the door again. Don't do this every time your cat goes in the carrier, though, because you still want her to feel that the carrier can be a quiet little hideaway when she wants to curl up and nap without being trapped.

For the next step, you're actually going to go somewhere, sort of. When your cat goes into the carrier, close the door, pick up the carrier, and walk across the room and back, then place the carrier back down in its original spot. Open the door and praise your cat. When she exits the carrier, have a piece of a treat ready for her or offer her a play session. Use your clicker to click and reward her for being calm in the carrier.

Gradually take your traveling cat a little farther in the house. Be daring and walk into another room and back. You can talk to your cat as you transport her throughout the house, but keep your tone casual and soothing. Bring her back to the original spot when the training session is finished. End every session on a positive note by offering either a piece of a treat, a portion of her meal, praise, petting, or a play session.

Now you're ready for a really big step. It's time to go into the car. Take your cat for a quick ride around the block and back home. End the session with something positive and rewarding. If your cat has previously associated the car ride only with a trip to the veterinarian, these little trips that don't result in being poked, prodded, or stuck with a needle will be quite a pleasant surprise.

If your cat has a history of getting carsick, it'll be a big help to take little drives around the neighborhood to build up her tolerance. Spray the inside corners of the carrier with *Feliway* about a half hour before putting your cat inside. When you return home, give your cat a little play session. Don't try to feed her right away because her stomach may need a little time to settle down first.

Build up to longer trips, such as taking your cat along for the ride when you go to the drive-through at the bank or the dry cleaner. Don't overdo the trips, but do enough so that your cat starts to learn that being in the carrier in the car isn't the end of the world. If you gradually build up her tolerance for this, it'll make it much easier if you ever have to do a long-distance trip with her.

Even after your cat has made peace with the carrier, keep it out for use as an extra sleeping area. There's also a very practical reason for keeping the carrier out and ready at all times. In the event of an emergency, you don't want to risk evacuating your home with a terrified cat in your arms. Have the carrier out and ready for action in case you ever have to take your cat to the veterinarian in an emergency or leave your house quickly.

Even though you've done all this great behavior modification work to help your cat learn to associate travel with things other than the veterinarian's office, there will come a time when that destination can't be avoided. The techniques you can use to make that experience less stressful appear a little later in this chapter.

The emergency technique for getting a carrier-hating cat into the carrier

You might be halfway through the behavior modification process of retraining your cat to the carrier when something comes up and you have to get her in the carrier right away. What's the best technique? Your previous method may have involved much risk of injury to yourself, lots of stress to both you and your cat, and an amazing display of strength on your cat's part. Attempting to put a cat in the carrier when that's the last place she wants to go usually reminds you just how fast and stubborn she is. It often also reminds you that you haven't trimmed her nails lately. There's a surefire way of getting your cat in the carrier without trauma when seconds matter.

Stand the kennel carrier on its back end so the entrance is now facing up. If your cat panics at the sight of the carrier, do this in a room away from the cat's view. Calmly scruff your cat with one hand and then grasp her hind legs with the other hand. Support her hindquarters with the hand holding her hind legs as you transport her to the carrier. Don't carry the weight of the cat with the hand holding the scruff. If you're unfamiliar with what it means to scruff your cat, there's loose skin on the back of her neck and you can gently but firmly grasp that. If you have a cat who'll bite when you attempt to put her in the carrier, then scruffing is the safest method in an emergency. You have to combine that with holding the hind legs and supporting the bottom of the cat, though, because the last thing you want is to have her flailing around in a desperate attempt to escape.

Carefully lower the cat into the upright carrier with her hindquarters first. As you lower her you can first remove the hand that's holding her hind legs and then remove the hand that's scruffing. This has to be done quickly. Once she's in, close the door. Latch the door immediately and then take your hand away. Place the carrier back in its normal position slowly and gently. If you were quick enough, you managed to get your cat into the carrier with the least amount of emotional trauma and with no injury to the feline or human involved.

LONG-DISTANCE CAR TRAVEL

You've gotten your cat used to the carrier, and now it's time for an unavoidable long-distance car trip. It's all about being prepared.

Don't attempt to take your cat on a long-distance car trip until you've gradually gotten her used to the experience of being in a car. Do the behavior modification technique described previously, taking her on short trips to get her comfortable with the motion of the car.

When it comes to giving a cat any form of sedation or antianxiety medication for travel, I'd advise against it. If you get your cat used to car travel in a gradual manner, she should make the adjustment just fine without any medication. Cats don't tend to get physically sick from car rides the way dogs do, but they do tend to get very anxious. That's why preplanning and behavior modification can make a world of difference. Also, if you have your cat secured in a carrier, she may meow and cry initially but should eventually settle down. Some medication can cause the cat to get disoriented and groggy. If your veterinarian has advised you that your cat would be better off being medicated, then be sure that the first time you give the medication isn't the day of the trip. Give a dose well in advance in case your cat has an adverse reaction to the medication. You don't want to be on the road and find yourself in an emergency situation with your cat. My advice, though, is to avoid the medication route and stick to behavior modification.

Catwise Pretrip Feeding Tip

 For long-distance car travel, feed your cat a light meal a couple of hours before the start of the trip. She can have small amounts of water right up until it's time to leave.

Even though your cat will be riding in a carrier, she should be wearing a collar with her current identification information. If you're moving, then her ID tag should have your new location's contact information on it. If you have a cell phone, that's the perfect number to have on the ID tag. Put identification on the carrier as well in case an emergency separates you from the cat. That way, somebody can get your contact information without having to reach into the carrier. If your cat is leash-and-harness-trained, put the harness on her for the car ride. This way, in addition to having proper identification in case an unforeseen accident happens, you also will have control if you have to take her out of the carrier to use the litter box, or for any other reason.

If your cat hasn't been trained to wear a collar or harness or to walk on a leash, the training technique can be found later in this chapter. Even if your cat lives strictly indoors, it's a good idea to have her comfortable with wearing a collar at the very least. Leash and harness training is valuable even for indoor cats just in case you do have to do long-distance travel.

You can use your cat's usual kennel-type carrier for the trip, but if you're going to be on the road for long stretches at a time, you may want to consider getting a larger carrier or even a dog crate. Dog crates can be easily assembled and then collapsed for storage. If you're going to be putting your cat in the back of your SUV, a dog crate would work well for a long drive. Drape a towel or sheet over the top so she feels as if she's somewhat hidden. Don't completely cover her, though, unless she's truly frightened. She may get some sense of security from being able to peek out and look at her family members in the car.

Line the carrier or crate with towels and have some extras with you in case of accidents. Pack plastic trash bags so you can bag up the soiled towels to be washed later. A pack of unscented baby wipes will also come in handy so you can clean messes on the inside of the carrier as well as on the cat's fur. Make sure the baby wipes are unscented and don't contain alcohol. The sensitive-formula ones created for newborns work best.

If you're using her regular carrier for a long-distance trip, you'll have to take occasional breaks to allow her to use the litter box. It's also a good idea to let her stretch her legs and have a few sips of water. This is where having her leash-and-harness-trained will be helpful because you'll have more control when you take her out of the carrier. Make sure the vehicle's doors and windows are closed when you let her out to use the litter box or to have a little water.

If you're using a large carrier or a dog crate, you'll probably be able to put a cage or travel-sized litter box in there with her. You can get either a plastic one or a disposable cardboard one.

When you're traveling long-distance, bring along your cat's brand of litter. Don't depend on the idea that you'll be able to find that brand at your destination. The last thing your cat needs is to have to adjust to an unfamiliar type of litter substrate on top of having to adjust to new surroundings.

In addition to the litter, bring along a slotted litter shovel and a container or plastic bag to store it in. You'll also need a scoop so you can fill the box with fresh litter. Sturdy plastic bags will be needed to store the waste that you scoop out of the box while you're on the road. You don't want to just dump urine clumps and cat feces into open trash cans.

Take along an adequate supply of your cat's food, especially if she's on prescription-formula food or one that's difficult to find. Don't assume you'll be able to get that exact brand at your destination. Bring along a scoop if using dry food and a spoon if using wet food. You'll also need her food and water bowls. Extra paper towels and plastic bags will make cleanup easier. If feeding canned food that doesn't have a peel-off or pop-top lid, you'll need to pack a can opener as well. You'll also need to bring along extra water for your cat. A change in water can cause an upset stomach. If your cat is sensitive to change, then she'll detect the change in the water's taste, so play it safe and bring an extra supply. If it makes it easier, start a transition process before the trip by adding bottled water to her regular water a little at a time. If you normally give her plain tap water, this transition will allow you to carry some bottled water with you as well as purchase some along the way, provided you stick with the major brands that are widely available. This way you'll always be able to offer your cat fresh water and the taste will be consistent. If your long-distance drive is for the purpose of making a permanent move to another state, then once you've settled into your new location, you can slowly transition her back to tap water if that's what you want to do.

If your cat has medium or long hair and your trip will take longer than one day, she'll need a little grooming at some point to prevent mats. Remember to pack her grooming supplies.

If your cat is on medication, plan in advance and refill any prescriptions that are running low. Pack the prescriptions in their original containers in case your cat needs medical attention during the trip. You don't want to have to rely on your memory concerning what the meds are and how much she takes.

If you're making a permanent move, plan ahead and get a copy of your cat's medical records to give to the veterinarian in your new hometown. Include any X-rays or test results your cat may have had. If your cat has been to a veterinary specialist in addition to your regular veterinarian, get a copy of those records as well. If you're going on a vacation with your cat or for a long-distance visit, it's still valuable to have a copy of your cat's medical records with you in case of an emergency. If she's under ongoing veterinarian care for an illness or injury, this will be extremely important. Even though you may have your current veterinarian's phone number, emergencies might take place after hours.

Place a picture of your cat with the medical records so that if the unthinkable should happen and your cat gets lost, you'll have a current photo to show people who may have seen her and so you can make flyers immediately.

Toys! Don't forget to pack some for your cat so you can continue your schedule of interactive play therapy when you get to your destination. Playtime is a wonderful stress reliever and will come in very handy in helping your cat transition to the new location. It's also a good way to help unkink those muscles after your cat has been cooped up in the car for a long time.

CATWISE CAUTION

Never leave your cat alone in a parked car. Even if the outside temperature doesn't seem too uncomfortable, the temperature inside the car can rise to 120 degrees in a few short minutes. Leaving the windows open at the top won't be adequate to protect your cat from heatstroke. Another reason not to leave your cat alone in a parked car is that it's an invitation for someone to steal her.

If you're going to be stopping at a motel or hotel overnight, or if your vacation destination involves a hotel stay, do your homework beforehand to make sure the hotel you choose accepts pets. More and more hotels are accepting pets, and some even go out of their way to make the pet's visit special. For more information on finding pet-friendly hotels, refer to the appendix.

When you arrive at the hotel, make sure the clerk at the front desk has made an official note of your cat's presence so the housekeeping and maintenance staff will be alerted. Some hotels have little magnetic signs to place on your room door near the lock informing the staff that there's a pet inside. If the hotel doesn't supply this, make your own little sign for the door.

It's best to arrange for housekeeping to service your room while you're there so you can place your cat in her carrier during that time. That's much safer than having someone enter your room when you aren't there unless you have your cat secured in a crate or large kennel. You can ask the person at the front desk to schedule housekeeping services at a specific time so you can be sure to be there. Whenever you leave your cat alone in the hotel room, put the DO NOT DISTURB sign on the door.

Check over your hotel room for potential kitty dangers and try to safeguard it as best as you can. Make sure your cat has her collar on with her identification that contains your cell-phone number just in case she escapes out the door. In a hotel with enclosed corridors, it probably won't be too difficult to track down which guest is the one with the cat, but if you're staying in a motel or hotel where your room opens directly to the outdoors, this identification will be crucial.

In addition to a few interactive toys, place some fun solo toys around the room. When traveling by car, it's also good to squeeze a corrugated cardboard scratching pad in there so your cat will have some form of scratching surface available to her.

Since the hotel room will smell totally unfamiliar to your cat, bring along the *Feliway* and use either the plug-in diffuser or the spray bottle to help your cat adjust to the surroundings more easily.

Be considerate of the housekeeping staff. Don't dump litter waste in the trash can without securely wrapping it in a plastic bag. Doing so will keep the room fresh-smelling, and prevent housekeeping from having to come in contact with your cat's waste.

If your cat meows, yowls, or cries while in the hotel room, be aware that it could be disturbing to other guests. Do play sessions with her, use *Feliway*, and try to set up the room in the most inviting and comfortable way for her. Leave the radio or TV on quietly when you leave the room. If your cat enjoys the cat entertainment DVDs, bring one along on the trip and pop it into the DVD player to keep her occupied just before you leave the room. Catnip may also be a help if your cat isn't adjusting well to the unfamiliar surroundings. Bring a little bag of good-quality catnip so you can offer some loose dried leaves to her or rub some on a few toys.

My cats absolutely love fleece pads, so I always make sure I've packed a couple when we travel. Placing them on the hotel bed or on a couple of chairs in the room usually creates instant comfort and security for my cats. If your cat has a favorite type of material that she enjoys curling up on or a cat bed, bring it along for her. I also leave the carriers open on the floor so my cats can use them as safe hideaways for sleeping. If you're using a dog crate, place a towel or some clothes over it so your cat will feel protected and hidden.

AIR TRAVEL

This is absolutely not a possibility until you have carrier-trained your cat. Even if you plan on having your cat travel in the cabin with you and not in the cargo section of the aircraft, she'll have to be confined to a carrier. The airline-approved carriers are even smaller than what you might normally use for her for car travel, so you must go through the process of getting her comfortable with being in a carrier. There are two extremely important reasons for doing the behavior modification. The first is to reduce the stress and anxiety she'll endure while traveling. The second (and this is a big one that's often overlooked) is that the cat will have to come out of the carrier during the security check at the airport. There's no getting around that, so if your cat freaks out or becomes extremely aggressive when in the carrier, the LAST place you're going to want to deal with that is in a crowded airport. Don't bypass the behavior modification process or it could result in tragedy. You need to retrain your cat to be comfortable both in the carrier and in a crowded place, and she needs to be leash-trained. This way, when you or the security personnel take your cat out of the carrier (some airports don't allow you to do it yourself), you'll have the extra assurance of having her connected to the leash.

Traveling by air also requires more preplanning in terms of making reservations for your cat and getting appropriate documentation. Some airlines allow small animals to fly as carry-on in the cabin with you, but some will accept pets only as cargo. You definitely want to take your cat onboard with you if at all possible. You'll need to make a separate reservation for her when you make your own flight reservation. Some airlines charge an additional fee, but it usually isn't very much. Make your reservations as soon as you know when your trip is going to be because there are only a certain number of pets allowed per aircraft. When you make your reservations, try to book a nonstop flight to reduce the amount of time your cat must remain in the carrier.

If your cat must fly as cargo, keep in mind that airlines have restrictions concerning weather. Your airline may deny boarding for your cat in extremely hot or cold temperatures. This is to ensure the safety of the animals during flight and during the time they will spend outdoors while waiting to be loaded onto the aircraft. Your airline may have restrictions during certain months of the year regardless of what the particular weather is that day.

Some airlines, such as Southwest, don't allow pet travel at all. If you're a frequent flier on a particular airline, it doesn't mean you'll be able to use that airline if you have to travel with your cat.

Specific documentation is required for feline air travel. Different airlines may have their own additional documentation requirements, but one form that's standard is the health certificate, which must be issued within ten days of your departure date. This is a certificate that your veterinarian must sign. He or she will have the forms in his or her office when you bring your cat in for the examination.

If you're planning to travel with your cat in the aircraft cabin, she must be in an airline-approved carrier that meets specific size requirements. It must be able to fit under the seat. You can buy airline-approved carriers in most pet supply stores. They come in hard plastic or soft-sided versions. Choose the type that your cat will be most comfortable in. Even though a soft-sided carrier might seem appealing, it may collapse around her when she's under the seat. Hard-sided carriers provide more safety in case of a sudden impact. Use your knowledge of your cat's security and comfort needs to determine which airline-approved carrier is best.

The carrier must have identification on it and it must also say *LIVE ANIMAL* somewhere on the outside.

If your cat will be flying as cargo, she must also be in an airline-approved carrier, though the carrier won't have to be as small since it won't be going under a seat. For cargo flight, you must use a hard carrier. There must be identification on the carrier with your name, address, and phone number, as well as a sign that says *LIVE ANIMAL*. There must also be clearly visible directional arrows that point to the carrier's correct side-up position. Food and water bowls must be firmly attached to the inside of the grille door on the carrier.

Catwise Preflight Feeding Tip

 Feed your cat a light meal four to six hours prior to the flight. Allow her to have small amounts of water up until the flight.

Get to the airport early to allow for the extra time it takes to check your cat through.

If you're going to be flying internationally, you need to contact your country of destination months in advance to be sure pets are allowed in, and to find out what the quarantine period is and what additional documentation may be required.

HOME ALONE KITTY: RETRAINING THE CAT WHO HATES PET SITTERS

If you have a cat who hates pet sitters and you're going away only for a night or two, you may be thinking you can bypass the whole problem by leaving your cat home alone. If your cat eats dry food and is free-fed, you might think this is an easy way out of the whole pet-sitting ordeal. Many people leave their cats alone for a couple of nights, right? In theory, you could leave your cat alone for a night or two, but I would advise against it. Wouldn't it be absolutely tragic if your cat got sick or injured during that time and no one was there to help her? How do you know that your cat isn't lonely or depressed or

anxious when her family suddenly disappears? Cats have the repu-
tation of being low-maintenance because they don't have to be
walked and can have food left out for nibbling, but that totally disre-
gards their emotional needs. With a little behavior modification,
you can make your cat more comfortable with having someone come
into the house to check on her. This will provide more peace of mind
on everyone's part, so you can have a more relaxing vacation knowing that your cat is safe at home.

Whether you ask your neighbor to check on your cat or hire a
professional pet sitter, it can be a nightmare if your cat hates the
person or goes into panic mode whenever she hears the key in the
lock. It doesn't have to be that way if you do a little preplanning and
make sure the pet sitter and your cat have developed some sort of
bond beforehand.

A mistake I often see made is that a cat owner will have someone
come over to take care of the cat whom the cat either has never met
or has seen only briefly. The pet sitter can be the sweetest person in
the whole world, and terribly fond of cats, but if your cat reacts negatively to strangers in the home, imagine how magnified that feeling
becomes when the stranger enters the home and YOU aren't there.
How does your cat know that the person entering the house isn't
there to do her harm? To top it off, this stranger is heading right for
areas that are solely the cat's, such as the litter box and the feeding
station. This stranger also often tries to track the cat down and make
an attempt at interaction. For a cat who has no fear of strangers, the
visitor's behavior will be fine, but for other cats it sends their stress-
o-meter into the danger zone.

Even if the pet sitter is a friend or neighbor who has been in your
home several times before, it doesn't mean your cat is comfortable
with the arrangement when you aren't at home. Much of her security
may come from being able to disappear when strangers normally
visit, but in the case of a pet sitter, she becomes the *target*.

If you hired a professional pet sitter, you may think you have done
all the right things by interviewing the person first and showing her

around the home well in advance of your trip. Depending on your cat's personality, though, that short interview may not have been sufficient enough for the pet sitter to gain your kitty's trust.

Use your knowledge of your cat's personality as you make arrangements for someone to pet-sit. Having someone come over once a day to scoop the box and put food in the bowl may not be enough if your cat has a tendency to get depressed or anxious when left alone for too long. The sex of the person may make a difference to your cat. Plan ahead as much as possible to limit the amount of stress your cat will go through during your absence.

When you choose the person to care for your cat, take the time to show him or her just how you manage the litter and the food. Be specific about aspects of your cat's care that will make a difference to your cat. I once had a client whose cat reacted very badly to the pet sitter because she remained in the kitchen after she placed the food bowl down. The cat was very nervous about having her in the room and refused to eat. Even seemingly minor things may make a big difference in your cat's level of comfort. For example, I have run across a few pet sitters who place the bowl of wet food down for the cats and then leave the bowl on the floor until the next visit. Your cat may not like the dirty dish sitting there on the floor, especially if she doesn't eat all of her food and it dries in the dish. If you change your cat's water daily, then make sure the pet sitter knows to do that and not just top off the dish with a little fresh water.

When you interview the person, conduct an interactive play session with your cat present if she isn't too frightened. That way you can show the pet sitter the technique you use for playtime. This can be a wonderful icebreaker for the pet sitter to gain your cat's trust. If your cat is up for it, hand the toy off to the pet sitter so he or she can do a little play session right then and there. Show the pet sitter where you store the interactive toys and be sure to stress that they must be put away after the play session.

If your cat simply fears anyone in the house, instruct the pet sitter not to try to track her down and entice her out of her hiding place. He or she needs to check on your cat to make sure she's safe, but trust won't be earned during their short daily or twice-daily visits, so the best thing is just to allow the cat to stay within her comfort zone. This is where preparing in advance by doing behavior modification to help your cat get more familiar and comfortable with the person who will be pet sitting can make a big difference. Even if your cat doesn't run to the door to greet the pet sitter, at least she'll feel safe in her own environment if she has had some past experience with the person that has been positive or even just neutral.

Even though most cats generally prefer being able to remain in their own homes when the cat owners travel as opposed to being placed in a boarding facility, it can still be a stressful experience for the cat to have someone enter her territory. The cat is already confused by the sudden absence of her family, so it's important for her daily routine to stay as normal as possible. If your cat is fed on a schedule and eats twice a day, then the pet sitter should make two visits daily. If that's not possible, you may want to purchase a timed feeding bowl. These are easy to find in most pet supply stores and online and will enable you to maintain your cat's normal feeding routine.

How the pet sitter smells may be a contributing factor in whether or not your cat is uncomfortable. A professional pet sitter who visits several other houses before coming to yours may have the scent of other animals on his or her clothes. That won't bother some cats, but it can be extremely upsetting to others. Your cat may be one of those who feels threatened by the scent of unfamiliar animals inside her territory. If you know your cat has a history of reacting badly to visitors who have cats of their own, and you've chosen a professional pet sitter, ask the person to change his or her clothes before coming into your home. In my line of work, I'm prepared for situations in which a client's cat may be uncomfortable if she detects the scent of other cats on me by always keeping several changes of clothes in my car, and I thoroughly wash my hands between clients. A professional pet sitter should be prepared for special requests. It's not too much to ask him or her to change clothes before coming to your home if you know your cat is very reactive. Another little trick is to have the person squirt a little *Feliway* onto the tips of his shoes and/or the hems of his pant legs. A good pet sitter understands that every animal has a different comfort level and will work with you to make the experience as positive as possible.

If you're asking a friend or neighbor for a favor in caring for your cat and you aren't financially compensating them, it can be more difficult to request special things, but don't shortchange your cat. If the pet-sitting experience is negative this time, it will be worse the next time. I'm sure there will be a favor you can return to the friend, so you can feel comfortable asking for special requests regarding your cat's care.

You may have a cat who doesn't run in fear when the pet sitter arrives but rather stands her ground and displays aggression. If your cat displays an aggressive posture to visitors in your home at a distance but doesn't take it any further, it's absolutely crucial that you instruct the pet sitter on how to behave when in your home. If your cat backs down when a visitor doesn't look directly at her or doesn't move toward her, then the pet sitter should just go about his or her business, ignoring the cat and not making any attempt to interact with her. If your cat is aggressive and actually pursues someone in the house, then a pet-sitting arrangement is not a safe one for the person caring for your cat. It also puts your cat in a position of feeling threatened, and without you there to provide security or do behavior modification, she may continue to remain anxious even after the pet sitter has left. In a home with more than one cat, this may lead to redirected aggression. In the case of an overtly aggressive cat, your best option is to have your cat boarded while you're gone. I almost always prefer that a cat remain in her own familiar surroundings when a cat owner goes away, but it's not a good idea when there's risk of injury to the caregiver or any of the other cats in the environment. Besides, in some cases, a cat who is hostile in her own territory may not be aggressive in the boarding environment.

BOARDING WOES

If your cat is used to travel, has been around other cats, and is okay with unfamiliar environments, then a boarding kennel may not bother her much at all. If she isn't used to being away from home, gets stressed in a cage environment, or is frightened or hostile in the presence of other cats, then boarding can be about as stressful as it gets in the cat world. In general, boarding takes away everything that's comforting and secure for the cat. She's without you, she's without her familiar environment, and she's now in an environment filled with threatening sounds, smells, and sights. Being in a cage can be extremely stressful because she has no hiding place and no ability to escape. Her litter box, food, and water bowls are within inches of each other. Nothing about this experience seems positive from a cat's point of view. But despite all the negatives, boarding is a very practical option for many cat owners, and in many cases is the only option.

As with everything else in life, there are good boarding facilities and bad ones. There are also boarding facilities that are more like pet spas than kennels, where your cat has a large condo, lots of room to play, interactive playtime with staff members, and maybe even her own television featuring the latest in cat entertainment DVDs. Because boarding creates anxiety for the cat and her owners, more animal-loving people are creating state-of-the-art boarding kennels. If you are fortunate enough to have one in your town and it's within your budget, it may make a big difference in helping your cat remain less anxious during your time away from her.

If one of those terrific boarding facilities isn't a possibility for you and your cat must be boarded in a typical cage environment, there are still things you can do to help reduce some of the anxiety. Always inspect the boarding facility before you commit to leaving your cat there. Find out how well trained the staff is and how the animals are monitored after hours. How clean is the facility? How quiet is it? Are the cats housed in a totally separate area from the dogs? What's the emergency procedure? If the boarding facility is not part of a veterinary clinic, how are sudden illnesses or injuries handled? When you're there to inspect the facility, pay attention to how the staff and the animals interact. Do the members of the staff seem to enjoy what they're doing and relate well to the boarded animals? Surprisingly, I have been in facilities that were strictly business—the staff didn't seem to have any desire to make the animals feel more at ease.

When you bring your cat to the facility, bring her own food and her own brand of litter. Your cat needs to be on her regular food to avoid any stomach upsets and also to avoid the added stress of a sudden change in diet. Even a change in litter can be traumatic, so regardless of whether or not the kennel supplies litter, bring the brand your cat is used to. Don't bring your cat's litter box, though, because an appropriately sized one will be supplied for your cat.

If your cat is on any medication, be sure to bring that along and include specific directions. For example, if a pill is to be given once a day, you want the staff to administer the pill at the same time of day that you normally do.

Pack a couple of shirts or towels that have your scent on them to be included in your cat's cage. This can provide just a little extra comfort and familiarity in an otherwise stressful environment.

Find out what type of daily exercise or interaction the staff provides for the cats boarded there. If your cat can be taken out of her cage for a daily interactive play session, that would be very beneficial. Many kennels have special play rooms set up where they take the cats one at a time for playtime. Find out what cleaning precautions are taken in these rooms. If the staff can do play sessions, pack a toy such as the *Cat Dancer* or the *Dragonfly* because they're easy to store and won't take up much room. If you bring your cat's current toys from home, purchase new ones to replace them because you may not want to bring the toys back home after they've picked up scents at the kennel.

If your cat is timid or you think she'll be frightened in the cage, find out if there's room to place a semicovered bed in the corner of the cage. At the very least, pack a few paper bags to use as hideaways. Open a paper bag and roll the edges back into a cuff as many times as needed to make the bag small enough to fit in the cage. Making a cuff around the edge of the bag will also make it sturdier and less likely to collapse. Place the bag on its side and put a small towel or shirt in there as a bed. Position the bag at an angle or sideways so the opening isn't directly facing the cage door. This will provide your cat with a little more security if she feels she's totally exposed.

For a cat who is completely over the edge with anxiety during the boarding process, a sheet of newspaper can be taped over the front of the cage. This may help if she's too nervous to venture out from her covered bed or paper bag even to use the litter box or eat a meal. Inquire about what the staff does to create more security for cats who are terrified.

Some boarding facilities keep *Feliway* spray on hand to use in the cages. If the boarding facility you chose doesn't do that, bring a bottle with you and spray the inside corners of the cage before placing the cat inside. Leave the bottle with the staff and ask them to spray the corners with one quick spritz once a day and after every time they clean out the cage or if your cat is transferred to another cage. It's best to spray the cage when the cat isn't in there to give it time to dry. A good time to do it is when the cat is removed for cage cleaning or playtime.

If there are particular calming techniques that you know work for your cat, or if there are certain things that create adverse reactions, inform the staff. For example, your cat may absolutely adore being scratched under the chin, and that may create instant purring on her part. Then again, your cat may like to be petted only on the back of the head and routinely attempts to bite if you touch her under the chin or on the front of the neck. This is important information for the staff to have. My two cats were feral when I rescued them, and although they're very well-adjusted, happy cats now, there were some specific petting techniques that had to be used with Bebe for a number of years. She would accept petting and absolutely love it as long as your hand approached from behind her and never over her head. If you attempted to pet the top of her head while she was facing you, she would swipe or try to bite. Although I never boarded her, there were times when she had to be hospitalized, and I had to make sure the clinic staff knew how to handle her. It would be natural for a technician to reach into the cage to pet her, but it would have ended in injury had I not given them proper instructions.

If you have more than one cat, keep in mind that even though they may be the best of friends at home, the stress of the boarding environment could cause hostility between them. If you want them to be boarded together in the same cage, make sure there's room at the facility to separate the cats should things turn sour. Also, if one of your cats has a tendency to display redirected aggression, especially at the sight of an unfamiliar cat in the yard, then there's a strong possibility that such aggression could be exhibited toward the companion cat in the same cage in a crowded kennel.

When you bring your cat home from the boarding facility, give her time to settle back into the home. Don't be hurt if she needs time before accepting hugs and kisses. What may matter most to her at the moment is checking out her environment to make sure it's the same as when she left it. If she needs to do this, don't interrupt the process. Let her regain her sense of security about her territory. She'll then be in a better frame of mind to turn her attention toward you. Don't offer her a huge welcome-home meal either, because she may still be a bit anxious over the whole experience of being away from home and now returning.

Immediately wash any towels or clothing that had been at the kennel as well as any that lined the carrier. Take the carrier apart, wash it thoroughly, and, after it has dried, give a couple squirts of *Feliway* in the corners and replace the carrier to its original position (which should be sitting open and ready in some room in your home).

If after being home for a while your cat still seems a little anxious and unsettled, engage her in an interactive play therapy session so she can work off those nerves in a positive way.

HOW TO REDUCE ANXIETY FOR VETERINARIAN VISITS

When it comes to travel destinations, this is definitely not on a cat's top-ten list. First, kitty starts out with the experience of seeing the dreaded carrier come out of the closet, and she knows that's never a good sign. After being chased around the house, she's captured, placed in the carrier, and whisked off for a ride in the car. If the only time the cat ever rides in the car is when she's headed to the veterinarian, then the pre–vet visit anxiety is already well under way. Finally, you reach the destination and kitty enters a building filled with the scents, sounds, and sights of unfamiliar animals. Perhaps the only seat left in the waiting room is the one next to the very large dog who is extremely curious about the little ball of fur hiding in the carrier. On top of the scents, sounds, and sights of unfamiliar animals, there's the occasional (or maybe not so occasional) shriek of a cat or yelp of a dog in pain heard from behind the examination-room door, perhaps accompanied by a hiss, growl, yowl, bark, and so forth. If kitty has had prior experience at the veterinarian's office, then she also knows there's a good chance she'll be poked, prodded, or stuck with a needle. *Gee, I can't imagine why she's not happy about going to the veterinarian's office!*

There are certain aspects of a veterinarian visit that just can't be changed, but there are some things you can do to reduce some of the stress for your cat. Every little bit helps.

If you don't regularly take your cat to the veterinarian, or are thinking of changing your current vet, see if there is a cats-only clinic in your area. It may make a big difference to your cat's comfort level if she doesn't have to sit in the waiting room with dogs. Cats-only clinics are usually set up in a way to minimize stress for the patients, and the staffs are very familiar with cat-handling techniques. If there isn't a cats-only clinic in your area, you may be able to find a clinic that separates the dog waiting area from the cat waiting room. When choosing a veterinarian clinic, though, what matters most are the veterinarian and the staff. Don't choose a clinic just because there's a separate waiting area for cats if you don't like the doctor, if the staff seems rude, or if the clinic appears dirty.

To help minimize waiting time, especially if there might be dogs in the waiting room, schedule appointments in the morning or just after the doctor's lunch hour. Unless it's urgent, try to avoid Saturday appointments or weekday appointments after five PM. You can call the receptionist and inquire about when the slowest times appear to be and choose that appointment if you have the flexibility in your schedule.

Another stress minimizer is to do the behavior modification described earlier in this chapter regarding your cat's association with the carrier and the car ride. These are two important steps, especially if your cat tends to be very fractious or panicky when the carrier appears in view.

Spray the carrier with *Feliway* about a half hour before placing your cat inside. Bring the bottle with you to spray the examination table at the veterinarian's office as well. Some clinics already engage in this practice, or at least keep the spray handy to spritz cages for hospitalized patients. If your cat reacts well to catnip, you can also bring a bit along to sprinkle on the examination table.

If your cat has a history of going ballistic in the waiting room, stay outside in the car with her until your appointment. If you have a mobile phone, call the clinic and tell the receptionist you're in the car in the parking lot and to please call when your cat is ready to be seen by the veterinarian. If you don't have a cell phone, run into the clinic and ask the receptionist to come to the door to alert you when it's your turn. If your cat is able to stay in the car with you and totally bypass the waiting-room trauma, that may help keep her anxiety at a more manageable level during the exam itself.

Many cats have what I call a window of opportunity. Some may be extremely anxious at first and need time to settle down before a veterinarian can handle them. For other cats, the window is short and quick, so the longer they remain in the exam room, the more worked up they get. If you know your cat's window of opportunity, inform your veterinarian. If her window is short and quick up front, your veterinarian should do all the examining and handling first and then engage in the discussions later. I once had a veterinarian who was a dear friend and always wanted to take the time when he first walked into the room to catch up on how my family was doing. My cat's window of opportunity was short and quick, and I had to let him know that so we could conduct our personal conversations after she was calmly back in her carrier.

In some multicat homes, when only one cat is going to the veterinarian, there may be some territorial aggression displayed when that kitty returns. Scent is a very strong recognition signal for cats, and when a cat returns from the veterinarian clinic, she doesn't smell like herself. To make matters worse, she smells like a place the cats view as threatening. For behavior modification techniques to help prevent hostility after a trip to the veterinarian, refer to chapter 8 in the section about *territorial aggression*.

LEASH TRAINING AN ADULT CAT

Even if you have never let your cat outdoors and don't plan to in the future, it's a good idea to leash-train her. At the very least, you'll be able to get her comfortable with wearing a harness, which will come in handy if you ever travel with her, as previously described in the sections on car travel and air travel.

Leash training is much easier done when the cat is young. If you're dealing with an older adult, you can't go too slowly! Plan on taking your time with all the individual phases of leash training. Don't stress out your cat or turn this into a battle of wills.

Just because you leash-train your cat doesn't mean you have to take her outside for a walk. Not every cat has the right temperament for being outdoors even under the most controlled circumstances. Timid cats aren't good candidates for outdoor leash walking. Cats who become aggressive in unfamiliar surroundings are also not good candidates. The type of outdoor environment around your home may also not be conducive to leash walking a cat. The training exercise is still worthwhile, though. You never know when a situation will arise in which having your cat comfortable in a harness could keep her safe if travel is necessary.

It's important to remember that leash walking a cat will in no way resemble walking a dog. If you ever do get to the point at which you take her outdoors for a walk on the leash, she'll probably want to stop and investigate every flower, leaf, or blade of grass. She's a hunter who is very tuned in to her environment, so her senses will be in overdrive. If you think that leash training her will enable the two of you to go trotting down the sidewalk the way your neighbor walks her poodle, you should readjust your expectations.

Before you begin training, you need the right equipment. Although your cat may wear a collar, it won't be acceptable for leash training. She needs a harness. There are two types of cat harnesses. One is a figure-eight design that loops around the neck and then around the body, just behind the armpits. The other type of harness is an H design, which fits like a sideways letter H on the body. An excellent alternative to a harness is a cat-walking jacket. This is a nylon jacket that fits around the cat's torso. I prefer using the walking jacket and find that cats accept it more quickly and seem to be more comfortable in it. Also, if you've adjusted it correctly, it's virtually impossible for the cat to slip out of it. I've seen cats slip out of harnesses, but I have yet to see one escape from a correctly adjusted walking jacket. Refer to the appendix for information on the walking jacket. The good thing is that you have options, so if your cat doesn't do well with one, you can try the other. Harnesses and walking jackets come in several sizes, so it's important to get the right fit.

When shopping for a leash, a very lightweight nylon one will do the trick. You don't need a chain or a leather leash. Thin, light nylon leashes are most appropriate for cats. Don't use a retractable leash either. If you do take your cat outdoors, you won't have her walking far in front of you. Because danger can lurk around any corner or your cat may suddenly get spooked, you'll want to walk right at her side so you can scoop her up instantly should the need arise.

The technique you'll use to help your cat become comfortable with the harness or walking jacket will require patience on your part. This has to be done in short, calm, positive steps. You'll also have to set aside at least two weeks of indoor behavior modification before you attempt to take her outside. Keep in mind that even if she does well in the house, it doesn't mean she's a good candidate for leash walking outdoors. As you go through this process, always keep your cat's temperament, comfort level, and health in mind.

The first step is just to place the harness or jacket on the floor so your cat can get used to the sight of it. If you have *Feliway*, you can give the harness or jacket one quick spritz. Another option is to put a clean sock on your hand and gently rub your cat around the mouth to pick up some of her facial pheromones, then give the harness or jacket a good rubdown with the sock.

After the harness or jacket has been around for a couple of days, put it on your cat loosely and then immediately distract her with a delicious meal. Don't make it so loose that it dangles down and bothers her as she walks, but don't attempt to tighten it the first few times you put it on her. Based on your cat's temperament, you may not even be able to fasten it at all the first couple of times you put it on her.

Keep the session short. As soon as the meal is over, take the harness or jacket off. What you're trying to accomplish is to build up her tolerance for wearing the harness or jacket gradually. The best way to do this is by distracting her with something positive. Do this a few times a day for several days and then you can gradually start to increase the amount of time she wears it.

Use the clicker when you put the harness or jacket on and then offer a reward. Every time you put the harness or jacket on her and she's calm, click and reward. If you aren't offering a portion of her meal during the harness/jacket training process, then make sure you have pieces of treats in your pocket and have your clicker handy.

Increase the amount of time your cat wears the harness or jacket each day. Don't attempt to attach the leash yet. Take as much time as your cat needs to get comfortable with this first stage.

CATWISE CLUE

It may be easier to put the harness or jacket on your cat if she's on an elevated surface. This will also make it easier for you to see the fasteners so you can be sure you have fitted it correctly.

When she can wear the harness or jacket without any problems, you can attach the leash for short periods. When she's attached to the leash, let it trail along behind her—don't try to hold on to it yet. It will only create panic if you try to tug on the leash in any way at this point. Use the click-and-reward system when you attach the leash. You can also offer her a portion of her meal or just have some pieces of treats handy to give her as she accepts being connected to the lightweight leash.

For the next stage, you're going to hold the leash, stand a little bit in front of her, and give a cue for her to walk up next to you. The verbal cue can be any word; just precede it with her name. So you might say, *"Fluffy, walk,"* or even, *"Fluffy, heel."* When you give the cue, lean down and show her that you have a treat in your hand. At this stage of leash training, I will tape the clicker to a spoon and have a little drop of wet food on the spoon's tip. This way I have the leash in one hand and the clicker/spoon combo in the other, so I don't have to fumble and end up marking the behavior too late. Show the cat the food on the spoon or the treat. As she walks toward it, click and reward. When you do this, don't tug on the leash. Let her be in control of the movement. After a few sessions of this stage of the training, you can start to give a very mild tug on the leash. The reason for this is so she gets used to the fact that there is, in fact, a tether attached to her. If she's going to have any sort of negative reaction to that realization, you want it to occur in the safety of your home and not outdoors. The normal position you'll take when walking your cat is to stand beside her or right behind her. This will reduce the chance that she could pull out of the harness or jacket if it wasn't fitted right or if she becomes frantic. It's important to stand beside or behind her to prevent an escape attempt because cats pull out of harnesses backward.

Continue your indoor training sessions until you're absolutely sure your cat is comfortable being on a leash and doesn't have any negative reactions if the leash is gently tugged.

If you're planning on taking your cat outdoors on the leash, she needs to be up-to-date on her vaccinations. Keep in mind that she'll also be at risk for parasite infestation, so she'll need flea and tick protection. Identification will also be very important. Even though she'll be on a leash, a mistake could happen and she could get out of your grasp.

When you go outdoors, bring along your clicker and your treats. If you have been using a trainer's treat bag or a fanny pack, load it up with all the tools you may need, such as a small container of wet food (I use little plastic containers similar to the type that holds film rolls), a spoon, some treats, and your clicker. Take along a soft-sided carrier with you as well. You can carry it on your shoulder like a duffle bag. This way, it won't get in the way as you're walking, but you'll have it nearby in case something frightens your cat. Trying to get back home with a fractious cat in your arms is dangerous for both you and your cat. With a carrier at the ready, you'll always be prepared and everyone can stay safe. At the very least, drape a thick towel over your shoulder before you head out with your cat so you'll have some way of safely scooping her up in an emergency and keeping her confined in your arms as you head back home. If the area in which you'll be walking your cat isn't fenced in, or if there's a reasonable chance that something or someone could cross your path, it's worth investing in a soft-sided carrier.

Don't venture far if you take your cat outdoors. Remember, this is all unfamiliar territory to her. She doesn't need to take a mile-long walk; she'll be very happy with a stroll around the house or even just around the deck or the backyard. The farther away from your own yard you go, the harder it'll be to bring her back home safely if something suddenly frightens her. Going farther away also increases the risk that you'll run into another cat or a dog.

CATWISE REMINDER

- Keep the experience calm, relaxed, and fun.
- Even though your demeanor will be relaxed, always keep an eye out for potential trouble.
- Double-check the harness or jacket before heading outside to be sure it's fitted properly.
- You're not walking a dog, so don't expect your cat to behave like one.
- Make sure your cat is protected against fleas and ticks.
- All vaccinations should be up-to-date.
- Don't leave the harness or jacket on your cat once you've returned indoors.
- Don't tie the leash to anything in order to confine your cat.

One thing that can happen after you start taking your cat outdoors for walks is that she may decide that anytime there's a door open in the house, she's free to wander through it. Once you've given your cat a taste of the outdoors, you have to make sure every family member is aware of the fact that kitty might not wait until it's leash-walking time to try to go outside. She may have decided to set her own schedule, and that would be very dangerous.

MOVING TO A NEW HOME

This is a stressful experience for humans, so imagine how over-the-top it can be for your cat. She had no idea that this was about to take place. All she knows is that, first, her world started changing drastically, with boxes coming in and things getting packed up and rearranged. Then she was whisked off to a totally unfamiliar environment. Since a cat is a territorial creature and takes comfort in the familiarity of her surroundings, this experience can be incredibly confusing and disorienting. It is confusing and stressful for most cats, no matter how old they are, but it's especially difficult for an older cat who has lived in the same environment all her life. So as you prepare for your move, you have to take your cat's needs into consideration and try to make the transition as smooth as possible. Even though you have so much to do and not enough time in which to do it, it will be much easier on everyone to help ease the cat through this now, rather than have to deal with a potentially severe behavior problem after the move.

Start early

The first big anxiety-provoking stage of moving may involve selling your own home. This means strangers will be coming into your home and invading all of your cat's territory. Keep your cat's temperament in mind throughout this process. If your cat is very sociable and doesn't have a problem with unfamiliar people in the home, then you'll be fine. If, however, your cat is frightened of visitors, make sure your cat's welfare is addressed as you go through the home-selling process. If you're doing an open house, your cat may be better off being boarded for the day, or staying at a neighbor's home. Perhaps a neighbor could set up one room in his or her home as a little sanctuary so your kitty can stay undisturbed during the hours of the open house. If your only option is to have your cat remain in your home during the open house, set her up in a quiet room and have a family member stay in there with her. This way, the family member can make sure potential buyers don't try to interact with the cat or get too close. Make sure the cat has several hideaway options in the room. If the cat really goes over-the-top with stress or displays aggression toward visitors, set her up in a large crate so she can have her litter box, water, food, and a cozy bed. Cover the crate or cage with a light towel so she can remain hidden. Leave a little space at the bottom for her to be able to see out.

Regardless of whether your cat was boarded, stayed at a neighbor's home, or remained in your home, take time after the open house to calm her. Use *Feliway* on corners of objects in the home so the cat will sense some familiarity again. If there was a lot of traffic on the carpet, vacuum before letting your cat back into the area and give the carpet a very light spritz of *Feliway* in a couple of the main areas. If your cat responds well to catnip, throw a little catnip party for her. Distract her from her anxiety with a little interactive play session if she's in the mood. Don't overdo the cuddling; that will only reinforce your cat's fear. Remain casual and calm as she walks around the house investigating any unfamiliar scents.

If you aren't doing an open house, but a real estate agent will be showing your home when you aren't around, make sure it's made clear that there's a cat in the house. I have known of instances in which cats were accidentally let outside. You may even want to set your cat up in a sanctuary room in your home, close the door, and put a sign on the door that warns people to be careful when opening the door so they don't let the cat out. That way, if your cat does manage to run out the door, it will only be out of an internal door and not the front door. You can also put a sign on the front door as a reminder to the real estate agent before he/she enters that there's a cat inside the house. Place a note on the inside of the front door as well, as a reminder for when the agent and the potential home buyer are leaving. If your cat gets very nervous around strangers, perhaps someone in your family or a neighbor can arrange to be in the home when the real estate agent shows the house.

Once the home is sold, the next anxiety-provoking stage is the packing. This is when your cat starts to wonder whether you've lost your mind because things in your home are being moved around and shoved into boxes. During this stage, her human family members aren't following the normal routine of playtime with her and are maybe even being late with dinner.

Let's start with the boxes. While a couple of boxes brought into the cat's home for playtime can be lots of fun and an opportunity for exploration, stacks and stacks of boxes coming into the home can start to be confusing. Take time out from your packing every now and then to engage your cat in a play session, especially if you see she's getting nervous about the changes taking place. Some cats may view the onslaught of boxes as a giant playground, but others may be frightened. Pay attention to your cat's body language so you can make adjustments along the way. The more you can maintain her normal schedule, the better. If you have a cat who is responding negatively to all of the unfamiliar boxes in the home, spray a little *Feliway* on the corners of them to help her find some comforting familiarity.

Your premove preparation time is also when you should be making sure your cat is comfortable with being in a carrier and is up-to-date on her vaccinations. If you don't have a carrier for your cat, you'll need one.

If you're moving out of town or far enough away that you'll no longer be using your current veterinarian, get a copy of your cat's medical records for the new veterinarian.

If your cat wears a collar, get an updated ID tag with your new contact information and put it on her the day of the move.

For an indoor/outdoor cat, the premove time can signal enough of a warning that the cat may not return home. As the move approaches, if things have been especially stressful for her, don't take the chance that she'll disappear. Start keeping your cat indoors well in advance of moving day. Don't count on the fact that she always returns home, because it would be a tragedy if you had to leave and kitty was nowhere to be found. I have known of cat owners who have actually let their cats out on moving day and then spent several desperate hours in search of them as the moving van was ready to go. Some of those people found their cats, but, sadly, some didn't.

Moving day

If your move is in town, you may want to board your cat at the veterinary clinic or a boarding facility while the movers are loading the van. It's very easy for a cat to slip out the door when someone is carrying out a large piece of furniture. If you think your cat will be terribly frightened by all the commotion, boarding her at the veterinary clinic may be the least stressful option. Another option is to ask a neighbor to allow your cat to stay at his or her home during the loading phase. You can also move everything out of one room first and then put your cat into that room and close the door. That way she can stay safe in there while people are going in and out of the house. If you choose that option, place a big sign on the door as a reminder to everyone that the room is empty of furniture and that there's a cat in there.

If you can't empty one room first, then perhaps you can save that room for last. Allow your cat to stay in there while everything else is being loaded. Then, when it's time to empty that room, place your cat in her carrier and put her in a quiet place while the last room is being dismantled and the furniture loaded onto the van.

If you have more than one bathroom in your home, keep your cat in there while the move takes place. Whatever your particular situation, make sure you have set up a safe and least-stressful holding area for your cat, because your mind will be on a million other things.

The new home

If you're able to be in the home before the actual physical move, use that time to establish where you'll set up your cat's sanctuary room, because you don't want to allow her to have the run of the place right away. It will be overwhelming for her to have to get to know the entire new house at once plus try to remember where her food and litter box are located.

Look around the house and make sure things are secure before you bring your cat in. If you're moving during warm weather and may be opening windows, are the screens secure and strong?

If you're moving into a previously lived-in home and there's carpet currently there, you may have some odor residue from previous pets. Bring along your black light and go over the home to check for areas where a cat may have sprayed. If you can detect any odor from old cat urine, you can bet that isn't going to sit very well with your cat. Take care of it ahead of time so that there's one less anxiety-provoking trigger that could cause behavior problems. Depending on how severe the stains and odors are, an enzymatic cleaner may do the job, or you may end up ripping out carpets and padding.

An in-town move may allow you to do some advance work to make some cat-friendly adjustments to the home. You may be able to bring some furniture over in advance, so you can set up a sanctuary room that'll be ready and waiting for your kitty.

When you do move your cat to the new home, spray *Feliway* on objects in the sanctuary room and also on any door frames. Make sure the sanctuary room has the cat's litter box on one side and the food and water bowls on the other side. There should also be hideaways so your kitty has a secure place to nap. You can leave the carrier out and open as an extra hiding place for her as well.

Keep your cat in the sanctuary room until she seems to be comfortable and unafraid. Depending on your individual cat, that could be a few hours to several days. Let your cat set the pace. If she's hiding, she's not ready to expand her horizons just yet.

When you do think it's time to let her see the rest of the home, do it in stages. Don't force her to try to establish her territory in an overwhelming way by having to get to know the entire house. Before you open the door to the sanctuary room, close off some other rooms. Use *Feliway* on corners in the house and on any new pieces of furniture purchased. Have your clicker and treats handy as well as an interactive toy. Open the sanctuary room door and allow your cat to come out at her own speed, and let her determine how far she wants to go. You can click and reward if she ventures out. As she comes out into the main part of the home, use an interactive toy to distract her if she starts to get nervous. Keep the sessions short if she seems nervous or unsure. It's better to do several short sessions a day and let her gradually get to know the new environment.

When she's out and about more often, keep the sanctuary room set up so she still has a secure place to retreat to if needed. In addition to the litter box in the sanctuary room, set up a litter box (or more than one) in the area(s) you've chosen as its permanent location. This way, your cat can get to know the other area while still having the security of the litter box in her sanctuary room.

If you've moved to a bigger home, keep in mind that you may need more litter boxes. If you've moved from a one-floor environment to a two-story or more home, you'll need a litter box on each level.

If your cat went outdoors in her previous home, this would be the perfect time to transition her to being exclusively indoors. If you absolutely insist on allowing her outdoors, don't do it for at least a month. Then, when you do start letting her out, have her on a leash so you can help her get to know her new environment. Keep in mind that there's nothing outside to remind her that this is her territory. In fact, she may have to face other cats who may not want another cat in the area. She may have to fight her way into the neighborhood. Seriously reconsider whether she should be allowed outdoors anymore.

11

Cat Versus Brush
Groom Your Cat and Live to Talk About It

Perhaps the thought of brushing your cat is totally laughable to you. In your opinion, your rough and tough cat who hunts in the backyard, keeps dogs twice his size out of his territory, and instills fear in the hearts of the veterinary staff at vaccination time can handle his own hygiene duties.

All cats, regardless of breed, age, type of coat, and even type of personality, need some degree of grooming maintenance. Some require much more than others, but you need to be able to get your hands on your cat every now and then without it being a battle that neighbors can hear three houses over.

Even if grooming time is dreaded by both you and your cat, it's never too late to change your approach and your cat's perception of the process.

LOOK AT YOUR CURRENT GROOMING TECHNIQUE FROM KITTY'S POINT OF VIEW

If you have a long-haired cat who has to be groomed every day but you haven't been keeping that schedule, when it comes time to brush him, there are probably more than a few mats to be removed. Mats can form in a very short amount of time, and if you don't do a light brushing every day, the session is guaranteed to be unpleasant because your cat knows it'll involve pulling, yanking, tugging, and perhaps even cutting. Much of that could be prevented by brushing a little bit every day.

If grooming is something neither you nor your cat enjoy, then when you do set aside time for the procedure, you may be taking too long. Some people think that once they have their cats restrained, they'll do everything at once to get it done with. That turns a grooming session into an intolerably long torture session for kitty.

The more a cat hates being brushed, the easier it becomes for a cat owner to restrain too much, get frustrated and angry, be too rough with the tools, or just abandon the process altogether.

If you didn't get your cat gradually acquainted with having his paws, ears, and other sensitive parts of his body touched when he was younger, then your attempts at grooming have probably been met with dread, fear, or even aggression. The sight of a grooming tool may have long ago became a signal to run for a spot from which it's practically impossible to be extricated by human hands.

Brushing and grooming sessions shouldn't be viewed with dread, yet many cats and cat owners engage in this bond-destroying ritual for years on end. Regardless of how long you and your cat have engaged in this test of wills, or even if you long ago gave up on any attempt to groom your cat, it's not too late to try to improve the situation.

Depending upon how well your cat was socialized, or how much work has to be done to get his coat mat-free, you may not be able to do complete grooming yourself. In some situations, it's best to leave the grooming to a professional. If your cat's coat has been neglected, let a professional groomer get it back in good shape, and then you can continue with daily maintenance. If your cat has never been receptive to touch contact with humans due to being feral, semiferal, or not having been socialized, then necessary procedures such as nail trimming and ear cleaning should be done by your veterinarian so they can be accomplished quickly and without injury to anyone.

Still, you should continue to work on trust-building behavior modification as described throughout this book. As you work on building trust, you may find that you can start some of the techniques described later in this chapter on brushing or getting the cat comfortable with having his paws handled.

HOW THE GROOMING SESSION SHOULD BE VIEWED BY KITTY AND THE CAT OWNER

This may be a stretch for you to imagine at this point, but the grooming session should be a time of trust and, if not enjoyable, should at least be easily tolerated.

In addition to brushing the coat and removing any mats, it's a time to check and trim nails. Ears should be checked to see if they need cleaning, and teeth should be brushed or an oral spray used. With some breeds, routine eye cleaning needs to be done as well.

The grooming session also allows you the opportunity to check over your cat's body. Since you'll be brushing and touching, you can check for any lumps or bumps, injuries, or tender areas. This is also the time when you can check ears and eyes for any sign of infection or problems. During tooth brushing or spraying the mouth with an oral rinse, you can check for red or inflamed gums, or loose or broken teeth.

Grooming can be a time of relaxation and enjoyment for the cat as he gets a nice massage and lots of petting. If he doesn't enjoy it all that much, he should at least be able to endure the process knowing it'll end very quickly. Finally, there should be a reward waiting for him at the end of the session, so that there's strong motivation to tolerate being brushed, fluffed, trimmed, and cleaned again next time.

THE RETRAINING PROCESS

Starting from scratch is exactly what you'll need to do. You have to change your cat's perception of the process through behavior modification.

Where you're going to groom your cat has to be decided. For the initial retraining and trust building, you can start with your cat on your lap or wherever the two of you feel most comfortable, but soon you'll have to decide on one spot. You may choose a table or other elevated surface so it'll be easier on your back. Just make sure it's an area where your cat is allowed so you don't send mixed messages by placing him up there for grooming, but chasing him off at other times of the day. If you have a long-haired cat and you need to check all over for mats and work on removing them, then an elevated surface will be much easier. For a short-haired cat who won't require much maintenance, you may decide that it's easier to do it with the cat in your lap. If you choose an elevated surface, you may want to put a rubber mat over the area so your cat has a secure surface to grip.

For right now, the sessions will be confined to showing your cat that being placed on the table or on your lap is a positive experience. Have your clicker handy. When he sits on your lap or on the table, click and reward. If you're not using a clicker, offer a piece of a treat when he's in the correct spot.

The first session is a trust-building experience that consists of just petting. If your cat is uncomfortable being touched or is sensitive about being touched in certain areas, you have to start by getting him comfortable with your fingers there. As an extension of petting or affection, gently touch his ears or the tops of his paws. If he's very sensitive about a particular area, do it just once and then move to a spot where he does enjoy being petted. If he's not comfortable having his paws touched, gently pet a paw one time and then give him a scratch under the chin or pet him behind the head. Calmly move back to the paw area for another light stroke or touch and then back to the chin or head again. Do the same with other sensitive areas, such as the ears.

In subsequent sessions, work up from just petting the paws to holding one lightly in your hand for a couple of seconds. Then go back to petting in the areas he likes. You can also use your clicker here. When you hold the paw, click and reward him. Do the same with other sensitive areas.

With the paws, you'll gradually start to hold the paw with your thumb on top and a couple of fingers on the paw pad so you can gently press to extend the claw. If your cat accepts that, click and reward. Also include petting of the areas he enjoys so the total experience is viewed positively.

With the ears, work up from just touching them to briefly holding the pinnae (the cone-shaped part). Click when you hold the ear and your cat is calm. Then reward him.

Since brushing the cat's teeth is an important part of good oral health—or at the very least, using an oral spray recommended by your veterinarian—your cat will have to become comfortable with your fingers there. Start by gently stroking him on the head and every once in a while stroking him along the side of the face. Always pet in the direction of the hair. Gently run your fingers along the sides of his mouth. During subsequent sessions, you'll work up to slipping your finger inside his lips so you can gently rub his gums. Click and reward each positive step, then return to petting in the areas your cat prefers.

Do these sessions during your normal times of cuddling and affection. When you're sitting on the sofa with your cat on your lap, incorporate some retraining exercises. It's the perfect time because your cat is relaxed and calm. Your demeanor must be calm and gentle as you do this. Think of it as an extension of petting so your body language will reflect that and not tense up. Talk to your cat in a very calm and comforting manner as well.

If your cat has a history of disliking the actual brushing process, use a grooming glove as part of your petting sessions. These gloves are a good way to retrain a cat to accept the feel of something other than your smooth hand on his fur.

If you have a long-haired cat who will need brushing in sensitive areas such as the armpits or tummy, you need to work on developing his tolerance for that if he has previously not allowed access to those spots. With your grooming glove on one hand, lift one paw up slightly with the other hand and then gently and quickly stroke his armpit with the grooming glove. Click and reward. Hold the clicker with the hand that's lifting up the paw. Use the same method to hold up both front paws with one hand and then gently stroke the tummy with the grooming glove. The tummy is the most sensitive place of all on the cat, but in the case of a long-haired breed, mats can form there as well, so you have to get him comfortable with the process. The technique I use is, with the cat facing away from me on a table, I lift up the front paws and lean toward the cat so he can feel he has support on his back. I then use my other hand to groom his tummy. For right now, though, just do a couple of strokes with the grooming glove and then let him sit back down. With a short-haired cat, it isn't as crucial to brush the stomach, but it's essential with a long-haired one. Remember to click and reward.

TIME FOR TOOLS

Once your cat is comfortable with having the different areas of his body touched, you'll start to incorporate the use of grooming tools. When you're dealing with a cat who hates being groomed, this must be done gradually and gently with one tool at a time. Don't attempt to trim nails, brush the cat, and clean his ears all in one session.

BRUSHING AND COMBING

If your cat hates being brushed but has accepted the grooming glove, you may want to begin with a soft-bristle brush. Start by petting him with your hand and then alternate one or two strokes with the brush. Go back to petting with your hand. Every once in a while use the brush until you can start to use it for more strokes. When you stroke your cat with the brush, use the clicker and then reward him. Keep in mind you won't be offering treats this way for the rest of his life, but for the retraining process you have to replace his negative associations with the idea that grooming benefits him.

Gradually build up to doing a few consecutive strokes with the brush before you click and reward. When you start brushing, do it in his preferred petting areas such as behind the head, under the chin, or along the back. Then, when you begin to incorporate one or two strokes in a sensitive area, go back to the desired areas immediately before your cat can focus too much on what he just allowed you to do. Increasing the number of strokes will be done over the course of several sessions. End each session on a positive note. If you can do only a few strokes before you sense his patience is wearing thin, stop and continue at some other time.

Once your cat is comfortable with the soft-bristle brush, you can start using a tool that's more appropriate for his particular coat. A very soft wire slicker brush usually works well for short-haired cats. Although this brush is very effective at removing dead hair, it can pinch if you use too much pressure. Use only light strokes with the slicker brush. Sometimes the reason a short-haired cat hates being brushed is because the brush is raked over his sensitive skin and down his spine or across his hip bones. Stroke the brush across the skin on your inner forearm to get a feel for how light your touch should be. If your cat has very short hair, skip the slicker brush and stick to the soft-bristle brush.

If your short-haired cat doesn't like the slicker brush, you can continue to use the soft-bristle brush or switch to a rubber brush. These brushes have rubber teeth that are very gentle on the cat's skin. If your cat likes the feeling of being massaged with the rubber brush, you can start to use it like a currycomb, moving it in circular motions to loosen all the dead hair in the coat. I've found that many cats who dislike the slicker wire brush will easily tolerate the rubber brush. After using it as a currycomb, finish off by brushing the hair in the direction it grows to smooth out the coat. Keep in mind that your cat may enjoy the rubber brush only as long as it goes in the direction of the hair, so if he doesn't let you use it as a currycomb, don't push the issue. Also, don't try using any other type of brush as a currycomb. All other brushes and combs should be used in the direction of the hair.

As you're working with the brush, whatever type it is, remember to keep the sessions short. It's always better to end the session before your cat starts to squirm or lose patience. If you end things on a positive note, you increase your chances of having the cat look forward to the process the next time.

As your short-haired cat becomes increasingly tolerant of the brush, you can give his coat a glossy finish to end the session by gently rubbing it with a chamois cloth in the direction of the hair. Cats with very short coats really look spectacular after a little chamois rub.

For a long-haired cat, it's best to start with a coat that's in good shape. If your cat has mats, have him professionally groomed. You don't want to attempt retraining if the first thing you have to do is tug on a mat. For a long-haired cat you'll need a large-tooth comb, a medium-tooth comb, and a pin brush. All of these products are easily found in your local pet supply store. Start with the large-tooth comb and gently and slowly comb in the areas in which your cat is the least sensitive. Click and reward as you comb. Later, when you're doing a real grooming session, you'll start at the base of the tail and work up in sections so you can check for mats, but you need to start where your cat enjoys being combed. Gradually, make a few strokes in other areas, and then go back to the tried-and-true desirable areas. Comb slowly because if you do run across a mat, you don't want to be tugging and yanking at it.

With a long-haired cat who hates grooming, don't try to do the whole coat in one session. Give him a break and do several short sessions in order to keep the experience positive.

As your long-haired cat builds up more acceptance of the grooming process, you'll move to the wide-tooth comb and then the medium-tooth comb. The wide-tooth comb is to check for mats. Once that comb goes through the hair smoothly, you can use the medium-tooth comb, and then finish off with the pin brush. If your cat doesn't like the pin brush, you can use a soft-bristle brush.

If you do come across a mat, don't just pull on it. Try to work it through with your fingers. A detangling spray made for cats, or a little cornstarch sprinkled on the mat, may help to ease it out without discomfort. The last resort is to cut it out. A cat's skin is very thin and sensitive, so it's very easy to lose track of where the mat ends and the skin begins. If you do have to cut a mat out, slide a comb between the mat and skin so you don't accidentally go too far. For added safety, use round-tip scissors. There are mat splitters available as well. You may prefer to use them. It may take a little trial and error for you to find the specific tools that work best for you and your cat. Don't attempt to cut a mat from a cat who is struggling and wiggling. In that case, let the groomer or your veterinarian do it because you can easily inflict injury. In addition to the pain you'll cause if you accidentally cut the skin, you'll also be setting your retraining back because the cat will once again have a negative association with the grooming process.

One type of comb that both long- and short-haired cats will need is a fine-tooth one. When it comes to checking for fleas, and removing them as well as their eggs, nothing works more effectively than a fine-tooth comb. It also removes dandruff and dirt to keep your cat's coat cleaner.

Once you've increased your cat's acceptance of being brushed, stay consistent with your grooming schedule. Long-haired cats need daily grooming and short-haired cats need it about once or twice a week to reduce the amount of dead hairs in their coat. The more loose hairs you remove, the less hairs your cat ingests through self-grooming. That may reduce the amount of hairballs you find on the carpet.

NAIL TRIMMING

I think it's safe to say that this is one procedure neither the cat nor the cat owner looks forward to. The best way to handle it is to get it over with quickly. If your cat doesn't like having his paws touched or has a negative association from previous painful experiences, then it's time to rethink your technique and do some retraining built around TLC.

As previously described, the retraining starts with getting your cat comfortable with having his paws touched. For some cats, this in itself will be a long and gradual process. Don't bypass it, though, because you can't trim the nails of a cat who is desperately attempting to get out of your grasp. If the cat is squirming, there's a great risk of clipping too much of the nail and causing pain, bleeding, and possible infection. There's also a risk of your getting scratched in the process, so take the time to do the TLC paw-touching technique first. Work up to the point at which you can press on the paw to extend the nail. Have your clicker handy so you can click and reward.

When you get to the point where you feel you can attempt to do some actual trimming, don't try to do all the nails at once. Be content with doing one or two now and then getting a couple more later. Ending a session on a positive note and before the cat's patience wears out are crucial to the retraining process.

Use a nail trimmer made for cat nails. Don't use human fingernail clippers because they aren't meant for the shape of the cat nail and they create a ragged edge. Don't use dog-nail trimmers either, because they're too big. You need the precision of the cat-nail trimmers so you can see exactly where you're making the cut.

Cats' nails contain a blood supply and nerves that start about midway down the nail, so you want to trim only the very tip that curves around. If your cat has light-colored nails, you may be able to see where the blood supply is. Just trim the tip and don't go beyond the curve. Wherever you think is the perfect line to cut, move the trimmer down toward the tip a bit more so you're cutting a little less than you think you need to. If your cat has previously hated nail trimming with a passion, then clip one nail and immediately click and reward. Do the same again at a later session. Work up to being able to trim two or three nails at a time. Let your cat set the pace.

When you trim the nails, remember to do the dewclaw that's in the typical thumb position. This nail doesn't touch the ground, so it never gets worn down.

The nails on the back paws need trimming as well, though they typically won't be as sharp as the front claws. The back claws have more opportunities to get worn down as the cat walks.

Your cat's nails must be trimmed on a regular basis (typically about once or twice a month) because if they continue to grow, they can curl back into the paw pad. As you might imagine, this is extremely painful and can lead to infection.

If you're frightened of trimming your cat's nails because you think you may clip too much, have your veterinarian show you how to do it. Once you've done it a few times, you'll feel more comfortable about the procedure.

Keep a bleed-stop powder made for pets in your grooming supply kit just in case a mistake happens. In a pinch you can also use cornstarch.

If your cat is declawed, keep in mind that the hind nails still need to be trimmed. Don't neglect to check them regularly.

EAR CLEANING

When you're grooming, take a peek inside the ears to make sure there isn't a lot of wax built up and there are no signs of parasites. If you see what looks like gritty black dirt, there's a good chance your cat has ear mites. Your veterinarian will have to prescribe a medication for use in the ears to kill the mites.

To clean the ears, take a cotton ball and wipe out the ear without going into the ear canal. Only wipe the inside of the ear flap. Don't use a cotton swab because you risk damaging the eardrum and could pack the ear wax farther down into the ear canal. There are commercial ear-cleaning pads and other products available. Before using them, make sure they're specified for use on cats, and, as an extra precaution, ask your veterinarian's opinion on which product is best for ear cleaning. If you feel your cat's ears need more specific attention, have your veterinarian check them.

If the ears look inflamed or have a discharge, see your veterinarian because the cat most likely has an ear infection. If your cat holds one or both ears in a T position, shakes his head a lot, or paws repeatedly at his ears, have him checked by the veterinarian because there may be an infection or he may have ear mites.

If you plan on using liquid ear cleaner in your cat's ears, check with your veterinarian first to make sure the specific product is appropriate for your cat.

TEETH CLEANING

Yes, you should clean your cat's teeth. That may seem amusing to you, but gingivitis and periodontal disease can cause much pain for your cat, and, if left untreated, the bacteria can get into the bloodstream and travel to the heart. It's a good idea to brush your cat's teeth on a daily basis. At the very least, do it three or four times a week. Once you get your cat used to the procedure, it won't take long at all.

You may be frightened by the thought of putting your fingers anywhere near the teeth of your feline snapping turtle, but it can be perfectly safe with a little training. If you haven't already starting getting your cat comfortable with having your fingers rub his mouth or his teeth, you'll have to do that. If needed, use clicker training to help your cat realize that being touched around the mouth will benefit him.

For teeth brushing, you'll need a toothpaste made especially for cats. Don't use human toothpaste because it's far too irritating to the cat's esophagus and stomach. Remember, he won't be spitting it out the way humans do. You can find pet toothpaste in your local pet supply store. Cat toothpaste comes flavored in appealing tastes for kitties, such as poultry or malt. You'll also need a pet toothbrush. They come in different sizes, so choose the smallest one. For a cat, you want a toothbrush that's very soft and small. There are also finger brushes available that fit over your index finger. They have little flexible plastic bristles for rubbing on the cat's teeth. You can also use a baby toothbrush. In addition to toothbrushes, there are tooth pads and sponges available for teeth cleaning. These disposable pads fit on the end of a handle and you use them in the same way as you would a toothbrush. You can even wrap a piece of pantyhose or soft gauze around your finger as a toothbrush.

To begin, dip the toothbrush or pad in a little chicken broth or some tuna water (not oil), then gently rub a couple of teeth. This process may help your cat get comfortable with the concept of having you rub his teeth because he'll be concentrating on the tasty flavor of the broth.

Once your cat is comfortable with that, you're ready for toothpaste. Put a small amount on your finger and let your cat taste it. Then put a small amount of toothpaste on the brush and gently wipe the outside surfaces of the teeth. For the first few sessions, don't try to clean all the teeth in one sitting. To help your cat learn to tolerate, or even enjoy, the process, do a couple of teeth and then click and reward him. Later in the day, try another session and do two more teeth. If you repeatedly end the sessions before your cat starts to squirm or get unhappy, you can gradually build up his tolerance for the process. Don't reward him for wiggling, hissing, or trying to escape. Only reward for positive behavior. It may seem counterproductive to be rewarding him with food when you're brushing his teeth, but remember that these early sessions are about retraining as much as they are about hygiene.

If brushing your cat's teeth proves to be completely impossible, ask your veterinarian about using an oral rinse. The rinse is sprayed or squirted into the mouth, and most cats tolerate the procedure quite well. To allow the rinse adequate time to work, don't feed your cat for at least one half hour afterward.

If you're diligent about regularly brushing your cat's teeth, you may be able to reduce the number of professional cleanings he will need from the veterinarian. This will reduce the number of times he'll have to be sedated, as cat dentals are done under anesthesia.

BATHING

If you have a short-haired cat, there's an excellent chance he'll never need a bath in his life. If he goes outdoors and gets dirty or if he has fleas, then he'll need to be bathed, but for the majority of short-haired cats, baths are unnecessary. The cat's tongue does an excellent job of keeping the coat clean and removing any debris. The saliva has an odor-neutralizing component in it, so after a tongue bath, the coat smells fresh and clean. If you bathe a cat who doesn't need it, you risk stripping the coat and skin of oil and causing dryness. It's also an unnecessary source of anxiety for your cat. If you have a long-haired cat, however, the occasional bath is needed.

If you've never bathed your cat and he needs one, or if you've done it in the past and it has left horrible memories for both of you, then tweaking your technique is in order.

Start by having the right tools. Purchase a shampoo that's appropriate for use on cats. Never use shampoo meant for humans, and even dog shampoos can contain ingredients not appropriate or safe for cats, so make sure you use only a cat shampoo. If you have a long-haired cat, you'll probably want a cream rinse or detangling rinse as well, but choose one meant only for cats.

Keep in mind that even the most mild-mannered cat may not take kindly to being bathed, so dress yourself appropriately. Regardless of how warm you may be, wear sturdy long sleeves to protect your arms from scratches. Yes, your sleeves will get wet, but a little wetness is easier to accept than scratches on the forearm. Wear long pants. If you have a plastic apron, you may want to wear that to reduce just how drenched you become.

You'll need a hose attachment for the bath or sink faucet, whichever one you plan to use for bathing. Some cats are fearful of the spray, so you may want to disconnect the sprayer part so that the water can come out in a quiet stream. If you don't have a hose attachment, use a large plastic (not glass) cup or pitcher to rinse your cat. If you use a hose with a sprayer, hold the sprayer close to the cat's body to reduce the noise.

If your cat is small, you may want to bathe her in the sink so it'll be easier on your back. Whether you choose the kitchen sink or the bathtub, make sure the room is quiet and warm. I like to bathe cats in the bathtub because I can close the door to keep the room warmer and prevent escape. The last thing you need is a wet cat covered in shampoo racing around your house. Your particular cat may view the bathtub as an ocean, so a sink may be better in your case.

I find that cats tend to feel less anxious if they have something to grip on to, so I place a bathmat on the bottom of the tub. If you are using the sink, place a plastic sink mat in there. Clear the adjoining countertops to prevent your cat from pulling something breakable into the sink.

You'll need a brush and a hair dryer. Use only a hair dryer that has a low setting, and, if possible, choose one that's relatively quiet. Have plenty of absorbent towels handy. Have more than you think you'll need because when you have a wet cat on your hands, it isn't the time to realize you need to go in search of an extra towel. A soft baby washcloth will be useful for cleaning around the face.

Brush your cat before bathing, especially if he has long hair. You must make sure the cat has no tangles or mats before getting his hair wet. Tangles will turn into tight mats if not addressed before the bath, and they are much harder to remove after being wet.

You may also want to trim your cat's nails in advance of the bath for your own safety.

Put a cotton ball in each of your cat's ears to prevent water from getting in there. If your cat is very small, you'll need to use half of a cotton ball in each ear. Have a few extra cotton balls nearby in case he shakes his head hard enough to send one flying into the water.

Put a tiny dot of plain ophthalmic ointment in each eye to protect them from shampoo irritation. Your veterinarian can provide you with this ointment or instruct you on what to use. A drop of mineral oil in each eye can be used if you're unable to get ophthalmic ointment.

When you bathe your cat, keep your demeanor very calm and re-assuring, but make sure you have a secure grip on him. Place the hose close to the cat's hair so there's less sound to frighten him. Make sure you have tested the temperature of the water against your inner fore-arm. Lukewarm water is generally most comfortable for a cat.

The amount of restraint to use when bathing your cat will depend on your specific kitty. With some cats, less is more, and they feel less anxious if you aren't using a death grip on them. You may find that your cat panics at first in the bath and then relaxes once he realizes he's safe. If he's starting to panic or is too difficult to hold, you may have to scruff him with one hand while washing with the other. For this reason it's very important to have all your tools and supplies handy, and be sure to open the shampoo bottle before starting the bath. Don't use too much restraint, but make sure you have control of the cat. Use your voice to reassure him and lean toward him to provide security.

Unless your cat has fleas, start bathing from the back and save the head for last, since he probably won't enjoy having his face and head get wet. If he has fleas, you should use a flea shampoo and start at the head; otherwise the fleas will run away from the water and into his ears, eyes, and mouth.

Use the soft baby washcloth to clean around his face. Don't suds up his face because you risk getting soap in his eyes and nose. Cats do an excellent job of keeping their faces clean, so a wipe with a damp washcloth will be sufficient. Don't pour water over your cat's face. After washing the face, rinse it by wiping it clean with a wet washcloth. If your long-haired cat has tear stains, use a product spe-cially made for that purpose. Don't just scrub the area, because you'll cause irritation.

Rinse, rinse, rinse. Any shampoo or cream rinse residue could cause skin irritation, so make sure you have removed all traces.

When the bath is over, remove the cotton balls from your cat's ears and wrap him securely in a towel. Use a blotting technique to dry your cat. Don't rub. Rubbing will create tangles and mats in long-haired cats. Rubbing can also break hairs. The paws usually absorb a tremendous amount of water, so blot them well. Once one towel is wet, remove it and wrap the cat in another dry towel. Keep blotting to absorb as much water as possible, changing towels as often as necessary.

For drying, set the hair dryer on low and use a soft-bristle brush as you dry. Don't use a comb because that's painful when the hair is wet. Don't aim the hair dryer directly in the cat's face and be sure to keep it far enough away from his skin. Be aware of how the hot air will feel against your cat's sensitive skin. Keep the dryer moving at all times so you aren't staying on one spot for too long.

If your cat is extremely difficult to keep still for drying, or if he's aggressive or terribly frightened, you can confine him to the bathroom until his coat is dry. You don't want a wet cat running through the house as he'll attract every speck of dust in your home. Cats with very short hair may not need to be blow-dried; just blot as much water as possible out of his coat. Long-haired cats, however, really do need the hair dryer, if at all possible. If you keep your house thermostat set low, then it's a good idea to dry your short-haired cat with the hair dryer as well so he doesn't get cold.

Despite your best efforts at bathing, brushing, and drying your cat, you'll likely notice him doing a very long self-grooming session afterward. Don't be insulted. Scent is very important to your cat and he'll want to neutralize any unfamiliar fragrance (the shampoo) and reestablish his own scent. Keep in mind that this may be a time when he ingests extra hair, so you may need to give him a little hairball-prevention gel afterward.

HAIRBALLS

Hack, hack, cough, cough, hack, hack. It's a sound most of us who live with cats know quite well. The very thing that makes cats so fastidious and clean also creates the unpleasant side effect of hairballs.

The surface of a cat's tongue contains backward-facing barbs. That's an efficient way to trap loose and dead hair in order to remove it from the coat, but the downside of this process is that because of the direction of the barbs, the cat is unable to spit the hair out. There's only one direction for the hair to go and that's down the throat and into the stomach.

Many cats are able to get rid of the hairballs by vomiting them back up. You may be quite familiar with the sight of your cat coughing up a hairball. Or maybe you've been surprised in the middle of the night by the soggy little hairball as you walked barefoot to the bathroom.

Small amounts of hair may be visible in the cat's stool if it wasn't vomited back up and managed to pass through the intestinal tract.

For many cats, though, the hairball doesn't get vomited back up or pass through the intestinal tract—it forms a blockage in the intestine. This is a serious situation and requires a trip to your veterinarian because the blockage may have to be surgically removed. If your cat has stopped eating and/or seems constipated and has not passed any stool in twenty-four hours, he may have a hairball blockage. If your cat doesn't normally have a bowel movement every day, it can be more difficult to watch for hairball blockages. It's important to be familiar with what is and isn't happening in the litter box so you can catch a potential problem in the early stage. There could be other underlying causes as well, so see your veterinarian immediately.

Common Signs of Hairballs*

- hacking and dry coughing
- appearance of a damp, cigar-shaped object on the floor
- lack of appetite in your cat
- appearance of hair in the cat's stool
- lethargy
- constipation

Signs of Potentially Serious Impaction*

- inability to pass stool
- diarrhea
- lethargy
- no appetite
- swollen abdomen
- crouched posture
- crying when picked up

*These signs can also indicate other underlying medical conditions.

If you have a cat who overgrooms, hairballs may be an ongoing problem. In a multicat home, your may think the hairballs you find are originating from your long-haired cat, but they could be coming from a short-haired cat who grooms the long-haired one.

To cut down on the number of hairballs your cat develops, get on a schedule of doing regular brushing. The more loose hair you capture in the brush, the less your cat will ingest.

There are commercial hairball prevention products that are very effective in helping the hairballs pass more easily. You can find hairball prevention pastes in your local pet supply store. Many veterinarians also sell these products. The pastes are mineral-oil-based. Mineral oil isn't absorbed through the digestive tract, so it lubricates the tract and helps the hairball pass through. The hairball prevention pastes are usually flavored to make them more palatable to cats. Since the mineral-oil-based hairball prevention products do not get absorbed into the system, they can interfere with normal digestion, so don't give them with food or right after your cat has eaten. Mineral oil can also interfere with the absorption of fat-soluble vitamins. The pastes should be administered between meals only. Plain mineral oil has no smell or taste, so it poses a tremendous risk to your cat because he could inhale it as you're trying to give it to him. Don't use any home remedy such as butter or other oils either, because they can create a secondary digestive problem and will get absorbed into the digestive tract without providing the necessary lubrication.

Your veterinarian will guide you on how much and how often to administer the hairball paste based on the severity of your cat's hairball problem. If the problem isn't bad, you can probably give the paste once or twice a week. Don't give it more than twice a week unless advised to do so by your veterinarian. Too much can cause digestive and thus nutritional problems.

The way to administer the paste is to put approximately a one-inch ribbon of it on your index finger and feed it to your cat. To ensure the paste gets into your cat's mouth, open his mouth with the same technique you would use for pilling, and gently scrape the hairball paste off your finger by running it across the ends of your cat's teeth. Let him close his mouth to swallow. If you hold his mouth closed, do so very loosely so he has enough room. If you clamp his mouth closed, he'll be unable to swallow the paste. If your cat doesn't like the taste and tends to spit it out, or if you're unable to open the cat's mouth enough, you can rub the paste along the side teeth, right inside the cheek pocket.

Some people have used the technique of wiping the paste on one of the cat's paws, since cats will almost always groom away whatever gets on their coats. The risk of this is that your cat may shake his paw first and the sticky paste will end up everywhere but in his mouth.

An alternative to using hairball paste is to feed your cat one of the hairball prevention formula foods. In order for the food to work, you must feed it to your cat exclusively. Don't use it if your cat is on a prescription formula food. If your cat is eating over-the-counter food and you want to try the hairball prevention formula, gradually introduce it by mixing a little new food into your cat's current brand. Stretch the transition out over about five days.

Increasing the fiber in your cat's diet may also help him pass the hairballs more easily. Ask your veterinarian about ways to do this for your particular cat. One way that works well for most cats is to use canned pumpkin. If you feed wet food, you can mix a little canned pumpkin into his dish—usually about one quarter to one half of a teaspoon, depending upon the size of your cat. Be sure to consult your veterinarian before making any dietary changes, though. Also, don't add too much canned pumpkin or any other source of fiber because excessive amounts can have disastrous intestinal consequences. Fiber increases should be done gradually to allow your cat's system to get used to them; otherwise he could end up with excess gas and diarrhea, which is unpleasant for everybody.

 CATWISE CLUE

Shedding is normal, but an excessive amount of shedding isn't. If you think your cat is shedding too much, consult your veterinarian. Also, if his coat is dry or dull, there may be an underlying medical problem. If your cat gets a clean bill of health, your veterinarian may recommend a change in diet or a fatty-acid supplement to improve the coat's condition.

12

Looking Ahead
Senior Cat Behavior

With advances in veterinary medicine and improvements in feline nutrition, cats are living much longer. Diagnostic tests and treatments that were unheard of for companion animals years ago are becoming more easily available in just about every part of the country.

With early diagnosis and compliance on the part of the cat owner in terms of administering medication and feeding appropriate food, a cat who once might not have lived to the age of ten could be enjoying her sixteenth year now.

 CATWISE CLUE

Cats are generally considered geriatric at about seven to ten years, depending on the cat and which veterinarian you ask.

Many things affect your cat's health in her senior years. A cat who hasn't been fed good food, or one who has spent the majority of her life outdoors, may have a tougher time during her senior years than an indoor cat fed a top-quality diet. Genetics also plays a big role, so even though you might have given your cat the very best care, certain diseases and disorders may still be inevitable.

When your cat was younger, you might have had a schedule of taking her to the veterinarian once a year for her routine vaccinations and exam. Now that she's in her senior years, the frequency of those visits should be increased to every six months. Early diagnosis can be the most important part of successful treatment for a variety of problems and diseases. Your veterinarian may also have a senior wellness program for his or her clients in which older animals get more extensive diagnostics. While some of these tests may not be within your budget, keep in mind that with early detection, the cost of maintaining your cat's health can be far less than if a diagnosis is made late in the game.

Tests Needed for Your Geriatric Cat

- Blood chemistry profile
- Complete blood count (provides information on white and red blood cells and platelets)
- Thyroid test
- Urinalysis
- Blood pressure check

BEHAVIOR AND PHYSICAL CHANGES

Behavior changes in older cats can range from relatively nonexistent to subtle to outright Jekyll and Hyde.

A cat who used to be sociable and loved affection may start displaying a cranky, cantankerous personality. A cat who was the big grouch of the house may now be settling into a more peaceful existence and showing more tolerance of other cats or family members. Your cat may now be showing a decrease in activity and spending more time sleeping in the sun than chasing imaginary prey. She may not show much of an interest in her scratching post or toys, or she may be using her post more than ever in order to get a full stretch to unkink those stiff joints.

Yowling, especially at night, is a relatively common behavior in older cats. It can be due to hyperthyroidism, age-related cognitive dysfunction, or confusion due to declining senses. If your old cat has started yowling, make sure she has had a thorough examination, including appropriate diagnostic tests to rule out any underlying medical cause. To ease her mind during the night, conduct a low-intensity play session so she'll be more inclined to sleep. It can often be confusing for the older cat when the house suddenly becomes dark and quiet at night. If your cat's vision has declined, that can add to her nighttime confusion. Leave some lights on, set some lights on timers, or use night-lights to provide comfort and familiarity and make it easier for her to navigate around the home.

If your cat yowls during the night, gently call out to her. She may be trying to locate you, and if you call to her, it may help her find her way back to you. You can also go and get her and set her up on your bed or in a cozy sleeping area in your bedroom.

If you think your cat may yowl when no one is at home during the day, or if you hear her yowling as you head out the door, leave a radio on or set your DVD player on a timer so she can watch a cat entertainment video, such as *Video Catnip*. Another option is to ask a neighbor to come in and visit with your cat every so often. If your cat enjoys the company of a neighbor's teenager and the child is responsible about entering your home and locking the door when he leaves, perhaps you could pay him to visit and play with your cat.

Use *Feliway Comfort Zone* in the environment to help your cat continue to make positive associations with his surroundings and to identify objects.

CATWISE CLUE

Although your cat may not be able to do the backflips and leaps she used to do in her youth, interactive playtime and solo play are still important aspects of her life. Modify the technique you use, if necessary, so your cat can still enjoy being the mighty hunter. Toy movements may need to be slower and the play sessions shorter. She may now enjoy just batting at a toy while lounging on the sofa. Set up solo activity toys and puzzle feeders to keep her mind engaged. It's more important now than ever.

Your cat's weight may be changing now that she's older. If she's less active, she may be putting on too much weight and that's very stressful for her joints. It also puts her at risk for arthritis, diabetes, and heart disease. Because her activity level has declined, you should talk to your veterinarian about whether her food portions should be adjusted. You may find that she now does better with smaller, more frequent meals. They may be easier on her stomach, and she won't feel the stress of having an empty tummy for too long. If your cat is physically fine, just overweight, then some increased activity is needed. Just because she's older doesn't mean she won't benefit from play therapy, activity toys, and a more enriching environment.

For other older cats, the problem isn't weight gain, but weight loss. Your cat's declining senses may be causing her to have less of an appetite. Since cats depend on their sense of smell to entice them into eating, a declining sense of smell may be causing her to walk away from the food bowl. One way to spark her appetite may be to warm the food slightly to release more aroma. You may also want to ask your veterinarian about adding a little warm chicken broth to wet food. Your veterinarian may decide to prescribe an appetite stimulant if your cat has stopped eating.

There are senior cat food formulas available over-the-counter and through prescription. Senior formulas have reduced calories as well as added antioxidants. They're also designed to be more easily digestible. Many of these senior foods also have increased fiber to aid gastrointestinal motility. Before switching your cat to a senior food, be sure you consult with your veterinarian. Some cats never need to transition to the senior formulas, whereas other cats truly benefit from them. Any change in diet is stressful for a cat and can cause digestive upset, so if your veterinarian does recommend a switch to a senior formula, do a gradual transition over the course of five to seven days.

Now is also the time to be diligent about your cat's oral health. Periodontal disease can result in infection from the gums traveling through your cat's bloodstream and ending up in vital organs. Brush your cat's teeth regularly or use a veterinarian-recommended oral rinse. Your cat may also need a professional cleaning. Because anesthesia is involved, your veterinarian will do a series of tests to determine how healthy your cat is before setting up the dental appointment. If your cat is in good health, there's very little risk involved in anesthesia. Complications from periodontal disease are more dangerous to your cat than the anesthesia is, so don't let your fear of anesthesia keep you from getting your cat's teeth properly cared for.

Look at your cat's eyes. You may notice they have a bluish tint or a cloudy appearance. This could be a sign of cataracts. Have your veterinarian check your cat's vision. If she does have decreased vision, it's important not to make changes in her environment. This isn't the time to rearrange furniture. Keep things as familiar as possible and your cat will do well navigating around the home.

Water is also a big issue with your geriatric cat. Some older cats start drinking less water when they really need to be increasing their consumption. Cats with chronic renal failure or diabetes need to drink a good amount of water each day. Step up your cleaning habits and make sure your cat's water bowl stays clean and filled with fresh water. Pay attention to how much she drinks. If you suspect she isn't drinking enough, consider getting a pet water fountain. Many cats enjoy playing with the water in the fountain and it entices them to drink more. If you think your cat might prefer a bubbling motion instead, there's a fountain called *The Bubbler*. The product is available at pet supply stores and online. If you use a pet water fountain, keep it clean and filled with the right amount of water. It's easy to forget about the fountain, and it can quickly become dried out or dirty.

MAKE ADJUSTMENTS AS NEEDED

Just because your cat may not be able to jump up to her favorite perches anymore doesn't mean she shouldn't have access to them. If there are some favorite elevated perches that she has always enjoyed, make it easier for her to reach them safely. You can construct a little ramp or carpeted stairway for her or buy one at your local pet supply store. More and more companies are making ramps and stairs for older animals, offering them the opportunity to still enjoy sitting in a sunny window or sleeping on the bed.

Your cat's tolerance for cold has probably decreased now that she's older, especially if she's underweight. Be sensitive to drafts around her feeding station, litter box, and favorite sleeping areas. Even if there isn't a draft, the day-to-day temperature in your home may not be as comfortable for her as it once was. There are heated pet beds available at pet supply stores and online that can provide a toasty little place for your cat to take one of her many afternoon naps. In addition to heated pet beds, many cats enjoy the warmth and softness of fleece bedding. If your cat would normally sleep on the open perch of a cat tree or on the bedspread, she may enjoy the surrounding warmth of a doughnut-shaped fleece bed that helps contain her body heat.

Your cat might have once been very particular about her grooming habits and had the sleekest coat of any feline, but as a geriatric kitty, she may be letting some of her daily hygiene slide. Even if you have a short-haired cat who never required much brushing, get a soft bristle brush and do a daily grooming session. In addition to assisting her in removing dead hair, you'll be providing a massage to stimulate circulation. The grooming also gives you the valuable opportunity to check for any suspicious lumps that may have suddenly appeared. Your cat may also not be as meticulous about what's going on in her hindquarter region. You may have to use a warm, soft, dampened cloth to help her clean any fecal matter or urine stains.

If your cat goes outdoors, it's now time to reconsider if she should be exclusively indoors. With declining senses and less ability to escape danger, your cat is at high risk. She's no match for a younger, tougher opponent now. There are also contagious diseases and parasites out there. Now isn't the time to compromise her health and immune system.

THE LITTER BOX

Litter box problems can easily show up in a geriatric cat. It may be that due to chronic renal failure or diabetes your cat simply can't make it to the box in time. Arthritis may make it too difficult for your cat to climb over a high-sided box or perch in a covered box. She also may just not have the bladder control she used to have. With a decrease in activity and a less efficient digestive system, constipation can also be a problem in older cats. Your cat may develop a litter box avoidance problem because she associates the pain of constipation or a urinary condition with the box itself. She also may just need to eliminate right where she is, even if it's far from the box. In a multicat home, your geriatric cat may be ambushed in the box or lose part of her claimed area to a young upstart companion cat.

As your cat shows signs of age, you need to reevaluate her litter box situation and make necessary modifications. If the covered litter box is creating discomfort, remove the lid. If your arthritic cat has difficulty getting over a high-sided box, replace it with a low-sided one. Use a litter-scatter mat in front of the box if you're concerned about how much litter your cat may send flying all over the floor.

Your older cat's aim may be a little off now and she may overshoot in the box. If she has arthritis, she may also be standing up more to urinate instead of squatting. Use *Catpaper* under and around the box to absorb any overspray. The *Catpaper* will protect your floors and carpet.

Increase the number of litter boxes and place them in more convenient, open areas. As your cat ages, the more remote the box, the more likely she'll have trouble remembering where it is. If your home has more than one level, have a litter box on each one in case your older kitty has difficulty going up and down stairs.

 CATWISE CLUE

When you scoop the litter box, use that as an opportunity to monitor your cat's health. Check for signs of diarrhea or constipation. Also, check the size of the urine clumps. If the size seems to be increasing, your cat may be in renal failure or may have diabetes. If the urine clumps are shrinking, she may have a urinary tract disorder or isn't drinking enough water. Either situation should be brought to your veterinarian's attention right away.

If your cat has become incontinent, or if she sleeps so soundly that she sometimes urinates in her sleep, cover her sleeping area with towels. If she does have decreased bladder control, examine her carefully on a regular basis because she may have dried urine on her fur or urine scalds on her tender skin. Look for red spots on the skin or signs of irritation.

FELINE COGNITIVE DISORDER

Another change to be aware of is called feline cognitive disorder. Similar to Alzheimer's disease, FCD is more serious than the normal brain deterioration that comes with age. FCD doesn't affect every cat, but if you suspect your cat's behavioral change isn't just normal aging, talk to your veterinarian.

Some Signs of FCD

• Excessive vocalization (especially at night)

• Disorientation

• Anxiety

• Nonrecognition of family members

• Elimination outside the litter box

• Change in normal sleeping patterns

• Changes in relationships with other pets in the home

• Pacing

• Uncharacteristic avoidance or dislike of physical interaction

FCD needs to be accurately diagnosed because your cat's behavior changes may be due to another underlying medical condition. For example, a sudden dislike of being touched may be due to arthritis. A change in litter box habits may be due to renal failure or hyperthyroidism. A change in personality could have hyperthyroidism as the underlying cause as well.

FCD will, unfortunately, progress. Medication may help slow the progression, however. Your veterinarian will guide you as to what's appropriate for your cat.

To help your cat during this time, keep the environment familiar. Don't rearrange furniture, and avoid making major changes in her life (no new pets, renovation, new furniture, and so forth) if at all possible. Increase the number of litter box locations in case your cat has trouble remembering where her box is.

A cat with FCD may need to be confined at night. At the very least, make sure doors are closed to rooms where she may hurt herself.

Continue to provide stimulation for your cat through interactive play therapy to help exercise her memory. Make sure your play sessions are appropriate for her physical capabilities and health.

OTHER COMPANION ANIMALS IN THE HOME

Sometimes the geriatric cat will lose her status in a multicat home, especially if she develops health problems. When a lower-ranking cat sees that the geriatric cat no longer poses much of a threat, there may be some takeover attempts. Other cats in the home may start pushing their way into the older cat's food bowl or taking over her favorite sleeping places.

Monitor the dynamics in your home to make sure your older kitty isn't becoming a victim. If she can still access high elevations, that may help her retain some of her status. Create stairs, ramps, or some other ways for her to still be able to get to her cherished elevated areas.

Watch what happens at the feeding stations. You may have to play security guard or set up some additional feeding stations to make sure your older cat can find a quiet and secure place for a meal.

If you're thinking that the addition of another cat might put a little spark back into your geriatric kitty, think very carefully before doing this. Many people make the mistake of getting a young kitten for a very old cat. Kittens don't have the sense of territory that an adult cat has and will end up in the older cat's face way too often. It can also be very stressful for an older cat to have to endure a kitten's endless energy. Stress is one of your cat's biggest enemies. The last thing your geriatric cat needs right now is the stress of having a young kitten around. Your cat's senior years are a time when she should feel relaxed, safe, and able to enjoy life with you without having to worry about a newcomer.

If you decide that your geriatric cat would truly benefit from a companion, follow the instructions in chapter 9 on how to do a proper introduction. Keep your cat's personality in mind when trying to match her with a companion. If she's sedentary and quiet in her senior years, she may do better with a cat who is also a bit older, or at least one who isn't racing around at top speed twenty-four hours a day.

SHOW PATIENCE AND TOLERANCE

Your cat depends on you to notice when something's wrong. She can't tell you that she's in pain or that her arthritis is acting up. She can't say that she has a horrible headache due to elevated blood pressure. You need to be very observant because noticing little things can make a huge difference in your cat's health and welfare.

Be tolerant of litter box mishaps, and other behavior problems. Set your kitty up to succeed in her later years by creating an elder kitty–friendly environment, monitoring her health, keeping tabs on the dynamics within a multipet home, and helping your cat remain active and vital.

ENJOY THIS TIME TOGETHER

These can be years of contentment, affection, and closeness. Your once high-speed kitty might now live life in the slow lane, but there's something to be said for a cat who's happiest when she's curled up in your lap. Enjoy the fact that she loves stretching out next to you when you're sitting down to read a magazine or watch TV. One of my most cherished memories of my twenty-year-old cat is the sound of his familiar purr. Through all our years together, his half-rattling, half-buzzing purr became my special bedtime lullaby. When I climbed into bed, turned out the light, and that one-of-a-kind purr revved up, all the stress of the day was forgotten.

Enjoy this time while you have it.

Appendix

Additional Reading

Johnson-Bennett, Pam. *Cat vs. Cat: Keeping Peace When You Have More Than One Cat.* New York: Penguin USA, 2004.

Johnson-Bennett, Pam. *Hiss and Tell: True Stories from the Files of a Cat Shrink.* New York: Penguin USA, 2001.

Johnson-Bennett, Pam. *Think Like a Cat: How to Raise a Well-Adjusted Cat—Not a Sour Puss.* New York: Penguin USA, 2000.

Visit Our Web Site

www.catbehaviorassociates.com

Animal Behavior Organizations

If you need professional help with your cat's behavior problem, you can find certified experts through the following organizations:

American College of Veterinary Behaviorists
www.dacvb.org

American Veterinary Society of Animal Behaviorists
www.avma.org/avsab

Animal Behavior Society
www.animalbehavior.org

International Association of Animal Behavior Consultants
www.iaabc.org

Veterinary Associations

American Association of Feline Practitioners
203 Towne Center Drive
Hillsborough, NJ 08844
800-204-3514
www.aafponline.org

American Holistic Veterinary Medical Association
2218 Old Emmorton Road
Bel Air, MD 21015
410-569-9795
www.ahvma.org

American Veterinary Medical Association
1931 North Meacham Road
Schaumburg, IL 60173-4360
847-925-8070
www.avma.org

Air Travel with Animals

The following Web sites provide information regarding requirements associated with air travel with your pet:

Animal and Plant Health Inspection Service
www.aphis.usda.gov

FAA
www.faa.gov/passengers/fly_pets/

Finding Pet-Friendly Accommodations

The following Web sites list pet-friendly hotels and also have additional travel information:

www.petfriendlytravel.com

www.petsonthego.com

www.petswelcome.com

www.travelpets.com

www.tripswithpets.com

Product Manufacturers

Angelical Cat Company
9311 NW 26th Place
Sunrise, FL 33322
954-747-3629
www.angelicalcat.com
(*a wide assortment of cat trees that can be customized*)

Bio-Pro Research
1701 Biotech Way
Sarasota, FL 34243
844-URINEOFF
www.urine-off.com
(*Urine-Off black light*)

BitBoost Systems
421 E. Drachman
Tucson, AZ 85705
www.bitboost.com
(*PawSense*)

Cat Dancer Products, Inc.
6145 Green Valley Road
Neenah, WI 54956
920-426-4330
www.catdancer.com
(*Cat Dancer, Cat Charmer, Catnip Cat Dancer—
a double-ended interactive toy*)

Catpaper
P.O. Box 6173
New York, NY 10150
866-545-9228
www.catpaper.com
(*Catpaper absorbent pads*)

Contech Electronics, Inc.
6582 Bryn Road

Victoria, BC VBM 1X6
Canada
800-767-8658
www.scatmat.com
(*ScareCrow sprinkler*)

Dorel Juvenile Group
Consumer Relations Department
P.O. Box 2609
Columbus, IN 47202
800-544-1108
www.safety1st.com
(*Safety 1st Toilet Roll Saver, as well as numerous styles of cabinet locks and other baby-proofing products that also work well for pets*)

Farnam Pet Products
301 W. Osborn Road
Phoenix, AZ 85013
800-234-2269
www.farnampet.com
(*Feliway Comfort Zone*)

Fe-Lines Inc.
888-697-2873
www.stickypaws.com
(*Sticky Paws*)

Folex Company
P.O. Box 575
Spring Valley, CA 91976
www.folexcompany.com
(*Folex*)

Go-Cat
3248 Mulliken Road
Charlotte, MI 48813
517-543-7519
www.go-cat.com
(*Da Bird and other interactive toys*)

Karen Pryor Clicker Training
49 River Street, #3

Waltham, MA 02453
800-472-5425
www.clickertraining.com
(*clickers, books on clicker training, plus other resources
for this type of training*)

Mammoth Pet
P.O. Box 1645
38 Laurel Mountain Road
Mammoth Lakes, CA 93546
888-738-2008
www.mammothpet.com
(*X-Mat training mat*)

MetPet.com
P.O. Box 230324
Tigard, OR 97281
800-966-1819
www.metpet.com
(*walking jacket*)

Mom Inventors, Inc.
P.O. Box 830
Alamo, CA 94507
866-376-1122
www.mominventors.com
(*TP Saver*)

Our Pet's Co.
1300 East Street
Fairport Harbor, OH 44077-5573
800-565-2695
www.ourpets.com
(*Play-N-Treat, Play-N-Squeak, and other cat toys*)

Panic Mouse, Inc.
42309 Winchester Road, Suite 1
Temecula, CA 92590
951-506-3643
www.panicmouseinc.com
(*Panic Mouse, a battery-operated toy*)

Pet Avision, Inc.
800-521-7898
www.cattv.com
e-mail: cattv@worldnet.att.net
(*Video Catnip and other cat entertainment videos and DVDs*)

Pets 'N' People
1815 Via El Prado, Suite 400
Redondo Beach, CA 90277
310-540-3737
(*Nature's Miracle, Nature's Miracle black light*)

Pill Pockets, Inc.
5132 Departure Drive
Raleigh, NC 27616
888-676-7455
www.pillpockets.com
(*Pill Pockets*)

Precious Cat Litters
4201 S. Navajo, Unit 1
Englewood, CO 80110
877-311-2287
www.preciouscat.com
(*Cat Attract litter*)

SmartCat, LLC
N. 144 W5660 Pioneer Road
Cedarburg, WI 53012
866-217-6278
www.esmartcat.com
(*Peek-a-Prize, SmartCat scratching post, as well as a very well-made litter scoop with holder*)

Stink Free, Inc.
7803 N. Kickapoo Street
Shawnee, OK 74804
800-824-5363
www.stinkfree.com
(*Stink Finder ultraviolet light*)

TopCat Products
4321 Oakcrest Lane
Hermitage, TN 37076
www.topcatproducts.com
866-874-1221
(*TopCat scratching post*)

Tots in Mind
215 South Broadway, Suite 312
Salem, NH 03079
800-626-0339
www.totsinmind.com
(*Cozy Crib Tent*)

Pet Sitter Organizations

National Association of Professional Pet Sitters
15000 Commerce Parkway, Suite C
Mt. Laurel, NJ 08054
856-439-0324
www.petsitters.org

Pet Sitters International
201 East King Street
King, NC 27021
336-983-9222
www.petsit.com

Index

abscesses, 19–20, 226
activity level, change in, 103, 207
adult cats, 250, 287
affection, 3, 280, 329, 356
affection areas, 88
aggression, 212–44, 261, 274, 306, 313, 320
    toward babies, 270
    biting in, 213–15
    elevation vs., 27
    fear, 7, 215–19
    in feline hyperesthesia, 128–29
    idiopathic, 235
    intercat, 219, 230–33
    maternal, 234–35
    new pets and, 108
    pain-induced, 225–26
    petting-induced, 214, 219–21
    play, 228–29
    and play therapy, 59, 62
    predatory, 229–30
    as reason for giving up cats, 212
    redirected, 221–25, 235, 310
    signals of, 8, 14
    territorial, 226–28, 313
    triggers to, 213
agitation, 14

air fresheners, 164
air hunting, 51, 54–55, 56
airplane-wing position, of ears, 8, 216
air travel, 300–302
allergies:
    of cats, 20, 42, 123
    to cats, 112
anal gland problems, 122
anemia, 20
antianxiety medication, 121, 126, 294
antibiotics, 19
antifreeze poisoning, 21
antioxidants, 349
anxiety, xxii, 3, 25, 61, 121, 123, 128, 161, 183, 193, 271, 280, 294, 303, 304, 307, 319, 338
appetite:
    changes in, 104, 119
    decrease in, 158, 349
    loss of, 107
appetite stimulants, 204, 349
arthritis, 46, 159, 207, 226, 349, 352, 354, 356
ASPCA, Web site of, 91
attention span, 78

babies, new, 149, 152, 162–63, 245
  advance preparations for, 264–66
  arrival of, 266–71
  crying of, 268
  fears about cats and, 267–68
baby food, 71, 203
baby gates, 242, 277
  for litter box security, 173, 262
back pain, 122
bags, paper, 40–41, 66, 90, 113, 230, 249, 259, 309
baking soda, 165
balance, 8, 13
bald patches, 123
balloons, 188
basements, 171
bathing, 338–41
bathrooms, 170
Bebe (cat), 309–10
beds, 249
bedtime, 33–34, 48, 279–80
begging, 101–2, 208
behavioral history, 138–39
behavior changes, in older cats, 347–48, 353–54
behavior modification, xix, xxii, 43, 58, 218, 242–44, 246, 254, 279–80
  catnip in, 68
  counterconditioning in, 108–9
  desensitization in, 108
  fear aggression and, 219
  for leash training, 315–17
  LIMA approach in, 87
  living conditions and, 17, 18
  in overcoming fear of visitors, 113–18
  play therapy and, 48, 59–60, 60–64
  for separation anxiety, 121
  total family, 139
  travel and, 287, 294, 300, 312
  treats in, 204
  urine odor vs., 144–46
  see also retraining

behavior problems, xix–xx, xxii, 35, 45, 47
  as communication, 1–2
belly-up posture, 5
beta-carotene, 12
Bielec, Frank, 40, 187
bird feeders, 36
birds, 263
biting, 13, 24, 213–15, 219, 246, 309–10
bitter antichew products, 127
black light, 145, 148, 323
bladder infections, 139, 157
blended families, 275–77
blood chemistry profile, 347
blood count, 347
blood pressure, 347, 356
blood tests, 235
boarding, 286, 305, 306, 307–10, 319, 322
body language:
  of cats, xx, 4–7, 16, 215, 221, 222, 241, 251, 275
  human, 129, 269, 329
boredom, 47, 102–4
bowls:
  cleaning up after eating, 210
  composition of, 197–98
  double, 198–99
  size and shape of, 196–97
  timed-feeding, 305
boxes, 41, 66, 230, 249, 259, 321
breakables, 41
brushes, 330–31, 332, 339, 341
brushing, 325–26, 329, 330–33, 351
Bubbler, The, 350
bunting, 3
Burmese cats, 126
butter, 132–33

car engines, 21
carnivores, obligate, 12
carpal whiskers, 10–11
carpet, on scratching posts, 184–85
carriers, 249–50, 260–61, 287–89, 295–96, 300, 311, 312, 317, 321, 324
  for air travel, 300–302

carriers (*continued*)
    emergency technique for, 293
    retraining to, 289–92
cars, 292, 311, 312
    long-distance travel in, 294–300
carsickness, 287, 292
cataracts, 350
Cat Attract, 166–67
cat beds, 35, 269
    semicovered, 31, 309
    thermal, 34
Cat Charmer, 52, 55, 274
cat cream rinse, 338, 340
Cat Dancer, 51–52, 55–56, 62,
    239–40, 308
cat detangling rinse, 338
cat-hoarding syndrome, 21
catnip, 67–69, 269, 299, 312, 320
    planting, 92
    play therapy and, 58, 68, 69, 105
    in scratching posts, 192
Catpaper, 156, 167, 352–53
cat-proofing, 276
cat sacks, 40–41
cat shampoo, 338, 340, 341
cat toothpaste, 336
cat trees, 27–29, 32, 33, 35–37, 40,
    43, 84, 88, 93, 113, 190–91,
    224, 232, 237, 259, 270, 272,
    277, 280, 281–82
cat-walking jackets, 314–18
catwalks, 37
certified behavior experts, 105, 120,
    122, 151, 235, 242–43, 261
certified trainers, 261
chamois cloth, 332
chattering, 15
chew toys, for dogs, 259
chicken broth, 349
children, 168, 245, 271–75, 276
    aggressive petting by, 225
    cat trees and, 29
    counter hopping and, 84–85
    fear aggression and, 218
    litter boxes and, 141, 172
    and pet-care responsibilities, 273
    reintroduction of cats and, 273–74
    toilet paper and, 94

chirping, 15
choking, 13
chronic renal failure, 39, 139, 157,
    206, 350, 352
clavicles, 4
claw conditioning, 32, 182
claws, extended, 231
clicker training, 70–78, 103, 218,
    232, 234, 238–39, 255, 266, 270
    advanced, 77–78, 282
    for carrier, 291
    in cat-dog reintroduction,
      259–60
    door dashing and, 88
    in grooming, 328, 330, 331, 334,
      336
    in leash training, 315–17
    in multicat home, 76–77
    in overcoming fear of visitors,
      114–16
    pilling and, 133
    for spraying, 154–55
climbing, 32, 35–37
cold, tolerance for, 351
collars, 294–95, 299, 314
color vision, 9
combs, 332, 333
communication, 245
    biting as, 213, 214
    by cats, xviii, 1–16, 245
    cat-to-cat, 147
    litter box problems and, 139
    scent, 250–53
    visual, 253–54
companion cats, 60
    in blended families, 275
    cats unsuited to having, 246
    introduction of, 227, 245,
      246–56; *see also*
      reintroduction
    loss of, 105–8
    older cats and, 355
    redirected aggression and,
      221–24, 310
    territorial aggression between,
      226–28
    see also multicat homes
compulsive behaviors, 103, 121–29

compulsive licking, 123–24
computers, 93–94
concordant signaling, 6
confidence, 45, 48, 105, 118, 124, 125, 127, 149
conflicting signaling, 6–7
constipation, 139, 164, 174, 273, 353
contagious diseases, 247
Cornish Rex cats, 169
counterconditioning, 108–9, 118
counters, 26, 33, 82–87
Cozy Crib Tent, 266
cream medication, 135–36
cribs, 265–66, 267–68
crib tents, 266
crouching, 5–6
curtain climbing, 93

Da Bird, 51, 54
D.A.P. (dog-appeasing pheromones), 258–59
declawing, 179–81
defecation:
    outside the box, 173–76
    problems with, 139–40
defensive aggression, 9, 212, 214, 216
    vocalization in, 15–16
defensive postures, 5, 6, 8
delayed reprimands, 150–51
depression, 45, 46, 51, 103, 104–5, 302, 304
desensitization, 108, 118
destructive behavior, xx–xxi, 48, 103, 119
deterrents:
    to scratching, 187–88, 192, 281
    to spraying, 156
dewclaw, 335
deworming, 247
diabetes, 39, 46, 139, 140, 157, 207, 349, 350, 352
diarrhea, 139, 164, 174, 273, 353
dining room, elimination in, 169–70
diseases, outdoor cats and, 19, 22
distraction, 127, 155, 239–40, 253, 256, 324
divorce, 107, 162
dog crates, 295–96, 300

dogs, 168, 294, 318
    affectionate postures of, 2
    begging by, 101
    in blended families, 275–77
    in boarding facilities, 308
    cat trees and, 29
    clicker training for, 70–78
    as companion animals, 60
    counter hopping and, 84–85
    fear aggression and, 219
    heartworm and, 20
    horizontal world of, 25
    litter boxes and, 141, 172–73, 261–63
    noses of, 11
    outdoor cats in confrontation with, 19
    Ping-Pong balls as hazardous to, 67
    proper cat protocol and, 259
    puzzle feeders and, 38
    redirected aggression toward, 221
    reintroduction to, 257–63
    separation anxiety and, 118, 243–44, 259
    tail wagging in, 14
    toilet paper and, 94
    in veterinary waiting rooms, 311–12
    walking of, 314, 318
door darters, 24
door dashing, 87–91
double-sided tape, 187–88
Dragonfly, 52, 55, 308
dry food, 38–39, 125, 126, 153–54, 197, 201, 203, 296, 302
DVDs, for cats, 39–40, 102, 118, 120, 269, 299, 307, 348

ear cleaning, 326, 327, 335–36
ear infections, 8, 336
early morning wake-ups, 97–101
ear medication, 137
ear mites, 8, 335–36
ears, 7–8, 16, 216, 220, 231, 272, 329, 335–36
earwax, 335

electrical cords, 41–42, 276
electronic containment systems, 18
Elizabethan collars, 123
emotional release, 32, 183–84
emotional trauma, 104
environmental circumstances, 16,
    17–25
environmental enrichment
    techniques, xxi, 25–44, 246,
    349
    compulsive behaviors and,
        122–23, 127
    separation anxiety and, 119–20
environmental modifications, 85,
    124–25, 218, 224, 237, 277
environmental stressors, 125,
    128–29, 147, 176
enzymatic cleaners, 144–46, 151, 323
escape:
    litter box and, 160, 161, 162, 170,
        171
    need for, 271, 275
exercise, 46
eye contact, 112, 114, 116
    avoidance of, 6, 216, 284
eye medication, 136
eyes, 8–9, 16, 216, 350
    cleaning of, 327

facial pheromones, 42–44
facial rubbing, 3, 42, 254
familiarity, environmental, 42–44
family members:
    introduction of new, xii, 142, 149,
        152, 162
    loss of, 105–7, 162
    transitions and, 245
fatty-acid supplements, 345
faucets, 96–97
fear, 9, 23, 58, 61, 63–64, 81,
        108–10, 228, 250, 261, 273, 274
    elevation and, 27
fear aggression, 7, 215–19
feathered toys, 65, 192
feeding, 195–211, 218, 267
    bowl bullies and, 204–5
    different diets and, 206
    weight reduction and, 207–10

feeding stations, 33, 85, 205, 206,
    249, 270–71, 272, 275, 277,
    322, 351
    adding stimulation to, 38
    litter boxes and, 171–72
    location of, 185, 263
    in multicat homes, 26, 86, 355
    obesity and, 47
feline alarm clocks, 99–101
feline cognitive disorder (FCD),
    348, 353–54
feline hyperesthesia, 127–29
Feliway, 42–43, 145–46, 249,
    251–53, 258, 264, 270, 285,
    290, 292, 299, 306, 309, 312,
    315, 320, 321, 323
Feliway Comfort Zone, 43, 107, 113,
    145–46, 151, 218, 233, 237,
    248, 348
female cats:
    as mothers, *see* queens
    spraying by, 3, 23, 146
fentanyl, 130
feral cats, 37, 309, 326
fetch, playing, 49
fiber, in diet, 126, 344–45, 349
fighting, playing vs., 231
fingers, not to be used as toys, 213,
    228–29, 275
finicky eating syndrome, 200–204
fishing pole toys, 38, 50, 51, 58, 192,
    213–14, 274–75
flank rubbing, 3–4
flashlight beams, 122
fleas, 20, 174, 278, 317, 318, 333,
    338, 340
flea shampoo, 340
fleece pads, 299, 351
flehmen reaction, 12
fluorescein capsules, 148
Folex, 145
food, 127, 196, 230, 236, 238, 250,
    253, 263, 273, 275, 290, 291,
    292, 294, 296, 302, 346
    appropriate type and quantity of,
        195, 196, 349
    fixed preferences, 200–204
    hairball prevention formula, 344

medication in, 130–31
as motivator, 253–54
outdoor cats and, 22
prescription, 202, 208, 296
reduced-calorie, 208–9
in retraining, 153–54
as reward in clicker training,
  70–71
senior cat formulas, 349–50
forward-facing posture, 6
free-feeding, 99, 101, 153–54, 203,
  205, 209, 233, 263, 283, 302
  begging and, 102
  clicker training and, 71
  pros and cons of, 199
Friskies Cat Habitat, 40
frostbite, 21
frustration, 8, 183
fun tricks, in clicker training,
  77–78
furniture:
  new, 151–52
  scratching of, 32, 178–79,
    186–88, 278, 281
fuzzy mice, 63, 69, 214, 239, 249

garages, 161–62, 171
glove toys, avoidance of, 50
*Grannick's Bitter Apple for Indoor
  Plants*, 92
grass, 39, 91
greeting place, 88
grief, 105–8
grooming, 13, 20, 46, 69, 88, 183,
  223–24, 278, 297, 325–45,
  351–52
  lack of, 103
  poisoning and, 21
  professional, 326, 332
  retraining for, 327–33
  see also overgrooming; self-
    grooming
grooming gloves, 329–30
ground hunting, 51
group play therapy, 239, 242,
  255
growling, 15–16, 216, 251
guest rooms, 112, 117, 264

hairballs, 15, 278, 333, 341–45
hair coat problems, 46
hair dryers, 339, 341
"Halloween cat" posture, *see*
  piloerection
hamsters, 263
harnesses, 313–18
heart disease, 46, 207, 349
heartworm, 20
heatstroke, 20, 298
hepatic lipidosis, 202
hideaways, 30–31, 113, 118, 236,
  237, 249, 280, 320, 324
hiding, 104, 232
hindquarters, presenting of, 2
hissing, 15, 115, 216, 251
hoop, jumping through, 77–78
hormones, 146
hotels, pet-friendly, 298–300
houseplants, 36, 39, 91–92, 276
  elimination in soil of,
    167–68
houses:
  cat during selling of, 319–20
  new, 322–24
  new items in, 151–52
  renovations of, 162
hunters, hunting:
  air, 51, 54–55, 56
  cats as, 2, 4, 45, 47, 207, 263, 314,
    349
  crepuscular, 8–9, 97
  equivalent for indoor cats,
    38
  eyes in, 8–9
  ground, 51
  outdoor cats and, 18–19, 20, 22,
    25, 37
  play and, 48–51, 53–55, 57–58,
    90, 97, 98–99, 103, 209
  toys and, 49
  whiskers in, 10–11
hygiene, 278
hyperthyroidism, 83, 123, 139, 157,
  348, 354

idiopathic aggression, 235
indoor air purifiers, 42

indoor cats, 18
　activity levels of, 207
　familiar environment for, 23
　lifespan of, 346
　outdoor cats in transition to,
　　24–25, 34, 43, 87, 156,
　　168–69, 324, 352
indoor gardens, 91–92
indoor vs. outdoor living, 17–25
inflammatory bowel disease, 139
intact cats, spraying by, 146
intact females, outdoors, 22
intact males, 279
　intercat aggression in, 230–31
　outdoors, 22, 286
　pheromones and, 12
interactive play therapy, xxi, 38,
　　48–49, 246, 280, 282, 292, 304
　for aggression, 218, 224, 230, 234
　boarding and, 307, 308, 310
　with children, 274–75
　for compulsive behaviors, 124
　depression and, 105
　early morning wake-ups and,
　　100–101
　fear of visitors and, 113–18
　for grieving, 107
　for introduction, 253
　low-intensity, for older cats,
　　348–49, 354
　and moving, 321
　multiple captures in, 56
　new babies and, 265, 267, 269–70
　nighttime activity and, 98–99
　for overweight cats, 209
　and rebuilding trust, 81
　in reintroduction, 236, 239–40
　for scratching post training, 192
　for separation anxiety, 119–20
　with spouse-avoiding cats, 285
　spraying and, 153
　techniques for, 52–56, 229
　toys for, 49–52
　travel and, 297–98, 299
　for wool sucking, 125, 127
interactive toys, 49–52, 113, 114,
　　117, 213, 214, 229, 253, 255–56,
　　299, 323–24

intercat aggression, 219, 230–33
intestinal blockage, from hairballs,
　　342, 343

Jacobson's organ, 11–12
jumping, 4

keyboard drawers, 93, 94
kidney infections, 39, 157, 226
killing bite, 54
kittens, 196, 215, 287, 288
　belly-up posture in, 5
　biting by, 213, 228
　deafness of, 15
　declawing of, 180
　fixed food preferences in, 201
　maternal aggression in
　　protection of, 234–35
　socialization of, 113, 217
　stimulation of, 102–3
　tail chasing in, 122
kitty greens, 127
Kitty Kong, 38–39

laser lights, 122
laundry rooms, 171
leash-and-harness training, 18,
　　234, 295–96, 300, 313–18
leashes, 259, 314, 316, 317, 318
liquid medication, 130, 134–35
litter (substrate), 43, 142, 250, 296
　additives to, 161
　aversion to, 159, 165–68
　clay, 164–65
　scented, 168
　scoopable, 164, 166, 167
　switching of, 166–68
litter box, 61, 91, 184, 224, 236, 248,
　　249–50, 252, 256, 272, 273,
　　275, 351
　additional locations for, 140, 142,
　　277, 353, 354
　as associated with pain, 158
　avoidance of, 139–40, 142, 212
　cats wanting separate, 175
　change in habits for, 104
　cleanliness of, 141–42, 158–59,
　　163–64, 165, 174, 267, 278, 281

covered, 159–60, 170, 173, 174–75, 262, 352

dogs and, 141, 172–73, 261–63

eliminating outside of, 46, 48, 119, 138–77, 244, 246, 278

environment of, 33, 142

in guest rooms, 112, 117

improving setup of, xxi, 140–42

location of, 142, 149–50, 155, 161–62, 169–72, 185, 264, 270, 280–81, 322, 323–24

need to escape and, 160, 161, 162, 170, 171

older cats and, 352–53, 354, 356

overcrowding and, 159

plastic liners for, 161

problems with, 44, 64, 85

retraining for, 138–77

security in, 146

self-cleaning and electronic, 160

size and type of, 159–60, 169

territory and, 149–50, 161, 162, 172–73, 226–27, 228, 232

in travel, 295, 296, 299

liver disease, 202, 208

long-haired cats:
    bathing of, 338–41
    fecal matter and, 174
    grooming of, 325–26, 328, 329–30, 332–33

lower urinary tract disease, 39

male cats:
    catnip and aggression in, 69
    intact, *see* intact males
    spraying by, 3, 23, 146
    urethra blockage in, 22

Manfredini, Lou, 40

marking, scratching as, 183

maternal aggression, 234–35

mats, hair, 325–26, 327, 328, 332–33

medical records, 297, 321

medical trauma, 104

medication, 129–36, 297, 308, 346
    antianxiety, 121, 126, 294
    for ear mites, 335
    in food, 11

megacolon, 139

meowing, 15, 208, 220

middening, 175–76

mind-set, changing of, 63–64

mineral oil, 340, 343

moaning, 15

moods:
    ears in, 8
    tail as indicator of, 13–14

mosquitoes, 20

motion toys, 67

mouth, 12

moving to a new home, 142, 152–53, 162, 275, 286, 287, 297, 319–24

multicat homes:
    aggression in, 6, 23, 226–28, 231–34, 313
    bedtime at, 34
    blended households and, 276
    bowl bullies in, 204–5
    cat perches in, 29–30
    clicker training in, 76
    counter hopping in, 84–85, 86
    feeding station in, 26, 205
    free-feeding in, 199, 205
    information gathering in, 7
    litter box issues in, 142, 159, 160, 170, 175–76
    loss and new hierarchy in, 106
    obesity and problems in, 46, 47
    older cats and, 355, 356
    play therapy in, 48, 58–60, 61, 62, 64
    scheduled feeding in, 199–200, 205
    scratching posts in, 186, 192–93
    spraying in, 146–49, 155
    status in, 27, 31, 46, 231, 233–34, 237, 355
    tail wrapping as sign of trust in, 14
    see also companion cats

murmuring, 15

Mylar crinkly balls, 63, 65–66, 68, 90, 102, 255

nail caps, 181–82

nail trimming, 69, 259, 278, 326, 327, 333–35, 339

nanny cams, 148
Nature's Miracle, 145
neutering, 146, 231
nighttime noises, 97–101
nose, 11–12
Nutri-Cal, 132–33

oat grass, 39, 92
obesity, 46–47, 101, 103, 199, 207
objects, fear of, 63–64
offensive aggression, 6, 9, 212, 236
    vocalization in, 16
ointment, 135–36
older cats, 36, 346–56
    arthritis and, 226
    increased lifespan of, 346
olfactory marking, 183
operant conditioning, 75, 154
ophthalmic ointment, 339–40
oral rinses, 329, 337, 350
outdoor cats, 36, 286
    bathing of, 338
    declawing incompatible with, 181
    environmental changes and,
        23–24
    fun anticipation vs. anxiety in, 25
    hazards facing, 18–23
    leash training and, 313–14, 317–18
    lifespan of, 346
    moving and, 321–22
    owners trained by, 24, 87–88
    spraying by, 150
    stimulation and, 37
    in transition to indoor-only life,
        24–25, 43, 87, 156, 168–69,
        324, 352
    as triggers for indoor cats'
        aggression, 222–25
    unseen injuries and abscesses in,
        19–20, 225–26, 232
outdoor enclosures, 18
outlet covers, 155–56
overgrooming, 103, 121, 123, 128, 208
overpopulation, 22
overweight, 82, 159, 206, 349

pain-induced aggression, 225–26
Panic Mouse, 67, 102, 269

parallel play, 59, 64
parasites, 20, 122, 123, 139, 173, 317,
    335
patches, medication in, 130
paws, touching of, 328–29, 334
Pawsense, 94
Peek-a-Prize, 38–39, 67, 100
Peke-faced cats, 196
penlights, 122
people:
    fear of, 110–18
    status-related aggression toward,
        233–34
perches, 37, 272, 351
perching, 35–37, 236
periodontal disease, 350
personal space, cats' need for,
    258–59, 272
pet beds, heated, 351
pet doors, 171, 173
pet sitters, 120, 302–6
petting, 81, 124, 128, 275, 284, 292,
    327, 328, 329, 330
    aggression induced by, 214,
        219–21
    babies learning to pet, 271
    biting and, 214
    in clicker training, 75
    style of, 221, 309–10
pet toothbrushes, 336–37
pet water fountains, 39, 92, 96–97,
    350–51
pheromones, 3, 107, 183
    dogs and, 258–59
    facial, 42–44, 113, 145–46, 151,
        252–53, 264–65, 285
    vomeronasal organ and, 12
physical trauma, 104
pica behavior, 124–27
pill guns, 131
pilling, 130–34
Pill Pockets, 131
piloerection, 6, 16, 216
Ping-Pong balls, 40, 63, 66–67,
    239, 255
pinnae, 329
plastic carpet runners, 85–86, 156,
    188

plastic licking, 123
play:
    interactive, *see* interactive play
        therapy
    lack of interest in, 104
    solo, 12, 38, 64–67, 214, 348
play aggression, 228–29
Play-N-Squeak mouse, 66, 90
Play-N-Treat balls, 38–39, 67, 100,
    210
play therapy, 45–64
    catnip and, 58, 68, 69
    door dashing and, 90
    interactive, *see* interactive play
        therapy
    in multicat homes, 48, 58–60
    redirection and, 61–63
    scheduling of, 57–58
poison, 20, 21
    houseplants as, 91
praise, 75, 259, 292
predatory aggression, 229–30
predatory mode, 9
prey, hazards in eating, 20
prey-drive, 25, 45, 47, 50–51, 54,
    62–64, 105, 119, 155, 214, 230
    sound and, 55–56
privacy, in litter boxes, 140–41, 160
Prozac, 243
psychogenic alopecia, 123
psychopharmacology:
    for aggression, 243–44
    for compulsive behaviors,
        122–23, 129
    for depression, 105
    for separation anxiety, 121
pumpkin, canned, 125–26,
    344–45
punishments, physical, 80–81
purring, 14–15, 356
    cessation of, 220
puzzle feeders, 38–39, 67, 100, 119,
    125, 126, 210, 230
puzzle games, 67

queens:
    maternal aggression by, 234–35
    purring by, 15

rabbits, 263
radios, 120, 249, 269, 299
ramps, 351
redirected aggression, 221–25, 235,
    251, 309
redirection, 61–63, 239–40, 256
reintroduction, 227, 235–42, 277
    to dogs, 257–63
renal failure, 140, 353, 354
reprimands, 154–55, 186
    delayed, 150–51
    physical, 214
restlessness, 119
retraining, 79–137
    approach to, 79–80
    begging, 101–2
    boredom and, 102–4
    to carriers, 287–93
    catnip in, 68
    for compulsive behaviors, 121–29
    computers and, 93–94
    consistency in, 34
    counter hopping and, 82–87
    curtain climbing and, 93
    depression and, 104–5
    door dashing and, 87–91
    faucets, 96–97
    fearful cats and, 108–10
    fear of visitors and, 110–18
    grief and, 105–8
    for grooming, 327–33
    litter box and, 138–77
    for nail clipping, 334
    nighttime noises and dawn wake-
        ups, 97–101
    pet sitters and, 302–6
    plant nibbling and, 91–92
    play in, 45, 58, 60–64
    rebuilding trust in, 80–81
    for scratching, 186–94
    separation anxiety and, 118–21
    toilet paper and, 94–95
    toilet water drinking and, 95–96
    for travel, 286–324
    see also behavior modification
rolling skin disease, 128
rope-wrapped scratching posts, 189
rough play, 274

rubbing, 3–4
rye grass, 39, 92

safety, 41–42, 84–85
saliva, deodorizing properties of, 13,
    338
sanctuary room, 152–53, 236–38,
    248–54, 256, 275, 281, 319,
    322–24
ScareCrow, 225
scent, 2–3, 250–53, 308, 313
    new babies and, 265, 266
    pet sitters and unfamiliar
        animals and, 305–6
schedule changes, separation
    anxiety and, 118–19
scheduled feeding, 83, 99, 126, 154,
    203, 205, 206, 233–34, 254,
    283–84, 305
    begging and, 102
    clicker training and, 71, 234
    pros and cons of, 199–200
    weekends and, 100–101
scratching, 14, 32, 178–94, 279,
    334
    of babies, 267–68
    emotional component of, 183–84
    as marking, 183
    need for, 179
    retraining for, 186–94
scratching pads, 190, 248, 281,
    299
scratching posts, 32, 37, 69, 90, 93,
    153, 179, 236, 248, 281
    about, 188–90
    cat trees as, 29
    location of, 185–86, 191
    number of, 186, 192–93
    replacement of, 193–94
    retraining to use, 191–94
    setup for, 184–86, 192–93
screened-in porches, litter boxes
    in, 161–62
scruffing, 293
secondhand smoke, 42
security, 2, 127, 170–71, 236
sedation, 294
seizures, 128

self-grooming, 219, 224, 333
    excessive, 119, 129
    lack of, 104
semiferal cats, 326
separation anxiety, 118–21, 128
shedding, 278, 345
short-haired cats:
    bathing of, 338, 341
    grooming of, 328, 330–33, 351
sideways-facing posture, 6
sisal-covered scratching posts,
    189–90, 192
skin cancer, 20
skin conditions, 46, 122, 123
skin twitching, 220
sleep habits, 103, 104
SmartCat, 189–90
socialization, 50, 113, 217, 253, 326
social maturity, 226, 231
socks, wool chewers and, 126–27
sofas, 27, 188, 193
solo play, 12, 38, 64–67, 214, 348
solo toys, 51, 107, 119, 269, 299
sound:
    as deterrent, 86, 94, 230
    and prey-drive, 55–56
    in toys, 65–66
spitting, 15
spouses, 245
    avoidance by cats of, 283–85
    cat-avoiding, 277–82
    new, 152, 162, 275
spraying, 2–3, 21, 61–63, 84–85,
    142–44, 145–51, 270, 323
    outdoor cats and, 23
    retraining for, 151–56
squirt bottles, 230, 233
stairways, 351
stalking, 229–30, 232
stare-downs, 149, 239
static electricity, 221
status-related aggression, 233–34
Sticky Paws, 93, 187–88, 281
Sticky Paws for Plants, 168
stimulation, 37–41, 124, 354
    lack of, 97
Stink Finder, 145
stones, 22, 139, 157

stool samples, 174
stress, 33, 45, 108, 121, 122, 123,
    124, 127, 142, 153, 162–63, 224,
    228, 245, 246, 247, 248, 250,
    253, 268, 286, 287, 292, 303,
    305, 310, 312, 319, 320, 355
  catnip for, 68, 69
stretching, 32
substrate, see litter
sunburn, 20
surge protectors, 156

table scraps, 101
tail, 5–6, 13–14
  chasing and chewing of, 122
  lashing or thumping of, 220
tapeworms, 20
target sticks, 74, 77, 115, 116, 259
tear stains, 340
teeth, 12
teeth cleaning, 327, 329, 336–38,
    350
territorial aggression, 226–28, 242,
    313
territory, cats and, 19, 232, 247–48,
    286, 319
Think Like a Cat (Johnson-Bennett),
    235
third eyelids, 9
thyroid tests, 347
ticks, 20, 317, 318
timers, lights for, 120
timid cats, 48, 313
  cat tree placements for, 36
  hideaways and tunnels for, 30–31
  play therapy and, 50–51, 67
toilet paper, 94–95
Toilet Paper Guard, 95
toilet training, cautions for, 176–77
tongue, 12–13, 342
TopCat Products, 189–90
touch sensitivity, 128
towel wrapping, for medication,
    134, 136, 137
toy mice, 42, 65
  catnip-infused, 40
  fuzzy, 63, 69, 214, 239, 249
  Panic Mouse, 67

Play-N-Squeak, 66
toys, 124, 155, 230, 236, 239–40,
    249, 254–56, 270, 281, 285,
    297, 349
  catnip in, 67
  as dead prey, 48–49
  feathered, 65
  fishing pole, 38, 50, 51, 58, 192,
    213–14, 274–75
  interactive, 49–52, 113, 114, 117,
    213, 214, 229, 253, 255–56,
    299, 322–24
  solo, 51, 107, 119, 269, 299
  sound in, 65–66
T position, of ears, 8, 216, 220, 272,
    336
TP Saver, 95
transdermal medication, 130
travel, retraining for, 286–324
treats, 218, 224, 230, 234, 238, 239,
    253, 255, 259, 266, 274, 280,
    290, 291, 292, 317, 328
  excessive, 204
  as reward in clicker training, 71,
    114, 115
triggers, 213
trilling, 15
trust, 2, 80–81
tuna water, 203
tunnels, 31–32, 40, 230, 237, 249
  as clicker training trick, 78
  for play, 67
TVs, 26, 40, 120, 269, 299
twitching, of ears, 8

underweight, 82
urethra, blockage of, 22
urinalysis, 139, 157, 347
urinary problems, litter box issues
    and, 139, 140
urinary tract problems, 22, 157, 158,
    353
urination:
  changes in amount of, 164, 273,
    353
  indiscriminate, 142–43,
    157–69
urine, blood in, 164

urine marking, 2–3, 43, 147, 212, 252
urine odor, 144–46, 279, 323
Urine-Off, 144–45
urine spraying, *see* spraying
urine stains, 144–46

vacations, 286–87
vaccinations, 19, 247, 317, 318, 321, 347
vacuum cleaners, fear of, 63–64, 109–10
vegetarianism, as inappropriate for cats, 12
verbal cues, 316
vertical space, xxi, 25–30, 205, 227–28, 232, 249, 355
veterinarians, 105, 120–24, 127, 139, 148, 151, 157, 174, 182, 195–96, 203, 207–8, 213, 226, 235, 242, 243, 297, 321, 326, 329, 335–37, 343–45
    cats-only, 311
    fear aggression and, 215, 216, 217
    fear of, 108, 111
    multicat households and aggression after trips to, 227–28, 313
    older cats and, 347, 349–50, 353–54
    stress and trips to, 286, 287, 290, 292, 311–13
veterinary clinics, 69
Video Catnip, 40, 348
vision, declining, 348, 350
visitors:
    for cats with separation anxiety, 120
    fear of, 29, 48, 61, 110–18, 246
    new babies and, 268–69
visual communication, 253–54
visual marking, 183
visual warning time, 171

vitamin A, 12
vocalization, 14–16, 24, 119, 158, 215, 216
    excessive, 128
    at night, 98
voice commands, for dogs, 258
vomeronasal organ, 11–12
vomiting, 119
V pilling position, 133, 134, 135, 136, 137

water, 196, 236, 294, 296–97, 302, 304, 350–51
    consumption of, 13, 119, 158, 353
    and pills, 132
    in toilet, 95–96
water bowls, 96, 273
water pistols, 225
water squirting:
    door dashing and, 89
    food snatching and, 102
weekday/weekend inconsistency, 100–101
weight changes, in older cats, 349
weight-management programs, 22
weight reduction, 47, 58
wet food, 125–26, 133, 197, 203, 296, 304, 345
    types of, 201
wheat grass, 39, 92
whiskers, 9–11, 16, 216
window perches, 29–30, 33, 113, 224, 269, 280
windows, 35–36
wood scratching posts, 189
wool chewing, wool sucking, 121, 124–27
worms, 174

X-Mat, 86, 93, 94, 188, 266

yogurt, 132
yowling, 348